Where China Meets India

Thant Myint-U was educated at Harvard and Cambridge Universities and later taught history for several years as a Fellow of Trinity College, Cambridge. He has also served on three United Nations peacekeeping operations, in Cambodia and the former Yugoslavia, as well as with the United Nations Secretariat in New York. He is the author of *The Making of Modern Burma* and *The River of Lost Footsteps: A Personal History of Burma*.

Further praise for *Where China Meets India*:

'A superb introduction to this region and the way Burma will play a key role in the emerging relationship between India and China.' *Times Literary Supplement*

'Brilliant . . . This magnificent book maps the extraordinary complexities of economy, politics, ethnicity and history bound up with the China-India border . . . It is beautifully written and . . . more like a thriller than a tragedy.' Chris Baker, *Bangkok Post*

'[Myint-U] travels widely in the borderlands of Burma, India and China, and gives a vivid sense not only of the ethnic diversity of all three countries, but of how the unimaginable — until a few years ago — changes are transforming lives.' John Casey, *Spectator*

'The compelling story of a land well placed, sandwiched between the world's fastest-growing and, arguably, most influential countries.' Petroc Trelawny, *Irish Times*

'The book possesses a heartfelt and welcome optimism, giving voice to a desire for connections that exceeds all notions of foreign policy, geopolitics or business and becomes, instead, about people encountering each other in all their glorious difference.' Siddhartha Deb, *Guardian*

'A bold thesis that puts Burma at the geopolitical heart of Asia.' *Wall Street Journal*

'Thant Myint-U . . . is in a perfect position to comment on the past, present and future of a country whose fate lies in the palms of its boisterous neighbours, and he does so in this fascinating book with skill and rare insight into the landscape of the twenty first century.' *Irish Examiner*

'Myint-U's talent with words is well known considering his last book, *The River of Lost Footsteps*, published in mid-2007 is arguably the best insight into modern Burma. His typical style of blending of travelogue, history, memoirs and accounts make his writing an interesting read for people of all backgrounds. Thankfully, he has not let us down on this too.' *Sunday Indian*

'Thant Myint-U . . . is in a perfect position to comment on the past, present and future of a country whose fate is intertwined with its boisterous neighbours, and he does so in this fascinating book with skill and rare insight.' *Oxford Times*

Where China Meets India

Burma and the
New Crossroads of Asia

THANT MYINT-U

faber and faber

First published in 2011
by Faber and Faber Limited
Bloomsbury House
74–77 Great Russell Street
London WC1B 3DA
This paperback edition first published in 2012

Typeset by Donald Sommerville
Printed and bound by CPI Group (UK) Ltd, Croydon, CR0 4YY

A CIP record for this book
is available from the British Library

ISBN 978-0-571-23964-1

To Sofia

Contents

Maps

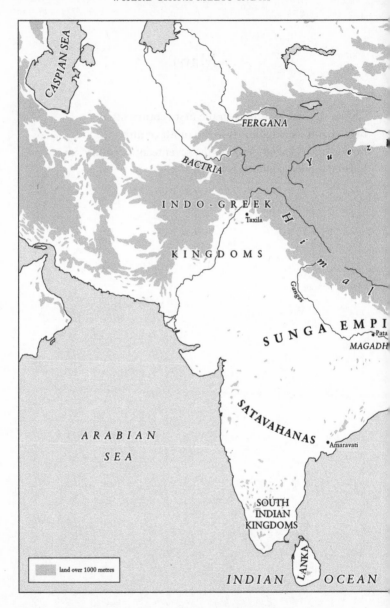

China, Burma, and India in the first century BC

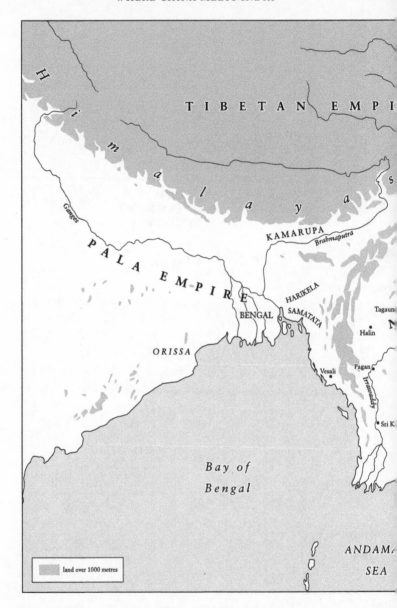

Burma and its neighbours in the ninth century AD

CHINA

(TANG DYNASTY)

Chengdu

Jiannan

Qianzhong

Dali

EASTERN
CUAN

ＡＯ   ＥＭＰＩＲＥ

WESTERN CUAN

Lingnan

Annam

(protectorate
of China)

ipunjaya

Mekong

DVARAVATI

KHMER KINGDOM

Angkor

CHAMPA

Indrapura

SOUTH
CHINA
SEA

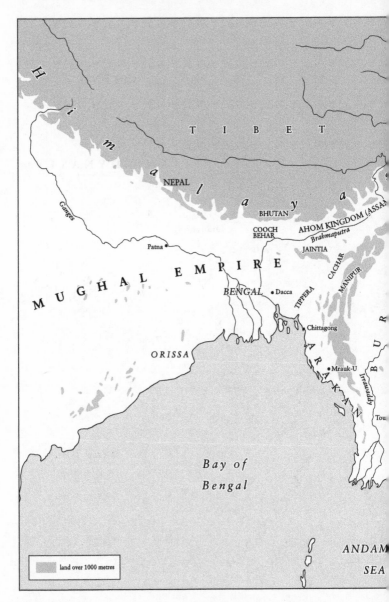

Burma and its neighbours in the seventeenth century

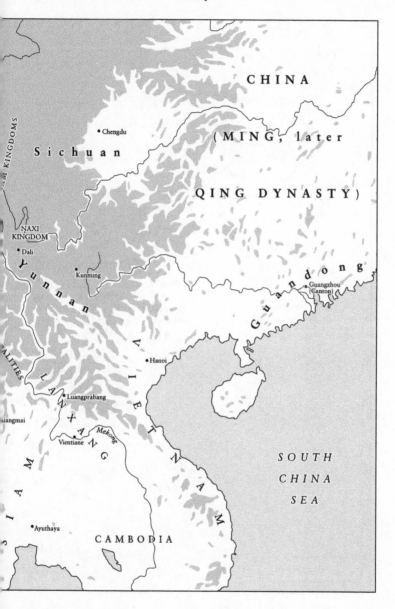

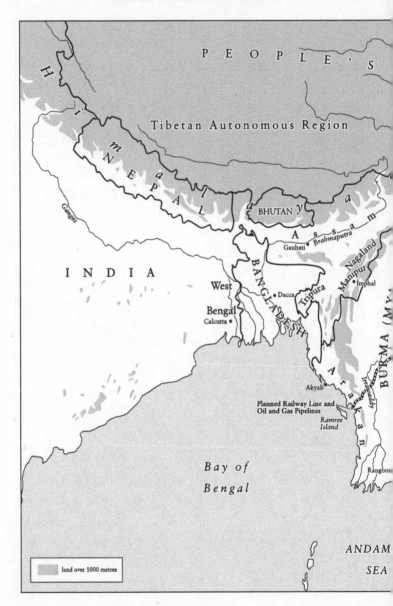

Burma and its neighbours in 2011

Prologue

In 122 BC, a special mission was dispatched by the emperor of China, a mission to find a rumoured southwest passage, one that was said to lead from his Middle Kingdom to the only recently discovered land of India and from India to the unfamiliar countries beyond.

A few years before, the explorer Zhang Qian had arrived back at the imperial court after a long and arduous journey along an already known northern route, reaching the limits of the known world. He had spent years in captivity at the hands of China's mortal enemies, the Xiongnu barbarians, before venturing across vast deserts and wastelands, to strange and outlandish places. He described the Fergana valley and the oasis towns along what would one day be known as the Silk Road, as well as his travels onwards to Bactria, in what is today Afghanistan, and which was then part of a flourishing Greek and Buddhist civilization. And he told of mysterious realms even further afield, like Persia and Mesopotamia, as well as 'Shendu' or India, a region 'hot and damp' where 'the inhabitants ride elephants when they go into battle'. These were kingdoms with their own cities and systems of writing and merchants who sailed the ocean.

And Zhang the explorer told them something even more astonishing: in the markets of Bactria, he had noticed merchandise – cloth and bamboo sticks – that had been made in the Chinese province of Shu. Shu is modern Sichuan, and in the extreme southwest of what was ancient China. Had other Chinese come this way before him? No, he was told, the products from Shu had come via India. It was a revelation and could only mean one thing: that there existed a southwesterly route, from China to the Indian world.

The existing northern way was treacherous and skirted the territory of the Xiongnu, fierce nomads who spoke a language akin to modern Turkish and Mongolian. Not long before, these nomads had defeated their rivals, called the Yuezhi, slaughtered the Yuezhi king and made his skull into a cup. A southwest passage would be a way around this menace. And direct contact with India could mean a grand alliance between China and India against the barbarians in between.

The expedition would not be a great success, however. The imperial envoys started off in Shu or Sichuan, and then travelled south over many months, up great cliffs and through narrow forest trails, braving tigers and giant snakes. Emperor Wu's Han dynasty ruled what is today eastern China and even held sway over much of modern Vietnam and Korea. The Pacific coastline was well known. But now they were deep in the interior, surrounded by alien tribes and uncertain how far India would be.

After first crossing the kingdom of Yelang, on the very margins of Chinese civilization, the envoys pushed further south, finally reaching the kingdom of Dian, in what is today the province of Yunnan, near Burma, and until then unknown to the imperial court. The king of Dian treated the envoys well but told them that their way onwards was blocked by another people, called the Kunming. They were forbidden to proceed. Quite possibly, the wily king of Dian wanted to protect his own commercial monopoly and the already thriving regional trade in everything from cowry shells to rhinoceros horns. He did, however, provide his visitors with additional information and told them that some thousand *li* further to the west there was yet another kingdom, called Dianyue, whose people rode elephants and where merchants from Shu sometimes went secretly to trade.

The emperor's original desire had been to open direct relations with India, and to outflank the Xiongnu by finding another route to the west. In this, he would fail. But in making contact with the kingdom of Dian, he began a millennia-long process that would finally bring China, by the end of the twentieth century, to the very borders of Burma, and bring the ancient dream of a direct passage to India within reach.

Geography sometimes changes. This can happen for natural reasons, such as when ocean levels fell during the last ice age, and connected Asia and America by land across what is now the Bering Sea. Or when rain patterns changed thousands of years ago, turning the once green and wet north of Africa into the virtually impassable Sahara Desert, and in this way separating much of that continent from the European world.

In modern times, man has also changed geography. In the nineteenth century, the Suez Canal joined the Mediterranean and the Indian Ocean, dramatically reducing the length of a journey from Europe to India and facilitating Western domination of Asia and Africa. And around the same time the first transcontinental railways were laid across North America, entrenching English-speaking control of the Pacific coast; other railways, across Siberia, would consolidate tsarist authority in the Far East.

When geography changes, old patterns of contact may disappear and new ones take hold, turning strangers into neighbours, and transforming backwaters into zones of strategic significance. Entire peoples face decline or vanish; others rise in importance.

Several years ago I began noticing the news reports of schemes that promised nothing less than a new map of Asia. There were plans from China to join the interior of that vast country to the shores of the Indian Ocean. New highways would slice through the highlands of Burma and link the Chinese hinterland directly both to India and to the warm waters of the Bay of Bengal. A great port would be constructed along the bay, where oil tankers would off-load African and Middle Eastern oil, to be transported along a new thousand-mile-long pipeline. There has even been talk of dredging the upper reaches of Burma's Irrawaddy River to allow giant cargo ships access to China's most remote inland regions.

There were reports from India, too, and Indian ambitions appeared no less modest. With their 'Look East' policy, successive Indian governments since the 1990s have sought to revive and strengthen age-old ties to the Far East, across the sea and overland across Burma, creating new connections over mountains and jungle. Just north of where China is building its pipeline, along the Burmese coast, India has planned to build another seaport, with a special road and waterway to link this port to its hitherto isolated northeastern states. There is even a proposal to reopen the Stilwell Road, built by the Allies at epic cost during the war against Japan and then abandoned, a road that would link the easternmost reaches of India with China's Yunnan province.

For millennia, India and China have been separated by near impenetrable jungle, deadly malaria, and fearsome animals, as well as by the Himalayas and the high wastelands of the Tibetan plateau. China and India have taken shape as entirely distinct civilizations, strikingly dissimilar in race, language and customs. To reach India from China or vice versa, monks, missionaries, traders and diplomats had to travel by camel and horse thousands of miles across the oasis towns and deserts of Central Asia and Afghanistan, or by ship over the Bay of Bengal and then through the Straits of Malacca to the South China Sea. The new schemes could change all that. Just as global economic power is shifting to the East, the geography of Asia is changing as well.

At the centre of this changing geography is Burma. I was born in New York City and educated in America and in England but my parents are Burmese and I have spent much time in Burma throughout my life. I am also a long-time student of Burmese history and so have seen the changing geography through a Burmese lens. Burma is not a small country; it is bigger than France in size, but its population of sixty million is tiny compared to the two and half billion combined population of its two massive neighbours. It borders to the east with China and India to the west. It stands exactly midway between Delhi and Bombay and Shanghai and Hong Kong. It is the missing link. It is also an unlikely twenty-first-century nexus. Its people are amongst the poorest in the world, governed until 2011 by the world's longest-lasting military dictatorship. What will be its fate, as India and China nudge closer together?

Some have predicted the making of a new Silk Road, like the one in ancient and medieval times that connected China to Central Asia and Europe. Others warn of a new Great Game, and rising conflict between the world's largest rising powers.

The schemes are also unfolding only after decades of tremendous violence and armed conflict throughout the region. In the West, it's normal when thinking of the past century to think of the two World Wars, following by the Cold War, and now, the post-Cold War world, with its economic and environmental challenges and the real and perceived threats of Islamic extremism. The view from Asia is slightly different. In Asia there was first the coming of colonial rule and then a long era of war and internal violence, lasting from the 1930s through the 1980s, from the Sino-Japanese war through the upheavals of the Indian partition, the wars of independence in Indonesia and Indochina, the Burmese civil war, the Korean war, the Indo-Pakistan wars and the wars in Vietnam, Laos and Cambodia. The generation now coming of age is the first to grow up in an Asia that is both post-colonial and (with a few small exceptions) post-war. New rivalries may fuel 21st-century nationalisms and lead to a new Great Game, but there is a great optimism nearly everywhere, at least amongst the middle classes and the elites that drive policy, a sense that history is on Asia's side and a desire to focus on future prosperity.

And a crossroads through Burma would not be a simple joining up of countries. Today's state borders are unlike any in history. The parts of China and India that are being drawn together are amongst the most far-flung regions of the two countries, regions of unparalleled ethnic and linguistic diversity, of forgotten kingdoms and isolated upland societies, that were, until recently beyond the control of Delhi or Beijing. They are also places where ballooning populations have only recently filled out a once very sparsely peopled and densely forested landscape: in the mid-19th century, Burma and the adjacent states and provinces of India and China were home to perhaps twelve million people in total. Today the same area, from India's Assam across Burma and China's Yunnan, is home to over 150 million. Next door is Bangladesh and India's West Bengal with another 230 million people combined, and on the other side China's Sichuan Basin, with 80 million more as well as the 30 million-strong mega-city of Chongqing. The forests in between – once almost impenetrable – are now practically gone. Frontiers are being pushed up against one another like never before and new countries are finding new neighbours.

Since I began this book in 2008, I have travelled extensively across upper Burma, to China's southwest and to India's northeast, through stunningly beautiful regions along the foothills of the eastern Himalayas, where glistening new shopping malls come today within striking range of mountain-top tribal communities barely touched by the modern world, and where the world's biggest democracy meets its biggest communist state.

This is Asia through the back door. We start in Rangoon.

Part One

THE BACK DOOR

Irrawaddy Dreaming

Before there was Rangoon, there was the Shwedagon pagoda. The legend goes something like this. Twenty-five centuries ago, two merchant brothers named Tapussa and Bhallika met the Buddha, by chance, just days after his Enlightenment at Bodh Gaya, in northern India. They heard his teachings on how to respond to the generally unsatisfactory nature of human experience. They became amongst his first followers, presenting him with an offering of rice cakes and honey and asking for a token of their encounter. The Buddha gave them eight strands of hair from his head. The Burmese believe that Tapussa and Bhallika were from lower Burma and that on their return home they placed the hairs in a jewelled casket and enshrined the casket deep within what would become the Shwedagon pagoda.

The pagoda sits today in the middle of Rangoon, a sprawling city of five million people, on the only hill for miles around. It is an enormous golden structure nearly 400 feet high, shaped something like an upside-down funnel, with an octagonal base, a rounded dome, and then a long spire. The lower sections are covered in gold leaf, the upper sections in plates of solid gold. Altogether the Shwedagon is said to be enveloped in no less than sixty tons of gold. 'More than in all the vaults of the Bank of England', the Burmese used to say during the days of British rule. At the top the spire is encrusted with thousands of precious stones as well as diamonds totalling 2,000 carats. Archaeologists and historians are uncertain about the true age of the Shwedagon. It is known that the pagoda (in its current form) was built in the fifteenth century, but that it was built on top of far older structures, likely dating back at least to the early centuries AD. A treasure chamber doubtless exists within its innermost recesses.

The Shwedagon can be seen from almost anywhere in the city, reflecting the sun by day and floodlit at night. There is perhaps no other city in the world as dominated, physically and spiritually, by a religious site as Rangoon is by the Shwedagon. Rudyard Kipling, after a visit in 1889, described it as 'a golden mystery' and 'a beautiful winking wonder that blazed in the sun'. Thirty-three years later, Somerset Maugham, who had stopped briefly in Rangoon, remembered that the Shwedagon 'rose superb, glistening with its gold like a sudden hope in the dark night of the soul'.

It was dusk when I arrived at the Shwedagon. Statues of two giant griffins or chinthés, the winged half-man half-lion creatures of Burmese mythology, guarded the base of the immense staircase that led up to the main platform. The stairs were made of teak, dark and smooth, and as wide as a street, lined on each side with little stalls, each selling flowers or incense or religious icons. The sellers, like most stallholders in Burma, were women, some with their children playing nearby.

A high roof covered the stairs and so it was only at the very top that the Shwedagon suddenly came into view, surrounded by a complex of dozens of smaller pagodas, pavilions, rest-houses, and shrines of different shapes and sizes, all laid out in no particular manner, the result of centuries of gradual augmentation. Many of the pavilions housed statues of the Buddha, big ones and small ones, the pillars of these pavilions covered in gold leaf or in glass mosaics. It was like a little city from a fairy tale.

Buddhism is the religion of an estimated 85 per cent of all people in Burma (the rest are mainly Christians and Muslims) and all Burmese Buddhists are meant to try to visit the Shwedagon at least once in their lifetime. I can't guess the number of people who were there that evening, certainly in the hundreds, probably in the thousands. Nearly all were wearing a sarong-like *longyi*, patterned and tied differently for men and women, together with a shirt or blouse. Most were probably from Rangoon, people coming after work, but at least some were villagers from far away, their *longyis* in less fashionable patterns and a little more threadbare. There were Buddhist monks as well, in rust-coloured robes, and nuns in pale pink. Everyone was in their bare feet, as is traditional and required at all sacred sites. The air was scented with jasmine and marigold, and at some shrines people were lighting little rows of flickering candles. I went into one of the larger pavilions where there were already a few other people, including an old lady, her eyes tightly closed and her long grey hair tied up in a bun, kneeling on the floor, their hands clasped together in prayer, facing the large statue of the Buddha in front of them. I first knelt as well and then touched my head and hands to the ground.

For some, Buddhism is primarily a philosophy, a guide to being happy and knowing how best to deal with the vicissitudes of life. A visit to the Shwedagon is an opportunity to be reminded of the Buddha's teachings, perhaps meditate quietly, or simply try to calm your mind after a hectic and stressful day.

For most Burmese, however, the Shwedagon is also a magical place. The faithful believe that somewhere beneath the gilded stupa are not only the hair relics of the historical Buddha, Siddhartha Gautama, but the relics of past Buddhas as well, from aeons ago: the staff of Kakusandha, the water filter of Konagamana, and a piece of the robe of Kassapa, and that all these relics impart the Shwedagon with supernatural power.

The Shwedagon is also the haunt of *weizzas* or wizards, Tantric adepts who have achieved special abilities (like everlasting youth or invisibility). There is a small pagoda, towards the southwest, decorated with the figures of wizards and necromancers from times past, where some believe invisible beings come to meditate. There is also a pavilion dedicated to Izza Gawna, a wizard and alchemist of medieval times, and a 'Shrine of the Sun and Moon', whose two Buddha statues are said to grant the wishes of all who come to pay their respects.

The pagoda has also played its role in Burmese history. To the north is the 'Victory Ground', an open area where people come to pray for success of any kind, religious or secular. Traditionally, kings and generals came here before leaving for war. More recently, it has been the place to begin political protests. One of the first was in 1920, when students camped here at the start of an anti-colonial campaign. There's a column nearby in their memory, with their names written not only in Burmese and English but also in Russian, a sign of the high hopes the anti-colonialists then had for the recent Bolshevik Revolution. And protesters have gathered here ever since. In September 2007, thousands of Buddhist monks led peaceful marches against the ruling military junta. The demonstrations lasted for several days and on each day the monks started here at the 'Victory Ground'. But at least in this case their wishes went unfulfilled as riot police eventually closed in, sealing off the Shwedagon complex, and violently ending the demonstrations.

There may be wizards and the occasional protestors, but there are still very few foreign tourists. I saw one that evening, looking relaxed, in khakis and T-shirt, sitting cross-legged with his camera on the marble floor, watching the Burmese go by. I may be biased, but I would rank the Shwedagon as easily an equal of any of the other great sites I have seen, including the pyramids in Mexico, Angkor Wat in Cambodia, or the Taj Mahal. Ralph Fitch was the first Englishman ever to come to Burma, in 1584 as the captain of 'the talle shippe Tyger' (the ship mentioned, some say, by Shakespeare in *Macbeth*), and he said of the Shwedagon: 'It is, as I suppose, the fairest place that doe bee in all the Worlde.' From the beginning of 1962 through the 1980s, it was difficult to travel to Burma and tourism was discouraged. That has changed and it is today easy to visit. But in the place of old government restrictions there are now boycott campaigns from overseas, campaigns that have called on would-be tourists to stay away from Burma, so as not to contribute to the coffers of the ruling generals. The boycotts have been terrible for the country's nascent tourism industry, but have had the benefit of keeping back the hordes that will almost certainly one day come.

It was dark by the time I climbed back down the stairs and walked to the busy roundabout in front, to hail a taxi and drive to the 365 Café.

Edward was a Burmese businessman in his late fifties, a strongly built man with thinning salt and pepper hair, who had worked for several years in Singapore, as an engineer, before returning to Rangoon, his home town. He had a Burmese name as well, but like many of his class and generation had received an English name at school. The Burmese name he used for any official purpose and was the way he introduced himself to any new acquaintances. But to old friends (he was an old friend of my family's), he had remained 'Edward'.

He was waiting for me when I arrived, dressed in a dark Hawaiian shirt and a Burmese *longyi*. He had a broad, almost Polynesian, face, and looked tanned and healthy. We spoke in a mix of Burmese and English. 'Business is bad,' he said. 'Sometimes I think I made a big mistake coming back. I should have stayed in Singapore or gone to America when I had the opportunity. My brother's there, you know, in San Diego. He offered to find me a job, ages ago. My mistake.'

Edward had suggested the 365 Café. It was downtown, on the ground floor of the Thamada or 'President' hotel. It was decorated in a bright international style, with comfortable faux-leather chairs, and had a menu that offered a mix of sandwiches and Asian dishes. Big glass windows covered an entire wall, and through them you could see a small car park, with a couple of old Japanese cars and a big truck filled with crates of orangeade bottles. Beyond the parking lot was the street, and then a tall hedge, and finally a red-brick church, looking exactly like a church in a small English town.

'We have nothing like a proper business environment,' he complained. 'The banking system's practically non-existent, there's corruption, and on top of that we've got sanctions!' He meant the sanctions Western governments had imposed to try to pressurize the ruling junta towards democratic reforms. They were amongst the toughest sanctions anywhere in the world, and included a prohibition of all Burmese exports to the US, a blocking of all loans to Burma by the World Bank and International Monetary Fund, and financial sanctions that essentially made it impossible for any Burmese company to do business in the West. He had tried his hand at different things, from setting up a furniture-making company to running a small hotel. 'The top guys can still make money, but for the rest of us, it's next to impossible. Why impose sanctions when the government already makes it so hard to make a decent living?'

Australia's Foreign Minister Alexander Downer once remarked that political progress in Burma was about as fast as glue flowing up a hill. And the news from Burma had rarely been good. In 1988, a massive pro-democracy uprising had been crushed. Two years later, the junta that was in power had held elections, but then ignored the results when the opposition scored a landslide victory. Burma rarely made the front pages, but when it did, it was usually about the continued house-arrest of Aung San Suu Kyi, the country's human-rights icon. There had been a fresh round of protests in 2007, and by the end of that year Amnesty International was estimating that no fewer than 2,000 political prisoners were languishing in the country's jails. And then, in 2008, the deadly Cyclone Nargis had left over 100,000 people dead. I was meeting Edward in late 2008, a few months after Nargis. It was hard not to be despondent. The little foreign tourism there had been was disappearing and the global recession was just beginning.

But what of relations with India and China, I asked? Their economies had been growing at light speed and were still growing, even during the recession. There were the plans to connect their economies with Burma. Edward hadn't thought about it very much. He was a man of the West. His father and grandfather had been educated in England and all his travels abroad, other than to Singapore and Bangkok, had been in the West. He had never set foot in India or China. He watched American movies, read English-language books, and hoped his kids would go to university in the US. He agreed that the world's economy was shifting eastward, but couldn't predict what its effect on Burma would be. This was the response I heard from many in Rangoon. Few seemed to be looking at the map. But there were others, elsewhere, who were not only looking at the map, but getting ready to change it.

More than a hundred years ago, it was the British who looked at the map, and had their own dreams of Asia's future. The British had seized Rangoon from the Burmese in 1852. And soon, in the clubs and boardrooms of London and Calcutta, there were dreams of the Irrawaddy River as a back door to the markets of China. Rangoon was then little more than a small town next to the Shwedagon, but it held a potentially strategic place. It sits along a branch of the Irrawaddy River, that starts far to the north, in the snow-covered peaks of the Himalayas, before descending a thousand miles and emptying into the Bay of Bengal, close to Rangoon.

The British were then the paramount power in India. From beachheads at Madras (also now known as Chennai), Bengal and Bombay, their East India Company had overwhelmed all rivals and established a complete hegemony over the subcontinent. The company already enjoyed lucrative trade with China, mainly involving the sale of British Indian opium in exchange for Chinese silver. But the British saw the obvious: Burma was what lay between their Indian Empire and the immense and still barely explored interior of China. They could sail around Singapore, but a passage through Burma might save time and lead to still more profits. In the decades that followed, soldiers, scientists and surveyors were sent out to map out the unknown borderlands, looking for new routes and attempting alliances with the remote princes and tribal chiefs they encountered.

The lure of China was strong, even then. In the 1890s, the adventurer and writer Archibald Ross Colquhoun had penned books such as *Across Chryse: Being A Journey of Exploration Through the South China Borderlands From Canton to Mandalay*, as well as his *China in Transformation*, which became a bestseller in London. He said that China was 'destined, before long, to be counted among the great world-powers' and pressed hard for the British to find a way from Burma into the heart of that enormous country. Another writer and former intelligence officer, H. R. Davies, made similar arguments: 'In an age when railways are penetrating to the most out-of-the-way places on the earth, it is impossible to suppose that India and China – the two most populous countries in the world – would remain without being connected by railway.' The Victorians thought big and there was even talk of an 'elevated railway' which would zoom across the jungle canopy and directly link Calcutta to the cities along China's Yangtze valley.

The French had similar dreams. A generation earlier, the explorers Ernest Doudart de Lagrée and Francis Garnier had travelled from Saigon up the Mekong in the hopes of finding a viable route to the Chinese interior, but they returned disappointed, Doudart de Lagrée dying from exhaustion and the formidable diseases contracted along the way. On a map the Mekong looked promising, but the French discovered that deep gorges and treacherous rapids would block any significant upriver traffic from their coastal bases in Indochina.

The British too eventually grasped the enormity of the physical challenge. A direct overland route from Calcutta was deemed impossible. From Bengal the Brahmaputra River ran for hundreds of miles northeast, but hundreds more miles of thickly forested and malarial mountains separated the upper Brahmaputra from the headwaters of the Irrawaddy and then China. The costs would be astronomical.

But what about going by the Irrawaddy itself? This seemed more promising. Ships could sail from Calcutta and Madras to newly conquered Rangoon and then off-load their cargo some-where up the river. Railways could then connect these upriver ports with China. In 1885, British forces had utterly defeated the army of the last king of Burma, Thibaw, and soon a railway line was being extended north and east from Mandalay, through the Shan Hills to within a stone's throw of the Chinese frontier.

The French explorer Prince Henri d'Orléans saw the potential and tried to warn his countrymen of the prize that he believed was coming within British reach. He was a grandson of King Louis-Philippe of France and a virulent anglophobe, famous in Europe for his sword duel against the Italian Prince Vittorio Emanuel (after Prince Henri had called the Italian soldiers in Abyssinia 'cowards'). In the 1890s Prince Henri had travelled from Siberia to Siam and then to Africa before returning to Asia and trekking along the China–Burma–India borderlands. He felt certain that this region, situated as it was between the world's two most populous regions, would one day be of huge significance, and only hated the fact that Britain and not France held the strategic land bridge – Burma – that lay in between.

The British, though, would find turning concept into reality far harder than anticipated. The problem was partly geographical and partly political. Yes, the last British outposts were now close to the Chinese frontier, but 'China proper' was still a long way away. Across the border were not the big cities of the Chinese interior but the wild and rugged province of Yunnan. Mountains, torrential rivers and deep ravines running a distance equal to that from Paris to Rome would still need to be traversed.

There were monumental political challenges as well. In China, a series of blood-soaked uprisings had left literally tens of millions dead, and the Manchu or Qing dynasty that had governed China for centuries was hobbling on its last legs. In the 1850s and 1860s, the Taiping Rebellion, led by a charismatic quasi-Christian leader named Hong Xiuquan (who believed in God, Christ, and himself as Christ's 'Little Brother'), had shaken Manchu rule to its very foundations. Meanwhile, in the southwest, Muslim rebels had grabbed control of Yunnan, the province next to Burma, and held the borderlands for years.

Beijing's authority over its distant provinces was weakening fast; warlords were replacing mandarins.

Burma was not going to be a back door to China, not yet.

By the beginning of the twentieth century, prospects of a road to China had been forgotten, and Rangoon, as the capital of British Burma, developed instead as a port for local exports – rice mainly, but also timber and petroleum oil. And in this way Rangoon grew rich. The Shwedagon remained at the centre of the new, sprawling city, with its tree-lined avenues, lakes and gardens, and the many and handsome homes of its official and business elite. Along the river to the south was a modern downtown, carefully laid out on a grid pattern, with its government and commercial offices, colonnaded shops and hotels, and rows of apartment blocks. A largely English administrative class presided over the colonial apparatus; Scots dominated trade. The big companies of the day – Steel Brothers (rice), the Bombay Burmah Trading Corporation (timber), Burmah Oil, and the Irrawaddy Flotilla Company, were all in Glaswegian hands. And millions of Indians, from every part of the subcontinent, streamed into Rangoon in search of new lives and new opportunities.

The British had initially hoped that Burma might be a back door to China. But for the Burmese, British rule led instead to a much closer connection with India than ever before. Rather than making Burma a separate colony (like Ceylon, now Sri Lanka), the one-time kingdom was annexed to British India, and governed as just another province, no different than, say, Bengal or the Punjab.

In the early twentieth century, Burma enjoyed a higher standard of living than India and was far less densely populated. And as the economy grew, there was a need for cheap labour as well as entrepreneurial and professional skills. All this came from India, with movement into Burma unchecked and for a long time positively encouraged. By the late 1920s Rangoon even exceeded New York as the greatest immigrant port in the world and this influx turned Rangoon into an Indian city, with the Burmese reduced to a minority. There was a mingling of peoples from every part of the subcontinent, from Bengali schoolteachers and Gujarati bankers, to Sikh policemen and Tamil merchants. There were Chinese too, and smaller communities of Europeans, Americans and even Latin Americans (the Chilean poet Pablo Neruda lived in Rangoon briefly in the 1920s). The Cambridge political economist and long-time Burma civil servant J. S. Furnivall invented the term 'plural society' to describe Rangoon's mix of nationalities. Steamships fastened Rangoon to Calcutta and then, with the start of air travel, Rangoon became a hub for all of Asia. Flights to Sydney from London on British Imperial Airways, or to Jakarta from Amsterdam on KLM, were all routed via Rangoon. World-class schools and a top-notch university helped create a cosmopolitan and politically active middle class.

But then this world came crashing down. First came the Japanese invasion and four years of bitter fighting, including the aerial bombing of Rangoon. Hundreds of thousands of Indians fled. Then in 1948 came independence from Britain, followed immediately by civil war, Rangoon itself at one point being besieged by rebel armies. And finally came the military take-over of 1962, which overthrew the last elected Burmese government and promptly shut off the country from the outside world. Many in the remaining Indian community, in particular the professional and business class, were expelled. This period of self-imposed isolation would last for a quarter of a century, and in the process Rangoon was remade in spirit from global entrepôt to backwater village, its stately if decrepit architecture the only sign of more affluent days.

Rangoon was my introduction to Asia. I first visited in 1974, on the occasion of my grandfather's funeral. I was then eight years old and was living with my family in New York. The country was in the full grip of General Ne Win's 'Burmese Way to Socialism', isolated, impoverished, with his army fighting little insurgencies in the hills. I would go back most years after that, sometimes for just a week or two, sometimes for the entire summer, spending time with my many relatives, in Rangoon and elsewhere in the country.

Rangoon in those days – in the late 1970s and early 1980s – seemed entirely cut off from the late twentieth century. There were few telephones or cars on the streets, almost no television (broadcasts were limited to a couple of hours a day), no super-markets or modern shops of any kind. It was easy then to imagine the days of the British Raj. There was the big red-brick High Court along Fytche Square and the Holy Trinity (Anglican) Cathedral nearby, the massive Secretariat complex further to the east, and the whitewashed neo-Palladian Customs House. There was the derelict building that had housed Rowe and Co., once a fashionable department store favoured by English and Scottish housewives. And the Empire Theatre, where John Gielgud had performed *Hamlet*. The Minto Mansions, a sprawling hotel that had boasted 'the only French chef in the Indies', was destroyed during the Second World War, but its competitor, the Strand, was still there, charging $20 a night to the trickle of visitors who still came. And near the intersection of Phayre Street and Merchant Street were the magnificent Edwardian buildings that had been home to Lloyds and the Hong Kong Shanghai Bank, Thomas Cook and the Irrawaddy Flotilla Company, all remaining, together with other smaller offices in a mix of art-deco and local styles, in what was perhaps one of the best-preserved colonial cityscapes anywhere in the world.

Rangoon was like a big empty movie set, the Burmese them-selves like supporting actors still hanging around after the main stars had left. It was a city waiting for a new role.

In 1988 nationwide protests came close to overthrowing the military regime, protests that saw hundreds of thousands take to the streets before they were brutally crushed. And in its aftermath a new junta was formed, maintaining an iron grip on power, but jettisoning the autarkic policies of its predecessors and beginning, tentatively at least, to open up the economy and the country to the outside world. General Ne Win, in charge since 1962, quietly faded into the background. A new leader, General Than Shwe, began consolidating his hold. Burmese socialism was dead. But what would come next?

New political forces had emerged in the aftermath of the failed 1988 uprising, and by 1990 these forces – united primarily by their hostility to military rule – had coalesced around the 'National League for Democracy', or NLD, led by Aung San Suu Kyi. At the height of the 1988 protests, the regime had promised 'multi-party elections' and in 1990 made good on their word. Why they did this remains somewhat of a mystery, given the enormous groundswell of opposition and talk of retribution. Perhaps they under-estimated the degree of public anger; perhaps they felt they had little choice but to proceed. The ruling junta likely hoped for a fractured parliament, one that the army could still dominate from behind the scenes. But when the NLD won a resounding 60 per cent of the vote, the regime prevaricated, without a clear plan, determined only not to cede power to their most outspoken foes.

The year after the election, the leader of the NLD, Aung San Suu Kyi, then in her mid-forties, was awarded the Nobel Peace Prize, propelling her to international stardom. A long-time Oxford housewife and the daughter of Burma's nationalist martyr General Aung San, she had returned to Burma shortly before the 1988 uprising, and then moved assertively into the political arena. Her tactics were inspired by Mahatma Gandhi and Martin Luther King, and she hoped that peaceful demonstrations would eventually melt military intransigence. She called for 'national unity' and spoke of a 'second struggle for independence'. She also called for the economic embargoes that were subsequently imposed by Western governments whilst at the same time asking for dialogue with the top army chiefs. Over the next twenty years, hundreds of her supporters would be jailed, and she herself would suffer long periods under house-arrest.

During the periods that she was free, people flocked to hear her speak. And she spoke in clear and simple terms about the importance of political freedom and respect for basic human rights. I had met her in 1987 when she was living in Oxford and I was in my final year at university. We talked about movies and old family friends and she struck me even then, in her living room, with books all around and her younger son, Kim, playing on the floor, as charismatic and self-assured. By the mid-1990s she was a world-famous icon, a challenge to the notion that democracy in Asia was a Western import, and the main protagonist in a morality play that set her and her movement against a thuggish and shadowy tyranny.

The generals, though, were unmoved. Sanctions strained relations with the West but they did little to convince the generals of a need to shift direction. And so the regime settled into the kind of authoritarian crony-capitalism familiar in the region, trading less with the West and more with the growing economies of the East, oblivious to the 'demands' for change from far-away London or Washington.

Rangoon acquired a veneer of normalcy, at least for those who could afford it. By the early 2000s, there were several well-appointed hotels, as well as cafés and restaurants ('Le Planteur' and 'L'Opera'), many set in renovated colonial bungalows and offering a range of world cuisines, from Italian to Korean. The new international airport was sleek and efficient, all light and glass and polished floors. New air-conditioned cinemas served up the latest Hollywood films and the first supermarkets and shopping malls sold the latest in international goods. There were even bars like 50th Street Bar and Grill, and Ginki Kids, with a big poster of Kurt Cobain on the wall, offering a selection of Thai snacks and draft beer. Satellite television was widely available and internet cafés sprouted up around town.

It was still, however, a poor city. There were many more cars but they were generally wrecks, old Nissans and Toyotas from the 1980s that almost anywhere else would have long ago wound up on the scrap heap. The pavements were potholed and whilst the old colonial buildings still seemed impressive, the newer ones tended to look mean and ill-made. Away from the city centre were poorer neighbourhoods still, with few social services and for many hours a day no electricity. It was not a grinding poverty. There were few beggars or homeless people. And people carried on as in any big city, walking to work or taking the bus, enjoying themselves with friends at a local teahouse, parents collecting their kids from school. But it was a poverty that seemed increasingly pointless, in what was a naturally rich and bountiful land.

And then came the tragedy.

On 2 May 2008 the city and the vast expanse of low-lying country-side to the west were battered by a cyclone of unprecedented size and ferocity. Cyclone Nargis swirled around the Bay of Bengal and then careered slowly across the flat delta of the Irrawaddy River, its 130 mile per hour winds driving a wall of water across the little villages and towns, much like the Boxing Day tsunami that had devastated Aceh in 2004. The results were catastrophic, by far the worst natural disaster in the history of Burma, killing over a hundred thousand people and making homeless and leaving utterly destitute millions of others. In Rangoon itself few people were killed but over ten thousand old trees were downed, roofs blown away and power lines destroyed.

American, British and French warships had appeared within days off the coast with offers of help. But after years of sanctions, vociferous condemnation, and active support for the opposition, Burma's generals were unsurprisingly reluctant to accept help from any Western military, all the more so after President Bush and First Lady Laura Bush separately renewed their condemnation of the regime less than forty-eight hours after the cyclone had struck. For three long weeks there was a stalemate, as the Burmese authorities prioritized their own security fears over the fate of millions of survivors; Burmese nationals were allowed to deliver aid, and all aid, including military-transported aid, was accepted from friendly governments (like India) but Westerners were kept from entering the disaster zone, including the UN disaster teams most needed. The small stream of aid reaching cyclone victims was nothing like what was required. There were then calls for forceful intervention as well as intensive diplomacy. Finally the junta agreed to a mechanism involving themselves, the United Nations, and the regional organization known as ASEAN (Association of Southeast Asian Nations). It was a face-saver for them, as well as a way of ensuring that no Western soldiers would set foot on Burmese soil. Dozens of UN agencies and international charities then began delivering food and medicines directly to affected communities. Luckily for everyone, a much feared 'second wave of deaths' from waterborne illness never materialized.

'It's shameful that funding for Burma has been so low', a long-time aid official in Rangoon told me. Burma receives less international assistance than any other developing country, about $4 [US] a year per person compared to ten times that for communist Laos next door. We were meeting over coffee in the lobby of the Chatrium Hotel, several months after Nargis. The Chatrium had become the hotel of choice for UN officials and the growing aid community, thanks to its central location, reasonable rates, and decent internet connection. The bigger trees nearby had been knocked down by the storm, but it was still pleasantly green outside. A sign out front said that a meeting on 'Food Security' was scheduled for 3 p.m. in the ballroom.

'Tens of thousands of people die every year from treatable diseases,' he said. 'Yes, the government is autocratic, but there are dozens of other places around the world, with equally bad governments, where we give far more in humanitarian aid.' Even aid for cyclone victims was low. Despite all the brouhaha at the time and calls for invasion to help these people, once there actually was opportunity to help directly, the money was less than forthcoming. Altogether, about half a billion dollars worth of assistance has been given to Cyclone Nargis victims, compared with the $10 billion that went into reconstructing Aceh after the tsunami. Everybody said they supported humanitarian aid to Burma's poorest. But in practice, Western governments generally shied away.

By 2009, though, there were some glimmers of possible change. The junta had embarked on what they called a 'Roadmap to Democracy', carefully scripted, and leading to a new constitution and a plan for fresh elections the following year. Many in the NLD rejected this constitution as being insufficiently democratic, more a device to sanctify rather than end military domination. Like past constitutions in Indonesia and Thailand, this one allotted a quarter of the seats in the legislature to the armed forces, providing future generals an effective veto in parliament. The president would only be indirectly elected, and the army would retain control over security-related ministries. All this provoked considerable debate. Not so much amongst ordinary people, who worried more about simply getting by, but amongst government officials, dissidents and other activists, aid workers and intellectuals, as well as the sizeable community of expatriates now living and working in Rangoon.

Some saw little more than an attempt to create a fig-leaf for continued military rule. 'How can we trust them! You'll see, they just want legitimacy, and to continue in power forever. We can't sacrifice our principles now, not for a constitution that is so far from what we've fought for all these years.' Others, however, saw an opportunity for change. 'Even a mixed civilian–military government is better than what we have now, which is pure army rule,' one university lecturer argued. 'What's the alternative? Revolution? It won't happen here! We need to be pragmatic. We need to move step by step, to broaden government, bring in new people, and focus on actual policies. The army has to be kept on board. Dreaming of instant democracy won't get us anywhere.'

In all my visits to Rangoon, these arguments were made to me many times by many people. Foreign diplomats, UN officials and what was left of the Burmese intelligentsia gathered around in receptions and dinners and speculated endlessly about the junta's latest actions or decrees. Distrust of the ruling generals was sky high. But with the ruling generals in their late sixties and seventies and at least the prospect of some kind of election and some kind of new government, there was also an air of transition.

There was a lot of talk about the minutiae of Burmese politics, but there was far less discussion of the much bigger drama that seemed to me to be unfolding all around. Far away in Europe and America there was constant speculation about 'the rise of India and China', and its effect on everything from climate change to jobs, to more generally on the world's economy and political order. There was nervousness that hundreds of years of Western domination was finally coming to an end and that different priorities and different values would need to be accommodated like never before. The West's entanglements in the Islamic world and the threats of terrorism were diverting attention in other directions, especially for foreign-policy and security establishments. But for business investors and others with a more long-term horizon, the emergence of a modernizing India and especially a modernizing China was unmistakably the most important issue of our lifetimes. Sitting one evening in my hotel room, I watched a panel on CNN debate what China's and India's continued economic growth would mean for the world. I wondered what it would mean for Burma and I knew that, although the focus in Rangoon was on internal politics, elsewhere others were beginning to look at Burma in a very different way.

In the heart of downtown Rangoon, close to the waterfront, is Mughal Street. In 1858, when the Indian Mutiny (or 'The First War of Indian Independence') was crushed, the last emperor, Bahadur Shah Zafar, was banished to Rangoon, where he lived in a small house next to the Shwedagon pagoda until his death four year later. His tomb has since become a Sufi shrine, attracting pilgrims as well as a regular stream of dignitaries from

India, Pakistan and Bangladesh. He brought with him dozens of courtiers and attendants and today many of the shopkeepers and others on Mughal Street claim descent from this exiled court. It's a broad street, running towards the river, with little girls in veils and boys in snow-white skullcaps on their way to a madrassa, several kebab shops and halal restaurants, as well as a surprising and sizeable concentration of optometrists. Walking around one morning I noticed a small medical clinic with a sign saying 'Trained in Edinburgh' and wondered what youthful memories of Scotland lingered behind.

There is in this part of Rangoon a wonderful mixing of cultures and religions from across the Indian subcontinent. The Indian population is now only a fraction of what it once was, and what is left is like a museum piece, a living remnant of a past connection. There is a grand banyan tree with statues and portraits of the Hindu gods Hanuman and Rama and the goddess Sita. And a few blocks away is the Mughal Shia mosque as well as several Sunni mosques, including ones belonging to the city's sizeable Bengali and Tamil Muslim communities. There's an eighteenth-century Armenian church, a Jain temple and a Parsi fire-temple, a temple to the Tantric goddess Kali and a multi-coloured temple to the Hindu elephant god Ganesh.

There is even a Jewish synagogue, the Musmeah Yeshua synagogue, right in the heart of the Muslim quarter. In the years before World War Two, Rangoon was home to over 2,000 Jews (out of a population of about half a million). The leading families, the Sophaers, the Cohens, and the Sassoons, were, like their cousins in India, from a mix of Ashkenazi and Sephardic backgrounds, but most were immigrants from Baghdad who had reached Burma in the late nineteenth century. There was a Judah Ezekiel street, named after an early settler, and Rangoon even had a Jewish mayor – David Sophaer – in the 1930s. They have now almost all left, all except for about twenty, for the US and Israel and elsewhere, but the handsome synagogue is still there, and recently refurbished. On a rainy afternoon, Moses

Samuels, the caretaker, proudly showed me the two Torahs that remained (dozens of others have been surreptitiously removed to Israel over the years), and I was introduced to his son, Sammy Samuels, back home after graduating from Yeshivah University in New York.

There is a long-standing Chinese community as well in Rangoon. They are not recent immigrants but the descendants of people who came from two directions: by sea and overland. The Chinese who came by sea were part of the worldwide Chinese diaspora, that stretched from Singapore to San Francisco. They were from the coastal provinces along China's southeast coast and spoke not the Mandarin Chinese of Beijing, but a mix of different southern dialects like Cantonese and Fukienese. The Cantonese in Rangoon were mainly artisans and were called by the Burmese 'the short sleeve' or *let-to* Chinese for the short-sleeve shirts they wore. The Fukienese were mainly merchants and were known as the 'long sleeve' or *let-shay* Chinese. Few Burmese cared to probe beyond these distinctions. As in most places, Chinese immigrants were industrious and seen as good businessmen. And, as many immigrants were single men, they normally took Burmese wives, a practice not particularly frowned upon and one that has led over the centuries to many in Rangoon having some Chinese ancestry. More than a hundred years ago, the top British official in Burma wrote of this group: 'Most mixed races in the East seem to inherit the vices of both parents, but [the mixed Chinese–Burmese] seems to have been endowed with the good qualities of both his father and his mother. He is intelligent, steady, and industrious, and decidedly superior in many ways to the pure Burman.' But except for these Chinese and mixed Chinese families, not many in Rangoon knew or cared much about China in those days. Nothing about China was taught in schools and most aspects of Chinese culture would have been a mystery to the average Burmese.

On the streets of downtown Rangoon, Indian and Chinese worlds nowadays appear almost in collision: the kebab shops and Hindu shrines, the bearded men and women in saris yielding almost entirely, after a heterogeneous zone of a block or two, to joss houses, men in baggy shorts and shop signs in Chinese characters. Chinatown is right next to the Indian quarter and has its noisy and crowded little restaurants and karaoke bars, an imposing Hokkien temple, and stores selling herbal medicine, offering acupuncture, and cut-price flights to Taiwan and Hong Kong.

This collision of the older Indian and Chinese worlds is a friendly and cosmopolitan one. But a much newer and far bigger collision, perhaps friendly as well, but with at least the potential for conflict, is fast approaching.

As British planners a century ago looked at the map and thought big thoughts, now Chinese planners have been doing the same. China's development has been concentrated on its eastern coast, from Beijing and Shanghai south towards Hong Kong. Yet to the west are still many poor and backward areas and these include areas with many non-Han Chinese minorities. The planners have been vexed by this gap between a prosperous east coast and a relatively underdeveloped interior. What China is lacking is its California, another coast that would provide its remote interior provinces with an outlet to the sea. Chinese academics have written about a 'Two Oceans' policy. The first ocean is the Pacific. The second would be the Indian Ocean. They didn't say that Burma would become China's California, but clearly they saw Burma as the bridge to the Bay of Bengal and the waters beyond.

They have also written about their 'Malacca Dilemma'. China is heavily dependent on foreign oil and approximately 80 per cent of these oil imports currently pass through the Straits of Malacca, near Singapore, one of the busiest shipping lanes in the world and just 1.7 miles across at the narrowest point. For Chinese strategists, the straits are a natural chokepoint, through which future enemies could cut off foreign energy supplies. An alternative route needs to be found. Burma again is a key.

In Rangoon itself there are few signs of a dramatic Chinese push south. On a flight in from Thailand in late 2008, I found myself sitting in the middle of a big group of middle-aged men who were speaking Mandarin, snapping photographs of one another, flipping through the duty-free catalogue (one bought a watch, the first time I've ever seen anyone buy a watch on a plane) and enjoying the free drinks and savoury snacks. A few hours later, at my hotel, I discovered that the group were a touring high-level delegation from Harbin, a northern Chinese city in what was once Manchuria, close to the Russian border. A big banner had been draped across the entrance that read 'Welcome to the Vice-Governor of Heilongjiang Province and Party' and I saw the same group lounging in the reception area, talking and smoking cigarettes. Otherwise I had seen very few other visitors from the People's Republic, only stories in the papers reporting on this and other visits from high-ranking officials and businessmen.

Chinese plans, though, aren't just talk. In the early 1990s the Burmese–Chinese border, after decades shut, was reopened to trade. Since then, an estimated one to two million Chinese have made their homes – temporary and permanent – in northern and northeast Burma. Chinese businesses have come to dominate much of the economy, with Chinese owning and running everything from small shops to big mining and construction firms. Roads have been built linking Chinese border towns to the valley of the Irrawaddy River and beyond. And much bigger plans are afoot. Reversing old British dreams, the Chinese have proposed connecting China to the Burmese coast by high-speed rail so that Chinese products could be shipped from new factories in the Chinese interior direct to the Indian Ocean. Massive hydroelectric dams are being built in Burma's far north that when completed will produce as much electricity as China's famous Three Gorges Dam, the vast majority of which will go to China. And most importantly of all, work has recently begun on an oil and gas pipeline that, in a couple of years, will start to transport Burma's newly found offshore gas to China's Yunnan province, as well as oil from the Middle East and Africa. It's a strategic hedge against the Straits of Malacca, one that may bring Chinese political influence right up to the Indian Ocean, for the first time in history.

This has worried the bureaucrats and politicians in New Delhi, Asia's other rising power. After a few years of all-out support for Burma's pro-democracy opposition, India reversed course in the mid-1990s, alarmed at China's growing influence with the junta. US- and UK-led sanctions had essentially dealt the West out of the game, but for Washington and London Burma was not particularly important and the price of failure not very high. For India, however, the costs of a Chinese-dominated Burma were unacceptable, and Delhi began to compete with Beijing for access and influence.

To many in Burma, India is in some ways a much more familiar place than China, in large part because of the ancient bonds of religion. An old aunt of mine recently spent a considerable part of her life savings to travel to India on a Buddhist pilgrimage, flying to Calcutta and then taking a bus with many other pilgrims to the sacred sites in Bihar related to the Buddha's birth, enlightenment and teaching. It was a dream of a lifetime. There is a natural or at least historical pull towards India that perhaps is not there with China. But it is unclear whether this will be a major factor going forward. The Indian government too has promised roads and new investments and trade has expanded considerably, but nothing on the scale of what is moving in from the northeast. The momentum for now is coming from Beijing.

The tea shop was on the ground floor of an old art-deco office building from the 1920s. Next door was a bookstore, with a billboard in front advertising Burmese translations of Obama's *Dreams from My Father*, Fareed Zakaria's *The Post-American World*, and Thomas Friedman's *Hot, Flat and Crowded*. And out front on the pavement was a man selling DVDs, the DVDs neatly arranged by category on a little folding table, and a woman next to him with ancient copies of *Life* and *National Geographic* stacked up on a dirty blanket on the ground. There was a smell of diesel from the ramshackle buses that passed by, as well as an occasional whiff of apples, from two large baskets, fresh from the Shan Hills, that were going for around 50 US cents each.

I was meeting old friends. Like nearly all men in Rangoon, they were avid followers of English Premier League football, and every now and then glanced at the Arsenal–Manchester City match showing on the small television screen at the far end of the shop. After a while I brought up Burma's relations with India and China. They said China was definitely a growing influence, on the government and on the economy, but that it was difficult to say exactly what impact both countries were having now. One was an academic. He said: 'I've read as well about all the different plans but it's not made any difference in Rangoon. We still don't even have proper electricity or running water! Being in between India and China should benefit us, and hopefully it will, but we have so many of our own problems to sort out first.'

Distance and Burma's long isolation meant that the great changes taking place at the other ends of Asia were not yet strongly felt. The Indian presence was like a relic of British times, far from the India of world-dominating software firms and Booker prize-winning authors. And the Chinese community in Rangoon was linked to a past diaspora, only tangentially tied to the rising superpower next door. The Burmese could still focus inward, but this inwardness, always before an option, would soon, I felt, no longer be possible. It seemed inevitable that the power and energy of the new China and the new India would eventually close in, for better or for worse, even if for now they remained like ocean swells far from shore.

Everybody, though, mentioned Mandalay. 'Mandalay's like a Chinese city now,' they said. I found this difficult to believe. I had been to Mandalay many times, as recently as 2004. It had been the seat of the last Burmese kings and about as sleepy a place as one can imagine. 'You won't believe the changes, the

Chinese have taken over,' I was told. I had already planned to visit Mandalay and over the next couple of weeks would travel there, and then across the Shan Hills to the Chinese border, along what had once been called the 'Burma Road'.

Cousins

When I was growing up and visiting Burma on holidays with my family, we would often take the train from Rangoon to Mandalay. The trains were old diesel trains with hard wooden seats, the windows kept open to let in the breeze. And from the windows we could see the villages in the distance, villages that looked like islands of tall trees, the little bamboo and wooden houses barely visible as we passed by, clusters of dark green set here and there amongst the fields. At the different stops men and women in faded *longyis* crowded beneath the windows to try and sell snacks and cups of tea and we would sometimes buy a simple dish, like biriani rice served on a banana leaf. It took at least fourteen hours to travel the 500 miles inland to Mandalay, but there must have been even slower trains, as the one we always took was called 'The Mandalay Express'.

This time, in early 2009, I went on a small propeller plane, run by Air Mandalay, one of the new private airlines. On boarding, I noticed that there were two uniformed army officers already in front and a Buddhist monk, sitting alongside them. These are the two special classes of people in the world of Burmese travel, who always receive an automatic upgrade. At least a few others on the flight were Chinese (I could hear them speaking Mandarin) and one was a Burmese girl in her twenties, with blue dyed hair and wearing a mini-skirt, a strange sight in a country where people still tend to dress fairly conservatively. Others looked like business-men and were carrying attaché cases. We all sat silently during the flight, as air hostesses in smart maroon outfits handed out copies of the government-run *New Light of Myanmar* and offered tiny sandwiches and a choice of Coke or Sprite in little plastic cups.

Burma is a fairly big country, the size of France and Britain combined, and from the plane I saw the wet paddy fields of the

Irrawaddy delta fade away, replaced first by forested hills, and then the savannah and scrublands of Upper Burma.

After about fifty minutes, we made an uneventful landing at Mandalay International Airport. 'International Airport' was a statement of ambition. Empty shops lined the big empty terminal and there were three baggage carousels, all to service just me and the two dozen or so other passengers. No other arrivals or departures that day were listed on the overhead information board. And as the rest of us waited for our luggage, I saw the Chinese men from the plane collecting a large crate of Johnny Walker Black Label whisky together with two sets of golf clubs, before speeding away in a waiting black Toyota Landcruiser into the dry and dusty landscape outside.

At first, Mandalay appeared reassuringly the same. From the airport I took a taxi to my hotel, a small place down a quiet residential street, and from there started on a long walk along the old palace wall. Mandalay is set on a plain, with the Irrawaddy to the west and the Shan Hills to the east. The palace complex itself was destroyed during the Second World War but the great walls still remained, a perfect square a mile long on each side, surrounded by a wide moat and then by whitewashed pavements and big trees. I remembered from my last trip that there had been a big red sign along the moat declaring in both Burmese and English the 'People's Desire' (with points like 'Crush all Internal and External Destructive Elements' and my favourite: 'Oppose Those Holding Negative Views'), but this was now obscured by greenery.

A giant chess board had been set up near one corner of the moat, and as I passed a small crowd was sitting and standing around watching a game. A few cars and bicycle rickshaws meandered along the adjacent road and nearby were old homes, in varying states of disrepair, as well as a few newer-looking restaurants and shops. The red-brick Methodist church looked unchanged as did the larger Anglican church, where in the 1860s King Mindon had sent some of his sons to be educated. A couple of dark, wiry men, shirtless and in kickboxing shorts, were jogging. Later that morning, a grand procession rolled past, led by a flat-bed truck with three little boys dressed like princes perched on top. On the next truck were a dozen or so traditional musicians, playing horns and drums, their music amplified by a loudspeaker. They were all on their way to a monastery (I presumed) where the pretend princes would be ordained as novice monks, probably for a just few days or weeks, a rite of passage for all Buddhist Burmese boys. Their parents, family and friends followed behind in a dozen or more slow-moving cars.

Just to the north, a few miles away, was Mandalay Hill, older than Mandalay itself. The hill is nearly a thousand feet high and rises like a cone above the otherwise entirely flat topography; 1,729 wooden steps go all the way to the top. Along the way up are many platforms and pavilions; some have pagodas, others monasteries and areas for quiet prayer and meditation. Women behind little tables sell flowers and pennants for visitors to leave at the many Buddha images, as well as savoury snacks like fried Indian samosas, and postcards for the few tourists who come. There are flame trees with blood-red flowers and rest areas with paintings, mainly from the nineteenth century, including some depicting the various Buddhist hells in gory detail, cartoon-like images of people being boiled in a vat or made to climb up cactus-like trees. And, close to the summit, there is a big statue of the Buddha, standing with an outstretched arm pointing towards the city below. According to legend the Buddha himself came to the hill and prophesied that a great Buddhist capital would one day be built.

There are many other historic and sacred sites within a day's drive of Mandalay, for the city was built in what was, for hundreds of years, the heartland of successive kingdoms. Early Burmese history is still hazy. But we know from recent archaeological work that this middle part of the Irrawaddy valley has been continuously inhabited for a very long time and that as early as the second millennium BC people in Upper Burma were already turning copper into bronze, growing rice and domesticating chickens and pigs, and were among the very first in the world to do so. By around the fifth century BC the first signs of ironworking had appeared and a few centuries later came the earliest attempts to irrigate this parched land. Big settlements and little walled towns were followed by the first kingdoms. Two hundred miles down the Irrawaddy from Mandalay, along a bend in the Irrawaddy River, are the ruins of Pagan (also spelled Bagan), where literally thousands of temples still remain, strewn across miles of near-desert terrain.

There were influences from many directions, and through the first millennium AD the links northward, towards what is today Yunnan in China, were strong. The Chinese, at least by the time of the Tang dynasty (roughly contemporaneous with the Dark Ages in Europe), knew of the kingdoms along the Irrawaddy, and Tang archives record that at the very beginning of the ninth century, a visiting troupe of musicians from Burma travelled to the Tang court and performed songs entitled 'The Victory of the Ram' and 'The Peacock King'. And the Tang were great connoisseurs of exotica, delighting in strange things, from dark-skinned dwarfs from the South Seas, to beautiful Turkish and Japanese dancing girls, to these outlandish performers from far-away Burma.

These early ties with China were important, but it was knowledge of India that would quicken and transform Burmese civilization. Today, in an age when many of us have flown or driven long distances by car, but have never ventured far by ship, we forget that in early times travelling by ship was often much easier and faster than going overland. Until very recently, the great cities of China lay months away from central Burma, an arduous and often fatal trek on foot or by mule. The overland road to India was equally difficult. But India was also across the sea, its vibrant eastern ports a quick and simple sail away. And it was from these ports, in Bengal, Orissa and the Coromandel

Coast, that new ideas and innovations, from mathematics and astronomy to notions of kingship to Buddhism itself, were eagerly imported. To this day, the Burmese word for university is *tekkatho*, a derivation of Taxila, a long-disappeared city in what is now the Swat valley, today a hotbed of Taliban activity, but once a great centre of Hellenistic and Buddhist learning.

It is important also to remember that these early Burmese kingdoms had nothing like the country's present borders. On a map today India, Burma, and China all meet up. But until the onset of British rule, no state power controlled the vast upland regions that separated the centres of Indian and Chinese authority. The Burmese kingdom was a little state in the middle of a thousand-mile stretch of peoples without any state, small chieftainships or tribal groups that owed no allegiance to a higher power.

The link with Indian ideas gave Burmese kings a leg up on their unlettered highland rivals. And a sense of being part of a wider world. Over the nineteenth century, Indian influence gave way to British colonialism, and then the long period of post-independence isolation. As the country opens up again, the question is whether China, rather than India, will become Burma's primary link to the wider world?

I met an old family friend, a teacher in his fifties, looking more haggard than his years, with a dark weathered face and light brown eyes, a descendant of an old aristocratic family, his ancestors having served in the court of the last king. He was living in poverty, as he had much of his life, on a schoolteacher's salary of about $30 a month, making some extra money, perhaps another $100, by providing private tuition in physics and chemistry. He lived in a tiny house, just steps from the old palace moat, and when I arrived he was with a student, both sitting cross-legged on a wooden platform, underneath a tree outside. The student left after a few minutes, and we moved into the house to talk over tea and biscuits. The floor was of hard dirt and an electric fan and a broken television set were the only modern appliances he had. A rickety bookcase was filled with dog-eared Burmese and English paperbacks, the spines of many of them held together with masking tape.

I asked him about the Chinese in Mandalay and he said Chinese immigration had led to lots of changes, more shops and economic activity generally, but that many native Burmese like him had not seen any improvement at all in their own lives and felt passed over:

The Chinese have moved in and the Burmese have had to move out. Very few other than the Chinese can afford to live downtown any more. They've bought land, torn down the buildings that were there and have built their own compounds. They prefer to live apart.

I had seen the enormous new houses on the way from the airport. They were all surrounded by high walls, many with coils of shiny new barbed wire on top. Through some of the front gates, I could also see impressive-looking satellite dishes sitting on neatly manicured lawns.

The Chinese sometimes arrive poor. Some started by just selling noodles on the street. But they work hard and move up. Most, though, came with many advantages, with money and contacts or easy access to loans through their own banks and networks, but the problem is not them, the problem is that we don't have a level playing field.

The better-off Chinese sent their children to English-language schools, he said. The Burmese teachers there were not even allowed to speak in Burmese. I had seen advertisements for these schools in a local magazine. One course was called the 'Cambridge Young Learners Programme'. Another the 'Pride International Education Centre' or 'PIEC'. The 'PIEC will led us to success! [*sic*]' said the advertisement. 'Singapore syllabus!' There was a cartoon drawing of Kipling's Mowgli alongside a picture of the school. 'We can't afford anything like this for our own kids.' He didn't blame the Chinese, but felt the entire system was unfair. I remembered an observation of a British visitor in the 1870s: 'There is a good deal of wealth in the commercial town, but it is in the hands of Chinese and Moguls, with whom the king was afraid to meddle. No Burman could get rich with safety.'

Mandalay had a certain energy that wasn't there in Rangoon. Away from Mandalay Hill, towards the old commercial centre, the shops were bustling with activity. Multi-coloured jeeps zipped around the streets and whereas scooters and motorcycles were banned in Rangoon, here they were allowed and they were everywhere. There was a north Indian look to many of the people, almost Middle Eastern or Mediterranean, and in general an amazing variety of racial types, from some that I might have guessed were Koreans to those with a more southern European look, to a couple who could have passed for native Australians. Policemen in white gloves directed traffic. There was a group of Buddhist nuns carrying lacquered parasols, Sikhs in bright orange turbans, and a wizened old hermit like someone out of a medieval fairy-tale, in threadbare coffee-coloured robes and a scraggy white beard.

The main market was crowded and dirty. In the mid-nineteenth century, when Mandalay was founded, this area had been the favourite camping ground of mule caravans coming down from Yunnan, bringing silver and silk in exchange for Burmese cotton. Then, around the start of the last century, a beautiful covered market was built, by an Italian architect, and though this ornate structure would survive war and fires, it was pulled down in the 1990s and replaced by the ugly concrete construction that now loomed over the dusty stalls and small shops below.

On a side street vendors were selling pots and pans and fresh vegetables. There was a row of shops piled high with construction material with names like 'Golden Lion Wire and Cable', 'Asia Metal Company' and 'Myanmar Wood Coating'. There were also four little stalls, all in a row, selling condoms and various sexual paraphernalia including blow-up dolls and herbal aphrodisiacs. Some of the devices were in worn cardboard boxes and several had, inexplicably, pictures on them of Harry Truman.

There were also many stores selling CDs and DVDs. I peeked into one and saw that in addition to Burmese and Western music, there was also a big section for monkish sermons. Mandalay is the monastic centre of Burma and there are still huge Buddhist monasteries both in Mandalay and in nearby towns, like Sagaing across the river. In Sagaing, the biggest monastery (where I had been on an earlier trip) has grown into a complex of training and research centres and even has a hundred-bed hospital, as well as the more traditional preaching and meditation halls. Some of the abbots who head these more important monasteries are sort of super-monks, well known across Burma and amongst the Burmese diaspora, travelling internationally, their lectures and sermons available on CDs. They are often on television. I saw one once at an airport terminal being greeted by well-wishers like visiting royalty, many of the waiting passengers and even airport staff coming around excitedly to pay their respects.

From the old commercial centre, the city had spread southward for several miles, along 78th Street. It had once been the neighbourhood of artisans and craftsmen, silversmiths and bronze-workers, some the descendants of captives from the court of Siam, brought over during the eighteenth-century wars. The area had become a Chinese preserve. There were no signs of any craftsmen now. Instead 78th Street had been transformed into a four-lane avenue, and was a mix of new developments and building sites, red dust billowing around, trucks and buses rumbling past. In place of the little wooden shops that I remembered from the 1980s, there were multi-storied concrete buildings, generally windowless with blue-tinted glass fronts that looked terrible and must have only magnified the heat inside. One of these buildings was the Great Wall Hotel. Unlike the hotel I stayed at, this big hotel had no Western tourists at all and many of the signs were written in Chinese. Several receptionists were crowded behind the counter and one told me the rooms were $22 a night and came with a free 'foot massage' at the 'foot massage centre' adjacent to the lobby. Across the street, a China Eastern Airlines billboard advertised a new direct flight – three times a week – from Kunming to Mandalay, starting soon. Another much more massive billboard advertised a condominium and retail complex that would be completed in late 2010. The billboard stretched a block long and hid the big hole in the ground that had been dug behind. It had a picture of the planned complex, with an immaculate street and pavement and little sports cars parked out in front. And beyond this commercial area were warehouses and small factories, almost all the way to the airport, about a 45-minute drive away. Mandalay wasn't quite the 'Chinese city' I was told it would be. But here, much more than in Rangoon, China's growing presence was plain to see.

There were three new shopping centres – an unheard of thing anywhere in Burma just a few years back. One had several floors, all air-conditioned and connected by escalators. On the top floor, past the clothes shops and food court, there was an internet café (Net Addict) where I was able to check my emails and catch up on the news. And on the ground floor was a very well stocked and brightly lit supermarket. In a country where most people have no electricity or running water and for whom shopping is a trip to an open-air market, these are novelties. The supermarket was like any normal supermarket in the US or UK, with many brands of cereal and canned soups to chose from, a large section for fresh meats and vegetables, and even a corner selling books and glossy fashion magazines. Unlike any supermarket in the US and UK, however, there was also a section selling monks' robes, neatly folded and wrapped into little wicker baskets. Monks themselves don't come in to buy these robes (they are not supposed to handle money at all, much less spend their days at the mall); they are meant for ordinary Buddhists who want to make an offering at a monastery. I saw one being sold, together with a six-pack of Diet Coke.

It was at a small café next to the supermarket that I had arranged to meet one of the older Chinese residents of the city, born in Burma to Chinese parents, a slender soft-spoken man in tortoise-shell glasses, and a distant relative by marriage. He was a doctor and had been in Rangoon at the time of the 1967 riots. He feared a backlash:

I would guess that Mandalay is at least a third Chinese now. [Mandalay has a population of about a million.] Twenty years ago we were perhaps 5 per cent of the population at most, and our families had been here for generations. We have close Burmese friends and relatives and love this country. Some of the new Chinese come from the border towns, others from inside Yunnan. Many others come from further away, from the southern provinces like Fujian and Jiangxi, but they come overland, not by sea like in the old days. A lot of the small factories are now owned by them, making sugar or pots and pans, you know, very basic things.

He smirked to suggest that there were none of the factories making robots or supersonic planes.

Many others are involving in logging and mining. The newcomers, from inside China, especially the ones here with proper papers, they don't really mix with us, let alone with the Burmese.

We ordered cappuccinos instead of the 'Iced Coffee and Blueberry Cheesecake' that was the $2 'special of the day'.

In Mandalay some of the top businessmen are still Burmese, not Chinese. One for example owns the two big hospitals here. There are also several important Indian businessmen, some Marwaris and Punjabis, and Tamils from South India whose families have been here for over a hundred years. But I think that will change; there is more and more money coming from inside China. And the new businessmen from China, they know how to work the system, because the system here is now almost the same as there. The Chinese like to say that we and the Burmese are *pauk-phaw*, cousins, descended from the same ancestors. But I'm not sure we are acting like good relatives. I worry that something will happen, and that the Burmese will turn against us.

Even our cappuccinos would have been beyond the means of ordinary Burmese in Mandalay. $2 was about the average daily wage in Burma and though my friend the teacher made more than that, a visit to a new café like this one would have been an unimaginable extravagance. The new Mandalay was an unequal place, with the new Chinese immigrants at the top of the pyramid.

It was also a mix of old and new. That evening, walking back to my hotel, I passed a brightly lit Nokia mobile phone shop, filled with Chinese punters carefully examining the newest models. But just a few feet away the paved road turned to a dirt one, and any signs of the twenty-first century disappeared amongst the candle-lit wooden houses. A young woman with a wet sarong tied across her breasts was bathing next to an outdoor well, stray dogs nearby.

It was all a far cry from what I knew was taking place in any medium-sized city in China, where shopping centres like the ones in Mandalay were being built almost literally by the day. But it was, in a way, an extension of what was happening in China, a spill-over from across the hills. And a spill-over from China was like a tidal wave in Burma and in Mandalay. The effects had been magnified as well by the complete absence of Western companies, the result of official sanctions and unofficial boycotts, as well as by the poor state of the Burmese economy more generally. There were no Starbucks or McDonald's or stores selling Apple computers, no Sheraton hotels, no Shell petrol stations. There were also few Burmese competitors. There was nothing intrinsically wrong with what the Chinese were doing. But the Chinese were entering a vacuum, and this once proud capital of a little kingdom, and later a city of British India, was being transformed into an outpost of the world's biggest industrial revolution. They were helping create an unequal society. It wasn't clear at all what the consequences might be.

Mandalay had been built as an act of defiance. In the 1850s, after two bruising wars against the British, Burma's penultimate ruler, King Mindon, had violently seized the throne from his half-brother. His ambition was to modernize what was left of the kingdom and in this way preserve its independence. He sent students to study abroad in India and Europe, imported steamships, built the first modern factories, laid telegraph lines and even developed a Burmese Morse code. He tried to create a professional army and reform government institutions, abolishing the old fiefdoms and taking the first steps towards a salaried bureaucracy. Embassies were dispatched to the West seeking treaties of friendship. It was all very similar to what was going on in contemporary Egypt under Mohammed Ali, in Japan under the Meiji, and in next door Siam (now Thailand) under King Mongut (the king of *The King and I*).

Mindon was not an anglophobe, but through his reforms he wanted to ensure that his country remained free of European aggression. Early in his reign, he decided to build a new capital – Mandalay – much to the shock of his ministers, who were happily ensconced in the old capital, Amarapura, about a dozen miles to the south. It was partly a military decision. Amarapura was right on the Irrawaddy, whereas the future site of Mandalay was two miles inland, just out of the reach of British gunboats. The moat and the massive earth-backed walls, walls that would withstand artillery and aerial bombardment nearly a century later, were designed to deter a British siege.

Mindon the modernizer was also Mindon the traditionalist. A devout Buddhist and a great patron of the faith, he is remembered best by Burmese for his innumerable acts of merit, from his sponsorship of monasteries and the building of pagodas, to his convening of an international Buddhist synod and the resulting review of ancient texts. He carefully performed the ceremonies required of a Burmese monarch and in the costumes and rituals of his court there was no hint of Western modernity. Mandalay was laid out according to age-old custom, as the best-ever rendering of a distinctly Burmese tradition, in a hope that this tradition might survive the Victorian age.

It was not to be. In 1885 a British expeditionary force annexed the kingdom, defeated a surprisingly robust guerrilla resistance, and abolished the ancient monarchy. Rangoon became the capital of all Burma and the focus of commercial attention, and Mandalay became a backwater, an upcountry town of no particular strategic significance. The walled inner city was renamed Fort Dufferin and became home to a small British garrison and the 'Upper Burma Club'. Within a generation, the old aristocracy withered away as a class and British judges, tax collectors and police superintendents were appointed in their place.

George Orwell lived in Mandalay in the early 1920s. He was fresh from school at Eton and had just joined the Imperial Police. He spent time collecting intelligence on the criminal gangs operating in the area (Burma had the highest crime rate of any part of the Indian Empire; some blamed the demise of religious education, others the 'wilful character' of the Burmese) and famously dismissed Mandalay as a rather disagreeable place. 'It is dusty and intolerably hot, and is said to have five main products all beginning with "P", namely pagodas, pariahs, pigs, priests and prostitutes.' Another denizen of Mandalay at the same time was a man named Captain Herbert Reginald Robinson, known as the 'most disreputable Englishman in Mandalay'. He and Orwell were friends. Robinson was a former military man who had become an opium addict and an occasional Buddhist monk. During his many opium-induced trances he believed he was discovering the secrets of the universe, but had a hard time remembering them later on. Once, he managed to scribble down one of his insights while still in a trance, but when he looked at the piece of paper the next morning all it said was 'The banana is great but the skin is greater'. Destitute, Robinson later tried to shoot himself in the head but managed only to blind himself. He eventually returned to England, retrained at the Massage School of the National Institute for the Blind, and ended his life as a physiotherapist in Tooting.

Today, there is little left of either Mindon's Mandalay or the Mandalay of George Orwell and Captain Robinson. On 4 April

1942 Japanese bombers turned the old city into a blackened ruin. The Japanese had invaded Burma three months before, part of their general assault on the Asian mainland, forcing a long British retreat over the mountains into India. Clare Boothe, the wife of Henry Luce, publisher of *Time* and *Life* magazines, and then a reporter in Burma, visited Mandalay two days after the bombing. She wrote:

Every house was burned down or still flaming and smoldering. A terrible stink arose from 2,000 bodies in the ruins of brick, plaster and twisted tin roofing. Only the smoke-grimed stone temple elephants on the scarred path were watching guard over the Road to Mandalay, while buzzards and carrion crows wheeled overhead. Bodies were lying on the streets and bobbing like rotten apples in the quiet green moat around the untouched fort

The British left Mandalay without a fight, but three years later were back, the Fourteenth Army under General Slim battling fierce Japanese resistance. The Fourteenth Army was a combined force of British, Indian, Gurkha and African troops – the African troops included Idi Amin, the future tyrant of Uganda, as well as a grandfather of the future President Barack Obama. The Allied air forces pummelled the Japanese while three divisions of the Fourteenth Army encircled Mandalay and then fought street to street, the now desperate Japanese snipers aiming straight for the heads of British officers.

After independence, Mandalay was partly rebuilt. But under General Ne Win's 'Burmese Road to Socialism', Mandalay, like Rangoon, deteriorated fast. There was no real development and no new infrastructure and much of Mandalay came to resemble an enormous rural community, with low wooden buildings and mean dirt roads. When I first visited in the 1980s, Mandalay seemed entirely forlorn, the great moat choked with water lilies, the Buddhist monks on foot far outnumbering the few antique cars and World War Two era Willys jeeps. There were no taxis and we often walked for miles from place to place or hired horse-drawn carriages (now all gone), the iron-rich dust covering the streets in a reddish hue. Around the same time, two big fires struck the city in succession, destroying thousands of homes and shops and what little architectural heritage was left.

And then, some time in the early 1990s, Mandalay's military rulers had the idea to build a facsimile of the old palace on the site of the original. The palace had been situated within enormous square walls, a mile long on each side, and was actually a tightly packed warren of pavilions and other buildings, each housing an audience hall or the private chambers of the king or other members of the royal family. Nearly all the structures were made of teak and other dark wood, intricately carved with ornate multi-storied roofs, the interiors decorated with gold leaf, lacquer, Persian rugs and glass mosaics. Everywhere were the markings of sovereignty and in the time of Mindon, and his successor Thibaw, the palace area would have been crowded with men and women in silk costumes and velvet slippers, walking here and there over the little footpaths and gardens. A British visitor in the nineteenth century remarked on the 'assembled lords in their brilliantly coloured clothes and tall rounded hats seated before their king like a field of wind-stirred tulips'. Another described the scene during a royal audience:

Here he sits on this throne, the enormous teak pillars holding up the darkened roof, his princes and ministers lying prostrate on the ground before him, the music of flutes and drums off to the side, the blue black mountains in the distance, like some sylvan lord in a fairy tale.

In a military dictatorship, a general's whim is quickly turned to reality, and the palace reproduction was completed within a couple of years. But what had first been constructed in teak was now constructed in concrete and then painted over in red and gold. The reason was understandable. Concrete would last longer than wood. Each individual structure was remade as an exact replica. But the overall impression was disappointing. In concrete, unpopulated and without the strange interiors, there was no sense of the original's fantastic and almost whimsical quality. At the rear of the site, in one of the larger pavilions, was a sort of museum with some of the old royal costumes on display in glass cases and a row of stiff portraits, photographs of the princes and ministers of the extinguished court. The rebuilding of the old palace would be the start of a trend, to underline Burma's pre-colonial past: other old palaces were rebuilt, statues of old kings erected in various towns, and news of archaeological discoveries eagerly announced.

It was perhaps, then, natural that the junta decided, some time in the early 2000s, to follow traditional practice and build a whole new capital as well – a couple of hundred miles south of Mandalay, in the old heartland of Upper Burma. Since about 2004, construction has continued almost non-stop; there are now several gargantuan public buildings (like the parliament that in 2010 was still be completed), a vast parade ground, many more smaller ministry offices, and literally hundreds of apartment blocks for civil servants, private homes for more senior officials, shopping centres, landscaped gardens, golf courses (ubiquitous in Burma since the days of Scottish traders) and even a zoo.

For junta supremo General Than Shwe, being remembered as the founder of the new capital (as Mindon is titled in the royal chronicles as 'the Founder of Mandalay') was almost certainly a key motivation. There were likely other motivations. The declared reason was that the new city, Naypyitaw, which in Burmese means simply means 'The Capital', was in a much more central geographical location than Rangoon. This is true. Naypyitaw is exactly half-way between Rangoon and Mandalay, and within easy reach of the restive Shan Hills and border areas further north and east. New roads have been built to provide it with easy access to different parts of the country. It is also far from the coast and the paranoia of the ruling generals about a possible American seaborne invasion cannot be under-estimated. And finally the new capital provides an insurrection-proof geography. Western media reports often refer to Naypyitaw as Burma's 'jungle capital' or, to add even greater mystery, its 'jungle hideout'. It is nothing of the kind. It is set amongst what was farmland, in an otherwise hot and dusty landscape, with the old British railway and logging town of Pyinmana now included within its boundaries.

The shift in capitals came without any warning. On the morning of 6 November 2005, the staff of all government ministries simply packed up and left, being told to do so just the day before. There had been rumours that a new administrative centre was in the making, but not much more. Even Beijing was caught unawares. The building of the new capital was a mark of the regime's nativist tendencies, the sudden move a reminder of its secrecy. And in not telling China beforehand, the regime signalled that, whatever Beijing wanted, they saw themselves as something other than a client state. The Chinese may have thought that in the Burmese regime, especially under Western sanctions, they had an easy and ready-made partner, but in this they would be frustrated.

Relations between the Burmese and Chinese governments today are good, at least on the surface, but it has not always been this way. In the late 1940s and 1950s Burma's leaders were keen to curry favour with the new People's Republic and became the very first country outside the Soviet bloc to recognize the new communist state. This was not so much the result of any ideological attraction (though many in the Burmese government were then of a left-wing bent), but an innate sense of the country's vulnerability next to a Chinese Goliath that had just been reborn after decades of civil war. The border was a somewhat arbitrary colonial one and Chinese maps were showing considerable swathes of northern and eastern Burma as part of their territory.

In 1949, as most of the defeated Nationalist army of Chiang Kai-shek retreated across the straits to Taiwan, another section slipped over into Burma, hoping to use Burma as a base for a recapture of China. Rangoon was fearful of Beijing's displeasure, attacking Nationalist bases, and building up its army to do so. Beijing's policy at the time was to court the Burmese and both sides made sure problems along the border did not get in the way of good relations. In 1960 the Burmese army and the Chinese People's Liberation Army even launched a joint operation along the border, effectively ending any serious threat from the Chinese Nationalists.

Later in the 1960s, however, relations between Burma and its big neighbour worsened dramatically. By the middle years of that decade, China had come under the grip of its Cultural Revolution, and radicals were trying actively to encourage communist insurgencies elsewhere in Asia. There was already a significant, home-grown, communist insurgency in Burma, but they were then on a back foot, with no real hope of armed victory. China's communist radicals wanted to change this. After a series of bloody internal purges, copycats of the kind taking place in China, the Communist Party of Burma converted itself into a Maoist organization, with a new batch of Chinese-trained leaders waiting just across the border. At the same time, the Chinese embassy in Rangoon began to stir up trouble. The embassy had been allowed to fund Chinese-language schools in Rangoon and these schools started teaching a Maoist curriculum, aimed at turning their students into Burma-based Red Guards, whilst at the same time Chinese embassy officials openly distributed copies of Mao's 'Little Red Book' and other propaganda. Tensions rose, not only with the Burmese government, but with the Burmese people generally.

Violence erupted in June 1967 after stories circulated of Chinese students assaulting their Burmese teachers, and for three days Chinese people and property were attacked by mobs all around Rangoon. Chinese schools were burnt down, together with the Chinese information centre, as well as ordinary homes and shops. A Chinese aid worker was knifed. Thousands of people tried to storm the embassy itself but were driven back by government troops who opened fire, wounding nine people.

Only armed patrols with machine guns were able to drive the population back indoors.

The reply from China was swift. Gargantuan crowds of more than 300,000 placard-waving Chinese gathered in the pouring rain outside the Burmese embassy in Beijing calling for the overthrow of the 'fascist' Burmese military regime. More importantly, Chinese support for the insurgent Communist Party of Burma swelled and in early 1968 a large force, ostensibly led by exiled Burmese communists but in fact officered by Chinese, crossed over from Yunnan and seized a big slice of territory in the eastern hills. It was nothing less than an invasion from China. At one point the communists were within striking range of Mandalay, stopped only by the tenacious resistance of the Burmese army. For twenty more years the fighting between the Burmese government and communist forces would continue, at great cost especially to the local civilian population. Only by the late 1970s, as the political scene in China changed, did Beijing ratchet down its support for the Communist Party of Burma. Both sides then took a pragmatic stance and relations slowly began to improve. By the mid-1980s there were talks about renewing trade and the first Chinese business scouts arrived in Mandalay, exploring opportunities. From then, relations, especially economic relations, would grow quickly. But the shadows of the past remained.

The new Chinese in Mandalay were entrepreneurs, taking advantage of the new openings, and over the coming days I saw them everywhere, shopping in the more expensive shops and eating in big groups in the Chinese restaurants all over town. At night they (the men, at least) frequented the many karaoke bars and massage parlours that had popped up near 78th Street. It's not always easy to distinguish a Burmese from a Chinese. The Burmese tend to be darker, with more rounded or deep-set eyes, and perhaps a narrower or more prominent nose, but the difference is sometimes slight, and in both countries there's a wide variety of appearances. But these new Chinese were easy to spot, never dressed in a Burmese *longyi* (as many of the Burma-born Chinese were), but in the somewhat baggy, Western-style clothes of modern China.

I met one by chance at the office of a friend. My friend ran a small import–export firm and the Chinese man, a businessman in a beige safari-suit, bowing and smiling, was just leaving. He spoke some English and he said he had been in Mandalay only a few months but was excited by the prospects. He said new roads and future railways would bring the two countries closer than ever before, lead to growing business ties, and better cooperation. He was looking at the possibility of investing in a factory (he didn't say what kind) and had been involved before in importing Burmese timber and gems. 'It's kind of a golden age for China–Burma relations', he said.

It was a confidence that came from feeling that history was on their side. And that their ways had proved better. Very recently, a 'Confucius Institute' was set up in Mandalay, one of several in Burma, providing language training as well as other courses about China. And in the same way that Western observers saw Burma's poverty and misgovernment and assumed Western models provided the answer, the Chinese did the same. I thought of an inscription, which I think is still there, on the wall of a nineteenth-century Chinese temple on the outskirts of Mandalay, that reads, 'Enlightenment finds its way even among the outer barbarians.'

The enormous influx of Chinese people and Chinese invest-ment in many ways parallels the Indian influx of similar (or even greater) size a century before. The Chinese were bringing in much-needed money and skills and the country could well benefit from closer contacts with its fast-developing neighbour. Being next to the biggest growth engine in the world could be an enormous boon. And, like many of the Indian immigrants in the early twentieth century, the Chinese immigrants of the early twenty-first saw Burma as a land of opportunity. They were not grand strategists or politicians. Many were far from rich and were seeking to improve their lives the only way they knew how. But the intensity of resentment from local people suggested that a backlash of sorts might not be far beyond the horizon. The Indians had come under the protection of colonial rule. And the Chinese were now coming into a Burma that was independent but lacked political freedom. People felt they had no choice but to accept what was happening and bide their time.

Draw a circle around Mandalay with a radius of only a little more than 700 miles. That circle reaches west over Bangladesh and across the hill states of India, to Assam, West Bengal, Orissa and Bihar; north and east to China's Yunnan and Sichuan provinces and parts of Tibet; and southward to cover most of Laos and Thailand. Within that circle are the homes of no fewer than 600 million people, nearly one in ten of all the people on the planet. And nearly all the people of this Mandalay-centric world are poor – the circle includes as many poor people as all the poor in sub-Saharan Africa. But there is also movement, energy, and uncertain futures. Poverty rates, on the Chinese side at least, are falling fast. Money is being made. On the opposite fringes of this world are Delhi and Beijing, but here in Mandalay it is Chinese influence that is clearly in the ascendancy.

By the time 2010 rolled around, work was already beginning on the oil and gas pipeline and as well as on an entire network of related highways and railways, cutting right past Mandalay on the way to the sea. It seemed on the surface that Burma would be drawn ever more tightly eastward. For the new visionaries of China, the map would soon be changed forever. But what of the Burmese government, the ruling junta? In the Western media they tend to be portrayed as lackeys of Beijing, a client regime that is happy to allow in a flood of Chinese people and goods. The relationship, however, is far more complex.

The Burma Road

To the west of Mandalay is the Irrawaddy River. To the east is a vast limestone plateau that rises suddenly and then extends all the way to the Yangtze River and the central provinces of China nearly a thousand miles away.

I hired a car and a driver. The car was a beat-up 1980s' Honda and the driver was a young man with white racing gloves who played Burmese rap music the entire way. The rap music phenomenon in Burma was something new to me. And as my personal exposure to new music more or less ended with university in the late 1980s, I am utterly unfamiliar with rap music even in the West and so could not really judge or appreciate what I was hearing. In the weeks ahead I would hear more Burmese rap music, at tea-shops and restaurants, and knew that it was very popular, with concerts by the better-known stars attracting hundreds, sometimes thousands of young people.

After a few miles, we had left Mandalay's dusty avenues and were on a bumpy road lined with shady trees, passing little hamlets and open fields, a brown and burnt countryside just after the harvest. Soon we began our ascent. The distance to Maymyo, our destination, was only forty-three miles, but it was 4,000 feet up the limestone cliffs. The road wound around and around, and after about twenty minutes, looking back, the great plain of the Irrawaddy was visible to a distance very far away, including Mandalay and the dozens of little towns all around, the gold of the innumerable and from here tiny-looking pagodas reflecting the afternoon sun. There was a place to stop to admire the view, a half-way point prosaically named '21 miles', and I saw there a Burmese family, their car parked, snapping photographs of each other against the imposing background.

Marco Polo, who never went to Burma but heard about it second-hand, described this area as 'a very unfrequented country, with great woods abounding in elephants and unicorns and a number of other wild beasts'. The Burma of the lowlands had faded away, and in its place were pine trees and red azaleas, more prosperous-looking farms and white picket fences. The heat and humidity gave way to clear skies and a cool breeze.

The Candacraig hotel looked exactly as I had remembered it from more than a dozen years before. An imposing mock-Tudor house with a gravel driveway and neatly tended grounds, it was probably not much different from how it was a hundred years ago, when it wasn't a hotel but a 'chummery' or 'bachelor's quarters' for the visiting (male) staff of the Bombay Burmah Trading Corporation, an important Scottish logging firm in its day.

There were elegant sliding doors and potted plants and a big teak staircase that led up to the six bedrooms upstairs. On the ground floor, there was a dining room to one side and a small bar on the other. Just outside (stepping out from the bar room) was a well-maintained tennis court, and later I would see four middle-aged Burmese men in whites enjoying a game of doubles. My bedroom was enormous, the size of a small Manhattan apartment, with newly made and not very attractive wooden furniture, a fireplace, a rusty bathroom, and an old creaky bed. There were no modern comforts, no television or anything that suggested the twenty-first or even the late twentieth century. It was very quiet and through the open windows I could only hear the sound of rustling leaves from the very tall trees overhead. I was the only guest.

I had arrived early and after some unpacking headed on foot towards the town centre, a couple of miles away. I walked down what had been Park Road, a winding road shaded by soaring pine trees, past homes whose owners long ago had named them 'Oakhurst', 'Ranelagh', 'East Ridge' and 'Penzille'. Some of these names were still visible on signs. Others I looked up later on an old map of Maymyo. There were all very grand, mainly red-brick, some with a vague Tudor effect and set on an acre or more of land. Some looked well kept with freshly cut grass; others were in poor condition as if no one had lived there for years.

A British writer a hundred years ago had written: 'To the Burmans of the plains, the climate is unsuited, but natives of Northern India, Gourkas [*sic*], and Europeans, who pay adequate attention to dress and dwelling houses enjoy excellent health.' I was a Burman (at least by ancestry) but to me the weather was perfect, sunny and cool, perhaps in the low sixties Fahrenheit. The British had tried very hard to evoke a sense of home but everywhere were reminders that this was not Britain – the eucalyptus trees and bougainvillea and the little lizards that were climbing up the walls at the hotel. And in this way, Maymyo seemed less like anything authentically British and more like attempts elsewhere to transport a sense of Britishness, say in North America, Australia or New Zealand.

Very near to where I was walking was where a British army officer named Colonel Henry Morshead had been mysteriously murdered in 1931. Colonel Morshead had served in France and in Waziristan and had been part of early expeditions up Mount Everest. In 1931 he was serving in Burma as Director of the Survey of India. One day, when he was on holiday in Maymyo, he went out for an early morning pony ride. About an hour later his pony returned, riderless and stained with blood. A search was begun at once and an entire battalion of Indian soldiers, Dogras and Madras Pioneers, was later sent into the forests close by. Colonel Morshead's body was finally found with two bullet wounds. Dacoits were suspected, but the murder remains a mystery. In Jeffrey Archer's recent novel *Paths to Glory*, Morshead appears as a character, killed in Maymyo in the last chapter, not by a mystery assailant, but by his wife's secret 'Pakistani lover'.

I passed 'Craddock Court' and then 'Croxton', both now hotels as well, the latter once the 'family holiday home' of the same Bombay Burmah Trading Corporation that had built the Candacraig. I had seen pictures from this time, of black-tie dinners and fair-haired children in costumes posing at fancy-dress parties. There was polo and other sports at the Maymyo

Gymkhana Club, amateur theatricals, and an endless round of parties during the high season. Standing in front of 'Croxton', with no one else around other than a very small Indian-looking man trimming the hedges, I had no trouble imagining that time, not as a glamorous Merchant Ivory film, but as real life, where the black tie dinner was followed by a climb up the wooden staircase to a rusty bathroom and an uncomfortable bed.

For the British, Burma was not very interesting in itself, but held an important geographical location, guarding India's eastern flank. In the 1820s an aggressive Burmese empire had threatened Britain's own expanding Indian possessions, taking Assam and Manipur (what is today India's 'Northeast') and menacing Bengal. The British were at first drawn in unwittingly, but then came to see control over the Irrawaddy valley and the adjacent hills as a vital part of their defence of India. Burma was a buffer against China as well as against the French, who were then moving up the Mekong River from Saigon.

Burma was also about making money. In addition to the rice, teak and oil of the lowlands, there were many other natural resources here in the highlands as well, ready to be exploited, including tungsten, silver, lead, copper, and zinc. The Scots dominated business, but profit-seekers came from all over the world. One was Herbert Hoover, about twenty years before he became president of the United States, who arrived in Burma as an up-and-coming partner of an international mining company. With a young family in tow, he even lived for a time in Maymyo and set up his own firm to make money from the silver mines recently identified near the Chinese border. He would write that the Burmese were 'the only truly happy and cheerful race in Asia'. He would also make millions for himself.

In pre-colonial times, demographics and geography kept both India and China far away. There were mountains and jungle and few people in the vast spaces in between Asia's big civilizations. But by the twentieth century this was changing. Populations were growing and filling in the landscape. And new technologies conquered once forbidding terrain. For most of British rule, the strategic and economic motives were still not there for Burma to become China's back door. Then in the 1930s the situation changed, as Japanese armies closed in on China's beleaguered Nationalist government from the east and Burma's strategic position became obvious for the whole world to see. The Allies would build the 'Burma Road' and then the 'Stilwell Road', desperate to connect India with China and keep Chinese forces supplied. It is these same roads that are now being remade, but for very different reasons.

For China the route that ran through Maymyo, from the Middle Kingdom to the plains of central Burma, had long been of some significance. Since ancient times Burma had been a source of precious commodities, like amber and jade. And under the final Burmese dynasty, large quantities of cotton and tea had also found their way to Chinese markets. Tea was indigenous to the hills just northeast of Maymyo, and the export of tea across the border was such an important part of the local economy that a Burmese minister in the early nineteenth century dismissed as 'preposterous' the British claim that there was tea in China too. Invading armies had also come this way. The Mongols had passed through in the thirteenth century, as did a great Chinese and Manchu force in the seventeenth century, sent to arrest and execute a renegade prince. In the 1700s the Manchus had invaded again, not once but four times, but each time were defeated by a spirited Burmese regime.

In British times the Chinese had turned inward, engulfed in civil war and warlordism. But in the 1930s, as Japanese armies swept through China's eastern coastline, Burma's military value skyrocketed, not only for the Chinese but for all the powers fighting Japanese expansion. Overnight, the country turned from backwater to strategic centre. For the British, Burma became an essential part of any plan to protect India from the Japanese. For the Americans, Burma was critical to continued access to

China and support for the armies of Chiang Kai-shek. And for the Japanese, Burma became a potential springboard to India and Asian domination.

Through the 1930s, Japanese armies had overrun the entire Chinese coastline, from Manchuria to Hong Kong. In 1937, after months of intense fighting, more than 200,000 Japanese imperial troops and naval aircraft had captured Shanghai (other than its Western enclaves) and by the end of 1937, the then capital Nanjing had itself been taken, leading to the killing of as many as 300,000 Chinese men, women and children. The industrial centre of Wuhan was next together with the cities of the south coast. Chiang Kai-shek withdrew his government to Chongqing along the middle Yangtze and continued a stubborn defence. The Chinese – both Chiang's Nationalist forces and the Communists under Mao Zedong – would soon be tying down no fewer than twenty Japanese divisions. As war between the US and the Axis powers approached, Washington was increasingly anxious to keep China in the fight. Sending help via China's own port cities was now impossible. A back door via Rangoon was the only option and the Burma Road was born.

From Rangoon, American war materials were sent by both truck and train up to Mandalay and then over the hills, from Maymyo to Lashio, the easternmost railway station in British Burma. A new road then joined Lashio to Chinese-held Kunming, more than 500 miles away. The road was built at literally break-neck speed, by 200,000 Chinese labourers using shovels, or sometimes nothing but their bare hands, to dig away at hills and mountains. At least 2,000 died in the process. But by 1938, where there had only been dirt tracks and jungle ravines, there was now a road capable of handling military lorries.

The war then came to Burma from the other direction. Beginning in December 1941, Emperor Hirohito's forces swept through almost all of southeast Asia, from Manila to Jakarta and Singapore, in a series of lightning conquests. For the Japanese, cutting the Burma Road had become a top priority and this they achieved by March 1942, after an invasion of Burma from Thailand and the capture of Rangoon. The British, caught unawares and with little preparation, then began a long northward withdrawal.

On 5 April in Maymyo, an American general, Joseph 'Vinegar Joe' Stilwell, met Chiang Kai-shek. Mrs Luce was there to interview Stilwell for a cover story in *Life* magazine and the British brought out kilted soldiers with bagpipes to welcome the Chinese leader and his wife, the Wellesley College educated 'Dragon Lady' Madame Chiang. The Chinese 5th, 6th and 66th Armies were then marching into Burma to join the anti-Japanese fight; 50,000 would soon die. In an innovative and never very satisfactory Allied arrangement, Stilwell had been placed (at least theoretically) in charge of the Chinese forces and appointed as Chiang's chief of staff. The American press were soon running enthusiastic headlines like 'Chinese Cavalry Rout Jap Panzers in Burma' and 'Look Out Hirohito!' But within days Mandalay too fell to the enemy and the British were in full retreat. Maymyo and Lashio were overrun and the Burma Road was gone.

The rapid collapse of its entire Far Eastern empire was a humiliating blow to British prestige. Plans were soon drawn up for a reconquest of Burma, to be followed by Malaya and Singapore. Few, however, believed that an overland invasion from India was possible, given the harsh terrain along the Burma–India border, and instead most British commanders favoured an amphibious assault on Rangoon. It would be a repeat of the East India Company's landing at Rangoon in 1824, which had caught by surprise the forces of the king of Burma. Winston Churchill pushed for Allied support, as without American planes and sea transport little would be possible. But the Americans were not interested. Roosevelt himself, whilst sympathetic to Indian desires for independence, was scathing in his views of the Burmese. He told Churchill:

I have never liked Burma or the Burmese! And you people must have had a terrible time with them for the past fifty years . . . I wish you could put the whole bunch of them into a frying pan with a wall around it and let them stew in their own juice.

For Washington, the main priority was not liberating Burma itself, but reopening the Burma Road. The US was now battling the Japanese across the Pacific and keeping the Chinese going was a top concern. Chiang Kai-shek's armies were not entirely isolated as American pilots had begun flying the 'Over the Hump', from Calcutta over the eastern Himalayas to Yunnan. But this was an extremely dangerous route and capable of transporting only a fraction of what had been possible via Rangoon. Overland access was urgently needed, but for this the recapture of Rangoon was unnecessary. Instead, the Americans wanted to construct a new road, leading from Ledo in Assam across the northern fringes of Burma to Yunnan. Assam was still firmly in British hands and a railway line ran close to the Burmese border. From there to China was dense jungle and mountains, one after another.

And so, over eighteen months, thousands of civilians and soldiers laboured day and night, in torrential rains, battling swarms of insects, leeches and deadly diseases, to build what would be known as the Ledo or Stilwell Road, a road that would skirt the base of the Himalayas and again provide direct access from India to China. Most of the soldiers involved were African-Americans, tasked with this gruelling and thankless job in part because their white superiors believed they had a natural 'night vision' that would allow them to work in dark jungle conditions. They were probably the first people of African descent ever in those remote hills and amongst the first Americans; for a while, the local Naga tribesmen assumed that all Americans were black.

Meanwhile, under the brilliant leadership of General Slim, the British Fourteenth Army pushed east from Manipur. At the August 1943 Quebec Conference of Roosevelt and Churchill, authorization had been given to reopening the Burma Road, but not to any specific re-invasion of Burma. But in 1944 the Japanese launched their own massive attack along the Burmese–Indian border, and Slim turned this potentially disastrous development into an opportunity, defending the Manipuri capital of Imphal, smashing the Japanese while their supply lines were overstretched, and then chasing them, first across the Chindwin River and then the Irrawaddy. Mandalay was encircled and then taken. Maymyo itself was recaptured in a dawn raid by a Gurkha battalion and part of the Welsh Regiment. Before they left, the Japanese rather gratuitously destroyed Government House in Maymyo, the stately summer home of British governors.

The Stilwell Road was finished and the Burma Road reopened, but only in time for this first (and so far only) direct passage from India to China to become redundant. In May 1945, the 17th Indian Division entered Rangoon unopposed and within three months the first atomic bombs were exploded over Hiroshima and Nagasaki. The Japanese Empire was no more.

The British quit Burma less than three years after the end of the war. With India's independence, Burma's strategic value as an eastern buffer was gone. The economy had been devastated by the war and all major infrastructure was in ruins. Malaya, Singapore and Hong Kong seemed like better bets for future profits. Even then, the British would have stayed and helped to restore the economy had it not been for an extra element: the emergence of a powerful and radical nationalist movement, determined to see the British out at any cost. Some were communists. Many others had collaborated with the Japanese, before turning against them towards the end. The country was awash in weapons and the young nationalists were armed and prepared for violence. With massive problems in India, Palestine and elsewhere, including at home, the British were in no mood to fight an insurrection in Burma. Pandit Nehru, India's new prime minister, had made clear that Indian troops would not be available to quell a Burmese nationalist revolt. The Labour government of Clement Attlee decided to do the prudent thing and on 4 January 1948 Burma became an independent republic. Soon the country was at civil war, and within twelve years a military junta would seize power, the beginning of decades of army rule.

By the 1960s, India, Burma and China had all turned inward. The Stilwell Road relapsed into jungle. The Burma Road led nowhere, with the border between Burma and China effectively closed. Nearly half a century would pass before it was resurrected, by the new and growing economies of Asia.

From the Candacraig it was about half an hour's walk to the town proper, where there was first a red-brick hospital, once run by the American Baptists, and then an Anglican church. Inside the church, a great tablet read:

To the Glory of God And In Memory Of The 10th Regiment Gurkhas Formerly First Burma Rifles This Sanctuary Has Been Presented By Their Brother Officers Relatives And Friends

Other British Army regiments – the Durham Light Infantry, the Duke of Wellington's Regiment, the Border Regiment – and the Royal Air Force all had smaller plaques with their insignia on the wall. Around the back, a group of parishioners were preparing for a church tea later that day. One of them, a small man in a floppy hat and sandals, said that the church had been built in 1912. He estimated that about seventy people still came to service every Sunday. Most, he said, were Burmese, but many were also of mixed ancestry, Anglo-Burmans and Anglo-Indians. He said he himself was of mixed Irish and Indian ancestry.

The church was at the top of the high street, called the Mall, about a mile long. I had seen an old postcard of the Mall in British days, with low wooden shop-houses, horse carriages, and a clock tower in the centre, and the Mall today looked almost exactly the same, except much more crowded, with several newer and taller buildings behind the original shops. The clock tower – 'the Purcell clock tower' – was still there as were the little horse carriages and a sign that must have been at least a century old that read 'Fancy Goods'. Together with the dusty streets and wooden buildings, they gave downtown Maymyo a Wild West atmosphere.

A large Sunni mosque stood to the side of the Mall. There was a northerly feel to the jumble of appearances on the street, decidedly not southeast Asian, as one might find in say Bangkok or Jakarta, but more north Indian, Nepali and Chinese, as well as Burmese. The Nepalis were partly descended from Gurkha soldiers who had been stationed there by the British and partly from the more general Nepalese diaspora that has extended from the Himalayas across Assam to Burma. A European strain was also sometimes visible as Maymyo had been a favourite place of retirement for the country's once sizeable Eurasian community.

Maymyo was famous for its strawberry fields (just outside the town) and there were baskets of strawberries on sale as well as apples and other fruits exotic in a country of mangoes, papayas and durian. 'Drink Cow's Milk Every Day for Good Health' read a sign at a milk shop. The Burmese generally don't drink milk and this too – a Nepali-run enterprise – was something unusual. It was now close to noon and there were lots of people filling the shops and walking up and down the pavement or speeding by on scooters and bicycles. A billboard advertised Iron Cross's upcoming 'Alpine Tour'. Iron Cross was the country's best known (heavy metal) band, and Alpine was a local bottled-water company that I assumed was sponsoring their concerts. Stalls offered tiny packets of things like instant coffee or washing powder and at one corner of the street a group of Indians huddled conspiratorially around what looked like the top of a fax machine. This was more familiar. It was a key part of the economy in every town: parts were sold, resold, mended, and sold again. There was a certain air of relative prosperity to Maymyo, at least seen here from the Mall, but there were also many destitute people. A couple of tiny street urchins wandered around begging for money. And women with Himalayan faces, in dirty and threadbare tribal costumes, sat on the side of the street, nursing their babies.

After a couple more hours of milling around, I decided to head back to the Candacraig. And instead of walking back I went to the clock tower and climbed into a horse carriage, powder-blue on the inside, with a driver who told me his family were Pathans, originally from what is now the Pakistan–Afghanistan border. The horse's hooves clattered on the cobblestones and soon I was back on the balcony of the hotel. I had told the receptionist that I would like to eat dinner in. Twenty years ago, the Candacraig was still run by a Mr Bernard, an Indian Christian who had worked there since colonial days, and I had enjoyed a meal of roast beef and Yorkshire pudding in the dining room. But Mr Bernard had died long since and the Burmese staff could only offer a simple meal of rice and curry, which I ate early, at sundown, the only sound a distant call to prayer from the mosque in town.

It was only on the second day that I noticed some of the more recent developments in Maymyo. To the north of town, away from the Candacraig, were a few fancy new hotels, including the 'Governor's House', a reproduction of Government House, where the British governor had lived during the 'hot weather', and which claimed to 'resurrect the legendary charm and grandeur of the 1920s and 1930s'. It was set on a hilltop and as there were no guests staying at the time, I persuaded the hotel staff to let me have a look around. The reproduction had been done well and though only a year or so old looked appropriately worn and weathered. There were framed black and white photographs from earlier times and a big room that I presumed in the original had been used for other purposes was now an indoor swimming pool. And in the foyer were life-sized mannequins of past British governors, like Sir Harcourt Butler and Sir Charles Innes, in frock coats and top hats, together with a fierce-looking Japanese soldier crouching a few feet away with a bayonet. Burmese people I later spoke to said many avoided the place, as it was rumoured to be haunted, with a ghostly old Englishman wandering around at night in the hall.

Nearby was a trendy-looking café (the Golden Triangle) serving excellent coffee, including coffee made from Burma's first coffee farms. And further away from the town centre, there were also bigger, newer homes, not unlike the Chinese houses in Mandalay, and 'resort' hotels, offering 'weekend spa packages'. Maymyo's salubrious climate was becoming increasingly attractive to well-off Burmese – army generals, businessmen and even the movie stars who often filmed here as well. A big draw for the holiday crowd were the Botanical Gardens. There was a man-made lake and paths that curved through the grassy slopes of flowers and trees. On the 150-acre site were said to be hundreds of different types of plants including more than 300 species of orchid. It was modelled on Kew Gardens and had been designed early in the last century by the amateur Irish botanist Lady Charlotte Wheeler Cuffe, though the construction work was done by Turkish prisoners captured during the First World War.

My last day in Maymyo was a Sunday, a day off for cadets from the Defence Services Academy, which sits just on the outskirts of town. They were everywhere that day, all in their neatly pressed forest-green uniforms and gleaming boots, skinny teenagers in crew cuts, many carrying little black attaché cases, their metal heel taps clicking as they walked by. I saw some getting haircuts and others having their pictures taken at the photographer's studio. They were in the little shops that offered long-distance phone calls and I saw them queuing up to call home. They examined the army kits (especially shoe polish) that hawkers were selling on the pavement. Others went to the cinema. I had lunch at a Chinese restaurant and I saw a few of them there, laughing and talking. There was a notice that said 'Cadets will absolutely (absolutely) not be allowed any alcohol', perhaps a sign of some recent disciplinary problems. But they all seemed polite as well as self-confident, enjoying their day off.

The enormous Defence Services Academy is the Burmese military's premier training facility, a sort of West Point or Sandhurst of Burma, offering a university-equivalent degree to aspiring officers. It had the look of a suburban American office complex, the headquarters of 'Acme Industries', with manicured lawns and well-scrubbed concrete and glass buildings. There was an imposing steel and granite gate in front, with a sign (in English) that read 'Training the Elite of the Future'. It was a reminder that, at least in the eyes of the Burmese officer corps, whatever happened, they were here to stay.

Burma's is the longest-lasting military dictatorship anywhere in the world. It is also a uniquely isolationist state that has gone through several different incarnations since the military coup of 1962 overthrew the last elected government. In its early years, the generals at the top, led by General Ne Win, were organized as the 'Revolutionary Council', overseeing their singularly disastrous 'Burmese Way to Socialism', cutting off nearly all contact with the outside world, expelling the Indian middle class, and nationalizing most businesses. At a time when parts of Asia were starting to zoom ahead, Burma fell far behind. Then came a new constitution, in 1975, based on those of the Soviet bloc, making Burma a 'Socialist Republic'. General Ne Win resigned his army commission but remained very much in charge, as 'Chairman of the Party', jettisoning some of the more extreme xenophobic policies. After the failed 1988 uprising, any pretence to socialism was thrown out the window, together with the constitution, and a new junta was formed, first calling itself the 'State Law and Order Restoration Council' (or SLORC, a James Bond-style acronym to rival Stalin's SMERSH), and then somewhat more demurely the 'State Peace and Development Council' (or SPDC).

It was this new SLORC/SPDC junta that began to unwind decades of isolation. General Ne Win, the tyrant of Burma since 1962, was fading into the background (he would later lose all power and end up under virtual house arrest before his death in 2002). And the new generation of generals, including several who had received military training in the US and UK, were eager at least to test out a more market-oriented, Western-leaning approach. They were not democrats. But they wanted to steer away from the ruinous economic policies of the past.

The state's finances were in dire straits. Foreign exchange reserves were close to zero and only a fire-sale of natural resources, mainly logging rights to Thai firms, avoided collapse. But soon, trade and investment policies were freed up, and a new wave of investment came in, from American and European companies, as well as from the region. Tourism was encouraged for the first time in decades, and hotels sprouted up everywhere, some owned by foreign businesses, others set up by local entrepreneurs. This was in the early 1990s when there was much talk of 'Asian Tigers' and other countries like India and Vietnam, still then no more prosperous than Burma, were also liberalizing their economic relations with the world.

But then things hit a brick wall. The government's own policies were partly to blame. The move to a free-market system was still half-hearted. More importantly, the generals at the top distrusted their own civilians, including and perhaps especially those educated overseas. This was in stark contrast to military regimes elsewhere in the region, South Korea for example, or Indonesia, that had followed the economic advice of civilian technocrats. But a big part of the problem was also the Western boycott calling for an end to any business dealings with Burma. Many in the US and Europe were keen to show support for the country's fledgling democracy movement and some argued, without much evidence or logic, that this was the best way to pressurize the generals, despite the fact that the generals were only starting, tentatively, to emerge from their own self-imposed isolation. As part of an official sanctions regime, all development aid was denied, making any moves towards greater economic reform much more difficult. By the mid-1990s the few Western companies that had waded in had begun to withdraw and prospective investors shied away. Momentum was already fading fast when, in 1997, there came both a formal US government ban on new American investment and the Asian financial crisis. Outside money dried up.

Except from China. Relations with China had begun improving from the 1980s and now went from strength to strength. The border was opened up for the first time in decades. In the early 1990s Beijing provided credit for military and other purchases estimated at well over a billion dollars in total. Chinese businesses didn't care less about the National League for Democracy or whether or not Burma was moving towards democratic government. And though the Asian financial crisis affected China as well, China's trade ties with Burma continued to expand.

Psychological support from Beijing was equally important, coming at a time when Western powers were cutting off long-standing military ties and just after US warships had appeared off the Rangoon coast. As Western rhetoric in favour of an immediate democratic transition became more shrill, China's steady declarations of friendship and pledges of 'non-interference in the internal affairs of Myanmar' rose in value. The more the British and the Americans berated the regime at the UN, the more Chinese diplomatic protection became essential to the regime's foreign policy.

Burma's generals were thankful for China's friendship. But they were the same generation of generals who had fought nearly all their lives against Chinese-backed communist insurgents (and, some believed, regular Chinese soldiers), seeing their men and fellow officers die by the hundreds. Several generals in the 1990s had been trained in the West and had fond memories of America. In their minds, something wasn't quite right. The Chinese wanted their friendship to lead to ever closer economic integration. But the junta started hedging their bets.

Fear is too strong a word. But an anxiety about China is deeply ingrained in Burmese thinking. There are the memories of past invasions. All schoolchildren learn of the Tayok-pyay-min, the 'king who ran away from the Chinese', the medieval ruler who feared an imminent Chinese assault and abandoned his capital. The defence of the kingdom from eighteenth-century Manchu invaders is celebrated in song and poetry. Though the main invasions from China were led by non-ethnic Chinese rulers – Mongols and Manchus – the Burmese rarely make the distinction. There is no special dislike of China or Chinese culture; dislike suggests a familiarity that is not there. Rather, there is a sense of the dangers of being next to an increasingly powerful and populous nation, whose internal wars and politics have time and again spilled over to wreak havoc on the much smaller country to the southwest.

Through the 1990s improved relations with the Americans and Europeans seemed unlikely. The 1990 election results were still fresh in people's minds. In 1995, Aung San Suu Kyi was freed after several years under house arrest and called again for the junta to hand over power to the winning NLD. This was never going to happen, but popular campaigns in the West, demonizing the regime and demanding tough punishments, strongly influenced any possibility of improved ties. China at the same time was offering more help, more arms sales, and big plans for closer relations.

The generals turned first to India to try to redress the balance. India, like America, had been a keen supporter of the pro-democracy opposition, but was now in the process of reversing policy. Frosty relations soon thawed and by 1995 the two armies were even undertaking a joint operation, 'Operation Golden Bird', to try to dislodge anti-Indian government militant groups sheltering on the Burmese side of the border. Military to military relations were scaled up. Trade ties increased significantly as well, but this trade was of a very different type to that with China. With China, the Burmese ran a huge official trade deficit, importing nearly all consumer goods from China and exporting logs and jade and other precious stones, much of this contraband, as well as heroin. With India, the Burmese had a big trade surplus, as clever entrepreneurs and market-savvy farmers began to grow beans (used to make Indian dal), exporting a billion dollars' worth by the early 2000s.

The generals also turned to their neighbours to the east and southeast, countries like Thailand, Malaysia, Singapore and Indonesia, grouped together as the 'Association of Southeast Asian Nations' or ASEAN. Some of these countries were also uneasy about China's free run in Burma and desired a balance. Burma wanted to join the group and this was accepted. Burmese leaders hoped that ASEAN membership would result in a major increase in investment; ASEAN leaders hoped the Burmese would at least compromise with the pro-democracy opposition, more to get Western pressure off their backs than anything else. The first didn't happen because of the Asian financial crisis. The second didn't happen because for the Burmese generals compromise, at least negotiated compromise with Aung San Suu Kyi, seemed unnecessary and potentially perilous, the upside very small, the downside much greater.

Then came the prospect of Burma as a major exporter of energy. Burma had once been a significant oil producer in the days before oil was found in Arabia and Persia. It was the Burmah Oil company that had given rise to British Petroleum or BP. By the 1950s, however, most of the oil fields had run dry and the isolationist government under General Ne Win had not bothered to invite outside exploration. This changed in the early 1990s and within a few years a considerable quantity, not of oil but natural gas, was discovered offshore. A potentially enormous amount more was waiting to be found. Proven reserves stand at about 10 trillion cubic feet, but estimates run as high as 90 trillion cubic feet, which would make the Burmese gas fields the tenth largest in the world, worth hundreds of billions of dollars.

The big oil companies lined up to develop the fields and win a share of the profits. Thailand was an initial beneficiary and the French company Total built a pipeline connecting one of the gas fields over the hills to near Bangkok, where it was turned into electricity. By 2006, the Burmese military government was receiving over $2 billion a year in revenue from these sales. Competition then heated up for access to another, bigger, field just to the west. A consortium including Indian and South Korean companies was involved in the development of the field, but no decision was taken at first about where the gas would go.

The Koreans wanted to liquefy the gas so that it could be sold to different customers around the world. India wanted a pipeline to its landlocked northeastern states or via Bangladesh to Calcutta. The Chinese wanted a pipeline too, but to their Yunnan province. There were years of opaque negotiations. The Burmese seemed to be edging towards either the Korean or Indian proposals. Then, in January 2006, the US and UK tabled a resolution at the United Nations Security Council condemning the junta's human-rights record and calling for talks with Aung San Suu Kyi. This would have been the first ever Security Council resolution on Burma, something the government could not easily ignore. The Chinese stepped in and vetoed the resolution. Two months later, news began to appear that the new gas pipeline would be built to China.

But the cement had not yet fully dried on Burma's new international orientation. No one in Burma wanted the country simply to be a client state of Beijing, and many in the ruling establishment had far greater personal ties westward than to China. Whereas English was widely spoken by the educated class, no Burmese person I knew spoke Chinese. People watched American movies and those with money aspired to send their children to school or university in the US, UK or Australia. Many had relatives across the English-speaking world.

In late 2008 and 2009 both Washington and the Burmese generals took some initial steps to improve relations. This had actually begun during the height of the crisis surrounding Cyclone Nargis, when the first planeload of American aid landing at Rangoon's airport included not only the head of the US government aid agency, but Admiral Timothy Keating, commander of the US Pacific Command, probably the most senior US military man to set foot in Burma since the Second World War. And the Americans, especially on the military side, were not unaware of China's growing influence and of how far their own influence had fallen over the past twenty years.

The incoming Obama administration said that 'engagement' with the authorities would complement continued 'sanctions' and soon the Burmese released over a hundred political prisoners and allowed senior US envoys to meet with Aung San Suu Kyi. Washington reciprocated through several small gestures, including a handshake between President Obama and the Burmese prime minister at a regional summit. For the Burmese, as a watershed approached in relations with China, there was curiosity to see whether a normalization of ties with the US was possible, and on what terms. But in the end the gap in expectations between the two sides was too large to bridge, and the interest in reaching a deal too tenuous. Washington found it difficult even to begin to relax sanctions without the generals starting a meaningful dialogue with Aung San Suu Kyi, yet this was probably the last thing they were willing to do.

'We know that India can't really balance China for us', one former Burmese officer told me:

We would like better relations with the Americans, but as long as they are only interested in 'regime change' [he used this term in English], there's really nothing to talk about. They say 'release Aung San Suu Kyi or do this or that and then we will see how we might want to improve ties with you, how we might decrease sanctions'. We don't like sanctions but we can live with them. We're asked to make risky concessions in return for vague promises. Maybe this works with other countries, but it won't work with us.

The relative decline of the West is often exaggerated. The West is still far richer, its universities second-to-none and the armed forces of the United States have no parallel. But here, in this small but strategic slice of Asia, the post-Western world is perhaps more evident than anywhere else. Walking around in Maymyo, the West seems more a memory and something very far away, sanctions and boycotts having kept out the businesses and aid programmes that would otherwise exist, leaving the landscape to be crafted by others. The money to be made, the fears to be addressed, the relations that need to be fostered, have become Asian, and close at hand.

And in this intra-Asian world, relations with China are paramount. Neither India nor the countries of southeast Asia have so far been able to compete with what China is offering and able to deliver. India is no further from Mandalay or even Maymyo than China, but contemporary Indian influences are practically non-existent. The Burmese leadership has been sceptical, and hedging its bets, but the country is being drawn into the Chinese economic orbit nonetheless. Will this continue? Will India ever become the 'balancer' of China in the region? Will American attempts to re-engage the junta bear fruit? From a distance, China's and India's stated desires to find new links to and across Burma seem straightforward, the question only of their relative prowess. But here it was clear that it wasn't all about Beijing and Delhi, and that Burmese fears and desires will also be a major factor in determining the future.

And there is an additional twist: Burma's unfinished civil war.

Lords of the Sunset

I had asked the staff at the Candacraig if they could organize a car and a driver to take me to Hsipaw, a little town to the east. It was along the road to China. I considered taking the train but train journeys in Burma are slow, unreliable, and either hot and stuffy or air-conditioned to near freezing. But the train ride from Maymyo to Hsipaw includes the once-famous Gokteik Gorge and a viaduct built a hundred years ago by Pennsylvania Steel across the jungle ravine. It was tempting, but in the end I decided I would see more from a car.

The next morning, a black 1960s Mercedes appeared, driven by an Indian-looking man with slicked-back hair. We agreed on a price of 10,000 Burmese kyat (about $10). The car had clearly seen better days but was comfortable enough. There was no rap music this time. The countryside from Maymyo was lovely, with big trees and rolling hills, and the air wonderfully fresh and cool. We passed a group of Indian Roman Catholic nuns walking along the road as well as many north-Indian-looking women, handsome and well-dressed, in trousers and long blouses, tending their little shops by the side of the road. There was even a Nepali Hindu shrine (I was later told there was a sizeable Nepali settlement in the area) and I saw men and women strolling around in formal Nepali dress as if on their way to a festival. We stopped for breakfast at a halal restaurant run by a Muslim family. There were two huge posters. One was of Mecca, the other of a Mediterranean-style villa with neo-classical columns and a red sports car in the driveway. We were now less than a day's drive from China, but there was little indication here of anything Chinese, only many reminders, from the faces of the people, that this was once a part of British India.

After an hour or so we reached the Gokteik Gorge, a deep and jagged canyon that sliced right through the countryside, and began snaking slowly down for miles, the two-lane road switching back and forth, the car making nearly 180-degree turns, finally crossing the narrow river over a wooden bridge, and then powering back up. The river was at 2,000 feet above sea level and the hills around were one or two thousand feet higher. Bunches of banana trees mixed with evergreens. There were big sixteen-wheel lorries, as well as cars and scooters, coming and going, and little shrines to local deities had been erected, some with fresh flowers and incense, as a way for drivers to ask for protection along particularly dangerous turns. From the river, I could see the great steel viaduct overhead in the distance. We had left 'Burma proper' and were now in the Shan Hills, the home of the Shan people, where for decades a series of small wars has devastated a once idyllic land.

The geography of Burma is important in understanding its history, its current ethnic make-up, and its possible futures. Its core, close to half the country in size and more than two-thirds in population, is the long and flat Irrawaddy valley, the home of the majority Burmese Buddhists or 'Burmans', extending a thousand miles from the river's upper reaches to the delta and the Bay of Bengal. To the west and north are mountain ranges, inhabited by other peoples, like the Naga and the Kachin, mainly Christians, extending up into the Himalayas. And to the east are the Shan Hills, actually a plateau about the size of England, with their own hills and mountains as well as lower-lying valleys. The Shan are the dominant people of the plateau and are also Buddhists. They are the second-largest ethnic group in the country, after the Burmese. But dozens of other peoples also live on the plateau, people like the Wa and the Palaung, who inhabit the higher elevations.

In the areas closer to the present China border, local chiefs in pre-colonial times often owed dual allegiances, to the Burmese crown as well as to the more distant imperial court in Beijing. Today, it is a region of near endless linguistic diversity where over recent decades little nationalisms have grown on top of one another, with new aspirations for statehood or self-determination sprouting up one underneath the other.

Burma's population is reckoned at around sixty million. No one really knows for sure how many people live in Burma, and how many belong to each of the various groups, or even how to categorize ethnicity more generally. Given the political and armed conflicts, it is in everyone's interest to play up or play down the population of a given group, depending on where one stands. And there has not been a comprehensive census since the one in 1931, part of the grand India-wide surveys that were carried out by colonial authorities every ten years. Since independence there have been censuses as well, but these have been only partial, as the country was still at civil war, and people in areas close to the fighting could not be fully counted.

Determining exactly how many of the sixty million are ethnic Burmese or Shan or anything else is even harder. There is really no answer. My parents are both Burmese, as were all four of my grandparents. All were Buddhists and all grew up speaking Burmese, both key markers of Burmese identity. But that's not really the whole story. My great-grandparents and more distant ancestors included people from both India and China, Buddhists and Muslims, as well as Shans from this area near China, and Mons, another major ethnic group, from the Irrawaddy delta. In any census, though, I would simply be listed as 'Burman' in the current, somewhat artificial lexicon.

And ethnicity in Burma is at least partly a choice. Many people speak more than one, sometimes several, languages, and even have more than one name, say a Burmese name as well as a Shan or a Chinese one. Religion could be a barrier to intermarriage and a clear sign of ethnic affiliation, but there are few hard and fast lines between Hindu, Buddhist and Chinese religious beliefs and practices; only Islam and Christianity tend to stand apart.

In Burma, in the past, and today, there are no strict restrictions on sex or marriage outside one's community – parental preferences perhaps, but no formal prohibitions or taboos. Foreign migrants – Indians, Chinese and Europeans – were and are overwhelmingly men; many found local wives and their children normally merged into the broader community. Some formed distinct little communities. In earlier times, there were communities of Armenians, Japanese (*ronin*, or rogue 'masterless' samurai from Nagasaki), Portuguese and even the descendants of the crew of a captured eighteenth-century French warship, but all became part of the Burmese melting pot, at least in the valley.

In the mountains it was different. Here the rough terrain meant that communities stayed more isolated from one another and an area of just a few miles could be home to many different languages, costumes and customs. The part of Burma where I was travelling was perhaps one of the most ethnically varied areas in the world, where ethnic and linguistic strains from many directions have jumbled up together, with literally dozens of distinct languages and hundreds of dialects, representing entirely unrelated language families, as different from each other as English and Estonian. Like the Caucasus at the other end of Asia, this is a mountain Babel which has long proved inimical to any centralizing authority.

As with early Burmese history, the early history of the Shan people is also murky. The Shan chronicles point to an ancient past, but no one really knows when or where either the 'Burmese' or the 'Shan' actually emerged as distinct ethnic groups, only that the earliest known examples of their writing first appeared in late medieval times. Before that time, we only have Chinese records that mention the troublesome groups living in this region, people who cultivated cinnamon and mined jade and who tattooed themselves and wore monkey hide as armour. The Chinese claimed some were cannibals.

'Shan' in Burmese is spelled 'Syam'. It's the same word as 'Siam', the old name for Thailand. And it's the word the Burmese use to refer to people who call themselves 'Tai'. And 'Tai' is just a different version of 'Thai', as in 'Thailand'. In China, there's a minority called the 'Dai' who live in the areas closest to Burma and who speak more or less the same language. The nuances are more confusing still, but the important thing to remember is this: 'Thai', 'Tai', 'Dai' and 'Shan' are all ways of referring to very similar languages and (to the extent that language helps define ethnicity) to a related group of people. These languages are not always mutually intelligible, but they are very closely related, at least as closely as the various Romance languages, Spanish, Italian and French. They include the Thai spoken in Bangkok, but also Lao, the slightly different tongue spoken in Laos. Some of the Shan dialects spoken in parts of Burma are almost identical to the Thai spoken in parts of northern Thailand, others the same as the Dai spoken across the border in China.

The Shan chronicles say that more than a thousand years ago two brothers, Khun Lung and Khun Lai, descended from heaven and became the kings of one of the little highland valleys. Their sons became the chiefs of nearby principalities, and their descendants became rulers of a vast region, from the Black River valley of northern Vietnam to the Brahmaputra valley of Assam in present-day India. It is a story of gradual expansion, which allowed the Shan in medieval times to challenge the domination of the older empires – Pagan in central Burma, Dali in Yunnan, and Angkor in Cambodia. By the fourteenth century, these Shan or Tai chiefs had extended their sway south towards modern-day Bangkok, to the country later known as Thailand, the land of the Tai.

There were periods when Shan dominion extended far and wide across mainland southeast Asia. But the Shans were never able to maintain any real unity. Instead of a single kingdom there were dozens of little principalities. At times the Shan submitted to Burmese authority and became close allies of the Burmese kings; at other times they offered some form of tribute but otherwise kept their distance. Some also sent tribute to the

Chinese emperor and received coveted titles in return. They were a middle people, expert in the art of balancing identities, playing off bigger powers, and benefiting from long-distance trade, including in arms and ideas.

The rulers of these Shan principalities styled themselves *saopha* or 'Lords of the Sky'. In Burmese, the same word is rendered *sawbwa*. The Burmese court also styled the more important ones *naywin bayin* or 'Lords of the Sunset'. They would send their sons to be educated at Ava and later Mandalay, and would offer their daughters to be one of the Burmese king's many dozen wives or concubines. In this way a tight cultural link was formed between the Burmese royal family and many of the Shan princely families, especially in those areas closest to Burma proper. The Shan courts became miniature versions of the Burmese court of Ava.

By the time the British arrived on the scene, there were a score of these little Shan principalities, scattered over the eastern hills. One of them was Hsipaw.

There were two or three dozen shops lining the main avenue that led from the river to the monastery – Hsipaw's main street. At a few little restaurants people sat both inside and on the dusty ground outside, under the shade of a tree, on tiny plastic stools, drinking and smoking and talking. One place had a couple of billiard tables. For the more affluent, there was also a Dohtawaddy Tennis Club (Dohtawaddy being the classical, Indian-derived name for Hsipaw), which was just a court and some rickety wooden benches. At a kiosk, fake DVDs were sold for about $1 each, with a little sign in front advertising *The Hurt Locker* and *Angels and Demons*.

Hsipaw had been founded in 1636 and in the late nineteenth century British visitors could still make out the outlines of an old wall and moat, buried under decades of jungle growth. But there was no sign now of anything particularly old. The little buildings that made up the centre of town seemed small and improvised, made of wood or sometimes just bamboo and thatch. I've rarely ever held a hammer in my hand and have next to no idea how a modern house is made, but looking at these simple structures I was fairly sure that I could build one myself.

Towards the end of the avenue was a cinema, also small. It couldn't have been more than ten feet high, and because the road was higher than the entrance, seemed almost like a bunker, half hidden underground. It was just one room, with the ticket seller out in front. The main set of doors was open, and I could see several rows of seats facing a screen. It was what I imagined an early twentieth-century cinema to be, the sort that would have a piano on the side adding music to the silent pictures. A few paces away was the town's lone bookstore, which doubled as the local office of the National League for Democracy. It was really just a stall with a couple of dozen English books displayed out front, and many more Burmese books, for rent as well as for sale, in the back. The Burmese are voracious readers, and the many Burmese novels, biographies and current affairs books, all printed on the cheapest possible paper and bound in what looked like masking tape, were all well-thumbed. Amongst the English-language selections was George Orwell's *Burmese Days* (available as a Penguin paperback) as well as a few English guide-books about Burma, some photocopies of the original stapled together, presumably for the occasional tourist who came by.

During the few days I was in Hsipaw, I got into the habit of eating at the same restaurant for nearly all my meals. It was the biggest one in town, which isn't saying much, where the main street joined the road heading towards China. It was airy and from the table at the corner that became my regular spot, I could watch what passed for a busy intersection. Just opposite the restaurant was a tall signpost with signs listing the distances to different places, like Rangoon or Mandalay, in miles and furlongs. Burma is one of only three countries left in the world (the United States and Liberia are the other two) where only imperial rather than metric measurements are used officially.

I had found the restaurant on my first night by following a group of well-heeled middle-aged Italians. They were with a Burmese guide, a young woman who spoke to them in what seemed to be fluent Italian. It was just after sunset and I was curious to see where she was leading them. They first stopped at a restaurant where I had initially thought of eating myself as it had been recommended by my guest-house. But it was closed for some reason and so the group kept walking on, with me a few discreet yards behind, in my *longyi* and flip-flops, looking like any other denizen of Hsipaw. Perhaps they thought I was a government spy. After a few minutes we came to the corner restaurant, the Italians taking one table and me the adjacent one, by the road. Over the meal I could overhear everything they were saying. As I know no Italian, I could not tell what they were talking about, but guessed from their smiles and hand gestures that they were often complementing the guide on the food. Every now and then enormous lorries loaded with the trunks of giant trees rumbled past, literally shaking the little restaurant. They were heading towards the border, only a few hours away.

Hsipaw seemed a tranquil place, barely touched by the violence and turmoil of the twentieth century, but appearances were deceiving. Japanese, Chinese, British, and even American soldiers had marched through this area during the Second World War. And since the early 1960s this entire part of the country had been engulfed in a complex web of armed conflicts, setting the Burmese army against local Shan armies, fighting for autonomy or independence, and communist rebels, fighting for a 'People's Republic of Burma'. The backwardness of the town had a reason: decades of war. Within a day's walk were villages still under the control of insurgent militias. Ceasefires were in place and Hsipaw and its environs were now peaceful enough for the odd tourist to visit and see the sights. The war was likely entering its final chapter. But it wasn't yet finished. Would China and growing Chinese influence play a role in ending the war? Or fuelling a new round of violence? The war was linked to rival notions of ethnic identity and nationalism. They also had roots in Burma's colonial past.

The British ruled Burma in two very different ways. In the lowlands of 'Burma Proper' – the Irrawaddy valley and the adjacent coastal areas – the British had imposed direct rule, abolishing the monarchy and replacing the aristocracy and local elite families with British civil servants and local clerks. From the 1920s in this 'Burma Proper', the British also began to introduce representative government. Political parties flourished and regular elections were held (with a very limited franchise). For a while parliament had only very limited powers, but under a constitution approved in 1935, the people of 'Burma Proper' were allowed to form a government that had authority over considerable areas of domestic policy. This followed the pace of reforms in India. By independence lowland Burma had considerable experience of often raucous party and parliamentary politics.

The highlands were treated very differently. Here the British kept the hereditary chiefs in power, doing away with some (those who had resisted colonial rule) whilst strengthening the power of others. As everywhere in the Empire, British political officers rationalized and systematized what had been a somewhat messy set of local chiefs and office-holders. By the early twentieth century, the Shan principalities were organized under thirty-four *sawbwas* in a strict 'Order of Precedence'. In the mountains were the lesser chiefs, of remote tribal peoples such as the Wa in the east, the Kachin in the north. The British supported their authority (in return for loyalty and a share of revenue) and many found that they could carry on much as before. Over time, Christian missionaries established schools and converted nearly all the various tribal people – not the Shan, who were devout Buddhists like the Burmese, but the mountain people, who had been animists. There was very little economic development. Almost no roads were built and only a single railway line from Mandalay to Lashio. But whereas lowland Burma became a cauldron of left-wing and nationalist politics, the hills were almost entirely peaceful. The British tended to trust these highland and now predominantly Christian people and recruited them into the Indian army and police, whilst excluding the ethnic Burmese. The various peoples of Burma thus went through very different experiences of colonial rule. At independence there would be intense mutual suspicion, followed by civil war.

The British first appeared in Hsipaw in early 1886. Mandalay had just fallen and British political officers were eager to secure the allegiance of the Shan rulers. The *sawbwa* of Hsipaw at the time was a man named Sao Hkun Hseng. A few years before he had fled to Siam, and then to Rangoon, trying to escape the political chaos and heavy tax demands from Mandalay that marked the final years before the British conquest. But he understood which way the wind was blowing and returned just in time to retake his home town and offer his submission to the new colonial masters, becoming the first *sawbwa* to do so. The British were then battling an unexpectedly tough guerrilla resistance (led by Burmese princes and pretenders) and were grateful to find new allies wherever they could. The British rewarded Sao Hkun Hseng by extending his authority over three little statelets nearby. Soon he was invited to London to visit the Queen.

He was succeeded by his son, Sao Hke. Sao Hke had been educated at the palace in Mandalay but was later sent to England to study as well, and on his return became a man of two worlds, no longer very happy to be confined to his little town. He told visiting Europeans and Americans that he was miserable, living in a place where almost no one else spoke English and where he was forced to live on 'an income insufficient for an English shopkeeper'. He wore Shan clothes – a turban and a tight jacket with baggy trousers – but replaced the traditional velvet slippers with English brogues. In 1905 he had a visitor in Herbert Hoover, who was there on a business trip for a mining company, hoping for the *sawbwa*'s help in exploiting the nearby silver mines. Hoover described Sao Hke's residence as a sort of 'frame building' with motifs 'reminiscent of Long Island' and saw the young prince as a tragic figure, caught between East and West, delighted only to be able to converse in English with outsiders who were not his British overlords. Sao Hke would later be knighted for his services.

After Sao Hke died in 1928, he was replaced by his son, Sao Ohn Kya, who had been educated at Rugby and Brasenose College, Oxford. By this time nearly all the major Shan chiefs were British-trained and were the only real aristocracy left in the country. They intermarried and several would become prominent diplomats and scholars after independence. The British superintendents who supervised them were universally charmed by them and their families, and by the Shan states in general, which they deemed the 'Switzerland of the East', with their rolling hills and temperate weather, an 'Asian Arcady'.

Just across the border, however, China was in the midst of war and communist revolution. Millions would die, millions more would be displaced. China was at a watershed. And, as has happened so often in history, monumental change in China would transform Burma as well.

When the British left Burma in 1948, they left the country in the hands of the men who had been on the extreme fringes of the student nationalist movement just a decade before. They were almost all Buddhists (by background if not practice) and ethnic Burmans. Before the Japanese invasion, they were not particularly important, but the war had radicalized society and they had seized the opportunity, first to collaborate with the Japanese and then to turn against them, in March 1945, just in time to avoid being arrested and hanged as Quislings. They included men like Aung San, father of Aung San Suu Kyi. They were immensely popular and even though they were still in their late twenties and early thirties stood head and shoulders above the older politicians, who were tarred as not having been daring enough. Aung San and many of his colleagues were then gunned down in 1947 in a still puzzling assassination plot, but others from the pool of ex-student radicals formed the first independent government. They would take Burma out of the British Commonwealth and launch the country down what was to be a not very happy path through the rest of the twentieth century.

Some on the British side had been worried about the fate of the Shan and other ethnic minorities in an independent Burma and suggested detaching the upland areas and keeping them as a British crown colony. British frontier officials were particularly fond of the hill peoples, such as the Karen along the Thai border, who had fought consistently and often very courageously against the Japanese. A commission was established to make recommendations on the future of the non-Burman regions in 1946. They asked representatives of the 'wild Wa', a particularly inaccessible tribal people in the mountains along the China border, for their views. The official report records this exchange:

'Do you want any association with other people?'
'We do not want to join anybody because in the past we have been very independent.'

'What do you want the future to be of the Wa States?'
'We have not thought about that because we are wild people. We never thought of the administrative future. We only think about ourselves.'

'Don't you want education, clothing, good food, good houses, hospitals, etc?'
'We are very wild people and we do not appreciate all these things.'

Other minorities, like the Shan, had far more sophisticated representation, and in talks between them and the up-and-coming political class in Rangoon, a deal was hammered out, through which a degree of autonomy was granted to the highlands as well as representation at the centre. There were promises of equality and an inclusive democracy.

But the country was soon wracked by civil war. Armed unrest started more or less as soon as the British left and was at first not an inter-ethnic conflict, but a fight between the Burmese army, dominated by ex-student politicians, and the Burmese communist party, led by a rival group of former student radicals. Before long, however, the civil war involved a dizzying array of factions, insurgencies and militias – from ethnic Karen soldiers once loyal to the British, to Islamic *mujahedeen* fighters demanding a separate state along what was then the East Pakistan border. By early 1949, just twelve months after independence from Britain, the new Burmese government seemed on the brink of collapse, barely in control of Rangoon itself, leaving the rest of the Irrawaddy valley a patchwork of insurgent armies and local militias.

The Shan states were at first blissfully uninvolved. Then, as has happened so many times in the past, upheaval in China washed across the border. By the end of 1949, Chiang Kai-shek's armies were in full retreat from Mao Zedong's communist juggernaut. Some made it across the straits to Taiwan, while others, cut off from the coast, marched southwest to Yunnan and then over the hills into Burma. It was a time-honoured strategy. In 1661, when the Manchus overran China, remnants of the Ming dynasty, led by the prince of Gui, had sought refuge at the then capital of Ava. For a while this was granted, but when a great Chinese army appeared under their formidable general, Wu Sangui, the Burmese king was quick to change his mind. The prince of Gui was handed over and then garrotted with a bow string by Wu Sangui himself.

This time the retreating forces neither asked nor received permission to enter Burma. Instead they stayed close up to the Chinese frontier and were backed, covertly, by both the US Central Intelligence Agency and the (right-wing anti-communist) government of Thailand. Chiang Kai-shek and his allies in Washington were hoping for nothing less than the recapture of China, and believed that bases in Burma could be crucial for success. Soon, a vast tract of land, complete with its own airstrips for flying men and cargo to and from Taiwan, was in

Chinese Nationalist hands. The Burmese were outraged. They turned to the UN but to no avail. The Burmese army was sent on the offensive. The eastern Shan states became a battlefield.

It would stay a battlefield for decades. CIA and Thai military support for the Chinese continued through the 1960s. By then these old fighters had become part of the scenery. Some eventually moved to Taiwan but many others married Shan or other local women and stayed. And those who stayed became central to an ever-expanding network of opium and heroin cartels. Over the late 1960s and 1970s warlords like Khun Sa, half Chinese and half Shan, and Lo Hsing-han, from the Chinese border enclave of Kokang, emerged as internationally wanted drug kingpins, battling the Burmese army as well as each other for control over what became known as 'The Golden Triangle'.

By then the Shans themselves had also joined the ranks of the insurgency. Before independence, the Shan *sawbwas* had agreed to join the new 'Union of Burma', provided they were allowed a degree of autonomy and, critically, an option to secede in ten years' time. This worked for a while. The Shan elite were very much part of the Rangoon scene, as members of parliament and government ministers and as highly respected scholars and professionals. The *sawbwa* of Yawnghwe served as the first (largely ceremonial) president of Burma, and for many years another Shan prince served as the country's foreign minister. But problems at home were growing. The fight against the Chinese Nationalists had militarized the Shan Hills, leading to army abuses against civilians. And new leftist political forces had sprung up to challenge the authority of the old aristocracy. Then came the military take-over in 1962. The *sawbwas* were arrested. The young US-educated *sawbwa* of Hsipaw at the time, Sao Kya Hseng, was never seen again. Some Shan aristocrats left the country (they have lived in exile ever since). Others joined the leadership of new Shan insurgencies. Local militias proliferated, with constantly shifting allegiances, all fuelled by the Vietnam War-era drug trade to America.

By the 1970s, Beijing was directly involved in the fighting, with its open and enthusiastic backing for the newly revived Burmese communist insurgency. The 'liberated zone' was right up against the border and China provided arms and ammunition, as well as 'volunteer' fighters and all manner of logistical support. To help stem the communist onslaught, Washington quietly scaled up aid, supplying dozens of helicopters and transport planes, and training Burmese military and intelligence officers in America. The combat was at times intense. Tens of thousands of civilians were displaced and their homes destroyed. In 1979–80, in operation 'King Conqueror', Burmese army battalions crossed the Salween River in an attempt to crush the insurgency but met ferocious resistance in the high frost-covered mountains, suffering as many as 5,000 casualties. Communist forces, numbering over 15,000, counter-attacked, taking the Shan towns of Muse and Mong Yawng. China was then trying to patch up relations with Rangoon but claimed its 'state-to-state friendship' was separate from its 'party-to-party support' for the Burmese rebels. Military expenditures were by then taking up over a third of the Burmese government's budget and were eating away at the country's very limited foreign exchange reserves.

The Burmese army eventually gained the upper hand. By the late 1980s, after a series of bloody campaigns, Burmese government forces managed to overwhelm the key remaining rebel strongholds and reach the Chinese border. This was when reform in China, under Deng Xiaoping, was already well under way, with party officials and a nascent business community in Yunnan eyeing the Burmese market. Hundreds of factories soon sprang up just across the frontier, producing goods developed specifically for Burmese consumers. Until then, most consumer products in Rangoon and Mandalay were smuggled in from Thailand. This would now change, with the Chinese besting foreign and local competitors alike.

In March 1989, the Burma Communist Party itself collapsed. Half a century of armed struggle was over. The end had begun with the mutiny of units from the town of Kokang, led by their ethnic Chinese commander Peng Jiasheng. Peng was heavily involved in the narcotics trade and more mercenary than Marxist. Within days the mutiny spread and by mid-April Peng and his co-conspirators had captured the communist headquarters and radio station. The erstwhile communist army then splintered into four smaller but still sizeable militias. The Burmese army reacted with speed. The regime's intelligence chief, General Khin Nyunt, enlisted both long-time opium warlord Lo Hsing-han and the bisexual war-lady Olive Yang, both ethnic Chinese from the borderlands. Through Lo's and Yang's help, ceasefire deals were soon struck between the Burmese army and all the ex-communist militia. This was all happening as the Berlin Wall was coming down and the Soviet Union collapsing. Few noticed internationally. But it heralded the end of what was arguably the longest-running war in the world. By the mid-1990s these ceasefires had been extended to nearly all the various ethnic insurgent groups around the country.

There was no more war, but nothing like peace. In offering the ceasefires Burma's military leaders had also promised development in the hills. Tighter Western sanctions and the cutting-off of United Nations and World Bank aid made it hard for them to keep their promise. It was this landscape that Chinese traders, businessmen and engineers began to roll into.

Just a little out of town is the beautiful Sakandar palace, a cream-coloured villa built by the Hsipaw prince in the 1910s, now forlorn, the gardens hopelessly overgrown. Closer to the middle of town, a newer palace, really just a grand British-style house, is still there, slightly better maintained, with a locked gate and few signs of any inhabitants. Until recently, a relative of the last *sawbwa* had welcomed tourists to the house, but he was arrested during a general crackdown on Shan dissidents in 2006.

Hsipaw had been a hub of Shan royal culture for generations, and under British rule had preserved many old traditions and rituals of the extinct Burmese court. But there was little obvious trace left of Shan culture in Hsipaw. The signs were all in Burmese, and unaccented Burmese was spoken by nearly everyone I met. Everyone was also wearing a Burmese *longyi*, or Chinese-made Western clothes. The baggy navy blue or brown cotton trousers traditionally worn by Shan men were nowhere to be seen.

There is an ancient Bawgyo pagoda on the outskirts of town. And at a festival in March every year the four sacred Buddha images enshrined in the pagoda are brought out to be venerated and re-gilded by large crowds. But it is no longer the more general celebration of Shan culture and patriotism that it was in the days of the *sawbwas*. Elsewhere the story is the same. In the early 1990s in Keng Tung, the main town of what had been a much larger Shan principality, the old palace was razed to the ground, in what can only be described as a gratuitous act of cultural destruction.

For the ruling junta the ceasefires meant that an all-out military solution was not an option, at least over the short term. But the ceasefires certainly didn't mean an end to their long-held ambition of a united Burma. Far from it. The idea of a federal system of government in which ethnic minority areas would enjoy autonomy as part of a loosely integrated union was anathema to top army officers. They had been trained to think that the disintegration of Burma along ethnic lines was both a real threat and the worst possible nightmare. It would invite foreign intervention and a return of colonial rule. Federalism – any compromise with demands for local autonomy – was the first step down that slippery slope. The ceasefires were a tactical retreat, nothing more.

And they saw an opportunity to push the boundaries of the Burmese state as far as possible, tie the local economies with the centre, and further the reach of the majority Burmese culture. All were viewed as related. Build more roads, encourage trade, and slowly other ethnic identities would dissipate. Through 'Burmanization' they would build a secure state.

There was a long history to this. Over centuries the Burmese language had expanded from its core areas along the middle Irrawaddy, together with a Burmese school of Buddhism derived from the ultra-conservative Theravada Buddhism of Ceylon. Peoples like the Kanyan, Pyu and Thet, mentioned in the old chronicles, no longer exist, absorbed into an evolving Burman tradition. In the eighteenth century, Burmese kings had annexed the ancient Mon-speaking kingdom around Rangoon, and the Mon became an ever-shrinking minority. There was a Burmese cultural frontier, and the hope of the military state was to expand this frontier to the very edge of the country.

Except now there was China on the other side. Though new roads were facilitating Burmese military and economic control of these hills, they were also opening the floodgates to power, money and influence from another direction. One frontier was collapsing into another.

The guest-house where I stayed was owned by a Chinese man from the border area of Kokang. Kokang is on the Burmese side, but its people are descended from Chinese migrants who settled in that mountainous region centuries ago. For generations they had been caravan muleteers. Now they ran car and lorry companies, plying the road from Mandalay to China. The guest-house was part of his mini-empire and he had done well, adding new structures to what had grown into a fairly large establishment, which catered to Western backpacker demands for clean rooms, energizing breakfasts, a ready supply of cold beer, and practical help in finding interesting places to see.

On my last day, I talked to a man I had met at the hotel, a small fair-complexioned man in his late thirties, who wore a baseball cap and leather jacket. He had been born in Hsipaw to a mixed Shan–Kachin family. He said his father was a businessman who had worked with Chinese traders and made sure that in addition to Burmese and Shan, his son learned Mandarin from an early age. After school he had won a scholarship to further his studies in Yunnan, the Chinese province next door, working there for a while before returning to Burma. He now owned a thriving shop in Mandalay and travelled regularly to China to buy the electronic goods that he would resell. He was successful. For him China was not a problem or a threat but an opportunity. And he had, in a way, become partly Chinese. He spoke fluent Chinese with the accent of Yunnan, and said he could cross over the border and travel easily in China without official documents. He had even taken a Chinese name, in addition to his Burmese and Shan names. 'In Mandalay I wear a *longyi*, listen to Burmese music, eat Burmese food and feel at home. Here in Hsipaw I see my old Shan friends and speak in Shan. In China, the Chinese think of me as purely Chinese.'

Along these frontier lands were people and peoples adept at navigating the multifaceted ethnic landscape and adopting different identities as it suited them. Whereas the Burmese tended to see the Chinese as resolutely alien, there were others, like the Shan, who had a much longer history of accommodation. From far away, Burma seemed a relatively minor missing link between China and India. Closer up, it was obvious that the fears and desires of the Burmese themselves and their military rulers, fears and desires rooted in old as well as recent history, were clearly important. And now there was this additional complexity, for the Burmese were not the only people in between, but part of a much greater ethnic mix, with other local peoples, shaping and adapting to the changing environment in their own ways. With the ceasefires and the new border openings, a very strange landscape was developing, of overlapping ethnicities, new politics, new warlords, and, perhaps, clues to Asia's future.

New Frontiers

To the north of Hsipaw, extending almost 500 miles to the edges of Tibet, were the Kachin Hills. I had been there once before, to the areas run by the Kachin Independence Army or KIA. This was around Christmas in 1991 and the war between the Burmese army and the KIA was still in full swing. I had gone there, secretly and not quite legally, from China in the back of a covered lorry. I was then twenty-five and a graduate student at university. And in travelling to KIA-held areas I took risks that I doubt very much I would take today. I gave over my passport, credit cards, and every piece of identification to my Kachin facilitators, and watched as they casually locked them away in a house I knew I could never find on my own, not in a million years.

At the time, much of China was still closed to tourists and I had to travel through a couple of these 'off-limits' areas. If caught at a checkpoint, I was told I should say that I was a Burmese merchant, in China for just a few days. A local ID card had been made for me. And, after a few anxious days on the road, I arrived at Pajau, then the Kachin insurgent headquarters, a rambling settlement of little bamboo huts and wooden houses set over a series of hilltops, China on the one side, Burma on the other.

The Kachins were devout Christians, mainly Baptists and Roman Catholics, and over the coming week I joined in their Christmas celebrations, listening to their carols, and watching a nativity play, alongside the hardened jungle fighters in green fatigues, their wives and children. The officers I met talked about their desire not for an independent state, but for an end to discrimination and some level of local autonomy. They spoke emotionally of the lives that had been lost in their struggle but were unclear what their next move should be. They were well aware of the changes already occurring in China.

I walked with my Kachin hosts into the surrounding hills. Everywhere the scenery was spectacular, lush valleys and crystal-clear streams, surrounded on every side by towering mountains. It was also freezing cold, especially at night, my warm clothes from England having been swapped for the KIA uniform and Chinese army coat that (my hosts said) allowed me to travel incognito despite the spies who lurked all around. From one hill, I could see Myitkyina, the largest town in the region and the Burmese army's local base. In the distance, I could also see where the N'Mai Hka and Mali Hka rivers flowed together to form the broad headwaters of the Irrawaddy. Later during my three-week stay, I travelled on a pony down towards Bhamo, an ancient border crossing with China. Further to the west, the Kachin controlled the famed jade mines at Hpakant, their major source of income, and I was shown big boulders that had been cut open to value the jade inside.

The territory controlled by the KIA was extensive, but I was told that there were places, hundreds of miles further to the north, that were so remote that they were beyond the reach of either the Burmese army or the Kachin insurgency. Sitting in my hut at Pajau, already feeling like I was at the very edge of the world, I thought often of these even more far-off tracts, at the edge of the Himalayas, whose people existed outside the pale of any government. They included small tribal communities, like the Rawang, crossbow hunters who speak a language more akin to Tibetan than Burmese. For the Rawang, who live in great poverty, even salt is a treasured commodity, and for salt they will hunt the few tigers left in the valleys and sell the skins and body parts to the few unscrupulous Chinese traders who make it over the icy passes.

The far northern regions are also home to the Tarons. They are the remnant of the only known pygmy race in mainland Asia. The men average about 4 ft 11 in (1.5 m) and the women are a few inches shorter. The British botanist Frank Kingdon-Ward met Taron villagers during his search for orchids in 1934 and referred to them ungraciously as 'one of nature's less successful experiments'. Today there are said to be only a few dozen left in Burma, perhaps only half a dozen of 'pure blood'.

Not long after I left, in 1993, the Kachin Independence Army, with its several thousand fighters, agreed to a ceasefire with the government army. Soon after, their leadership moved down from the mountainside and established a new headquarters at Laiza, a little village that quickly became a bustling border town. The KIA were allowed to keep their arms, and since then the territory they control has been in a sort of limbo; efforts at a permanent peace deal have so far been unsuccessful. The Burmese army is not far away and there are Burmese battalions here and there, interspersed with battalions of the Kachin army. But political limbo has not precluded business, especially cross-border business with China, and over the following years jade mines, toll roads and relentless logging have kept powerful men of every faction equally comfortable. A new political economy has emerged, with both sides – Burmese and Kachin – tied to China's increasing presence.

This time, rather than heading north to the Kachin Hills, I went east, further along the Burma Road. It was an area that had been at the epicentre of the civil war for over a quarter of a century, from the 1960s to the ceasefires of the late 1980s and early 1990s. Some of the rebel militias were led by Shan nationalists, fighting for a separate homeland. Others were led by opium warlords. Others were a mix. There were pro-government militias and anti-government ones and some swapped sides depending on what suited their wallets the best at any given time. And there was the army of the Burma Communist Party, with its bases pressed up against the Chinese border. As in the Kachin Hills, the fighting in this region – the northern and eastern Shan states – had halted as well. And here too there was no stability, only a more complicated array of armed battalions.

Lashio was the main town in the area, about a hundred miles from the China border, a town much bigger than Hsipaw, and the terminus of the old British Burma Railways line. Lashio had figured prominently as a stopover on the old Burma Road, and had even featured in the John Wayne epic *Flying Tigers*, a not-quite-accurate account of American derring-do in the fight against the Japanese.

When I was a teenager and visiting Mandalay, I often thought about going to Lashio – we were said to have distant relatives there – but I never did. It was then the back of beyond. The train took forever and few other than army officers and drug lords travelled there by car. Communist insurgents controlled the hills around and beyond Lashio, together with an assortment of other rebel groups like the Shan State Army and opium-trafficking militias. A Burmese army garrison was quartered in town, but the writ of the regional commander barely extended a few miles into the lush and green countryside.

I travelled from Hsipaw to Lashio in a 'shared taxi' together with a Chinese family, speeding along a well-paved road, me in the front seat, a middle-aged woman and her two young children sitting in the back. They were returning from a three-day trip to Mandalay and were going home to Lashio. The woman, neat and fair-complexioned, spoke some Burmese, haltingly and heavily accented. She spoke politely to the taxi driver in Shan and he joked with them and teased the children. She said she had been visiting relatives in Mandalay and doing some shopping. I remembered the mall and the supermarket and imagined her browsing the aisles. I had squeezed my small bag in the boot, next to their several suitcases and a large plastic toy plane. The kids were quiet and well behaved and dressed in Western style, in trainers and shorts. We stopped briefly along the way at a restaurant called 'The Panda'. She told me that she and her husband had come from Yunnan ten years before. They saw Burma as a chance to improve their lives and create a better future for their children. Her husband was a businessman, 'buying and selling'. I thought of the Yunnan I knew of the early 1990s, still rough, cut off. But this little family appeared more refined and from a less cut-throat world.

Once in Lashio, it was easy to tell that we were entering a much more Chinese world than anything I had ever seen before in Burma. It was just after the Chinese New Year, and we drove down street after street of houses, each in their own little walled compounds, decorated with red banners and 'Happy New Year' signs in yellow Chinese characters. The taxi pulled into one of these compounds, and up to a modest single-storey house, surrounded by a garden and small trees. There was a child's tricycle out front, and I could see a television screen flickering just inside through the sliding glass doors. An elderly man and a younger woman came out to greet them, with broad smiles, embracing the children and helping them with their things.

From there the taxi drove me past a school and hospital and a government telecommunications centre, all set along a broad and well-maintained tree-lined avenue. There were also several churches. The Shan themselves, like the Burmese, are overwhelmingly Buddhist, but there were many Kachin in Lashio as well. There was a red-brick Kachin Baptist church, with a decorated Christmas tree outside, as well as a Roman Catholic one. During the early twentieth century, missionaries had been active in this area, especially the Roman Catholics. In the 1930s a group of Italian priests, later joined by a growing number of nuns, were using Lashio as a base, running schools and boarding houses and nurseries and medical clinics. From here they had ventured east across the Salween, into the then barely explored mountains, and across into China. They flourished even under military rule. In 1975 the Vatican entrusted Lashio to the Salesian Order and in 1990 a Burmese priest, Monsignor Charles Bo, had been appointed the first bishop of the newly created diocese of Lashio.

Other than the churches and a few pagodas and Buddhist monasteries, there was very little in Lashio that dated back to even the 1970s. This was partly the result of a monstrous inferno in 1988, perhaps one of the worst anywhere in the world in the twentieth century. Lashio then had a population of around 200,000. The disaster had started as a little kitchen fire, but within two hours the blaze had engulfed more than 2,000 buildings. Buildings in Lashio are not the same as buildings in, say, New York – many of the destroyed structures were small wooden houses and shops. But it was still an unusually fierce fire and left 113 people dead and tens of thousands injured or homeless.

I had arrived on a rainy day and the new town centre that has developed over the past several years looked muddy and unattractive. The streets here were in bad condition, strewn with rubbish no one would collect. The market area was a heap of flimsy looking two-storey concrete buildings, each with dozens of shops offering cheap Chinese goods and piles of second-hand clothes. One shop offered a range of cosmetics, and had a large advertisement for Jing Lon skin-whitening cream. Jing Lon was a Chinese brand, but whitening creams produced by more familiar brands like Noxema are readily found in cities all around the region, from Kyoto to Karachi. A fair complexion is the desired complexion in Burma, as it is everywhere in Asia, particularly for women, and these new melanin-suppressing ointments were extremely popular.

I watched a woman in ragged tribal clothes, just outside the shop, with two tiny children in tow, counting a handful of filthy banknotes of very small denomination, altogether amounting perhaps to the equivalent of $1, and then peering around to see what she might buy. Any of the cosmetics in the shop would have cost many times what she had, but there were hawkers on the pavement in front offering much cheaper wares. She looked at a soiled T-shirt, then a block of sandalwood (sandalwood paste is traditionally used as a sunblock), examining each item very closely, before leaving without making a purchase.

As I was coming into town I had seen white Toyota Land-cruisers belonging to the UN's World Food Programme or WFP, the international agency that specializes in delivering emergency food aid in disaster and war-torn situations. WFP had a field office in Lashio and had been given permission by the military government to run programmes in the area. This was a relatively new thing, both the desire of international aid agencies (and the Western governments that fund them) to provide humanitarian assistance in Burma, and the willingness of the authorities to allow outside aid to be delivered directly. Twenty years ago, UNICEF's country director in Burma had warned of a 'silent emergency' affecting the country's children, and had argued that help for the poorest should not have to wait for democratic change. His appeals were largely ignored. At the time, and for many years after, Western governments shied away from giving any aid to Burma, eager to see economic sanctions bite, and the Burmese army didn't particularly want foreigners (especially Western foreigners) trooping around the countryside, close to rebel lines.

Only slowly did a different view gain the upper hand. There was a growing appreciation of the severity of humanitarian needs in Burma and this information was used to persuade governments in Europe and elsewhere that the plight of Burma's poorest people should no longer play second fiddle to political concerns. A third of all Burma's sixty million people were living on $1 a day or less, and at least as many were living on only a little more. Millions were malnourished and millions of children were stunted in their growth. Any other country in a similar situation would have received far more help from the West.

The Burmese regime was always in favour of development assistance, but this they saw mainly in terms of big projects, new roads, new bridges, new schools, new hospitals. They had worried that 'humanitarian assistance' was closely linked to notions of 'humanitarian intervention', and would be a stepping stone towards other kinds of unwanted attention. But they, too, became increasingly aware of the depth of need and over time became more comfortable with several of the agencies, like WFP, which was then given access to once off-limits areas. UN surveys had shown that there were desperately poor people in areas all around the country. But amongst the poorest of the poor were the tribal peoples in the hills to the east of Lashio, the one-time war zone that was now China's doorstep to Burma.

China was once much worse off than Burma. In the 1930s Burma's per capita GDP was at least twice that of China's. By the 1960s China had caught up. Today, China's per capita GDP is at least six times greater. And in the absence of Western trade and investment, it was China that was now driving Burma's development. American and European sanctions meant that the Western involvement in this part of the country was limited almost exclusively to the provision of humanitarian aid. China, though, was unrestrained, investing in infrastructure projects, building roads and dams, cutting down teak forests, mining for jade, and selling its own consumer goods. The net result was that few jobs were being created for local people and a more unequal society was being established.

For the ruling generals, the pride of Lashio was a replica of Rangoon's Shwedagon pagoda, built just on the edge of town. It looked exactly the same as the original, though it was smaller, with no other pagodas or shrines around it, and it was hollow. The inside was cavernous and brightly lit; the floor was covered in rugs, and on the walls were frescoes of well-known Buddhist structures from elsewhere in the country. All were simply painted and in bright colours, like a mural on the wall of a nursery school. And at the end of this series of frescoes was a framed white sign that listed them all, as 'Great Religious Structures' in Burma. They were listed and categorized chronologically. First were a few from the medieval Pagan period, a few from the subsequent Ava period and so on, until the period of the current military government, which had the largest number of all. The point was clear: this is a government that supports Buddhism, and is unrivalled in doing so.

The messaging continued. An inner circle displayed scenes from the life and past lives of the Buddha, fairly common in pagodas and monasteries, so nothing very special. But an innermost circle featured a collection of about ten or so statues of the Buddha, large ones, in shining gold. They were impressive, and little carpets gave worshippers a chance to prostrate themselves in front of each image. Written underneath the images were the names of various top generals and their wives, the military couples likely the donors of the statues. I imagine they had trooped in together as part of a grand televised ceremony, in a public demonstration of their piety, as well as to make merit for their own future incarnations.

And in a way the replica was part of the grand state-building project. As in Stalin's Russia, where every Soviet Socialist Republic had to have its own opera house, in contemporary Burma a replica of the Shwedagon was an aspect of the regime's ambition for these far-flung towns. It was part of exporting 'Burmese' Buddhism to the outer, minority-inhabited regions, but it was also part of establishing a grid of national institutions.

The replica was also a sort of monument to a war that was almost won. Lashio had been at the epicentre of decades of counter-insurgency. Burma's top generals had seen many of their fellow officers and men killed in the cruel fighting that had taken place over decades. Battles never heard of outside the country are etched in their minds. Perhaps more than many others, they see a difference between the situation of thirty years ago, when the Shan hills were literally in a state of anarchy, and today, when the guns are largely silent. And here, on a hill spur overlooking this once besieged city, was an emblem of their ethnic identity and their anti-communism. The new pagoda in Lashio was called Yan-taing-aung or, loosely, 'We Win All Our Fights'.

Lashio sits in a valley over two and a half thousand feet above sea level. The area was once very prosperous and before British rule the valley around Lashio had been a hub of Burmese royal authority, a Burmese governor lording it over his charges from a hilltop fort nearby. These were the days when caravan journeys from the inland cities of China to Mandalay took many weeks or months and Lashio provided an important stopover. Tea and silver were then plentiful in the local markets. By the mid-nineteenth century there was also some opium. Opium poppies are not indigenous to the region, but are actually an import, from very long ago, from western Europe, where they grew wild in Roman times. The Arabs brought them to Asia in the eighth century AD and a thousand years later the British were harvesting opium in India and shipping the increasingly popular drug to China. It was around this time that opium first appeared on the scene in Burma as well, theoretically banned, but usually tolerated.

When the British first arrived in Lashio in the 1880s, they found the entire valley in ruins, the result of years of rebellion and attacks from highland tribes. It was, however, still a natural seat of local government, and the new colonial masters chose Lashio for the headquarters of their 'Northern Shan States'. The 'Superintendent of the Northern Shan States', normally a young Englishman, was stationed in Lashio, together with a garrison of Indian soldiers and military police. His job was to keep the peace, ensure the local chiefs were well-behaved and paying their taxes, and occasionally fly the Union Jack along the Chinese frontier.

During the early decades of the twentieth century Lashio was a not very important frontier town, with China about a hundred miles away along a single dirt road. It was a quiet frontier. Whilst India's Northwest Frontier along the borders of Afghanistan conjured images of dashing cavalry charges and Great Game intrigues, this eastern frontier of the Indian Empire was a sort of dead end, with no real threat on the other side, only a small stream of mule caravans and impoverished tribal peoples.

This changed during the Japanese war, when Lashio occupied a key strategic position along the Burma Road. The Japanese took the town in late April 1942 and three years later, when the Allied counter-offensive was in full swing, Lashio lay on the march from northern Burma, already in British hands, to Mandalay. Chinese armies in the area were under the American command of Lieutenant General Daniel Sultan, of Oxford, Mississippi, who first seized the important Baldwin silver and lead mines twenty-two miles to the northwest, mines big enough to supply all the lead needed by the Japanese war machine. The Americans then bombed Lashio from the sky, before British Indian troops retook the town in April 1945. Lashio and its environs were then quickly forgotten by the outside world.

Only now, seven decades after the building of the Burma road, is the area around Lashio becoming critical again for China. Soon the town will sit astride the future pipeline, carrying up to 20 per cent of China's imported oil, the new rail line transporting goods bound for Europe. Renewed fighting anywhere nearby would be a disaster. Lashio is today the headquarters of the Burmese Northeast Regional Commander', a major general whose division-strength command is in charge of managing relations with the myriad armed groups nearby. If there is a new offensive, Lashio will be the launchpad.

With the ceasefires, some of the ethnic insurgent leaders had hoped for compromise. Many had once advocated independence from Burma. Now they said they only wanted a 'federal system' of government, with equal rights for all citizens and a degree of local autonomy. But the idea of 'federalism' was never something the Burmese army leadership was going to accept. It spelled weakness and fragility, a recipe for an eventual break-up of the country.

With a federal system this country will fall apart within ten years. Look at the map! We're a small country. Why should we stay divided in a hundred little pieces? Many countries have had to forge unity by force. Only then can we survive. Otherwise we'll be eaten up by the Chinese. The foreigners will criticize us, but they are hypocrites. They've all done the same thing.

I was talking to a recently retired army colonel, a man with a dark leathery face and big hands. He was wearing a pale blue shirt and an old *longyi*, but it was easy to picture him in jungle fatigues, marching his men over the hills. He believed that the civil war would end not through some recognition of ethnic difference, but through assimilation. Roads and railways would grid the nation together. Trade and a single system of education would slowly but surely weaken local difference.

In a way, the Burmese army's policies towards their opponents were the direct opposite of the policy of Western governments towards the ruling junta. Western governments had employed economic embargoes and diplomatic isolation, hoping that by shunning the Burmese generals, the generals would eventually come around. They didn't. The Burmese army employed very different tactics. They fêted their erstwhile foes, calling them 'leaders of the national races'. They took them to the big cities, created new desires and allowed them to enrich themselves. Business links, even illicit ones, were actively promoted. They did this knowing that it would sap the insurgents' strength as fighting organizations. By 2010 the Burmese army was in a far stronger position than when the ceasefires were first agreed.

Under the new constitution, some power would be devolved to local governments, each with their own semi-elected legislatures. It would be far from a federal system and the real authority of the local governments would be heavily circumscribed. But it was a small concession to ethnic minority leaders who had been fighting for genuine self-determination.

The Burmese military leadership also offered the ex-insurgent armies a deal on their future armed status: reorganize your men into a 'Border Guard Force', that will partly be officered by us and that will ultimately come under our authority. It meant a partial but not complete integration with the Burmese army. Acceptance would mean sweet business deals and a place for former rebel leaders in the new order. Some of the smaller militias accepted. The rest have not, so far.

What has emerged over the past twenty years has been neither war nor peace, but a weird half-way house, still dominated by men of violence, an almost medieval world of rival fiefdoms, some owing allegiances to a distant overlord, a complex web of feuds and fealties, the idea of a modern state still set far in the future.

To the southeast of Lashio is the territory the United Wa State Army or UWSA, boasting more than 30,000 armed men backed by armour and artillery and even surface-to-air missiles. The Wa were once a very remote people, like the Rawang. As late as the 1930s, British control over their mountain fastness was incomplete. The British divided them into the 'Tame Wa' and the 'Wild Wa'. The difference to the colonial administrators was that the latter wore (almost) no clothes and were infamous as head-hunters, living in earthen tunnels along the crests of the higher ranges. Today, though, the Wa are big players in the Burma–China borderlands. Their army is one of the largest private armies in the world, with as many soldiers as the Taliban, controlling a territory larger than Belgium. In the 1990s they were the world's largest producers and traffickers in heroin but have more recently turned to methamphetamines to help fund their mini-state.

More importantly, the Wa are no longer living at the back of beyond, but on the margins of China, the emerging superpower. Under their ceasefire with the Burmese army, they are allowed to keep their guns and their autonomy. To enter the Wa zone from Burma proper there are checkpoints and Burmese soldiers are not allowed. But there is no border with China. Coming from Lashio a couple of hours away, the dirt roads become Chinese highways. And much of the Wa zone is on the Chinese electricity grid, and even its internet and mobile phone grid. Blackberrys don't work in Rangoon but they do in the Wa area. Their leaders are mainly China-born Wa (there is a Wa minority in China as well), have Chinese names, and send their kids to school in China. They are rich and enjoy continued if discreet support from the local Chinese authorities across the unmarked frontier. It's a stunning reversal in Burma's geography. What had been remote is now closer to the new centre. What were muddy mountain hamlets are now more modern than Rangoon, once a rival of Singapore.

Even stranger an entity than the territory of the United Wa State Army is the town of Mongla further south, along the Mekong and adjacent to Laos. A one-time communist rebel base, Mongla transformed itself over the 1990s into a sleazy holiday destination for Chinese tourists, complete with casinos, transvestite cabarets, 24-hour restaurants and nightclubs, and brothels featuring women from across Asia and even Russia and the Ukraine. Officially, the area around Mongla is called the Shan State 4th Special Region. Its leader Lin Mingxian was a Chinese Red Guard radical during the Cultural Revolution, who joined the Burmese communist insurgency as a 'volunteer', rising up to be the commander of '815 War Zone'. When the ceasefires were agreed, he kept his own militia, carved out his own little niche and went hard to work. By the early 2000s, thousands of Chinese were flocking across the border to Mongla every day and the money was rolling in.

Lin built a massive Miami Beach-style mansion in pastel colours on a bluff overlooking his fiefdom. He entertained visiting Chinese and Burmese VIPs at the huge casino halls, some with a hundred gaming tables or more. Unlike the wrecks plying the streets in Rangoon, here there were gleaming new SUVs. He encouraged prostitution but policed it, setting up a special red-light district with mandatory and regular health checks. Russian women were said to command 50 per cent more than the local ladies. To show his drug-trafficking days were behind him, Lin erected an Anti-Narcotics Museum, also in bright pink. As in the Wa zone, Mongla became an Alice in Wonderland world, where the back of beyond was suddenly transformed through its connection with China into a mini-metropolis.

But some of the Chinese higher-ups were not very happy. Hundreds of their officials had been siphoning off money from public accounts to spend (and often lose) at Lin Mingxian's gambling dens. Tens, perhaps hundreds of millions of dollars were streaming into Mongla, most of it illegally (and off the Chinese government's books). When the daughter of a high-ranking party official lost a quarter of a million dollars during a weekend jaunt to Mongla, Beijing decided to take action.

In January 2005, units of the Chinese People's Liberation Army crossed over into Mongla ('Operation Blue Arrow'), shut down the casinos and sealed the border. But in a remarkable feat of entrepreneurship, Lin, the former communist radical, turned crisis into opportunity by taking his operation online. By 2007 he had built more than two dozen new casinos nearby but these were connected to cameras with fast internet connections. Anyone in China can now place a bet of up to a million dollars online without setting foot in this once far-flung corner of Burma.

It was through this deeply fractured world, full of distrust and with long traditions of violence, that the Chinese began to move into Burma. Warlords, businessmen, ethnic leaders, and military men – most of those in power were a mix of all four. When the border first opened up in the 1980s, the first sign of the new China was the flood of cheap Chinese goods into Burmese markets, coming via Lashio and then on to Mandalay. Then came the logging, on a gargantuan scale. The forests of Burma's north and east were mercilessly chopped down, with hundreds of lorries a day ferrying huge teak and other hardwood logs to waiting Chinese sawmills. The jade mines of the Kachin Hills were another big attraction. Burmese jade has been highly prized in China for centuries and with the end of fighting ever greater quantities could be transported across to Yunnan and then to markets in Hong Kong and elsewhere. There was also of course the trade in heroin, long a staple of the Golden Triangle, which in the 1990s fed a growing number of Chinese addicts. By the early 2000s, the border trade was worth billions of dollars a year. Over 2010 and early 2011 the sale of Burmese jade to China was worth more than $4 billion.

There are also enormous new Chinese-owned and run plantations, many growing rubber. Other plantations, some thousands of acres in size, grow rubber, sugar cane, cassava and pineapples. Chinese businessmen 'rent' the land from local authorities. The small-time farmers who were there – Burmese, Kachins, Shans and others – have had no choice but to vacate their land, receiving minimal compensation in return. No one knows how many thousands of people may have been displaced so far.

There are other commodities as well. The Chinese, like the Romans, infamously eat everything, the more exotic the better, and see medicinal or aphrodisiac value in the rarest animals. Burma's forests had been home to many endangered species, from snow leopards to rhinos. All are now being hunted and shipped across to impatient customers over the border. For years the New York conservationist Alan Rabinowitz has worked tirelessly to protect Burma's surviving tigers and in this he has had some success, persuading the government to designate huge areas of the far north as sanctuaries. But implementing even the best of plans has been almost impossible, given the enormous disparity between the incomes of local would-be poachers and the prices being offered by Chinese buyers. Mongla has become a key hub. A report in 2010 by TRAFFIC, an international network fighting illicit trafficking in wildlife, said that they had found the skin of a clouded leopard, pieces of elephant hide, containers with bear bile extracted from live animals, and a dead silver pheasant, as well as parts of many other endangered species in the Mongla market. The tiger parts they found included entire skins, bones, paws, penises and teeth. Chinese customers come to buy what they want, for themselves or for resale in China. One speciality is 'tiger-bone wine', costing $88 for a small bottle, and said to be a health-boosting tonic. It can even be ordered by telephone for delivery to the Chinese town of Daluo across the border.

Women as well have become a commodity. Since 1978, couples in China's cities have been to restricted to only one child as part of a draconian and successful effort at limiting the country's population. Nearly all preferred a son, and often chose to terminate pregnancies rather than having a daughter as their only child. What this has meant a generation on is that there are now forty million more men in China than women, or forty million men who will need to find a wife outside China if they are to marry at all. For Burma (where there is no similar gender discrimination), it has meant a boom in the illegal trafficking of women to China. The trafficked girls and women are often sold to men in poor Chinese villages for whom the going rate of 20,000 to 40,000 yuan (about $3,000 to $6,000) is a bargain, compared to the dowry that they would need to pay for a Chinese bride. The women are usually tricked into believing they are going to a new job in China. A few manage to escape.

But all these things pale in magnitude in comparison to the new plans that are being drawn up. And the most important plans involve the thing that industrializing China really needs most from the outside world: energy.

There is the oil and gas that will soon be delivered by the new pipeline. There are also Burma's great rivers, the Irrawaddy and especially the Salween, that rush down from their Himalayan and Tibetan sources to the Bay of Bengal. Neither has been dammed and the Salween is the longest pristine river system in the world, with a diversity of plant and animal life that has only begun to be explored. It won't last much longer. Over the past few years China's state-owned enterprises have negotiated agreements with the Burmese junta to build a giant $9 billion 7.1 gigawatt hydropower station across the Salween. Another project, already under way, will dam the Irrawaddy just north of Myitkyina. Ten thousand or so Chinese workers have arrived to carry out the construction, living in their own camp, in rows of little wooden houses. Other projects aim to dam the Salween further downstream. Altogether, if realized, these will provide more than 20 gigawatts of electricity. To put this into perspective, Burma today consumes less than a tenth that amount; 20 gigawatts is about what is consumed by all of Thailand. Some of the new electricity will stay in Burma, but the vast majority will be exported to China. A dam financed by the World Bank is required to do an extensive environmental impact study, but the World Bank is not allowed by Western governments to operate in Burma. There is no doubt that Burma desperately needs electricity, that these dams will provide this electricity (some smaller ones already do so), and that the sale of electricity could be a vital money-earner in future. But the potential environmental consequences could be catastrophic, not only for this area, but further downriver, impacting on the tens of millions of people who depend on the Irrawaddy and the Salween for their survival.

Lashio's Guan Yin temple is the biggest Chinese temple in Burma. Guan Yin is the Chinese personification of mercy and seen as the Chinese version of Avalokitesvara, the bodhisattva of compassion in the Mahayana Buddhist pantheon. It was a holiday and the place was packed with families, many just strolling around, many in traditional Chinese cloth shoes. There were monks and little novices, all shaven-headed, not in the familiar brown robes of Burmese Buddhist monks, but in the slate-grey kimono-style robes of China. A series of impressive stone staircases led from one outdoor plaza to the next, until they reached the main temple with a tiered roof and three massive images of Guan Yin. There were offerings of incense and candles and Chinese men and women with their eyes tightly shut made wishes before the statues. Little whiffs of dark smoke drifted upwards. To the side was an ancestor hall, where offerings could be made to one's ancestors. On the side wall was a giant painting telling the story of the Monkey King.

Outside, on the lower plaza, was a small Ferris wheel. Kids were running around everywhere, many of the boys brandishing toy guns. Some of the girls were dressed in pink princess costumes. Parents bought Italian ices for their children and sugar-cane juice for themselves. Everyone was eating watermelon. Here and there little grey-robed novices, no more than nine or ten years old, were running around as well, though without the toy guns; if they became too raucous, a monk would come by and quietly discipline them. The more well-to-do had cameras and snapped posed photographs of their families, with the green Shan Hills in the background.

From the temple I took a taxi downtown to talk to a Chinese businessman whose contact details I had been given in Mandalay. He didn't live in Lashio but was there for a couple of weeks, supervising the construction of a plastics factory. 'I hope Western sanctions will remain forever,' he said. He was short and plump and had a smooth round face. It was getting dark and we were in a small restaurant, drinking Johnny Walker whisky on ice and eating roasted peanuts from a little lacquer bowl.

I know, maybe it's not a good thing, but they help us, a lot. There are so many Chinese in Lashio now. There is talk of opening an Institute of Confucian Studies here too. I think the government will allow this. Why not? It will be good for Burma's political development. They don't need democracy, not for a while. But they need to improve their government. I think Confucian ideas will help.

He was originally from Hubei, far in the interior of China, and clearly saw Burma as a backward place, but one with potential. When we got up to leave, he said, 'You know, I've been here for a while now, and I have feelings for your people. They deserve better.'

Was China the emerging superpower going to be a responsible neighbour, quietly making possible an end to decades of war, building infrastructure, investing in the economy, and bringing Burma into the twenty-first century? Or was China a plundering behemoth, grasping everything within its reach, without concern for the environment or the rights of individuals or communities? For a poor country like Burma, being next to China, the economic powerhouse of the world, should be a huge advantage – but will it? At a time when Chinese influence around the world was starting to be felt more strongly than ever, Burma was the canary in the coalmine.

When I was looking at the map a few years ago, the story of China's and India's attempts to find new connections to and across Burma seemed a straightforward one. But the situation in Burma was complex and Burma, as much as China or India, was shaping the direction of what was to come. Western sanctions had pushed the country's ruling junta ever closer to Beijing and had created an unusually privileged environment for Chinese business. The Burmese government's alliance with China was a tactical move, but would it become permanent, sealing in a future for Burma as a raw material exporter to China? And here, along the frontier, the situation was incredibly complicated, with multiple armed groups and ceasefires that remained tenuous at best, even as China began to pour billions of dollars into new infrastructure. Would China be able to navigate the world of Burmese politics to its advantage?

America was hovering on the edge. So far at least, attempts by the US government to talk to the Burmese have not delivered much. Early in his administration, President Obama called for a new partnership with Beijing, but by 2010 relations between the current and rising superpower were tense, and a more competitive dynamic was emerging. Burma was a low priority for American policy-makers and so it was perhaps unsurprising that Beijing rather than Washington was moulding the local environment. Things could change, but for now Burma seems to offer a prime example of declining US influence in the region.

And what of India? Trade between Burma and India was growing, if not as rapidly as with China. But the nature of this trade was entirely different, based on a $1 billion Burmese export of beans and pulses and the import of Indian pharmaceuticals and a few other products. The trade was carried out via Rangoon and not across the long land border. The two governments have talked of improving road connections, and of India building a new port on Burma's Arakan coast. But by 2010 there was little beyond talk, and there was clearly not the same momentum in India–Burma relations as between Burma and China. We will later see the reasons why this was the case.

Most importantly there was China itself. Its motivations were still a mystery to me. I knew something of the old history of Yunnan, the province just on the other side of the border, but it was difficult in my mind to relate the colourful and romantic histories I had read to the aggressive capitalism streaming over the frontier.

From Lashio a better road, almost a highway, snaked through the hills to Muse. It was built and maintained as a toll road by a company called Asia World, owned by the son-in-law of none other than Lo Hsing-han, the 1970s Lashio opium warlord. Checkpoints lined the way. Truckloads of watermelons, grown on the new plantations, careered eastward. Muse was the border crossing, with big green-roofed warehouses and customs houses on the Burmese side and a modern skyline of office towers and high-rise hotels, the bright lights of China, on the other. For me, though, this was the end of the line. I had no permission to cross the border and would have to backtrack to Rangoon before going by air, first to Beijing and then to the other side of the Burma–China frontier. I would travel across Yunnan province, in China's far southwest, to places I had been before, nearly twenty years ago, as well as others I had long wanted to see, a land of forgotten kingdoms and lost civilizations, now China's springboard to Burma and beyond.

Part Two

SOUTHWESTERN BARBARIANS

The Malacca Dilemma

Around the time that Alexander the Great was preparing to conquer the known world, in the fourth century BC, Hui Wen, the king of Qin, was also expanding his domains, laying the basis for an empire that would grow and expand to the present day. This was during China's 'Warring States' period. The country had not yet been unified and Hui Wen's kingdom was only one of several feudal states that were constantly fighting one another for supremacy. Qin was situated just beyond the Yellow River, a dry and dusty region adjacent to the Gobi Desert. To the south was the kingdom of Shu, located where Sichuan province is today, entirely different in language and customs, as well as rich and fertile. Hui Wen's main aim was to incorporate his other rivals to the east, but he was convinced by his advisors that by first adding Shu to his domains he would gain the strategic edge he wanted. He needed, however, to come up with a clever plan, as there were rugged mountains between the two kingdoms and no road through which to march his armoured crossbow-wielding legions.

He decided on a ruse. Qin already had diplomatic ties with Shu and had sent women to the ruler of Shu to become his concubines. According to Chinese chroniclers, this Shu ruler had also fallen madly in love with a transvestite from the far north and had become distraught when the transvestite died. The Qin court regarded him as a greedy and lecherous clown. There were also rumours of dissension within the Shu regime. For Hui Wen the turmoil presented an opportunity and he had his men construct statues of cows made of stone and placed them in an area of Qin where he knew visiting Shu ambassadors would see them. He also had blocks of gold placed near the statues, so it would seem (said the Chinese annals) that the cows were excreting gold. The plan worked. The ruler of Shu soon heard of the golden cowpats and requested that he be sent a few of these miraculous cows. Hui Wen replied that he would be happy to present them as a gift but that he would first need to build a special road through the mountains, as the cows were delicate and needed to be transported with care. The Shu ruler accepted. The result was the 'Stone Cattle Road', an amazing feat of early engineering, with huge wooden planks laid on top of great vertical beams, bored straight into the mountainside. And as soon as the road was completed, the Qin launched their invasion, and permanently annexed the land of Shu. It was a step towards the creation of the first Chinese empire, and a major expansion southwest towards new and alien domains.

In the late 1970s, the Chinese Communist Party embarked on a series of epic reforms, reforms that liberalized the economy while maintaining strict political control. They would unleash market forces and propel China into the first rank of global economic powers. Under the growing authority of party leader Deng Xiaoping, the system of people's communes that had been the bedrock of daily life and economic activity in the countryside was ended, private business was encouraged, and villagers were allowed to leave their old homes and travel as they wished in search of jobs. New Special Economic Zones were established to attract foreign capital. All this was a drastic departure from the policies of the recent past, policies that had led to widespread famine, entrenched poverty, and little or no room for individual freedom. In the early 1990s, after conservatives threatened a reversal, Deng underlined the communist state's new commitment to a market economy, telling the nation that 'to get rich is glorious', reinvigorating reform efforts and setting the stage for what has now been three decades of unprecedented growth.

The results of China's reforms are well known. Manufacturing, especially for sales abroad, has skyrocketed. According to official statistics, the country has enjoyed export-led growth rates of 8–15 per cent a year since the early 1990s, even during the recent recession. In late 2010, China's economy overtook Japan's as the second biggest in the world, after the United States. Chinese reserves of foreign currency stand at well over $2 trillion, by far the largest in the world, and Chinese per capita GDP has increased twelve-fold over the past twenty years. Only 10 per cent of the population now live below the official poverty line, compared to 64 per cent before the reforms began in 1978. Life expectancy has increased dramatically and a country that was 80 per cent illiterate half a century ago now enjoys a literacy rate approaching 90 per cent.

Literally hundreds of millions of people have moved from the countryside to China's ever-expanding mega-cities, especially along the southeastern coast, in what has been the greatest migration in human history. In the process, the percentage of Chinese people living in urban areas has grown from 18 per cent to 39 per cent. Across China in 1978, there was one phone for every 2,000 people and one TV for every 3,000. In 2011, 83 per cent of all Chinese had a telephone and more than a third were internet users. All this has been complemented by immense works of infrastructure, from the fastest trains in the world to dozens of world-class airports to entire cities levelled and rebuilt. At the beginning of Deng's reforms, Shanghai had three buildings over twenty storeys tall. Today it has more than 2,000. An industrial revolution of a scale and intensity never before experienced is today transforming the lives of the 1.3 billion people who live in the People's Republic.

I have had a long fascination with China. Growing up, I lived for several years in Thailand and travelled often with my family to places in southeast Asia, like Singapore and Penang, where Chinese culture was an enduring part of the local scene. This was the world of the overseas Chinese, whose diaspora, now totalling over sixty million people, extends around the globe.

Until very recently, nearly all overseas Chinese had originated from the southeast coast of China; the ancestors of nearly all Chinese-Americans, for example, come from a sliver of territory along the Pearl River delta (near Guangzhou and Hong Kong). It is as if all people of European descent outside Europe came only from Norway or Portugal. Living in Thailand I gained a familiarity with the culture of this small part of China, the food, the dialects, the appearance of the people, but not at all with the rest of the vast Chinese nation. The People's Republic was then in the final years of the Cultural Revolution and at the very start of Deng Xiaoping's reforms; there were no real opportunities to travel there as a tourist.

At university in America I took many classes in Chinese history and politics and an intensive course in Mandarin. My first visit to mainland China was in 1991, to Yunnan, on my way to the Burmese border. But it was only later, in the early 2000s, that I made my first trips to Beijing and the other big cities of the coast. By then, China's ultra-fast development was already well under way. When I went again in 2009, the pace of change had become even faster, and like everybody else I could only be impressed by the transformations taking place.

There was the new Beijing airport terminal, spacious and hyper-efficient, with an immigration officer so polite and soft-spoken that I couldn't tell whether she was asking an official question or just being friendly. 'Are you staying long?' 'Where are you from originally?' 'Is this your first time in China?' 'Have a good time!' The terminal, built in time for the 2008 Beijing Olympics, was bigger than all five London Heathrow terminals combined and had been voted by *Conde Nast Traveller* as the 'best airport in the world'. Altogether, more than $30 billion had been spent on Olympic venues and related infrastructure. There was the new 90,000-person capacity National Stadium, known as the 'Bird's Nest' for its striking design, with an outer skeleton of 42,000 tons of intertwined steel covering an inner 'skin' of double-layered plastic which keeps out the wind and rain and filters UVA light. Nearby was the National Aquatics Centre, in the form of a semi-transparent cube, with a surface that gives the impression of giant connected bubbles, and the National Theatre, a huge egg-shaped glass and titanium structure surrounded by water. On my first morning back, I walked for miles along the broad and immaculate pavements, across big plazas and past one shopping mall and office building after another. Everything seemed planned and orderly, the car traffic and pedestrian crowds dwarfed by the monumental architecture around them.

Beijing sits near the edge of the Chinese world. To the south are the speakers of the many different Chinese dialects – languages really, as different from one another as French from Spanish – stretching all the way from the Yellow River basin to Vietnam and Burma, more than 2,000 miles away, the distance from Paris to Cairo. But just a hundred miles or so to the north is the Gobi Desert and the Great Wall, and on the other side the grasslands of Mongolia and the vast arc of Mongolian and Turkish-speaking peoples (the Mongolian and Turkish languages are closely related) that reaches from the Arctic Circle to the Aegean Sea.

Beijing is also an old city. The Mongols, who conquered China from the north, were the first to make the area their capital. The Ming emperors who replaced them decided to rule China from the same region and founded Beijing at the beginning of the fifteenth century. Its name means 'Northern Capital' and it has remained the capital of China ever since, with only a few short interruptions. And over the intervening centuries it has been the administrative hub of vast empires and republics as well as one of the most populous cities in the world. Today, the Beijing municipal area – about the size of the greater metropolitan area of New York – is home to twenty-two million people.

There is, however, little sense of an old place or of organic growth or accretion. Instead, the overwhelming feeling is of a designed space, looking forward to the future, confidently and without nostalgia. Near my hotel was the financial district with the offices of over a thousand different firms, international ones like Goldman Sachs and UBS as well as Chinese ones like the People's Bank of China, the steel and glass towers all lined up as if on parade. Unlike Manhattan or central London, it's not a jumble of the ultra-modern with the old. In the 1950s many parts of Beijing were torn down, the leafy courtyards and cobblestone alleys replaced by grey and boxy Soviet-style buildings and broad stately avenues. Much more has been demolished over the past twenty years. Soon, almost nothing more than a few decades old will be left.

The main commercial area is along Wangfujing, Beijing's equivalent of Fifth Avenue or Bond Street. A Chinese city usually conjures up images of teeming masses, pushing and elbowing along narrow streets. But Wangfujing is entirely pedestrianized, its wide expanse barely filled by the well-dressed shoppers ambling along. For hundreds of years it was lined with princely residences. Today there is one mall or department store after another. I walked past The Place with signs for Mango and French Connection out front, as well as a huge outdoor screen showing random clips of fashion shows. Next door was a higher-end mall, with advertisements for Gucci, Coach and Marc Jacobs. And off to the side was Snack Street with neatly organized stalls offering a variety of Chinese specialities, from crispy sesame cakes to the more exotic 'silk worms on a stick' and 'starfish fried in shark oil'. For the less adventurous there was also a McDonald's and a Kentucky Fried Chicken (by far the most popular fast-food chain in China). It was a cool spring day, but many of the women on the street were carrying umbrellas to protect themselves from the sun; here too, porcelain-white skin was seen as a key ingredient of feminine beauty.

To the south was Tiananmen Square. A portrait of Chairman Mao still hangs over the square. The square had been expanded in the early 1950s to serve as the principal parade ground for the People's Liberation Army. During the late 1960s, hundreds of thousands of impassioned people in identical Mao suits, feverishly waving their little red books of Mao's quotations, gathered to hear the chairman's calls for a 'Cultural Revolution' against the old and existing order. In 1989, equally large crowds calling for democratic change had assembled here, before being crushed by tanks and automatic weapons.

On my second day, with some free time on my hands, I went to see Chairman Mao's embalmed body, which is kept in a special mausoleum on the other side of Tiananmen Square from the Forbidden City. I joined a large crowd of Chinese people, quietly shuffling along, past the entrance area where I bought a ticket as if to a movie, and then into a big hall where there were dozens of bouquets and bunches of flowers. In little groups we were then ushered into a smaller, darkened room, to within a yard of so of the Great Helmsman himself, stiff and waxy. A woman next to me was silently weeping as if overcome with emotion. We were allowed just a few seconds each to look, before having to pop out of the back door and into the bright sunshine outside.

There is a selective preservation of the past in Beijing. There is Mao's photograph over Tiananmen Square (the only place I saw a photograph of him anywhere in China) and the mausoleum. Parts of the old city wall have been kept or even recreated. The homes of 'good' Chinese writers from the nineteenth and early twentieth century are museums. And there is the Forbidden City itself, the enormous palace complex of the old emperors, with its mustard-coloured tiled roofs and vermilion walls, a reminder of 'feudal' oppression of days gone by, but perhaps as well a sign of pride in the country's imperial greatness. There is a desire too to demonstrate the antiquity of Chinese civilization, which some like to believe is more ancient than any other. At one end of Wangfujing was the Oriental Plaza, called 'a city-in-a-city', with several shopping complexes and a Hyatt Hotel. When the plaza was being built a few years ago, an eagle-eyed postgraduate student of Beijing University named Yue Shenyang happened to pass along the construction site and spotted a black charcoal mark on the dusty ground. He dug around and found the broken bones of animals as well as stone tools. They are today kept in glass cases in a small museum created on site, next to a life-size statue of a dark-skinned but Chinese-looking woman, bare-breasted and in a furry loincloth, nursing her baby. A pamphlet I was given said: 'The discovery of palaeoanthropology relic in Wangfujing is the first time around the world discovering palaeo-anthropology in the downtown of an international metropolis . . . Further discretion is advised.'

In November 2006 Chinese state television aired a twelve-part series called *The Rise of Great Powers*. The series outlined the histories of different countries that became 'great powers' and was based on research by a team of Chinese historians. This was seen as a change in China, where any hint of superpower aspirations were kept tightly locked away. Just two years before, President Hu Jintao had used the term 'peaceful rise' but even this was seen by some as too provocative. The series began with an account of Portugal in the fifteenth century and ended with the present-day United States. With a dramatic soundtrack in the background, the deep-voiced narrator warned of the mistakes made by Germany and Japan, whilst also drawing attention to those strategies worthy of emulation, such as the development of Britain's navy to secure its overseas trade. Queen Isabella was praised for her risk-taking as well as Abraham Lincoln for his efforts to 'preserve national unity'. The research team were said to have briefed the Communist Party Politburo on their findings.

China's economic strength was shaping global markets. Closer to home, there was a security dimension as well. China was traditionally a continental power and in the nineteenth century its Qing dynasty navy had been entirely outclassed by British warships during the Opium Wars, forcing Beijing to cede Hong Kong and open up the country to Western commerce. China had not had a blue-water fleet since 1433 when a giant armada under Admiral Zheng He had sailed through the Straits of Malacca and around the Indian Ocean. Around the same time, however, the

Oirat Mongols under Esen Tayisi were crushing Chinese defences along the Great Wall. Attention had to be turned inland. There was no looking back. In 1497–9 Vasco da Gama navigated around the Cape of Good Hope, beginning what would be 500 years of Western domination of Asian waters, first by the Portuguese, then the Dutch, French, British and finally the Americans. Twenty-first-century China was keen to take to the seas. Since the end of the Cold War, US naval forces directed by its Pacific Command in Hawaii have controlled the sea lanes from the Sea of Japan to the Persian Gulf. Would growing Chinese power upset the applecart? The Americans for one were increasingly worried.

Just before I was in Beijing there had been a curious stand-off between an American navy ship, the USS *Impeccable*, and five Chinese-flagged vessels not far from China's southeast coast. The Americans were increasing their surveillance of Chinese submarines (the *Impeccable* was a submarine-hunter), and this in turn had angered the Chinese. The five ships had steered dangerously close, waving Chinese flags and demanding that the American ship leave the area. When the Americans resorted to fire hoses to try to force their pursuers back, the Chinese crew on deck stripped to their underwear (presumably the better to withstand the sprays of water directed against them) and continued their chase. The Pentagon claimed harassment. The Chinese were unapologetic. In the *China Daily*, Vice-Admiral Jin Mao was quoted as saying that the *Impeccable* was a spy ship, up to no good. 'It's like a man with a criminal record wandering just outside the gate of a family home,' he said. The Chinese website Danwei went further, saying the *Impeccable* was like 'something in which a James Bond villain would plan world domination'.

India, too, was concerned about the prospects of China as a military superpower. Relations have not been good for decades and the 1,200-mile-long Himalayan border is still not demarcated. China claims India's northeastern state of Arunachal Pradesh as 'South Tibet' and part of China, and has long bristled at New Delhi's hosting of the Dalai Lama and the Tibetan government-in-exile. China has armed forces of over two million men, India over one million; both have a nuclear arsenal.

Whilst the Americans were more concerned about Chinese objectives in the western Pacific, India's focus was naturally on the Indian Ocean. While I was in China, I read on the internet an article in the *Guardian* by Brahma Chellaney, professor of strategic studies at Delhi's Centre for Policy Research. He said:

China wants to be the pre-eminent power in Asia and whether Asia ends up multipolar or unipolar will be determined by what happens in the Indian Ocean. Currently there is a power vacuum there and the Chinese want to fill it.

A recent *Time* magazine cover story was entitled 'Burma: The New Great Game'. The original Great Game was the nineteenth- and early twentieth-century competition between tsarist Russia and imperial Britain for supremacy over Central Asia. Analysts argued that a similar 'tournament of shadows', as the Great Game was also called, was beginning to be waged around the Indian Ocean. India and China certainly seemed to be vying for influence. In Pakistan, Sri Lanka, Bangladesh, Nepal, and of course Burma, all the countries along India's periphery, China was busy cultivating commercial ties and building infrastructure. The flag could easily follow trade as it had for past 'Great Powers'. Some said it was just a matter of time before China displaced America as the main naval power in the western Pacific and established itself, militarily as well as economically, around the Indian Ocean as well.

I asked a Chinese scholar of the region what he thought of this line of reasoning. He was, perhaps unsurprisingly, dismissive.

This is not Europe in 1914. We don't need to replicate the Western experience of rivalry and war. China is still a poor country, India is a poor country. All these countries near us, Nepal, Bangladesh, are poor. We all need development. We should think of cooperation, not competition.

Others were more blunt. 'The Americans just want to keep China down,' said a Chinese friend. He had studied in London and was now working for a big multinational company. He was tall and at fifty still boyish-looking in his jeans and lime-green Ralph Lauren sweater. We were have dinner at the Middle 8th, a fashionable restaurant in Sanlitun. Sanlitun is a neighbourhood to the east of the centre of Beijing that had been the hub of the local nightclub scene since the 1990s (and the haunt of mini-skirted working girls from Mongolia and Russia until they had been cleared out for the Olympics). There were many bars along the tree-lined street, including Paddy O'Shea's, the Q Bar and the Apothecary, as well as restaurants and cafés, some with tables and white plastic chairs set on the pavement outside. The Middle 8th specialized in food from Yunnan, with a menu that included several mushroom dishes. It was noisy and brightly lit and the crowd inside, a mix of Chinese and Westerners, were mostly young and expensively dressed.

Over a dish of 'fried boletus edulis with shrimp', my friend argued that the Americans had prejudged them, already vilifying them as the future enemy and making plans accordingly, cementing ties with Tokyo and other Pacific nations, drawing closer to New Delhi, and selling sophisticated arms to Taiwan. The US was maintaining fleets and bases around the world, invading countries, and had a defence budget equal to all other countries put together. He didn't understand how Americans could possibly see China as the more dangerous power.

Others I met in Beijing echoed this view. In 2009, the US military spent $738 billion on defence and homeland security. Estimates for China's annual military budget vary considerably, ranging from $69.5 billion to $150 billion. There was annoyance at the thought that China could be a threat to anyone and protests that China was only seeking a 'peaceful rise'. I mentioned Deng Xiaoping's advice to the Communist Party, well remembered in China, to 'hide our capabilities, bide our time'. In many countries there was anxiety about what would happen, if not now, then in a decade or so when capabilities would no longer need to be hidden. They said there would be no new imperialism. A better life for the Chinese people was all that was desired. If it meant growing ties with markets and governments around the world, that was China's own business. The rest of the world would just have to adjust.

Whatever the truth of China's ambitions overseas, it is also clear that in the late 2000s China's leadership was still extremely worried about the sustainability of its recent gains. The world recession of 2008 did not knock the Chinese economy in the same way as in the West and indeed seemed to underline the feeling that the future could be rosier in China than elsewhere. But there were big problems lurking under the surface, from rampant official corruption to China's basic dependence on exports to a now anaemic American market. There were two other major worries as well.

The first was the huge and growing divide between the haves and have-nots and between a prosperous east coast and a still poor rural interior. A provincial breakdown of China's current GDP per capita shows this divide clearly. At the very top of the table of provinces, municipalities, and Special Economic Zones, way above the rest, is Hong Kong with $44,000 per capita, compared with a national average of $6,000. A per capita income of $44,000 places Hong Kong roughly on par with many industrialized countries, including the United States. Then there are the big eastern and coastal cities like Beijing and Shanghai, where the per capita GDP is less than half of Hong Kong's, but still very high by international standards at about $18,000 a year, placing them at about the same level as Poland or Hungary. Per capita income in Guangdong, also on the east coast, is about the same as Brazil's at $10,000 a year.

But move inland and the numbers change dramatically. First come the provinces like Shaanxi, closer to the centre of China, with per capita income at about the national average, comparable to Egypt or Guatemala. Then there are the very poor ones. All are clustered in the west and southwest. Yunnan is third from the bottom, with about $3,400 a year in per capita GDP (at the bottom of the list is Guizhou, next door), about the same as Vietnam and the Philippines.

And so we have a gigantic east to west slide in income levels, from US levels of prosperity to levels not much different from the poorer agrarian countries of southeast Asia. For the Chinese government's strategic thinkers, the need to narrow the gap between rich and poor, east coast and interior, was a top priority, and looking at the map, they concluded a big reason for the southwest's poverty was its distance from the sea and lack of easy access to international trade. Some 90 per cent of international investment had been targeted at coastal cities. It was these cities that were booming. Future development had to mean creating new infrastructure, including airports and motorways that would more efficiently link the poorer provinces to the eastern seaboard.

But there seemed another way to ameliorate this coast–interior divide. And that was to make China a 'bi-coastal' nation. China's 'Western Development Strategy' was officially inaugurated in 1999 and related to this was the idea of a connection through Burma to the Indian Ocean. It was an idea that was championed first by academics, and then by policy-makers. Development of the west would require massive investment in infrastructure and over the past decade tens of billions of dollars have already been spent. Easy access to the Indian Ocean would be a significant plus; on this everyone agreed. The problem was making it happen. It meant first and foremost bringing the Burmese military junta on board.

There was a second problem as well: managing the country's ethnic diversity at a time of fast economic and social change. From afar, China seems like a giant monolithic society. Most will know that Tibet is in the far west of the People's Republic, and will perhaps have heard or read about the Uighurs in the northwest and the recent violent clashes there between Uighur Muslims and the majority or 'Han' Chinese. But few outsiders appreciate the full complexity of China's ethnic picture or the importance placed by Chinese policy-makers on the integration of China's disparate ethnic communities. The Han Chinese are basically the people who speak one (or more) of the many Chinese dialects and who see themselves as part of a Chinese tradition, stretching back to the old Han dynasty of ancient times and beyond. But there are many ethnic minorities who speak entirely different languages and identify themselves with other traditions. These ethnic minorities account for 7 per cent of the total population. Which doesn't sound like much. But that's still more than a hundred million people, equal to the populations of France and Spain combined. And these minority nationalities are the majority or near majority in over half of China's territory.

There's Xinjiang in the far west with its vast reserves of oil and natural gas. And the huge Tibetan plateau, not just what is today the Tibetan 'Autonomous Region' but also Qinghai, and the historically Tibetan-speaking areas now annexed to Gansu, Sichuan and Yunnan provinces. Then there's Yunnan in the southwest and the adjacent minority regions in Guangxi and Guangdong, together home to more than forty million non-Han people, from minorities few in the West have ever heard of, like the Naxi, Yi and Dai.

China's rulers know that within living memory what is today China was a led by a hotchpotch of warlords and local military commanders, or under the control of independent and non-Chinese rulers. Their answer to the threat of ethnic division has been different at different times, but in recent decades the answer has largely been the same as the answer to everything – sustained economic growth. With more jobs and better jobs, other problems will be manageable and will vanish over time. Burma is next to China's biggest concentration of ethnic minorities, Yunnan, and Beijing's Burma policy has been dictated first and foremost by what will help Yunnan's economy move forward. This too meant dealing with the Burmese military junta.

Chess was invented in India and exported to Europe. In China, however, the principal board game has long been *weiqi*, known in the West by its Japanese name, Go. And in Go, victory comes to the player who can surround the pieces of his opponent. It was a mix of internal challenges that appeared to be leading China back down the Burma Road. But would China, like the Europeans who acquired Africa in a 'fit of absent-mindedness', one day emerge in control, on Indian's eastern flank and on top of the sea lanes of the world?

Over the past twenty years, China has emerged as the Burmese government's top foreign friend and supporter. China has provided hundreds of millions of dollars worth of military hardware, including planes and tanks, as well as crucial diplomatic protection at the United Nations and elsewhere. Trade has risen to all-time highs with official figures now placing bilateral trade at over $2 billion a year; the real figure, including contraband, is doubtless far greater. Together with a growing array of investments, the Burmese economy is today tied more closely to China's than at any other time in modern history. High-ranking Chinese party leaders, generals, ministers and provincial officials routinely visit Burma, and Burmese military brass are often seen in the official media touring Chinese cities.

China's policy is about as different from the American and European policy of economic sanctions and diplomatic condemnation as possible, and this difference is not too surprising. It's hard to see how promoting democracy would ever be very high priority for Beijing. It's also worth remembering that during much of the Cold War, roles had been reversed. In those days, especially in the late 1960s and 1970s, it was Washington that was the Burmese military government's best friend abroad, providing military training and welcoming its then dictator General Ne Win to Washington (he made a quick visit to Lyndon Johnson's White House before a week in Maui playing golf). China for its part was denouncing Burma's generals as 'fascists' and actively plotting the regime's overthrow, not only through sanctions and rhetoric, but through all-out backing for the communist insurgency. This was at a time when China was providing help for communist movements throughout southeast Asia. Only with the consolidation in power of Deng Xiaoping and like-minded reformers did the focus turned solidly to economic development at home, not to revolution abroad. Export of Maoism ended and the search for markets began. Human rights were never on the agenda.

As China's industrial revolution gained pace, so did its hunger for the natural resources necessary to fuel its continued growth. The countries of the developed world have been the big buyers of new Chinese goods, but it has mainly been poorer countries (and a few well-endowed rich ones like Australia) that have been the focus of Beijing's desire to lock in its energy and mineral needs for the future. In many parts of Africa, places that had long been the preserve of former colonial powers, Chinese firms are buying mines, building roads, and in general spending billions of dollars, without so much as a peep about 'good governance', gender equality, or other issues often linked to Western aid.

Burma, though, is not just another foreign country. Unlike other new-found trading partners, it occupies a critical space on China's southwestern flank, right next to its densest concentration of ethnic minorities. Borders easily become blurred. For Beijing's leaders, securing markets near and far has been of crucial importance. But of even greater importance has been ensuring internal stability, including and especially in ethnic minority areas.

The Chinese view Western policy towards Burma as hypo-critical and self-defeating. Hypocritical because they see Western governments, when it suits their interests, propping up regimes elsewhere which are just as tyrannical, if not more so, and self-defeating because Western sanctions and boycotts have only removed what leverage they would otherwise have. But this does not mean that Beijing will push for a change in the American or European approach. At one level, they would like to see Western sanctions lifted, believing that a more prosperous Burma, connected to international markets, will help ensure stability and that this will be good in the long run for China as well. But they also clearly see the huge advantage that sanctions (and related boycott campaigns) have given to their own business interests by removing economic rivals from the scene. Why work to bring in their competitors?

Behind these practical considerations, however, is a more philosophical position. In the West, even after recent experiences in Iraq and Afghanistan, there is still a strong feeling that problems elsewhere – civil wars, repressive governments – can be fixed with the right dose of international help. The Chinese have little experience meddling far away, and are much less certain of the efficacy of what they would term foreign interference. 'The Burmese have their problems, but we've all had our problems and we've had to find our own way out. It's better to leave them alone. Look at where China was not long ago. It wouldn't have helped at all if foreign governments tried to tell us what to do,' I was told by a Chinese analyst. This was a firmly held conviction that dovetailed well with less altruistic motives.

At times I sensed that at least some in Chinese officialdom were no longer sure of this approach, and veered towards a more paternalistic attitude. Perhaps the Burmese are different? Perhaps they do need some help? In 2007, when monk-led demonstrations in Rangoon dominated international news for a couple of weeks, the Chinese were nervous. 'Our leaders want to find a solution to this Burma issue once and for all,' a Chinese journalist said to me at the time. But then the story faded from the TV screens and it was back to business as usual.

Meanwhile, business as usual was acquiring a new dimension. China by 2009 was not the China that had first reached out to Burma in the late 1980s. The recent global financial crisis had severely weakened Western economies, but China was emerging relatively unscathed and more confident than ever. It had lots of money in the bank and was on a frenetic shopping spree for raw materials. Economic relations with Burma were moved into high gear.

By early 2010 construction had begun on the oil and gas pipelines that would connect China's southwest across Burma to the Bay of Bengal. They would run from Mandalay past Ruili, first to Yunnan and then onwards to the Guangxi Autonomous Region and to the mega-city of Chongqing. All three were places targeted in the 'Western Development Strategy'. Like the huge hydroelectric projects on the Irrawaddy and Salween that were also moving forward, the pipelines from Burma would ensure the energy needed for ever faster industrialization. The pipelines had a strategic dimension as well, and were a part of resolving what President Hu Jintao in 2003 called 'The Malacca Dilemma'. China's oil needs are growing by the day, and imports of oil, from Africa and the Middle East, are all currently shipped via the Straits of Malacca and Singapore. Chinese strategists were worried about pirate attacks along the Straits, but were even more worried that, in the event of a future conflict with the United States or India, a few enemy warships could easily block essential oil supplies. A conduit through Burma was a way out of the dilemma.

The trouble for China was that the situation in Burma was not quite stable. A new constitution, one that included regular elections, was about to be implemented, yet overall political reconciliation seemed far away. And the Chinese, especially the Chinese security establishment, knew better than anyone else that much of the north and east of the country lay in the hands of armed groups other than the Burmese army. In 2009, much to the chagrin of Beijing, the junta had launched a lightning attack on one of these groups, sending tens of thousands of ethnic Chinese fleeing across the border. Was China really going to place so much strategic weight, not to mention international prestige, on a country whose future remained uncertain? Some Chinese analysts were unconcerned. 'If we were going to be worried about any neighbouring country, it would be Pakistan, not Burma,' one told me. 'Burma's in a far better situation.'

In general it seems that a mix of pragmatic considerations is shaping China's Burma policy. There were the internal challenges for which Burma as a bridge to the sea was at least part of the answer, as well as the desire, in some quarters of Beijing at least, to exploit the withdrawal of the West from Burma and in the process gain influence on India's flank. But there was a deeper history as well, that seems to have been entirely overlooked: the history of China's southwestern frontier.

One way of seeing China is not so much as a rising superpower but a re-emerging one. The country was, for centuries until the 1800s, the biggest economy in the world (with the possible exception of Mughal India) and arguably the most technologically advanced. From this viewpoint, what is happening now is simply a return to an ancient status quo. The Chinese often view themselves as heirs to a unique and unbroken tradition stretching back thousands of years to the earliest Bronze-Age dynasties, a leading world civilization, perhaps the leading world civilization, whose pre-eminence was only on occasion interrupted by barbarian invasions and by the more recent and shameful period of Western domination, but which is now on the road to recovering its rightful position.

But China is actually not a fixed geographical entity. And we need to remember that the China of today, and the borders of the People's Republic, are very much a creation of the twentieth century and do not necessarily correspond to the China of previous eras. There is a frontier history, often sidelined, that is perhaps becoming important again.

Chinese civilization started along the Yellow River, not far from present-day Beijing and the open plains of what is now Mongolia. Millet was first domesticated there, perhaps 10,000 years ago, and it was in that arid and windswept land that the first Chinese writing appeared, written on oracle bones, heated and cracked turtle bones used to divine the future. When the 'First Emperor' Shi Huang Ti – a successor of King Hui Wen of Qin – unified the Chinese world in the third century BC, it was still a relatively small world, one that had expanded beyond its

Yellow River base, but was only a small portion of China today, maybe a quarter.

No one understands exactly how the Chinese language and Chinese culture then spread from this core around the Yellow River. Superior agricultural technology is likely to have been an important factor. Advanced farming meant more people, and, perhaps, a steady stream of Chinese speakers migrating southward, from the cold and dry north, first towards the Yangtze River valley, and then further, into the steamy jungles of what is now southern China. The earlier peoples of these new regions spoke entirely different languages, including ones ancestral (or closely related) to modern Thai, Cambodian and Vietnamese. The people of the Wu kingdom, for example, around present-day Shanghai, likely spoke a language akin to modern Thai and the Shan dialects of Burma. And the people of the kingdom of Yue, based near present-day Hong Kong, spoke an Austro-Asiatic language, similar to Vietnamese. In their trading emporiums by the South China Sea the Yue dealt in imported ivory from as far away as Africa and frankincense from Arabia. The Chinese saw the Yue as outlandish foreigners, eating on banana leaves and living amidst malarial swamps.

At its height, ancient Chinese imperial control extended across much of the present eastern half of the country, including the long coastline. This was roughly during the time of the Roman Empire, during the first centuries AD. Gradually, local kings and courts and tribal peoples were incorporated politically and integrated culturally and linguistically. What had been the kingdom of Yue, for example, would remain part of every successive Chinese dynasty, its people eventually losing their distinct identity. Their original languages gradually disappeared and were replaced by Chinese dialects such as Cantonese and Hokkien, dialects that were influenced by long contact with the now extinct aboriginal tongues. Only the southernmost Han imperial possession, Vietnam, would regain its independence (after a thousand years of Chinese rule) and the Vietnamese have fiercely guarded this independence ever since.

To the southwest, towards Burma and Tibet, is a different frontier history. The valley of the Yangtze River snakes hundreds of miles, from near Shanghai on the coast, to the great gorges beyond Yichang. Further on is the Sichuan basin, once the land of Shu, today home to over eighty million Chinese people. Since the building of the Stone Cattle Road, immigrants have streamed in from the harsher climates of the Yellow and Wei River valleys to this new Chinese province, which would become famous for its linens and mines of copper, iron ore and salt, and which has been part of every Chinese empire ever since.

Beyond Sichuan, though, were ever-higher mountains and upland valleys, ending finally in Tibet and Burma. As in south China, there was a moving frontier. But it is a much more recent frontier. Whereas Sichuan and south China were more or less fully incorporated into China by medieval times, large parts of the southwest, an area three times the size of France, were still outside any real Chinese control well into the twentieth century. For much of the southwest, the history of the past hundred years has been not only the history of war and communist rule, but also the history of its integration with 'China proper'.

Along the Burmese borderlands, one could say that it is a process that is still continuing. In Burma, the picture has been of China as a juggernaut, rolling in and intent on supremacy. And from further away, China's ties with the junta have been lumped together with its relations with other 'rogue' states like North Korea and Sudan, sinister and inscrutable, or set within an emerging 'Great Game' with India. The domestic considerations are little understood, nor the actual dynamics motivating Sino-Burmese ties. And entirely ignored is China's frontier history and the situation in Yunnan.

From Beijing, Yunnan's capital, Kunming, is a three-hour flight away, across the Chinese hinterland and over increasingly high mountain terrain. It is the province next to Burma, almost equal in size and population, and the engine of China's drive towards the Bay of Bengal. I knew Yunnan a little from a trip there in the early 1990s. I also knew Yunnan as a place where independent kingdoms and upland chiefs had long resisted Beijing's control. What role did Yunnan now play in China's policy towards Burma and the region? I wanted to put the pieces together.

South of the Clouds

Yunnan for centuries was China's wild southwest. It was a land of outlaws and miscreants and exotic religious sects, a place where musket-slinging Han settlers battled bow and arrow-wielding tribesmen and aliens from beyond the pale. Its jungle-clad mountains teemed with fearsome animals and its torrential rivers, thousand-foot cliffs and deadly miasmas deterred all but the hardiest of frontiersmen. The Chinese made a distinction between the barbarians who were 'cooked' and those who were 'uncooked'. The cooked ones had come to accept the superiority of Chinese ways, learned the Chinese language and were well on their way to being Han Chinese themselves. Well into modern times, however, Yunnan was still full of the rawest barbarians possible, people with bizarre sexual mores, hostile to any imperial authority. Beyond them were the even stranger kingdoms of the Mien or Burmese, and on the other side of the Mien, the western sea.

Today, Yunnan, which means 'South of the Clouds', is a province of the People's Republic, about 152,000 square miles in size (a little bigger than Germany) and with a population approaching fifty million. It's an area rich in natural resources, relatively under-populated, and home to the largest concentration of minority peoples anywhere in the country. Nearly 40 per cent of Yunnan's people are today classed as non-Han. The Irrawaddy, the Mekong, the Yangtze and the Pearl Rivers all descend from the Tibetan plateau through Yunnan, and the province's hydro-electric potential, now quickly and controversially being realized, is enormous. Yunnan is also China's biggest producer of tobacco and flowers, as well as aluminium, lead, zinc and tin. Marco Polo, who visited in the late thirteenth century, commented on Yunnan's great salt mines, for which the area was famous, together with its silver and, later, its opium. It has long been renowned as well for its tea, and more recently for its coffee, first introduced a hundred years ago by a French priest from Vietnam. Nestlé and Maxwell House have started to buy coffee here for export and Starbucks has even introduced a new 'South of the Clouds' blend at its more than 500 outlets around China. The dark forests that had frightened early Han settlers have now largely been cut down, but Yunnan is still a place of great natural beauty, with rolling hills in the east and mountain valleys, turquoise-blue lakes and snow-covered peaks to the west, on the approaches to Tibet and at the edge of the Himalayas.

Kunming is the capital of Yunnan province and had been my introduction to China. This was in 1991, when I was on my way to the insurgent-held areas of Burma's Kachin Hills. It was winter, and though the temperature in this 'City of Eternal Spring' was mild, it was also grey and cloudy, a morning mist obscuring the big construction sites and new skyscrapers that were set at long intervals along broad and half-deserted avenues. I was coming from steamy and frenetic Bangkok and Kunming at the time seemed neat and clean and nondescript, a city of cyclists in black cloth shoes, old men and women chatting away on park benches, and pavements lined with small, evenly spaced and carefully tended trees. There were almost no Westerners and I don't remember coming across anyone who spoke English.

It was a city with a rich and colourful past. In the early twentieth century, when European influence in Asia was at its peak, the British and the French had vied for access and influence, and the French had built a train line, connecting Kunming with their port of Haiphong, near Hanoi. And when the Japanese invaded China in the 1930s, thousands of refugees from the coast, many of them well-to-do professionals and businessmen, flooded into this distant corner of the country, some bringing with them whole factories that had been dismantled and were to be reassembled beyond the range of Japanese bombers. Entire universities were even evacuated as well to Kunming, and this one-time frontier town began to take on a cosmopolitan air. The Burma Road carried supplies from Rangoon and Calcutta, as well as war-profiteers and spies. There were American military men too, airmen who flew missions against the Japanese and special operations agents from Detachment 101 of the Office of Strategic Services (a predecessor of the CIA) who trekked from Kunming to the Vietnamese highlands to make contact with the anti-Japanese Viet Minh guerrillas under Ho Chi Minh. It was only in 1949, under China's new communist rulers, that all ties with the outside were severed, ushering in a period of isolation that would last more than a quarter of a century.

The traces of the earlier city are now more or less gone. There are a few temples, churches and mosques, but nearly everything else has been razed to the ground in a headlong rush for modernization. Some old neighbourhoods were still intact when I visited in 1991, but by the mid-1990s the speed of development had quickened. The old commercial street called Wuchenglu, with its rows of wooden shop-houses, was demolished, and soon after the wonderful assortment of early twentieth-century buildings along Jinbilu, many in the languid French Indochina style, were torn down as well, developers sparing only the old Roman Catholic cathedral, the Cathedral of the Sacred Heart of Jesus.

And when I went back in 2009, Kunming, like the rest of China, had changed beyond recognition. It was now crowded and noisy, a bustling city of apartment blocks and shopping malls and traffic jams, with sometimes surprisingly modish people, the women in mini-skirts and knee-length boots, the men in dark Western suits or black leather jackets.

My hotel was at a busy street corner, not far from an expansive central plaza around which were half a dozen shopping malls. And my room, on the eighteenth floor and with a big window looking out onto the neon lights below, was like a hotel room anywhere, except for the thermos of hot water (people in China like to sip hot water) and a television that had only

Chinese-language channels. Unlike in Burma, English-language satellite news channels like CNN are not available in most Chinese provincial hotels, and for a few minutes I watched part of a Chinese game show, which seemed to involve women and children rushing around a supermarket, finding and piling goods into their shopping cart as quickly as possible.

All the nearby rooms were occupied by what I assumed was a big extended family. They kept their doors wide open, talking loudly to each other across the hallway; I thought at first that they were about to check out and were yelling because they were late for a flight or a train. But soon I realized that they had turned my section of the floor into a multi-roomed family unit, walking up and down and across the corridor as if it were home, their yelling part of normal conversation. On my way to the lift, I peeked into the rooms and saw people of all ages, the men in their underwear, sitting on the bed or on the sofa, slurping noodles and watching TV. Over the coming weeks, this would become a familiar sight in many of the places I stayed.

In the morning there was a big breakfast buffet on the ground floor. There were dozens of men, very few women (I was later told most of the hotel guests were businessmen from other parts of Yunnan), wolfing down steaming hot bowls of soup, together with little white pork-filled buns and hard-boiled eggs. Some poured sugar into glasses of hot milk. The brightly lit and windowless room had a sort of neoclassical design with mock-Corinthian columns, and 'Amazing Grace' played quietly in the background. The hotel gift shop sold jade that I knew had come from Burma.

On the street outside, older women matter-of-factly handed out cards with the telephone numbers of prostitutes. And in this tobacco capital of China, everyone smoked. People smoked everywhere in the hotel, even in the lift. And walking on the pavement were groups of men, all puffing away with little clouds of smoke rising above them. Cigarettes were often set in little plastic filters, and some held them like opium pipes, not between two fingers but grasped in the palms of their hands.

There were shops and shopping everywhere and shopping centres lined the main avenues. *Transformers 2* was playing at one of the main cinemas and a block-long construction site nearby was shielded by a sign promising a new 'mega complex' with condos and an 'IMAX Theatre Multiplex'. The sign had a picture of George Soros and the slogan in bold letters: 'More Detail Reflect Global Business Style'.

Not far away, along a boulevard of tall buildings, was a stone house. It was here that the American General Stilwell had met with Chiang Kai-shek during the Japanese war. It was simply called 'The Stone House' and the downstairs was now a restaurant, with a notice in English next to the entrance: 'Known for its good food'. There was a garden to the side with a little pond, and around the pond about a dozen old men and women, sitting on benches, silent, enjoying the afternoon sun. Most looked like they were at least seventy, old enough to have seen the stone house in its heyday, perhaps even to have caught a glimpse of Stilwell and the generalissimo through the window. The house had been the centre of government in the 1940s, even in the early years after the communist take-over, at a time when Kunming was still a collection of dirt roads. Now there was a shopping mall next door, glass and steel, with Zegna, Ralph Lauren and Mont Blanc stores downstairs and large billboards outside for Elizabeth Arden and Dior.

A friend who was visiting from Hong Kong told me over drinks that evening at the hotel:

We have to remember how traumatic life was for so many until just thirty years ago, the war, the Cultural Revolution. The old want to forget the past, and the young know nothing else but the stability and progress you see today. I wonder if it's a little like the West in the 1960s, a quarter-century after World War Two, with a younger generation that have no sense of how bad things can be.

There were few obvious signs of anyone other than Han Chinese. Yunnan once had a large Muslim population, but the only 'mosque' I came across was on the top floor of a building which also housed a 'Disney Mickey-Mouse' store selling toys and clothes for kids. There were some Muslim men in skullcaps, and occasionally on the streets I could see the aquiline faces of Turkish Central Asia. I was told there were other mosques, including a restored mosque first constructed in the time of the Mongols, but that most were on the outskirts of town.

Many people wore quite creatively put together outfits, like a mix of clothes from vintage shops. There was hardly anyone in the once ubiquitous Mao jacket. Some were in leather cowboy hats, which seemed all the rage. Men also wore old, worn, European-style suits like tramps from the 1930s. An old man, selling apples on the pavement, was in a faded but still elegant navy suit, his hair slicked back like a movie star from another time. Less elegantly dressed was a group whom I suspected from their dark skin and curly hair might be Wa tribesmen from the hills near Burma. They looked wild on the streets of Kunming, like Native Americans visiting Dodge City.

Here and there were little hints of a different past. There were giant bronze statues on the way from the airport, statues of strangely clad people that mimicked an earlier tradition, and a tourist display board on one street with pictures of women wearing sarongs as in Burma and Thailand. And in my hotel lobby there was a huge mural featuring black-skinned natives in feathered headdresses playing primitive-looking drums. Bare-breasted women danced in the background and both the men and women were portrayed as robust and muscular. They were not meant to be pointers to a separate political history, but a suggestion to visitors that this was a picturesque and excitingly unfamiliar part of China. They were like the leis offered to tourists when arriving in Hawaii, telling visitors they were somewhere exotic, but still safely within their own country.

Two thousand years ago, when Chinese imperial forces first began venturing in this direction, Yunnan was *terra incognita*.

There were strong contacts between Yunnan and the pre-Chinese cultures of Sichuan and quite possibly with the pastoral peoples further north as well, along the Ordos Loop of the Yellow River and even the Turkish and Scythian grasslands beyond. But there were important ties as well in the other direction, to what are now Burma, Thailand, Vietnam and Laos. In the late centuries BC, a flourishing Bronze-Age civilization existed along the shores of Lake Dian, not far from modern Kunming, and very similar bronze artefacts, including magnificent bronze ceremonial drums, have been found in Yunnan, as they have been in many areas of mainland southeast Asia. Men of distinction were buried with containers filled with cowry shells, an important currency across much of Asia before the use of silver for money, the cowries having come all the way from the Maldives in the Indian Ocean, via Burma and the Bay of Bengal.

Early trade between the Chinese and the people of Yunnan included trade in barbarian slaves and in the little horses for which Yunnan was prized, and these were exchanged for iron tools and weapons made in Chinese Sichuan. In the Chinese classical book *Account of the Southwest Barbarians*, the people living in the Kunming area were described as a component of a broader confederacy, called Mimo, a confederacy that extended over a thousand miles, all the way to what is now the Indian border. The people of Mimo were said to dress their hair in a bun-shaped topknot (like Burmese men until the late nineteenth century). It was a military society, very hierarchical, the elites connected in a still poorly understood way to other equestrian elites from the steppe worlds of inner Asia.

During the height of the Han dynasty, the Chinese, based far to the north, were able to co-opt or overwhelm rulers in the area, establishing military outposts or what they called 'commanderies' right up to the Burma border. It wasn't a complete conquest but a scattering of authority in a sea of native rulers. A road linking their domains was first called The Five Foot Road and then (after some improvements) the slightly grander and more sinister-sounding Southwest Barbarian Way. This was around the same time that the Romans ruled Britain. And like the Romans in Britain, the Chinese in Yunnan doubtless made an impact on local people, awing them with their superior technologies, martial prowess and lavish lifestyle. But when their empire collapsed in the third century, the Chinese withdrew completely, setting the stage for the rise of new and entirely independent, non-Chinese states. About a hundred years after the Anglo-Saxon kingdoms were first established in Britain, a new kingdom was founded in Yunnan, known to the Chinese as Nanzhao, a kingdom that by the ninth century would grow into an empire, one of the most powerful in the medieval world.

In the thirteenth century Marco Polo visited the area around Kunming and understood that he was in a place outside Chinese civilization, with strong links to other parts of Asia. He described the main city in the region, which he called Karajang, and wrote that it was 'a great and noble city, in which are numerous mer-chants and craftsmen. The people are of sundry kinds, for there are not only Saracens and Idolaters, but also Nestorian Christians.' Nestorian Christianity was then widespread in Central Asia and was the state religion of the Khitans, a Turkish people to China's west whose king, Yelu Dashi, was the inspiration for the legend of Prester John, the Christian king of the Orient who would one day vanquish Islam. Marco Polo explained that the people of Karajang 'ride long like Frenchmen' and that they didn't eat 'wheaten bread' like the Chinese, but 'rice they eat and they make of it sundry messes'.

Marco Polo had come to Yunnan in the train of Mongol conquerors. The Mongols had crushed Yunnan's rulers and incorporated the entire region around Kunming into their vast Eurasian empire, stretching then from Poland to the Sea of Japan. A good portion of Yunnan's ruling class would become Mongol and Turkish by descent. When the Mongols were replaced a hundred years later by the new Ming dynasty in China, Yunnan as well fell under Ming control. It was then, in the early fifteenth century, that Kunming was founded as the main garrison town and local capital. This was the beginning of real Chinese rule in Yunnan.

It was the start of Chinese rule, but over a region that was not yet Chinese. The Han Chinese population in Yunnan was tiny, but would increase quickly, not just here but throughout what is today the 'the southwest'. A frontier was created, not unlike the American frontier a few centuries later, where military garrisons and expanding settler towns grew up amongst native and tribal communities.

The Yao were one of these native communities. They had once lived just south of the Yangtze River, in what is now the middle of China. In the twelfth century, however, this area (modern Hunan province) was still the frontier and the Yao were being pushed south by growing numbers of Han Chinese, themselves often refugees fleeing Mongol incursions. There was frequent violence between the Yao and Chinese newcomers, who were cutting down once dense forests to make room for intensive rice cultivation and shipping out the timber. Wild elephants, once plentiful, died out or retreated southwest. Some Yao rulers were co-opted by the Chinese and recognized as *tusi*, the Chinese term for a native chief. On paper, the Ming Chinese empire now seemed to extend all the way from the Yangtze River to Burma, but all along the way imperial control was often limited to fortified stockades, with large areas still governed by *tusi* or home to 'uncooked' barbarians.

This would gradually change. In the decades just before the Europeans first began their colonization of America, the Chinese were intensifying their colonization of the southwest. The Yao made their last stand at the Great Vine Gorge, in what is now the Guangxi Autonomous Region. Later Chinese chronicles state that in 1450–6, Yao forces under a chief known as Big Dog Hou 'attacked and ruined prefectures and countries, appearing and then disappearing again among the mountains and valleys'. Offers of reward for his capture proved useless and the president of the ministry of war, Wang Hong, observed that dealing with Big Dog was 'like dealing with a spoiled child: the more indulgence was shown to him, the more he would howl. If he were not flogged until the blood flowed, he would not stop howling.' No fewer than 160,000 soldiers were directed at Big Dog's headquarters. The Chinese emerged victorious. Sixteen hundred prisoners were taken alive, more than 7,300 others killed and decapitated.

Under the later Manchu or Qing dynasty, the southwest was further consolidated. Emperor Yongzheng's policy was to 'bring the chieftains into the system', a massive and brutal integration of non-Han areas. There were to be no more places where the state's 'whip, although long, could not strike'. Native *tusi* alliances were partly abolished and their territory incorporated as new prefectures. Autonomous Yao militias were forcefully disbanded.

Another native people were the Miao. In 1726 at the Battle of Mount Leigong, more than 10,000 Miao were said to have had their heads chopped off and more than 400,000 starved to death. In 1797, yet another people, known as the Buyu, attempted to throw off the Chinese yoke, leading to thousands being either burned to death or beheaded. In 1855, the same year Chief Billy Bowlegs was leading the last stand of the Seminole people against the US Army in Florida, Zhang Xiumei, a Miao, led a massive uprising that temporarily controlled all of eastern and southern Guizhou. When he was eventually defeated in 1872, countless numbers of his people were massacred. These revolts would continue well into the twentieth century. There are still more than ten million Miao people and four million Yao people in China today, roughly as many as there are Swedes in Sweden and Danes in Denmark, but almost insignificant in number compared to the huge Han Chinese population, and virtually invisible from the outside.

By the nineteenth century, hundreds of thousands of Han settlers were pushing further southwest to Yunnan as well. Many of these settlers were from the cold and arid north and brought with them the northern Chinese dialect that is today the basis for Mandarin. Today, the Chinese dialects spoken along the southeast coast – like Cantonese and Hokkien – are entirely unintelligible to Mandarin speakers, a sign of their ancient divergence. But the difference today between the Chinese spoken in Beijing and the Chinese spoken in Yunnan is slight, a matter of accent more than anything else, comparable to the difference between the English of London and New York.

It was a new frontier and a frontier that was moving. In Yunnan too there would be rebellions and uprisings by native peoples. Yunnan became a sort of Chinese Siberia, a place of settlement and economic opportunity, but also of exile for political troublemakers. One was Yang Shen, a prominent Ming dynasty scholar and poet. He was involved in the Great Rites Controversy of 1524 (involving the succession of the new Jiajing emperor) and was banished to Yunnan where he spent the next thirty years. There he was welcomed by the local literati and wrote at length about his new home. He is particularly remembered for his essay 'Roaming Atop Diancang Mountain', in which he embraced the idea of the Yunnan frontier. He wrote:

The Chinese are a truly cosmopolitan people, the heirs of all mankind, of the entire world. The Han are just one of the ethnic groups in the empire, and we include many different types of people. In Yunnan alone there are over twenty other non-Han native peoples. So long as they accept the emperor's rule, they are Chinese.

There was a time, in the late nineteenth and early twentieth centuries, when India was expanding towards China and not the other way around. It was, of course, an India that was under British rule, but there was an Indian component nonetheless. Burma was then firmly part of the Indian Empire and British Indian troops – Dogras from the Jammu Hills, Jats and Sikhs from the Punjab, and Gurkhas from Nepal – manned outposts on the edge of Yunnan. From their bases in Rangoon and Calcutta, networks of Indian merchants, Gujaratis, Tamils and Marwaris, explored trade links into China. British India saw Tibet as part of its 'sphere of influence' and western Yunnan as well was seen as part of its expanding backyard. Beijing was then barely in control of most of Yunnan and over long periods lost control completely to local hereditary rulers and warlords.

The most important of these warlords was Long Yun, who dominated the province from 1927 to 1945. China was then in anarchy, the country divided between the Nationalists under Chiang Kai-shek, the Communists under Mao Zedong and a host of provincial armies. It was the age of the warlords. Elsewhere in China there was the 'Dogmeat General', Zhang Zongchang, who ruled Shandong province, nicknamed 'Dogmeat' after his favourite summer dish, a giant well over six feet tall who kept a harem of Chinese, Korean, Japanese, French and Russian concubines, and even, according to a contemporary journalist, 'one bedraggled female who said she was an American'. Manchuria was the personal fief of the 'Young Marshal' (son of 'the Old Marshal') and morphine addict Zhang Xueliang. He would become famous for the 'Xian Incident', in which he kidnapped Generalissimo Chiang Kai-shek in a botched attempt to force Chiang into a united front with Mao Zedong and the communists, against the Japanese. He was arrested and would spend the next half century of his life in detention, before moving to Hawaii and dying there in 2001, aged 100. There were many others equally colourful, like the 'Philosopher Warlord', Wu Peifu, in Hubei, so-called because he had received a classical education, and the Methodist 'Christian General' Feng Yuxiang, who fancied himself the Oliver Cromwell of China.

Long Yun himself, the warlord of Yunnan, was a one-eyed, bespectacled, thin-faced autocrat whose name meant 'Dragon Cloud'. He was not a Han Chinese but a member of an aristocratic Black Yi family, the Black Yi being one of the more prominent minority peoples in Yunnan, heirs of a long tradition that went back to the medieval Nanzhao kingdom. He would rule Yunnan from 1927 until he was finally ousted by Chiang Kai-shek in late 1945. He had his own army of over 100,000 men and even his own currency and allowed American aid meant for the war effort to pass through his territory, though redirecting a not insignificant amount into his private coffers. He also controlled the biggest opium crop in the world.

Long Yun brooked little dissent but nevertheless permitted the many academics who flocked to Kunming considerable intellectual freedom. In 1939 he even responded positively to a plan to resettle 100,000 European Jews in Yunnan, a plan that never materialized, its backers in Germany seeing it as worthy but 'too visionary'.

He would be overthrown in 1949 and exiled to Hong Kong, only to return to China after the communist take-over and be awarded high office in the People's Consultative Conference. His two sons migrated to the US where for years they ran a restaurant business in Washington DC and Cambridge, Massachusetts. By this time, the People's Liberation Army was steamrollering over the final areas of Nationalist and warlord resistance. Over the coming years Beijing's control would finally run along the entire Burma–Yunnan frontier, for the first time in history. On the other side of the frontier was no longer the British Indian Empire, but a newly independent Burma, soon to drift into civil war.

The Han Chinese have traditionally viewed the indigenous people of the region in a less than flattering light: 'Their written language, resembling worms tied in knots, makes no sense at all,' remarked one nineteenth-century observer. 'They reek with unbelievable stench' and 'like wolves, they dine on raw meat, and are fierce in nature', said another. But the communists had to think a little differently. In the mid-1930s, Mao Zedong had led his embattled communist party fighters on their 'Long March', walking hundreds of miles from the coast, where they were being wiped out, deep into the interior, hounded every step by the then superior Nationalist armies and barely surviving as a coherent force. Their retreat took them to Yunnan and to many other areas where the Han Chinese were either a minority or were nowhere to be seen. They needed the help of these non-Chinese peoples, and came to see them as 'little brothers' who could be enlisted to the revolutionary cause. Later, once the revolution was won, they turned to Stalinist ideas about nationality, and embarked on a 'nationality classification project' to place the various non-Chinese peoples into a single all-encompassing scheme. In theory they were regarded as different nationalities, with rights to varying degrees of self-governance. In practice, few had any choice but to accept the new order and a degree of control from Beijing that was unprecedented.

For a while, there was a softly-softly approach to dealing with minorities, in Yunnan and elsewhere. Much of the province was incredibly remote from the centres of Chinese power. In 1950 it still took a month to travel from Kunming to the Burmese border, malaria was rampant, and much of western Yunnan home to only a negligible Han Chinese population. 'Autonomous zones' were set up as well as local border militias, and communist party workers set about distributing seeds and agricultural tools and improving markets and roads, hoping to win over minority support. A Minority Nationalities Institute was established in 1951 to train ethnic minority cadres, but, as late as 1953, *tusi* were still presented with seals of office, as in the old days of the Ming and the Manchus. In the hills there was resistance, often fierce resistance, as People's Liberation Army units moved into areas that had never before come under Beijing's sway.

Direct rule intensified. In 1957 there was a left-wing turn and the native chiefs were stripped of all their remaining privileges. Minority peoples in general were told they were to receive no special treatment, no special autonomy. 'All must travel the socialist road together.' Land reform began on a large scale and people throughout Yunnan were told to join new cooperatives. This was the same time as the Great Leap Forward in the rest of China, an attempt to jump-start industrial production and collectivize agriculture. It would lead to economic chaos, famine, and millions, possibly tens of millions, of deaths nationwide. Yunnan suffered terribly. Many native rulers fled to Burma, then a beacon of openness and relative modernity.

The Cultural Revolution came next. In the mid-1960s there were attacks on 'Little Nation Chauvinism'. Anyone in traditional clothes was fined. Ethnic festivals were banned or transformed into political rallies. The Raoshanling festival of the indigenous Bai people, for example, which is a three-day event honouring their deities, was made into the Festival of the Three Constantly Read Articles, with each day devoted to mass recitals of one of Mao's essays. All around the country, hundreds of thousands died during these years. An estimated 500,000 people were detained in Yunnan alone and nearly 7,000 became the victims of 'enforced suicide'.

There were incidents of extreme violence. Anything that was seen as different from mainstream culture was maligned and attacked, and that included the practice of Islam, still widespread in parts of Yunnan. All over China mosques became places of extreme harassment, as Muslims were forced under pain of death to raise pigs and eat pork.

In the town of Shadian, not far from Kunming, the local people fought back. Shadian people had a long tradition of blacksmithing and weapons manufacture, going back to medieval times when their ancestors had arrived in Yunnan with the Mongol and Turkish garrisons of Kublai Khan. The town had produced many accomplished Islamic scholars and was where one of the first translations of the Koran into Chinese had been written. During the tail end of the Cultural Revolution, in 1975, the local men made their own guns and organized a Muslim paramilitary force. They battled the all-Han militia that had also been set up. Policemen were sent to deal with the violence and were killed. Finally, in July that year, the town was attacked by several regiments of the People's Liberation Army, supported by heavy artillery and airpower. The town was effectively destroyed and nearly 2,000 men, women and children are believed to have been killed in what was the only ethnic uprising during the Cultural Revolution.

By the time China began opening up to the outside world a few years later, there was no hint of minority protest in Yunnan, only an overwhelming desire for something different.

I spent part of my few days in Kunming attending a seminar on Burma at one of the local universities. I have attended many seminars on Burma in America and Europe and the headline topic is almost always some variant of 'The Future of Democracy in Burma'. Here the agenda centred much more on mapping and understanding what was actually happening in the country and less on working backwards from a specific policy ambition. Several of the Chinese academics spoke Burmese well and were knowledgeable on the nitty-gritty of specific issues, from the Burmese army's relations with individual militias to cross-border trade. They were close to the action.

The university was on the edge of town and was leafy and tranquil, with impressive lecture halls and students bicycling around, not very different, in appearance at least, from a New England college campus. It was here that the warlord Long Yun had allowed refugee intellectuals to study and teach, at a time when the heartland of the country was in the grip of Japanese invaders. The scholars I met were all exceedingly hospitable, treating me and other seminar participants to many meals, where the several courses of food were complemented by endless rounds of mao-tai toasts. They were funny and unpretentious and laughed often at themselves. There was also a handful of Burmese students present, from a mix of ethnic backgrounds, all on scholarships and fluent in Chinese. They seemed somewhat awed by their situation, and asked me quietly for advice on their studies and their future.

During a guided tour I was shown an older building in a traditional Chinese style, with stone walls and a sloping roof. It was an examination hall built centuries ago, I was told, before the rest of the campus. Inside were little rooms, like cells, each with a life-size mannequin of a Chinese scholar, in a layered silk robe and black hat, seated behind a wooden desk. Candidates for the civil service would live here for days in isolation to write their exams. There was a small bed in the room as well as a tiny child-size toilet.

One evening I went to a trendy restaurant nearby called Salvador's. The menu served quesadillas and falafel as well as gourmet coffees. It was a favourite of Western tourists and the few expats who lived here. A student I met said:

Yunnan's the kind of place where people come to get away from it all, to get away from the rat race back east. Many people like me come to the university to study and then decide to stay on. It's cheaper here, the people are friendly, and there's not all the pressure to make money. It's very laid back.

Others were less laid back. On my last day in Kunming I met a businessman connected to one of the big government-owned corporations. He was in his early forties, a heavy-set man with thick black hair and glasses. He was originally from Tianjin, in the northeast near Beijing, but had made Kunming his home. He was very optimistic about Yunnan's future and enthusiastic about its growing links with the rest of Asia, including Burma. 'The Yunnan government has a very clear development strategy,' he said. 'Yunnan will be made into China's gateway to South Asia and southeast Asia.' It was about as straightforward an exposition as I had heard so far.

There were two aims. One was to raise living standards for everyone. The other was to make sure that local minority groups stayed happy and felt they were benefiting from China's economic progress. Traditionally, he said, the main problem in Yunnan was its location, in the extreme southwest and far from the big ports. The government's idea was to solve this problem by expanding links southward as well as improving transport links to the Chinese coast. Many different schemes were being developed that would tie Yunnan to Cambodia, Laos, Vietnam, Thailand and Burma, and further west to Bangladesh and India. All involved multi-billion-dollar investments in infrastructure. All meant Yunnan becoming the new regional hub.

Railways were a big part of the plan. A high-speed rail line will connect Kunming to Shanghai, nearly 1,240 miles away, and help bind this once isolated region more closely into the national economy. From Kunming, existing rail lines will be upgraded and new ones laid. One line would travel southwest to Ruili on the Burma border and then onward to Rangoon, with a branch extending directly to the sea, near Ramree Island. There is hope that this will one day be high-speed as well, running at 120 miles an hour over the entire route (Kunming is almost equidistant between Rangoon and Shanghai). A second line would head in a more southerly direction, connecting Kunming with the Laos capital Vientiane and proceed from there to Bangkok. The trains would move across once inaccessible mountain terrain, through tunnels yet to be created. Well over $20 billion would be spent. Ties with southeast Asia were already growing fast. By 2010, trade between China and southeast Asia was approaching $300 billion a year, but most of this was transported by sea. Cargo from Burma, Laos and Thailand could only move by lorry up and down the intervening mountains. Costs – in time and money – would drop precipitously.

It wasn't all about roads and railways either. Yunnan was aggressively developing its own industries, from tobacco to steel, readying itself to be a major exporter not only to Burma, as it was now, but to the entire tier of countries to its south. Part of the pipeline from Burma will stop near here, in the Kunming suburb of Anning, where $3.4 billion is being spent on a refinery capable of handling over 220,000 barrels a day. It will be complete by 2013.

Tourism will also be a big draw. Yunnan has great natural beauty and a year-round temperate climate and was being carefully branded as an unspoiled and exotic location within China for Chinese as well as foreign tourists. The businessman said: 'People will come here on holiday, maybe with their wives or girlfriends and have a good feeling about Yunnan. Then they will want to spend time here and invest their money.'

The ideas seemed sound, though it wasn't clear that they could easily be realized. So far, at least, things seemed to be going according to plan, but possible roadblocks were not difficult to see.

Around the time I was in China, a big scandal was being exposed in the city of Chongqing, Chiang Kai-shek's old wartime capital (then usually spelled Chungking), now metamorphosed beyond recognition like every other city in China, with a forest of skyscrapers to rival Manhattan. It's not part of Yunnan but just to the north, perched along steep cliffs overlooking the Yangtze River. In theory it's the world's largest city, with thirty million people, but that's partly because the surrounding districts with many satellite towns have been included in its vast metropolitan area. In any case it's still a mega-city, one that many in the Chinese leadership hope will attract billions of dollars more investment and one day rival Shanghai. In late 2009, a five-month long special police probe uncovered an enormous criminal network that reached to the very heights of local government.

Dozens of people were arrested, including the deputy police commissioner himself, Wen Qiang, who was charged with having received over $15 million in bribes in return for protecting criminal bosses throughout Chongqing. Some 25,000 police from outside the local jurisdiction had to be brought in for the crack-down, raiding illegal arms factories and netting nearly 2,000 firearms. Graft and racketeering involved a scandalous mix of both criminal and communist party chiefs, who ran gambling dens and brothels like the White House club in the basement of the Marriott Hotel. The 'Godmother of Chongqing' was a fifty-something-year-old woman named Xie Caiping, who was married to the deputy police commissioner's brother. She was said to have kept a private stable of sixteen young men as lovers and zoomed around town in one of her fleet of Ferraris and Lamborghinis until her arrest.

There was no similar public scandal in Kunming. But it was hard to believe that serious corruption wasn't a problem in Yunnan as well. After all, across the border in Burma were the ex-insurgent armies, a less than squeaky clean army regime, a multi-billion dollar drugs industry, and trafficking in all manner of contraband from people to precious stones. I was told in Kunming that it was impossible for central authorities to maintain the sort of tight supervision they would like over a country of China's size. Local officials and local businesses often did what they wanted and knew well how to circumvent the system. Criminal networks were bound to flourish.

Another major problem is the tremendous stress on the local environment caused by recent development. This was true in Yunnan as well as in many parts of China. In 2010 Yunnan would experience the worst drought in living memory, one that left eight million people short of drinking water and devastated billions of dollars worth of crops. Though this may well have been the consequence of global climate conditions, many suspected that the massive deforestation of the countryside was at least partly to blame. In areas close to Burma, more than 95 per cent of forest cover has been cut down over the past thirty years and much of the cleared land turned into rubber plantations (rubber trees are known for their insatiable thirst). Huge dams may also have been a culprit. The same year saw unprecedented drought conditions in Burma, Laos and Thailand as well and people and governments in these countries began to think more carefully about their riparian rights and Yunnan's upstream management. There was a growing environmental consciousness in China too. Further deforestation or the building of environment-wrecking dams in Yunnan would no longer be an easy sell.

I enquired about all these things but the businessman was undeterred in his enthusiasm. 'We'll find a way!' he said. And when I asked about plans for India, he became even more excited and explained his vision for a 'Southern Silk Road'. Current trade between India and China, a fairly modest $60 billion in value, takes place almost entirely by sea, via Singapore and the Straits of Malacca. 'A new road across Burma will mean a journey from Kunming to Calcutta could be made in just three or four days instead of ten! With a railroad, it could be made in 48 hours!' Down the street, work was beginning on a 72-storey twin-tower complex, projected to be the biggest building in Yunnan, with a five-star hotel, 'amusement and leisure facilities', and 'Grade-A office space'. It was to be called South Asia Gate and Kunming's commercial centre for trade with Burma, India and beyond.

He saw the future relationship with India solely in terms of trade. India currently runs a big deficit with China. It exports are mainly iron ore for China's steel mills and other raw materials. China in return sells manufactured goods. Yunnan stood to benefit immensely. For the businessman at least there was no hint of geopolitics or an unfolding Great Game with India, only money. 'Yunnan is still poor, but this will change, fast.'

In ancient and medieval times, Yunnan had been a crossroads of sorts, linking the Chinese empires to the north with Tibet, India, Burma and other places to the southwest. It was now becoming a hub again, but as an integral part of China. Would its old cultures and civilizations have any bearing on the future? From Kunming I travelled on to Dali, the capital of the last independent kingdom of Yunnan.

Gandhara

I had been in Dali once before, in early 1992, during the same trip that took me to Kunming and then the China–Burma border. Tourism was still new to Yunnan then, with many 'out of bounds' areas, but Dali had been open for a few years and had already become a little gathering place for backpackers. The choice of accommodation, though, was still very limited. Two or three 'guest-houses' had been set aside for foreigners, simple concrete buildings constructed around a courtyard, each with a number and no name. They were reasonably clean, with unadorned walls, wooden beds, and thin foam mattresses. They were also very cheap (a few dollars a night). The simplicity of accommodation added to the sense of being off the beaten track and in a place where everything was still untouched by global tourism. There were a couple of private eateries and these served the kind of fare familiar in backpacker havens elsewhere in Asia, like banana pancakes and lassi, and omelettes and ice-cold beer. I tried out the 'Shiatsu' massage clinic that had just opened up and received a very painful massage from a mute giant with enormous hands.

The town was beautiful, like a small town in Montana or Colorado in early winter, dry and cold, with the great cobalt sky and snow-covered mountains dwarfing the simple little streets and houses. I can't remember any Chinese tourists, only a handful of Westerners in anoraks and hiking boots (and me the only Burmese, I am certain) and an equal number of Japanese. The Japanese were of a special kind: adventurous and keen to experience whatever was on offer. I remember seeing a couple of them, with long wild-looking hair, in greatcoats and long felt boots, sunburned and smiling, walking into one of our backpacker eateries. They were trying hard to blend into the surroundings and looked almost Tibetan and I guessed that they had just come from a many-day trek further north, perhaps on horseback,

On that trip, I had come to Dali from Kunming via Xiaguan. Xiaguan was the local city and was at the south end of the enormous Lake Dali. Dali was the 'old town', several miles to the north and on the west bank of the same lake. I had spent a first night in Xiaguan: an entirely grey and cheerless place, the staff at the hotel disinterested, the carpets stained. There was almost no cooked food to be found anywhere and even at the hotel there was only a Chinese menu at the grubby restaurant, with no possibility of an English translation. I managed to get a local soup, which was more or less a layer of oil on top of boiling water with a few unidentifiable lumps of vegetables thrown in. I ate some popcorn I had bought from a street vendor to round off my meal.

Bleak Xiaguan and then charming Dali, both along a vast lake, is what I had remembered. But now, looking out the window from my bus, I was hard pressed to recognize anything I saw. The street we were on wound past the lake's edge and there were small sporty cars driving past at a leisurely speed. Just beyond was a promenade lined with lampposts and flowering potted plants, cafés along the waterfront, and many well-heeled people. On the other side of the street were elegant apartments, with balconies facing the lake and the mountains in the distance. There were no yachts, but one could almost imagine being in Switzerland, on the shores of Lake Geneva. 'This is Xiaguan,' said the Chinese man sitting next to me and indeed, a moment later, I saw signs in English and Chinese saying the same. We drove by big office towers, shopping centres and high-rise hotels until, after about twenty minutes, we were before the massive stone walls of Dali itself.

It was immediately apparent that a big part of Dali had been converted into the sort of place young Western tourists are habitually drawn to, like Khao San Road in Bangkok or Thamel in Kathmandu, but with Chinese characteristics. Where there had been just a couple of basic guest-houses twenty years ago, there were now dozens of small hotels, restaurants and cafés, and shops selling everything from Mao-era souvenirs to bootlegged CDs and DVDs. All this was centred on what was called Yangren Jie, or 'Westerner Street', just off the main high street. There was the Bad Monkey bar, the Phoenix pub with 'The Best Fish and Chips in Dali', and pizza places one after another. But unlike Bangkok or Kathmandu, everything was clean and wholesome, with no suggestion of prostitution, no beggars, everything orderly and well-managed. It was as if some central authority had said: 'Let's create a street just for Westerners. We'll give them everything they want, including fish and chips and pizza. But let's keep it clean. No drugs, no prostitution. And we'll try to keep them separate from everyone else.' Which is probably what happened. Westerner Street was a big success and now the Western-oriented establishments were spilling over into nearby alleys. There were travel agencies and places offering tours and bicycles for hire. One afternoon, tired from travelling and wanting something familiar, I found a café that offered free movies. There was a little library of DVDs downstairs at the café itself, and upstairs was a very comfortable living room with a huge flat screen television with a DVD player and a fine sunny view out the window. There was no one else there. For about three dollars I had a pleasant Chinese lunch, and then spent a couple of relaxing hours lounging in a big sofa, drinking beer and watching *Sideways* for the second time.

There were many Western tourists here, but outside Westerner Street they were overwhelmed by the multitude of Chinese tourists who flowed into Dali every day, day trippers mainly who preferred to spend the night at Xiaguan's more impersonal modern hotels. The pedestrian was king in Dali and few cars and no buses were allowed within Dali's newly restored stone walls. The old Dali of the early 1990s had been refitted into a sort of movie set (and indeed movies are now often filmed here). A great gate (which I didn't remember from my first visit) marked the entrance to the south and a wide cobblestone avenue led to a central plaza where popcorn was sold at a kiosk. The same avenue then continued for over a mile. The shop-houses all had wooden façades and sloping roofs with dark-blue glazed tiles.

Dali was touted as the main city of the Bai people and the Bai Autonomous Prefecture. The Bai are classed as a Yunnan 'minority nationality' and there are reckoned to be about two million Bai people altogether, both in this area and elsewhere in the province. They have their own language (Bai is thought to be distantly related to both Burmese and Tibetan), though most ethnic Bai are now either bilingual or speak only Mandarin. And everywhere in Dali were women in what were said to be authentic Bai costumes, with thin white cotton trousers and embroidered pastel-coloured waistcoats, selling souvenirs at the more touristy shops (which were nearly all the shops), working as waitresses at the bigger restaurants, receptionists at the hotels, and as ticket-sellers at all the sites.

For much of its early history, Burma's neighbour to the northeast was not China, but the independent kingdom of Yunnan, with Dali as its capital. And from the eighth to the thirteenth centuries this kingdom was a power in its own right, at times allying itself with the Tibetan empire to its west, at times with China's Tang and Song dynasties. Its mounted armies ventured deep into what is today Burma and may have been behind the founding of its medieval city of Pagan. We don't know what the people of Yunnan called themselves ('Yunnan' itself is a relatively new word). The Chinese called their ruler the Nanzhao, the Lord of the South, and this became the name of the kingdom as well.

Yunnan had come under partial Han Chinese authority in ancient times, but in the third century AD the last of the Chinese garrisons withdrew, leaving Yunnan to its mix of native peoples. Amongst these peoples would have been some of the ancestors of the modern Burmese, as well as the minority peoples of Yunnan today, speaking a range of languages and dialects. In the ninth century, the Chinese ethnographer Fan Cho compiled the *Man Shu*, or 'Book of the Southern Barbarians', in which he described Yunnan's different communities. There were, he said, various Wu-man or 'black southern barbarians', so-called after their dark complexions. Many were pastoral folk, tending goats and sheep, and slowly drifting southward, along the many river valleys, from the Tibetan marches down to the hot and arid plains of Burma. Some of the barbarians 'were plentiful all over the mountain wilds'. Others were 'brave, fierce, nimble and active ... they bred horses, white or piebald, and trained the wild mulberry to make the finest bows'. Still another group included women who 'only like milk and cream' and who are 'fat and white and fond of gadding about'. To Chinese eyes they were not a particularly hygienic lot, but cheerful nonetheless. One tribe known as the Mo-man were said to live their lives without ever washing their hands or faces. 'Men and women all wear sheep-skins. Their custom is to like drinking liquor, and singing and dancing.'

From Dali, around the time of the Islamic conquest of Spain, the Nanzhao ruler had unified six nearby principalities into a single state and then had gone on to mobilize these diverse tribal communities. From the start it was a militaristic state, expanding energetically in every direction. In these early medieval times, eastern Asia was dominated by two great powers: China and Tibet. The Tibetans were the upstart power, but at the height of their imperial reach. For some time Nanzhao fought alongside the equally aggressive Tibetans. In 755, when China was wracked by internal rebellion, the Tibetans and Nanzhao joined together to pillage Chinese cities.

Later, the Chinese managed to break apart the Tibet–Nanzhao alliance. Tibetan expansion was then a big headache for the Chinese court and the Chinese were trying for a policy of continental encirclement, aiming to bring together the Turks and Arabs to the west, the Indians to the south and Nanzhao to the southeast, in a grand coalition to crush Lhasa. 'Using barbarians against barbarians' was a time-honoured Chinese creed. When a combined Nanzhao–Chinese army defeated a Tibetan force near the present-day Burmese border, the Tibetan side included captives from as far away as Samarkand and Arabs from the Abbasid caliphate, men from the court of Harun al-Rashid and *A Thousand and One Nights*, taken prisoner on a Yunnan hillside together with 20,000 suits of armour. In appreciation, the Chinese received Nanzhao's envoys as representatives of a high-ranking kingdom, ahead of Japan, welcoming them with an honour guard of war-elephants and presenting exotic gifts.

The Nanzhao were then at the pinnacle of their power. They invaded south to Burma, plundering the little walled towns of the Irrawaddy valley, and perhaps even reaching the distant and sandy shores of the Bay of Bengal. During a period of supreme confidence they would even break their pact with China, attacking Chinese-controlled Hanoi, and marching over the mountains into Sichuan and sacking the city of Chengdu. All this from Dali, where the ruler of Nanzhao sat on his throne, swathed in tiger-skins, 'red and black with stripes deep and luminous, from the finest tigers in the highest and remotest mountains'.

When the Nanzhao dynasty eventually fell it was more because of internal intrigue than external pressure. The whole royal family was wiped out in a power struggle in 902, and was replaced by a slightly more modest regime, still based at Dali. By then Buddhism had a firm grip on local society and the kings of Dali emerged as committed patrons of the faith. The capital itself became an important centre of Buddhist learning. The links with Burma were strong, and the new Burmese kingdom at Pagan most likely developed in the shadow of Dali's influence. And via Burma there would have been ties as well to India, then divided into Hindu and Buddhist kingdoms, on the eve of the Muslim invasions.

The kings of Dali adopted the name Gandhara for their realm. It's the same word as Kandahar in modern-day Afghanistan and remains the literary Burmese name for Yunnan. Gandhara was once an almost mythical Buddhist land, straddling the present Pakistan–Afghanistan frontier at the time of Alexander the

Great, and was remembered long afterwards as a place of profound scholarship, governed by sages, peaceful and devout. The Dali kings even styled themselves as descendants of the great Indian and Buddhist emperor Asoka, who had reigned in the third century BC, seeing themselves as part of a fraternity of Buddhist states, from middle India to Ceylon to Vietnam.

Dali also associated itself with Mithila, the important commercial and religious centre once home to the Buddha himself, the New York of the ancient Indian world, with 'store-houses filled, and sixteen thousand dancing girls and treasure with wealth in plenty'. Other great Buddhist sites were also transposed, metaphorically, to the surrounding landscape. A cave on the other side of Lake Dali became the famed Kukkutapada cave (the original is in north India) where the monk Maha Kasyapa is believed to be waiting in a trance for the coming of the next Buddha. Next to the cave is said to be a stupa with relics of the Buddha's great disciple Ananda as well as the Pippala cave where the First Council of Buddhism was held. In this way, Dali became a facsimile of the holy land. As with the later kings of Burma, the kings of Dali wanted an Indian pedigree, and claimed descent from that greatest of Indian emperors, Asoka. The Persian scholar Rashid al-Din wrote that the king of Gandhara styled himself maharaja.

A variety of Buddhist schools flourished here. Chan Buddhism, better known in the West by its Japanese pronunciation, Zen, was a preferred school. Zen had begun in the seventh century within the Chinese Buddhist world as a reaction to the never-ending production line of monastic texts, commentaries, philosophical debates, images and rituals that its founders believed were choking off a more practical way to salvation. They hated all intellectualization and systematizations and often refused to write anything down. Their sayings were purposely cryptic and their style of teaching known as 'strange words and stranger actions'. Later, Tantric Buddhism, an import from both Bengal and Tibet, gained the upper hand. Its leaders were the Azhali, originally adepts in yoga and arcane rituals, who were believed to command supernatural powers. In Burma they would be known as the Ari, infamous for their heterodox ways and sexual licentiousness.

The Yunnan of old was a Yunnan that looked in different directions for ideas and inspiration, a link between China and the Indian world.

At the Three Pagodas complex, men and women were putting on clothes chosen from a rack of Chinese costumes and then posing for a cameraman, who sold the photos for a few yuan each. The pagodas had been the most important place of worship in the old Dali kingdom. They had been designed in a similar style to their contemporary, the Giant Wild Goose pagoda, built by the Tang emperors, and the Chongsheng monastery next door was once a leading centre of Tantric knowledge.

But now the gates were crowded with costumed people, hoping not for enlightenment but only for a photo with the iconic pagodas in the background. It was a hot late-summer day and many of the families were in shorts, the men and boys in baseball caps. There was a long approach to the pagodas themselves, undulating grassy lawns on each side, a couple of cold drink and ice-cream vendors, and like everywhere in Dali, the constant buzz of happy, holidaying people, the smell of cut fresh grass and the sound of lawnmowers in the distance.

Beyond the Three Pagodas was a newly restored temple with a gargantuan golden statue of Avalokitesvara, the bodhisattva of compassion. Even here there were little souvenir shops. But compared to the big crowds outside, there were only a few people, families wandering in and out, some offering incense, more it seemed as an amusement than anything else.

There were other choices for the tourist. But I skipped the two main ones. One was Nanzhao-style Island and the other was the Dali Deva Naga Film Studio. Both were big money earners, packaging what was different about Yunnan within the framework of China as one harmonious family.

The creation of amusement parks to represent ethnic traditions is now fairly widespread in China. The most famous such place is the Nationalities Park in Beijing, a combination of museum and fairground, where Han Chinese dress up in minority outfits. 'Nationalities Park' was originally translated into English as 'Racist Park', before it was quickly changed. Other similar ventures proliferated and Nanzhao-style Island was established in the mid-1990s, around the same time as the China Folk Culture Villages in Shenzhen (near Hong Kong).

The more recent parks are more interactive. In Burma, Laos and Thailand, people celebrate the new year (in April according to local calendars) by splashing water on one another as part of a several-days-long festival. The Dai people in southern Yunnan have the same tradition, and for years Chinese tourists have gone to the Dai area in growing numbers to see this curious spectacle. But one astute businessman decided what works for a few days a year could work year around, and so created a sort of human reserve, where every day is Dai New Year's Day. For a fee, tourists can stay in one of four villages (with staff dressed up as Dai), and witness a never-ending new year's celebration, including constant water splashing and all-round revelry.

Some parks no longer even have an ethnic dimension. While in Dali, I read in a local tourist guide about the Dwarf Empire, located twenty-five miles from Kunming. Part of the Ecological Garden of Butterfly, the Dwarf Empire is a theme park where about eighty or so dwarfs ranging from little over two feet to four feet three inches tall parade around in different costumes (not necessarily ethnic ones) and entertain visitors by singing, playing unusual musical instruments, break-dancing to techno music, and performing various tricks. Closer to Dali, a huge Disneyland-style amusement is planned for the near future. All will be part of Yunnan's scheme to be the leisure capital of China's massively growing tourist market.

*

Seven hundred years before the present wave of tourists was an altogether different wave, of Mongols, Turks and Islam. The Mongol conquest of Yunnan in the thirteenth century brought this hitherto independent kingdom for the first time under Beijing's control and began a process of integration into 'China proper' that has continued to today. The Mongol conquest also brought an astonishingly diverse influx of mainly Muslim peoples, from across their Eurasian domains.

Though the invasion forces were ultimately under Mongol command, many of the officers and most of the soldiers were Turks or people from further west. The force that invaded Burma for example is said to have included no fewer than 14,000 men of the erstwhile Persian Khwarezmid empire, under their own commander Yalu Beg. Others came to garrison the new possession. They included Turks from Samarkand, Bokhara, Merv and Nishpur. They also included tribal peoples like the Kipchaks and even Bulgars from the lower Volga. Yunnan itself had been conquered by the Mongol Prince Uriyangkadai who had also conquered Baghdad, and his forces most likely included captive soldiers from the Abbasid caliphate as well as southern Russia and the Ukraine.

There were even more exotic immigrants. They included the Alans – a Sarmatian tribe today known as the Ossetians – who had submitted to the Mongols and had provided a thousand warriors for the personal bodyguard of the Great Khan. A son of the Alan chief, Nicholas, took part in the conquest of Yunnan, and men from the North Caucasus were posted along the Burmese borderland.

A member of the Mongol imperial clan, Prince Hugeshi, was appointed 'prince of Yunnan' whilst the old ruling family, the Duans, were allowed to stay in Dali and keep the title of 'maharaja'. The Muslim newcomers, based at Dali, became extremely powerful and the most powerful of them all was a native of Bokhara named Sayyid Ajall Shams al-Din Omar. He claimed descent from the emir of Bokhara (though some say his family were originally from Cairo) and by the late 1250s he was a rising star in the Mongol establishment. He served in Baghdad and in China and was appointed as the top administrator in Yunnan in the 1270s. Today the Muslims of Yunnan regard him as the founder of their community, a wise and benevolent ruler who 'pacified and comforted' the peoples of Yunnan.

Sayyid Ajall was officially the Director of Political Affairs of the Regional Secretariat of Yunnan, about as bureaucratic a title as one can imagine in medieval times. According to Chinese records, he introduced new agricultural technologies, constructed irrigation systems, and tried to raise living standards. Though a Muslim, he built or rebuilt Confucian temples and created a Confucian education system. His contemporary, He Hongzuo, the Regional Superintendent of Confucian Studies, wrote that through his efforts 'the orang-utans and butcherbirds became unicorns and phoenixes and their felts and furs were exchanged for gowns and caps'. There were many other civilizing missions on China's periphery but only in Yunnan was one conducted under Muslim (and essentially Turkish Muslim) leadership.

In this way, Yunnan became known to the Islamic world. When Sayyid Ajall died in 1279 he was succeeded by his son Nasir al-Din who governed for five years and led the invasion of Burma. His younger brother became the Transport Commissioner and the entire family entrenched their influence. There were still very few Han Chinese in Yunnan and the growing Muslim community began to excel as long-distance traders as well. In the early fourteenth century, the great Persian Jewish historian Rashid al-Din Hamadani stated that the Dali region had become exclusively Muslim.

This was at a time not only of Islamic expansion but specifically Turkish Islamic expansion worldwide. The Ottomans would capture Constantinople only a hundred years later, but already their distant cousins were sweeping across Central Asia and across the north Indian plains. At a time when Sayyid Ajall and his men were at the pinnacle of their influence in Yunnan, from the other end of the Himalayas Turkish cavalrymen were careering down the Ganges valley, to the very edge of Bengal, just a few hundred miles away. Only Burma separated these two Turkish-speaking worlds.

Burma was then a no-go zone, for all but the most intrepid merchants and adventurers. Some Muslims from Yunnan did travel via Burma to reach the Indian Ocean, mainly pilgrims on their way to Mecca. Marco Polo, who was in Yunnan in the 1280s, never made it further than Dali. He had come to China across the desert wastes of Central Asia. When he returned he went by sea, from southeast China to Java to the Persian Gulf. Even Marco Polo chose not to travel overland across Burma, so forbidding was the landscape between Yunnan and India. This was a fact of geography that would remain for centuries, one that is only changing now.

The faces on the streets of Dali were the faces of southern Chinese, the kind long familiar in southeast Asia and more recently in cities around the world, from Vancouver to Melbourne. But here and there were very different faces, faces of the Tibetan borderlands and Upper Burma. They were much darker-skinned and with bonier features and scruffy hair. They wore baggy ill-cut clothes, in faded dark colours. They were not tourists. Instead they looked like time-travellers. They were the people I had seen everywhere in Dali twenty years ago, but now looked lost in the sea of camera-slinging, T-shirt and trainers-wearing people.

There were a few other remnants of old Dali. One afternoon, I turned off one of the main pedestrian avenues into a side lane and then an old courtyard, shaded by the branches of big trees. Here were old grey- and white-haired men and women, playing mah-jong and drinking tea, most in washed out navy-blue Mao suits and black cloth shoes. Some sat in beach chairs, enjoying long drags on cigarettes or reading little paperback books. On the far side of the courtyard was a community centre, there since before the tourist rush and still shielded from it, with a billiards room, unused, and a reading room, with a few books and an ancient computer and a framed portrait of Albert Einstein.

Further along, inside a narrower alley, was a simple run-down guest-house that could have been the one I stayed in seventeen years before. Then it was winter and I had been offered a choice of People's Guest House Number 1 or Number 2. Back then, everyone was in Mao suits or second-hand army clothes. It was in Dali that I bought a Chinese PLA overcoat and hat for my further adventures, pleased to be fitting in. The nearby mountains were then covered in snow, like a little town in the Rockies, wonderfully peaceful and secluded.

My nostalgia trip didn't last long. I turned another corner and was back amongst another mighty throng of pedestrians, hundreds of them shouting cheerfully at each other, yelling into their mobile phones, eating ice cream, smoking, holding hands, and every few steps pausing for a picture. I slipped into a café, with posters of Che Guevara and Bob Marley on the wall, and ordered an outrageously expensive cup of coffee. Dali was rich; its past was forgotten.

When a new Chinese dynasty, the Ming, overthrew the Mongols in 1368, the Mongols retreated north to their grassy homeland, but also tried for a while to keep their hold over Dali and the rest of Yunnan. The new Ming rulers, however, would have none of it and sent envoys to Yunnan to demand that these renegade Mongols surrender, dispatching five embassies altogether between 1369 and 1375. The Mongols refused, even killing some of the envoys, until an enormous expedition of over 300,000 men was sent to annex Yunnan by force.

The Mongols were soon defeated. The once ruling Duan family, who had maintained a sort of ceremonial position during Mongol rule, now requested autonomy, but this too was turned down by the Ming generals. The head of the Duan family and his two sons were captured and taken to the Chinese city of Nanjing. One son was sent to a frontier station along the Great Wall; the other was assigned as an official at a port city along the Yangtze. This was the end of the royal lineage that had ruled Nanzhao in the tenth century and had maintained Dali as a beacon of Buddhism for nearly 400 years.

In their place, the Ming emperor Zhu Yuanzhang appointed Mu Ying as the 'duke of Yunnan'. Mu Ying was a distinguished general and had helped lead the campaign against the remnant Mongol forces. He was also Zhu Yuanzhang's adopted son and before Zhu Yuanzhang's rise to power, the two men had been poor together. Mu Ying was now trusted to govern this distant but important frontier and placed above the normal military and civilian administrators. It was to be an hereditary position, and in the decades to come the Mu family would become enormously wealthy and powerful landowners throughout the province.

As in Mongol times, immigration followed conquest, but now, rather than Persians, Turks and Central Asians, an immense wave of Han Chinese arrived in Yunnan for the first time. They were a motley bunch. Nearly 300,000 were soldiers who had come with the Ming invasion, only to be left behind to garrison the southwest, together with their wives and children. Other immigrants included farmers in search of land, merchants, political exiles and criminals. This colonization under the Ming may have brought over a million settlers in total, which made it one of the largest and most sustained official migrations in Chinese history. Migration would only intensify under the Manchu dynasty that succeeded the Ming, as people poured in to take advantage of new economic opportunities, in particular in the mining industry and trade with Burma. They brought with them their northern speech, and today the main dialect spoken in Yunnan is a variant of Mandarin, as in Beijing. Many were brash and aggressive, appropriating land and mining rights. They were egged on by imperial agents, and between 1775 and 1850, Yunnan's population ballooned from approximately four million people to ten million. By then Yunnan was home to three very different communities: the new Han Chinese settlers, the descendants of earlier Muslim immigrants, and the different native peoples. In the late 1850s, there would be an explosion of inter-ethnic violence.

Conflict between the Han Chinese settlers and old communities in Yunnan, both Muslim and non-Muslim, had been brewing for years and government officials invariably sided with the Han Chinese. In 1839, seventeen Muslims were massacred by a government-organized militia and in 1845 Chinese secret societies carried out a three-day rampage that left scores of Muslims dead or wounded. The tipping point came in 1856 when the Chinese heartland was itself in the grip of a gargantuan civil war, with Manchu forces battling Taiping rebels across the country. In May of that year, local officials joined by Chinese townspeople undertook a systematic pogrom in Kunming, killing up to 7,000 Muslims, including women and children, destroying mosques and calling for the extermination of Muslims throughout Yunnan. It was the beginning of a genocidal operation that would forever change the make-up of the southwestern frontier.

The Muslims fought back. There were reprisals against the Han Chinese, and by September Muslim-led militias had captured Dali. Under their leader Du Wenxiu, they declared a new and independent kingdom and Du Wenxiu became 'Sultan Suleiman'. As imperial forces lost their grip on major towns and then struggled to maintain supply and communication lines with central China, there seemed at least a chance that a restored Yunnan state would survive. The rebellion was known as the 'Panthay Rebellion' after the Burmese word *Panthay* for the Muslims of Yunnan.

Du Wenxiu was then in his mid-thirties. He had been born to an elite Muslim family in the town of Baoshan close to the Burmese border. He had received a classical Chinese education and even studied for the imperial civil service. He now styled himself Generalissimo and Sultan of All the Faithful, establishing madrassa schools in areas under his control, encouraging Arabic teaching, and printing the first Koran in Chinese. He sent envoys to the Burmese king, Mindon, who sympathized with the Yunnanese rebels (whom he saw as the true 'natives' of Yunnan), but who in fear of China imposed trade sanctions against the Dali regime. He also sent representatives to Calcutta and his son 'Prince Hassan' to London, hoping in vain for British recognition and guns.

By the late 1860s, however, the prospects for lasting independence had dimmed. The Taiping had been crushed, and Manchu forces were able to concentrate on the recapture of Yunnan. One by one Muslim-held towns were overrun, and the people in them slaughtered, until by Christmas 1872 Manchu troops, supported by French gunners, were at the outskirts of Dali itself, surrounding the ancient city. Du Wenxiu decided to surrender himself in the hope that this would prevent a wholesale massacre. On 15 January 1878, dressed in his best robes, he was carried in his palanquin to the Chinese commander. Along the way he swallowed a fatal dose of opium. His wife and children poisoned themselves. Some accounts say he was dead by the time he reached the Chinese lines. Others say he was still alive and pleaded for the lives of his followers. He was decapitated, and his head was encased in honey and sent to the emperor.

No one knows how many were then killed. There was no mercy. The Chinese government says 10,000 were executed. Others say that 30,000 were killed out of Dali's total population of 50,000. Hundreds drowned trying to swim across Erhai Lake. Others fled into the hills to be chased down by Manchu cavalry. For decades afterwards, European travellers to Yunnan noticed the desolation of the countryside, the many ruined towns and depopulated cities. Thousands of Panthay Muslims found their way to Burma where they still form a sizeable community, especially in the Shan hills, in Maymyo and Mandalay. In Yunnan itself, the demographic tide had swung decisively in favour of the Han Chinese.

Du Wenxiu's house has been made into a museum. And when I went there on a sunny afternoon, kids dripping ice lollies on the floor, it looked like any prosperous Chinese house of the nineteenth century, with a courtyard and tiled roofs, and rusty weapons on display. In some of the rooms were maps and photographs, with captions describing the revolt. It was presented not as a Muslim rebellion but as a 'revolutionary peasant uprising'. Du himself was called a 'peasant general'.

There were few other signs of Dali's Islamic heritage. Opposite the side entrance to my hotel, along a small alleyway, there were a few halal restaurants with signs written in Arabic script, and in these restaurants there were men in skull-caps, and women in head-scarves, like the other time-travellers, seemingly in a parallel universe to the tourists just beyond their doorstep. The past has been neatly packaged in Dali and the amusement parks and renovated religious sites are key props in the attempt to create a more unified society. The new wave of tourists, perhaps like the settlers of earlier times, are helping refashion the old southwest into an integral part of the new and rising China.

It was hard not to regret the disappearance of the older cultures. But it was also difficult to blame the Chinese. Tourism was lifting up the local economy, creating jobs, and helping reduce poverty. And what was taking root in Yunnan was not anything particularly Chinese, but just an aspect of global consumer culture. Nearly everywhere in Asia this consumerism was on the rise, symbolized best by the colossal shopping malls that had now pushed out from their earliest beachheads in Singapore and Hong Kong to these more remote corners of the continent.

I thought of what was a few hundred miles away on the other side of the border, the impoverished Burma of insurgency, ceasefires, and counter-insurgency. There were the roads being built, the dams, the big mining projects. But I wondered whether it would be Chinese tourism and allied consumerism that in the end would reshape the landscape. Yunnan's tourists were actually still few, by Chinese standards. But within years they could grow into the tens of millions. How many of these would soon visit Burma as well? In the late nineteenth century, the first railway companies operating to California had been instrumental in promoting West Coast tourism. The China–Burma rail line is primarily meant to facilitate trade in goods. Perhaps mass tourism would follow too.

Analysts of Burma have long wondered how peace might finally come to Burma. Will it be a victory for the Burmese army? Or a victory for its ethnic insurgent foes? But what if neither happens, at least not for decades more, and instead a dozen new shopping malls, tourist attractions, amusement parks, and a flood of Chinese tourist dollars transforms all of northern Burma? Not a formal peace, but a changed way of life. This was something I had not considered before. Perhaps it was a new kind of frontier.

I was now close to Burma, and what remained between Dali and the frontier were a couple of mountain prefectures, home to peoples closely related to those on the other side. Peter Goulart, a Russian who lived in Yunnan in the 1940s, wrote that the area's 'secluded ravines and icy mountains' had for centuries been 'the cradle and deathbed of nations'. One of these nations was the ancient kingdom of the Naxi, centred on the town of Lijiang, and the inspiration for Shangri-La in James Hilton's 1933 novel *Lost Horizon*. I went there next.

Shangri-La

China is like a series of giant steps, ascending over a thousand miles from its eastern seaboard to the Tibetan uplands, the roof of the world, where elevations average over 12,000 feet. Geologically, Yunnan is part of the Yunnan–Guizhou plateau, the last big step before Tibet, a crush of mountain ranges and deep ravines. The Salween, the Mekong and the Yangtze Rivers all descend in torrents from the snow-peaked mountains in the west of Yunnan, the Salween heading straight south to empty at Moulmein, on the Bay of Bengal, the Mekong snaking its way through Thailand, Laos, Cambodia and Vietnam, and the Yangtze heading east, through the Chinese heartland, to Shanghai. A fourth great river, the Brahmaputra, starts in an eastward direction from Tibet, before making a U-turn in Yunnan, carving out the Assam valley, and then spilling into the Indian Ocean near Calcutta.

One might imagine that these great river links would have bound Yunnan closely with the wider world. But they have not, as they can only be navigated for short stretches. Narrow gorges and violent cataracts have meant that access to Yunnan has until very recent times been only by foot, or by mule train, and many of its remarkably diverse peoples and cultures, perched up in their own mountain communities and speaking languages known only to them, have had little regular contact with anyone else.

From Dali the old caravan route to Tibet headed north, through the mountain passes, freezing cold in winter. The town of Lijiang was an important stop along the way. I went by bus. The journey once took two or three days, and up until the 1950s caravans had to be guarded against bandit attacks. But now the way from Dali to Lijiang is safe and easy, part of the new and immense system of expressways that are knitting China together from one end to the other. The first Chinese expressway wasn't build until 1988 and until the middle 1990s only a few had been completed. Today, however, the network of expressways is 40,000 miles long, second only to the United States and catching up fast. The bus I took had comfortable reclining chairs and a movie was shown on a screen up front. The trip was over in less than three hours.

And when we reached the Lijiang plain it seemed like a little world unto itself, surrounded on every side by uninterrupted mountains. There were miles of russet-coloured fields and small sturdy houses, several with satellite dishes and motorcycles or scooters parked out front. Roses, primroses and other flowers grew wild alongside the roadside. We were 7,200 feet above sea level. There was a Himalayan feel to the climate, the air was cold and fresh and the mountains peaks, several miles away, were covered in snow.

Until the communist take-over in the 1940s, the dominant people of the Lijiang valley were the Naxi (sometimes spelled Nakhi), one of the fifty-six 'nationalities' officially recognized by the People's Republic of China. They are a very small nationality, with fewer than 300,000 people, tiny not only compared to the Han Chinese majority (with 1.2 billion plus) but even to other minority peoples in Yunnan. Their language, also called Naxi, is grouped by linguists as part of the Tibeto-Burman language family, and is thought to be closer to Burmese than Tibetan, a hint of an ancient and now entirely forgotten relationship.

The ancestors of today's Naxi likely arrived in the Lijiang area from somewhere further north, along the craggy edges of Tibet, and until very recent times the Naxi had enjoyed trading links with Lhasa and via Lhasa with India along what was known as the Horse and Tea Road. Farmers in the valley grew rice and vegetables, while people in the highlands grew maize and wheat and tended goats, horses and yak.

They were an entirely independent people until the thirteenth century, when a Mongol army under Kublai Khan cantered into the valley as part of a grand pincer move against China's Sung dynasty. At that time, the Mongol empire was in the ascendant, lording over a vast region from Korea to the oasis towns of the Silk Road to Persia and the Arab world. At the other end of the steppe, they had just defeated a combined army of the king of Hungary and the Teutonic Knights, crossed the Danube and reached the gates of Vienna. They had also subdued all of northern China, but the Sung still held the south of the country, from the Yangtze River to Vietnam. For forty years the Mongols and the Chinese were at war.

Then the Mongol leader Kublai Khan changed tactics. He reckoned that to conquer the Sung he first had to outflank them and seize the Sichuan basin, to the west of the Chinese heartland. And to outflank Chinese forces in Sichuan, he first had to command the mountain valleys to Sichuan's southwest. This included the Naxi kingdom. And so, in 1253, a huge Mongol-led force marched south through the icy passes, crossing the Dadu River north of Lijiang, and annexing the little chieftainships they encountered along the way. With each victory, selected Mongol officers were ordered to remain behind, taking local women as wives; up to the twentieth century there would be chiefly families descended from these marriages, the only patrilineal clans in an otherwise matrilineal society.

The Mongols then rode to where Lijiang is today. The ancestors of the Naxi, seeing which way the wind was blowing, offered their help, providing the invaders with goatskin rafts and guiding them to the Old Stone Bridge at Dayan, their principal settlement. The chief of the Mu clan, the Naxi ruler, submitted to Mongol authority and was allowed to keep his position. In thanks, the Mongols left half of the orchestra that was accompanying them, a gift of music to their newest vassals.

From the bus station a taxi had taken me to the edge of the 'old town'. Taxis and most other vehicles were not allowed in. To one side of me was a four-lane street with lots of traffic and modern shops, most of them selling car parts and construction equipment, and to the other was an unbroken row of small chocolate-coloured wooden buildings, all in a traditional Chinese style, with shutters and decorated roofs. A cobblestone road led though a big ceremonial gateway and then into a maze of more wooden buildings. Every few feet there were lampposts with hanging red lanterns and old gas lamps. It was easy to imagine Mongol horsemen suddenly appearing around the corner, fresh from battle with Teutonic Knights.

Old town Lijiang is a reconstruction. In February 1996 an earthquake measuring 7.0 on the Richter scale destroyed much of what was there, killing 200 people and injuring 14,000 others, many seriously. Nearly 300,000 people were forced out of their damaged homes. Hundreds of aftershocks followed. Landslides destroyed more homes in the mountains nearby. Lijiang had to be rebuilt and the flimsy concrete towers that had sprung up over the 1980s and early 1990s were replaced with sturdier lower-rise buildings and more traditional single-family dwellings. With help from the World Bank, the old town was restored, with new old-looking streets, bridges and canals. In 1999, Lijiang 'old town' was designated a UNESCO World Heritage Site. The boom in domestic tourism soon followed.

My hotel was in a quiet alley, but steps away there were legions of Chinese tourists, strolling up and down the high street. The old town had been rebuilt as a sort of movie set cum amusement park, like Dali, a place for Chinese visitors to walk around, eat, shop, and feel like they were in a strange and distant place. The high street was at least a mile long, lined with dozens of souvenir shops. At one end of the high street was the 'Old Stone Bridge', reconstructed, so the tourist pamphlets said, at the very place where the Mongols had tethered their ponies and pitched their tents. Right next to it was an enormous wooden watermill. There were other, smaller watermills elsewhere, as well as many canals, some substantial, with a footbridge to cross, others no bigger than a drain. The water was sparkling clean. Actually everything was spotless, including the several public toilets, and even the wood on the buildings looked like it had been recently varnished. In keeping with the exotic look, the salespeople, nearly all women, wore the Naxi costume, a sort of bright blue smock with black cloth shoes and a cap, like a coif in a Flemish painting. There were shops selling locally made paper, silver, leather goods, and the tea, yogurts and cheeses that were the specialities of Lijiang.

For the first couple of days in Lijiang, my walks were essentially confined to the 'old town'. The high street led to a central plaza, from which there were a couple of other big streets and lots of little alleyways. The tourists, almost all Asian from their appearance and (I would guess) overwhelmingly Chinese, stuck close to the main avenues. The side streets just a few feet away were practically empty.

The Naxi kingdom had been ruled by the same Mu clan since medieval times. The time of the Manchu or Qing dynasty in China – the seventeenth to nineteenth centuries – was the heyday of the regional tea trade and a time when the Naxi kingdom and its Mu rulers had prospered. They were a leading force along the Tibet and Yunnan borderlands and acted as a bridge between the Tibetan and Chinese worlds. The royal family were well versed in Chinese culture and the Confucian classics and wrote Chinese poetry and essays, and a family library housed their accumulated works. They were not Chinese or controlled by China, but their elites were drawn tightly into Beijing's cultural orbit.

The palace was now a museum. It too had been heavily damaged during the earthquake and had since been remade. It looked like a small version of the Forbidden City in Beijing: the courtyard, the wide whitewashed steps, the open throne room and multi-tiered roof looked the same. The main difference seemed to be the tiger skin that draped the throne, an odd touch on an otherwise Chinese scene. The tourist brochures referred to the palace as the 'Mu House' as, I suppose, a palace would underline the kingdom's once independent status. The Mu, from the Chinese perspective, were a local ruling clan, natives granted permission to govern by the distant imperial court.

The Naxi have a wonderful and unique writing system, centuries old. For the most part, they use simple pictograms, cartoonish, almost childlike in their representations of words. A cartoon-like picture of a friendly-looking tiger means 'tiger', for example, whilst a more abstract concept, like 'marriage' is shown by two stick-figures, one lying on top of another, inside a house. All along the high street were little shops selling images of the Naxi script – on scrolls, on prints for framing, on postcards and on T-shirts.

None of the salespeople, though, seemed particularly interested in tempting customers, and sat in their shops watching television or nibbling on a snack. I spoke to a few of them in my very basic Chinese and learned that none were actually Naxi. They were Chinese or Bai, from Dali or elsewhere in Yunnan. They were in Lijiang for work, to make money and said they wore Naxi costumes to please the tourists.

The only 'real' Naxi I saw that first day were in the central square. They were four old men, all with wispy grey hair, two in tortoiseshell glasses, sitting on benches that circled a tree, enjoying the afternoon sun, chatting, dressed in Mao suits and navy greatcoats, their canes resting by their sides. Occasionally, another old man would walk past and there were hearty greetings. They would have been teenagers or young men around the time of the communist revolution, and would have remembered the old Lijiang, and this central square at a time when there were no Chinese and no tourists, only the occasional Tibetan horse-trader or tea-merchant, fresh from braving the bandit-infested mountain passes and looking for an inn for the night.

Now the square was packed but the old men seemed unaffected by all the people swirling around. I crept over and sat down on one of the benches. One of the old men in halting Mandarin asked me where I was from. I said 'Mien Dien', meaning 'Burma' in Chinese. He smiled, and repeated 'Mien Dien', but Burma didn't seem to mean anything special to him. The Naxi and the Burmese doubtless shared a common ancestry, some of the ancestors of the Burmese having come from the same Tibetan marchlands as the people of Lijiang. From Lijiang the Burmese border was only a hundred miles away, but the intervening mountains were as great a barrier as the Sahara was in separating Tunis from Timbuktu. Even in legend the old connections were not remembered.

Just then a group of women of mixed ages, all in Naxi clothes, gathered in the middle of the square. A boom box was placed on the ground and soon the women were dancing (really just swaying back and forth) to what I assumed were Naxi folk tunes. The Chinese tourists were thrilled. Hundreds of cameras snapped away.

On the other side of the square, there were other treats in store. A tall, very dark-skinned, decidedly non-Chinese-looking man in a Tibetan-style fur hat and knee-high felt boots posed next to his horse. Next to him was another man, with a hawk. For a fee, tourists were allowed to mount the horse or hold the hawk and have their picture taken. 'We wanted to have a special place for our honeymoon and we chose Lijiang,' said a Chinese visitor. 'It's like paradise here, so different from home, and the people on horses are amazing.'

There was a wide choice of restaurants catering to tourists. A couple of times I went to the Blue Papaya Café, not far from the central square. The menu listed dishes by their health function and included special local dishes. Some were purported to 'invigorate the circulation of blood, bright eyes, relieves pain and internal heat'. There was a 'Lijiang Ham and Chicken with Gastrodia Elata Hot Pot'. Hot pots seemed to be a local standard and the menu explained that 'Gastrodia elata grows in deep mountains by valleys and is an Orchidaceae perennial that grows off of mulberry trees.' There was a whole page devoted to 'Insects and Worm Dishes' including 'Bee Pupa and Fried Dragonfly'. 'Yak Meat with Lemon on Budock Fungis (a sort of aquatic mushroom)' was also available. For the less adventurous, 'Vegetarian Pizza' was also on offer.

Later, passing through a narrow alley, I saw a stunning young woman in a short lemon-coloured dress modelling for a photographer against a stone wall. Lijiang, I was told, was often used for fashion shoots and even by filmmakers wanting a background different from the modern office blocks elsewhere or needing to recreate historical scenes. A once non-Chinese city had come to represent all of China's past.

The old Naxi kingdom had emerged in a world that no longer exists. It was founded during the time of Byzantium and the Vikings in Europe, the Crusaders and the Baghdad caliphate. To its immediate east were their kinsmen in the kingdom of Dali, ruling over much of today's Yunnan. A few hundred miles to the south were the ancestors of the first Burmese, a new people who were just establishing a foothold along the Irrawaddy valley. And to the west was the great Tibetan empire that then stretched all the way to the desert cities of Central Asia.

To the north, in the area that is now Gansu province, near Mongolia, was another kingdom, a much bigger one, the kingdom of the Tanguts. The Tanguts spoke a language, like Naxi, that was also related both to Tibetan and to Burmese. A thousand years ago they dominated the overland trade between China proper and Central Asia, over the Silk Road, including trade in the war-horses that were essential to the Chinese as they sought to fend off Mongol attacks. Though heavily drawn to things Chinese, the Tanguts sought as well to maintain a separate identity. Their king in the early eleventh century decreed that all his countrymen had to adopt a new and severe hairstyle, something like a tonsure, to mark themselves as different from the Han Chinese next door. They knew they were coming under Chinese influence, but were keen to keep their independence. They were devout Buddhists and called their kingdom by the wonderfully outlandish name Phiow-bjij-lhjij-lhjij, which translates roughly as 'The Great State of the White and the Lofty'. Their end came with the Mongols. They had incurred the wrath of Genghis Khan, who then died at a siege of their capital. But the Mongols pressed on, overwhelming the Tanguts and decimating their kingdom so thoroughly, slaughtering untold hundreds of thousands of people, that next to nothing was known of them until Russian and British archaeologists discovered their lost cities, buried deep under the desert sands, in the early twentieth century.

Further back in time, the links between this world of Tibeto-Burman speaking peoples and the Chinese civilization to the east become more tenuous. Two thousand years ago much of what is today Yunnan was the home of a still little-understood Bronze-Age culture known as the Dian, based near modern-day Kunming, where their tombs were first found a hundred years ago. They were known at the time to the Han dynasty and were said by the contemporary Chinese official and court historian Sima Qian to have become willing allies of the Chinese in their campaigns against Vietnam. In the first century BC, during the Chinese search for a southwest passage to India, the Dian came under tremendous military pressure, finally allowing China to establish outposts very close to where the Burmese border is today.

Exactly who the Dian were, no one knows as they did not leave any written records. But in their tombs archaeologists have discovered other evidence of their civilization, including magnificent bronze drums, engraved images of war and human sacrifice. On some of these drums, their rivals to the east – the pig-tailed Kunming people – are shown being captured and beheaded by triumphant bun-haired Dians.

Going further back, the nature and fate of local civilizations become more mysterious still. In 1986, construction workers in the village of Sanxingdui, in western Sichuan, not far from Lijiang, accidentally came across burial pits containing thousands of bronze, jade and gold objects of high quality, some of enormous size, together with elephant tusks and stone implements. They include eerie masks with big eyes and long protruding noses. They were remarkable not only for their antiquity (they were dated to around 1200 BC) but also for their entirely unknown style. According to traditional textbooks, Chinese civilization at that time was confined to the Yellow River basin, a thousand miles northeast. But here in the southwest was another, wholly distinct civilization, seemingly unconnected. Until this discovery, Sichuan, like Yunnan, had been assumed to have been a cultural backwater, the realm of barbarous tribes, like Scandinavia at the time of the Greeks. Some speculate that the people of Sanxingdui were the ancestors of some of today's Tibeto-Burman-speaking peoples, though little is known for certain. Their civilization may have been a direct forerunner of the later Tibeto-Burman-speaking kingdoms, such as Yelang and Dian, which flourished in Guizhou and Yunnan 2,000 years ago. But no written records have been found. It is a lost civilization.

There are other mysteries. From Lijiang the pasturelands extend north to western Sichuan, the ancient site of the San-xingdui, and then to the desert world of what is today Xinjiang or Chinese Turkestan. The people of Xinjiang are now a mix of Uighurs, who speak a Turkish language, and recent Han Chinese immigrants. But until medieval times, the people of this area spoke Tocharian, an Indo-European language, much closer to Iranian and even English than Chinese. Here have been found the mummified remains of people whose physical features and clothes suggest an affinity with (for want of a better word) the 'Caucasian' peoples further west. Chinese officialdom are not keen to stress the racial heterogeneity of the region's past or encourage new theories that there may have been a significant number of Indo-European speakers on the very edges of ancient China, Indo-Europeans who may have brought with them chariot technology, something the Chinese would like to think they developed themselves.

Pliny the Elder records that an embassy from Taprobane (Ceylon) to Emperor Claudius described a place called 'Seres', somewhere in the direction of China, whose inhabitants 'exceeded the ordinary human height, had flaxen hair, and blue eyes, and made an uncouth sort of noise by way of talking'. Some speculate that this have been a reference to the ancient Caucasian populations of the Tarim Basin. No one knows. Many of today's Uighurs, though speaking Turkish, carry features that could be the result of an ancient admixture with these long-time inhabitants. Some even suggest that the genetic legacy of these people reaches further south, to Yunnan and the Burma borderlands.

In Tibet, too, there are echoes of prehistoric migrations, dating back millennia. For a long time scholars believed that the Tibetan plateau, so high and inaccessible, was one of the last places to be inhabited by humans. But very recent research is showing something radically different, that parts of Tibet, not far from Lijiang, were places of refuge during the dramatic climate changes of more than 10,000 years ago. Other research suggests that people today speaking Tibetan, Burmese and related languages like Naxi may be connected not only to their neighbours in Asia, but through the Bering Straits to the final wave of Siberians who journeyed to the New World.

Lost races and civilizations would give rise to medieval kingdoms, followed by Mongol domination and, only in modern times, the coming of the Han Chinese.

One evening, I decided to try a 'must-see' attraction in Lijiang: the Naxi Orchestra, an orchestra of old men, some Naxi, most well into their eighties. They were advertised as 'proud guardians of centuries-old ceremonial music that had once flourished throughout China' but now survived only in 'these isolated foot-hills of southern China'. I bought a ticket at the entrance and walked past a hall with photographs of the famous people who have heard them perform on tour, from Norway's King Harald to Chris Patten, the former governor of Hong Kong. The concert hall was large and less than half-full and when I arrived the old men were already gathering on stage. They wore plimsolls with their silk robes and several were wearing ski-jackets as well to protect them from the draught.

One of the musicians spoke in both Chinese and English (there was a scattering of non-Chinese-looking tourists), making jokes and introducing the various pieces. I know little about Chinese music, but the music the Naxi orchestra played did not seem particularly different from classical Chinese music I had heard elsewhere. He explained, however, that they were using special and antique instruments, and that they were part of a tradition that had arrived with the armies of Kublai Khan. They still played songs from medieval times, he said, and were the last in China to do so. During the Cultural Revolution, the performers had to bury their instruments to keep them from being destroyed. By the late 1980s they were performing publicly again, and now were a big draw.

Another attraction was the Dongba Museum on the outskirts of town. The Dongba are the priests and scholars of the Naxi people. The Naxi have their own peculiar tradition, perhaps related to the indigenous Bon religion of Tibet. The Dongba are keepers of traditional knowledge and perform a ritual function, leading important ceremonies. Their scriptures, some over a thousand years old, are written in their hieroglyphic script, and include hundreds of works of history, medicine, astronomy, literature and philosophy, very few of which have been translated into English.

During the Cultural Revolution the Dongba had been persecuted as 'cow devils and snake spirits'. Now they were propped up as a tourist attraction. There wasn't much to see at the museum, which seemed a sleepy place (I was there at lunchtime), with 'ritual instruments' stored behind glass cases. I saw a list of some of their epics and they included 'The Migration of the Herdsmen' and 'The War Between Black and White'. The museum area was said to be a sacred site of Naxi culture, but nothing very sacred seemed to be happening when I was there, only a few Chinese tourists paying Dongba priests in conical hats to write their names or even a funny saying in their hieroglyphic script.

Over the past ten years the number of tourists visiting Lijiang has increased from fewer than two million a year to nearly five million. It is hard to see how the town can avoid becoming anything other than an amusement park. Overall, the number of tourists arriving in Yunnan is estimated at well into the tens of millions a year (overwhelmingly domestic tourists), and new airports, railways and six-lane highways are springing up by the month. The tourist industry has become a fifth of the province's economy. Given the extreme poverty and violent repression of not so long ago, perhaps people don't mind putting on a show or having their culture made into a lure for money. It was hard to say. One of the Dongba priests who spoke some English smiled when I asked him this. 'Without the tourists I'll have no income,' he said, 'but I hate writing for them, I feel it's an insult to our traditions.'

It wasn't until my second day in Lijiang that I fully emerged from the old town and into 'the new city'. My first night I had made it as far as the Stone Bridge and the giant watermill. I knew then that I was at the edge of the old town and that a more normal city was just ahead: I could see cars and the lights of a Kentucky Fried Chicken in the distance. But I was discouraged by the swarm of people in front of me taking pictures of the watermill and turned around.

On this second day, though, I took a side route out into the ordinary world (I thought of Jim Carrey in *The Truman Show*), and was soon braving traffic, not a single costumed person in sight. The weather was perfect, cool and sunny, and snow swirled around the 17,000-foot Jade Dragon Snow Mountain ahead of me. The new city looked as prosperous as any town in Europe or North America. On the pavement, men and women were selling baked potatoes everywhere and sticks with grilled meat. Some of the sellers were Muslim Uighurs in skullcaps and leather jackets. Everyone seemed to know one another. There was an easy informality. Groups were chatting away, people greeting one another. The faces were different than in the old town, darker and longer and more Tibetan. Many of the people could easily have been Burmese. In a huge car park, Naxi or Tibetan men and women were loading giant lorries with wicker baskets full of vegetables. A shop nearby sold jeans, another sold kitchen appliances. Loud techno music boomed out from a third shop, selling CDs.

The Naxi kingdom was essentially unknown in the West until the early twentieth century, when two men, the American botanist Joseph Rock and the White Russian doctor Peter Goullart, lived and travelled around the area. Rock was the son of an Austrian manservant and from an early age took to a life at sea. He journeyed around the world before winding up in Hawaii, where, without any training, he established himself as the local botanical authority. He wrote three books on local flora and then in the 1920s went to Burma in search of a plant to cure leprosy.

It was during his travels in the Burma–Yunnan borderlands that he 'discovered' Lijiang and from Lijiang ventured on to the even more remote and smaller kingdoms of Muli, Choni and Yungning, studying plants and sending off thousands of specimens to European gardens. In 1933, he told a *New York Times* reporter that the Naxi were 'one of the extraordinary races or tribes surviving in the world today'. An article he wrote around that time in *National Geographic* would inspire the American novelist James Hilton to invent 'Shangri-la' for his novel *Lost Horizon*. Rock's subsequent book *The Ancient Na-Khi Kingdom of South-West China* was perhaps one of the most eccentric ever published by Harvard University Press, with strange digressions and pages of genealogies. Ezra Pound was a fan and drew on Rock's writings for his Cantos.

A couple of Westerners, despite warnings, ventured ever further, towards the Liangshan Mountains that formed the border between Yunnan and Sichuan, then notorious for its brigands and hostile Yi tribal peoples. They were Teddy and

Kermit Roosevelt, sons of the former president, who came on a hunting expedition in 1928. They were amongst the first Westerners ever to see a panda. They also become the first to kill one, an old male who didn't know that he should fear the Americans and 'that didn't even make a sound when it was shot'. The panda was later stuffed and sent to the Field Museum of Natural History in Chicago.

Part of this countryside north of Lijiang is also home to the closely related but more rustic Mosuo people. The Chinese have long been fascinated by the idea of female warriors and tales of gender equality in these distant southwestern lands, and even more fascinated by accounts of local sexual promiscuity. The Mosuo have a special reputation for sexual promiscuity and this too is now being used to attract the tourist yuan.

Mosuo society is matrilineal and women have traditionally enjoyed a strong, perhaps even dominant place. The Mosuo live with their extended families, with many generations cohabiting in a single house and often in a single large room. Older girls and young women, however, may have their own private 'bedrooms' and if a woman is interested in a man, she may invite him to come and sleep with her – it's a private affair, conducted after dark.

The woman is free to change lovers whenever and as often as she likes, but in general relationships are monogamous and long-lasting; each partner stays with his or her own family and there is no economic side to the relationship, no claim on each other's money or property. It's known as *zouhun* or a 'walking marriage'. If a child is born, the father, if he is known, will normally have little or no responsibility for the child's upbringing. The child belongs to the mother's family and she and her relatives, including her brothers and other male relatives, bring up the boy or girl.

During the Cultural Revolution, the Mosuo were pressured to give up their 'walking marriages' and marry 'normally' instead. Many did, but they have since returned to their traditional ways.

Though the Han Chinese are strictly patrilineal themselves, accounts of these Mosuo ways are to them probably not very surprising, as they fit in well with traditional descriptions of the southwest barbarian. In the early fourteenth century, Li Jing, who was then an imperial official, Deputy Pacification Commissioner and Bearer of the Tiger Tablet, wrote down some first-hand observations. He remarked that in an area south of Lijiang, the women 'plucked their eyebrows and eyelashes and wove their hair into two coils' and that they, rather than the local men, did most of the work. Virginity was not prized, he said, and the local women were free to have sex with men as they wished. Virginity was even a disadvantage for a woman looking for marriage. They were 'as profligate as dogs and swine' and if a woman died before marriage, all the men who had had sexual relations with her held up a banner at her funeral. If the banners numbered a hundred or more, the woman was considered especially beautiful. Her parents would lament: 'How could we have known that our daughter who is loved by so many men would have died so young?'

A hundred years earlier, Marco Polo had written about sexual relations in the kingdom of Caindu, also in Yunnan:

I must tell you of a custom they have in this country regarding their women. No man considers himself wronged if a foreigner, or any other man, dishonours his wife, or daughter, or sister, or any woman of his family, but on the contrary he deems such intercourses a piece of good fortune.

Today, Yunnan tourism officials are happy to exploit this reputation of promiscuity. The posters on the shores of Lugu Lake, the heart of the Mosuo region, proclaim in English: 'The Kingdom of Women'. In Chinese, too, the billboards had once read 'Nu Guo' or 'The Women's Kingdom' but perhaps this was seen as not tempting enough and so officials changed the name to 'Nuer Guo' or 'The Girls' Kingdom'.

One evening at the Rembrandt Café in Lijiang I met a few Chinese men, young men visiting as tourists, who told me about the draw of Lugo Lake, the promise of exotic women and free sex. 'They have walking marriages there,' said one. 'I'm really hoping to have a walking marriage.' Some were less optimistic but all believed that the minority women in Yunnan were different from Chinese women. 'We will go and have a look tomorrow. Maybe we will be lucky in the kingdom of the girls.'

More than a year before I was in Yunnan, widespread protests had broken out in Tibet against Beijing's rule. They began on 10 March 2008, with hundreds of Buddhist monks in Lhasa calling for the release of other monks who were already in detention; they grew quickly and then turned violent, with Tibetans attacking Han Chinese property and people. To the astonishment of the authorities, the protests spread beyond Lhasa and what the Chinese government has demarcated as the Tibetan Autonomous Region, into the much wider Tibetan-speaking area. There was bloody unrest in parts of Gansu province, near Mongolia, and along the old Silk Road, as well as further south in Sichuan, very close to Yunnan, where Tibetan monks clashed with police. The outcome of these skirmishes was never in doubt and a wave of arrests and incarceration soon followed.

Tibet has had a complex relationship with successive Beijing-based dynasties over the centuries. Until medieval times, Tibet was either a single independent empire in its own right, or a medley of smaller but still independent states. During the period of Mongol domination over nearly all Eurasia, Tibet came under indirect Mongol rule, accepting Mongol suzerainty, but was never directly administered by the Mongols as was, say, China or Russia. It was an intimate relationship nonetheless, with many in the Mongol leadership eventually converting to Tibetan Buddhism. Today Mongolians who profess any religion are nearly all Buddhists of the Tibetan school.

It was only in modern times, under the Manchu or Qing dynasty, that Beijing began to exert real sovereignty over the Tibetans, partly out of a desire to keep the British, then just over the

Himalayas in India, at bay. The Manchus were Tibetan Buddhists as well and held Tibetan culture in the highest regard. Then, in the early twentieth century, with China in chaos, Tibetan areas in the east came under the control of different, often non-Tibetan, warlords, while on the Tibetan plateau itself a Lhasa-based regime declared itself independent of any outside power.

This period of modern independence did not last long. In October 1950, only a year after the communist take-over of China, soldiers of the People's Liberation Army marched into Tibet, quickly overwhelming the small Tibetan army. The Chinese then tried to win over the Tibetans, treating locals well, improving infrastructure and distributing money and goods, maintaining the Dalai Lama in his position and even welcoming him to Beijing. This was very much in line with Chinese policy in Yunnan and other non-Han regions at the time. In 1951, Tibetan and Chinese representatives signed a seventeen-point agreement that allowed the Chinese to enter Lhasa peacefully whilst respecting local autonomy.

The agreement was valid only for the area viewed as Tibet proper. In the eastern Tibetan areas like Kham and Amdo no such autonomy was even discussed, and early attempts at integration were met by stubborn local resistance. Brutal reprisals followed. Tibetan fighters in Kham soon solicited and received covert help from the CIA, which was then arming remnant Chinese Nationalist forces along the Burma–China border, and was looking for any opportunity to destabilize America's new Cold War foe. In 1959, the unrest finally spread to Lhasa, leading to open revolt, and the deaths of thousands, perhaps tens of thousands, of people. The Dalai Lama himself escaped to India where he has lived in exile ever since.

The past fifty years have been the first time in history that Beijing has administered Tibet directly. From a Han Chinese and communist perspective, direct rule has brought many advantages, with new roads and schools and hospitals and all the other benefits of modernity. The grip of parasitical landowners has been removed and other 'feudal elements' smashed, and a theocracy has been turned into a 'people's democracy' with greater equality and an opportunity for Tibetans to participate as citizens of the world's emerging superpower.

Many Tibetans, however, see the story very differently. The flight of the Dalai Lama was followed by the Cultural Revolution of the 1960s, in which Tibetan Buddhist monasteries, some with priceless collections of art and manuscripts, were destroyed, monks were defrocked, and Tibetan culture in general 'struggled against' as worse than useless. No one knows precisely how many people were killed. And even though recent economic development has brought higher living standards to many, it is seen as the progress of an alien power, one whose values and worldview are entirely different from those of the still ardently Buddhist Tibetan people.

July 2009 saw another round of ethnic protests in China, this time by the Uighur people in the far western territory of Xinjiang. The Uighurs are a Turkish-speaking people who migrated to what is now Xinjiang in early medieval times. Today, the Uighurs remain distinct from the Han Chinese not only in language and religion, but also in racial appearance; many could easily be mistaken for their distant Turkish cousins in Anatolia and by blood are likely linked to the ancient Indo-European peoples who inhabited the region before them. They were once devout Buddhists, and at one time their khanate stretched from the Caspian Sea to Manchuria; they were major participants in the great networks of Buddhist art and scholarship that then existed along the old Silk Road. Some later become Manicheans, before the vast majority converted in late medieval times to Islam. A proud tradition of Muslim scholarship followed. Like the Tibetans, the Uighurs eventually fell under the thumb of the Manchus in Beijing.

And also like the Tibetans, when the Manchu dynasty was overthrown and China plunged into anarchy, the Uighurs attempted to reassert their independence, their leaders in 1933 even proclaiming an 'East Turkistan Republic' based in their western-most town of Kashgar. But this was short-lived. Just as the Soviet Union saw itself as the rightful heir of the Tsarist Empire, the People's Republic of China was determined to exert its control over all parts of the former Manchu Empire's far-flung domains. The Uighur region is rich in oil and gas and other mineral wealth and Han Chinese migrants by the million have been encouraged to move to Xinjiang ('The New Frontier'). What had been an ethnic Chinese presence of around 7 per cent in 1949 is 40 per cent today. The Uighurs will soon be a minority in their ancient homeland.

The latest round of violence actually started in southeastern China, near Hong Kong, where fights had broken out earlier in 2009 between Uighurs at a toy factory and their Chinese co-workers. News of the fighting then spread back home, where ethnic tensions had long been simmering, setting off days of first peaceful protests and then rioting in the local capital Urumqi (which is about half Uighur, half Chinese). Chinese civilians and property were violently attacked. Nearly 200 people died and well over a thousand were injured in the fighting and crackdown that followed. It was another jolt to the system, as there could be no greater nightmare for Beijing's party bosses than a China that goes the way of the Soviet Union, splintering along ethnic lines.

Will Yunnan suffer the kind of ethnic violence recently seen in Tibet and Xinjiang? It seems unlikely.

In Yunnan the minority nationalities are much more jumbled together. In Tibet, nearly the entire population are either Tibetan or recent Chinese immigrants. In Xinjiang, nearly all are either Uighurs or Han Chinese. In Yunnan there are dozens of different minority nationalities interspersed across the province. There might be Yi, Bai, Hani and other villages all within a few miles of one another. In addition, their identities are sometimes blurred, and some of the groups – like the Yi – are actually composed of many sub-groups, including sub-groups that might not see themselves as Yi at all. Many who are classified as non-Han, like the Zhuang for example, are also much more assimilated into mainstream Chinese culture than the Tibetans and Uighurs, the ethnic frontier in Yunnan being centuries older than the frontier further west, towards Lhasa and Kashgar. Muslims, who led the last great revolts during the nineteenth century, are today far fewer in number and there has been no known resistance to Beijing's rule in this area for at least a quarter of a century.

Beijing is keenly focused on keeping Yunnan's minorities happy. Billions of yuan have been spent on new infrastructure, incomes are rising and poverty rates falling. Minority cultures are no longer under attack and there is far more cultural freedom than in the recent past. Local officials are drawn from the ranks of local communities. And, whereas in China proper a strict one-child-per-family policy has been rigorously enforced for decades, minority nationalities in Yunnan are free to have as many children as they like.

It was certainly hard to conceive of trouble in Lijiang, awash with tourists and new money, and next to impossible to imagine that the little Naxi kingdom would one day again be independent.

But history seldom moves in a straight line and stranger things have happened. Who would have thought as late as the 1980s that the small countries in the Caucasus like Georgia, Armenia and Azerbaijan would break away from Moscow, then face rebellions from even smaller nationalities within, prompting European and United Nations mediators and peacekeepers to intervene? Stability in China has been based first and foremost on the phenomenal economic growth of recent times, and no one can say for certain what might happen if that economic growth suddenly came to a halt.

Closer to the Burma border, very different realities are merging into one another – one war-torn, military-dominated, ethnically fractured and the other under the single control of the Chinese Communist Party, newly capitalist, and in the process of being reshaped by consumerism and tourism. Sometime after this trip, I spoke to a friend who was Shan and a long-time supporter of self-determination for ethnic minority peoples in Burma. I asked him how he thought Shan people in Burma felt, seeing the rapid improvements in living standards enjoyed by their cousins on the other side. 'They are increasingly attracted to what is happening in China, and say that in Yunnan there is at least development, perhaps a better model.' A better model? The pull of Chinese culture has always been strong and the pull of China was now supercharged.

But war and conflict have their own pull as well. And the situation in Burma was reaching new levels of complexity. In 2010, events along the border, close to the crossing at Ruili, would shock Beijing.

Between China and the Deep Blue Sea

From Lijiang I backtracked to Dali and then took a bus down the old Burma Road, now National Highway 65. For centuries this area had marked the very limits of Chinese imperial administration and it was easy to see why. We crossed one mountain range after another, some with peaks over 15,000 feet high, the valleys as far as 9,000 feet below, snaking around the mountain bases or going by tunnels that cut right through. Occasionally it was possible to see into the distance, the rest of the highway down below looking like a long and jagged wound, exposing the grey rock beneath the otherwise lush and forested hillsides. Other times, we were right in between the mountains and all we could see were walls of green on either side. Tiny makeshift houses made of stone or brick were occasionally perched on steep slopes. There were two drivers. One was a chubby middle-aged man who drove fast and eagerly overtook the vehicles, mainly heavily loaded lorries, that lumbered ahead. The other was a determined-looking young woman, expressionless, who drove more cautiously. When the man was driving, Chinese pop music blared from the loudspeakers up front. When the woman was driving, a movie played on the television screen overhead, the sound turned off.

About midway, we crossed two of the world's longest rivers, the Mekong and the Salween, within a couple of hours of each other. We then began our descent, 5,000 feet altogether, moving from an alpine to a subtropical landscape. There were innumerable fields of rice, some terraced along the hillsides, like enormous emerald-coloured stairs. The air became moist and along the roadside were clumps of banana trees and bamboo. The houses were no longer of stone but of wood and bamboo. Late at night, we arrived at the town of Ruili (population 140,000). Burma was a few miles away.

*

I had been to Ruili once before, in 1991, on my way to the Kachin Hills. The town had just been opened to foreign tourists and was my last stop before sneaking over the border into insurgent-held Burma. The single guest-house that allowed foreigners was spartan, each room like a cell with a cot-like bed and a small plastic-top table with a thermos of hot water.

Nothing I remember from that trip seemed still to exist. Ruili was then a poor and backward place, with a couple of streets of shops selling very little except Burmese jade and other contraband. The town was in the grip of an HIV epidemic, partly the result of prostitution, but more the result of widespread heroin addiction. Addicts were everywhere, stick-thin men and women in rags, filthy, lying on the pavement or propped up against a wall.

There were also many hair salons. The enforced uniformity of the Mao years was then still very recent, and though Shanghai and other big cities were becoming more fashion-conscious by the day, in Ruili the desire to catch up with their more trendy cousins to the east had not yet been matched by any home-grown talent, either for hair-cutting or for fixing the permanent waves that had become very popular. Across the border 'The Burmese Way to Socialism' had never been particularly constraining on women's hairstyles and a small corps of Burmese stylists had made their way to Ruili and were running profitable little businesses.

I have no recollection of where that guest-house or the Burmese hair salons were, but I doubt they still exist. Nothing looked the same. Twenty-first-century Ruili had overwhelmed its earlier incarnation and was now a town of wide palm-tree-lined boulevards and glass-fronted shops selling Armani clothes and Rolex watches. Futuristic-looking hotels, some more than twenty storeys high, overlooked the blue-green Shan hills to the south. At about $50 a night, mine was considered one of the best in town. Out front was a long black stretch limousine, the longest limousine I've seen anywhere in the world.

The receptionists were clearly not used to foreigners, as no one spoke English. But they were polite and friendly, gesturing and speaking slowly in Mandarin, and I had no problem checking in. On the wall behind them was a line of clocks set to London, Rangoon, Tokyo, Beijing and New York time. To one side was a vast lobby, with marble floors, and sets of black sofas and glass tables. Sitting at one set of sofas were men in short sleeves, smoking, drinking whisky, and speaking a language I didn't recognize but which I thought might be Jingpo (one of the main languages in the area, the same as Kachin in Burmese).

A bellhop in a red uniform showed me upstairs. My room was cold (literally) and impersonal, the way most people in Asia like their hotel rooms to be. After the bellhop left I studied the hotel brochure and saw that in addition to the basic singles and doubles (I had taken a single, called a 'Deluxe'), there were various classes of suites. The most expensive was called 'The Administrator's Suite'. The pictures showed a wood and leather swivel chair and a big wooden desk, at the back of which were bookcases with a few scattered books. The brand-new television showed only Chinese channels. Downstairs, there was not only a massage parlour, as in every Chinese hotel, but an entire massage floor.

Ruili is the biggest crossing between Burma and China. It sits along a muddy river of the same name that marks the frontier in this area. The entire Sino-Burmese frontier is long, about a third of the length of the US–Canadian border (excluding Alaska) or about two-thirds the US–Mexican border, and almost entirely mountainous, the Ruili plain being an exception. There are several legal crossings now, and many more illegal ones. No government really controls the border, and the Burmese and Chinese governments share authority with the various militias and ex-insurgent outfits on the Burmese side, as well as with their own sometimes unruly, almost always difficult to supervise, local soldiers and officials.

Though the Ruili River marks most of the border in this area, there is a slice of land on the other side that is still part of China, connected by a long bridge to Ruili proper. I learned that it was called Jiegao, or 'old town', though there didn't seem to be anything old about it. Instead, it was more or less a big outdoor mall, with a central square and several blocks of shops, restaurants and offices on every side. Many of the shops were Burmese, much more prosperous-looking than anything I had seen in Burma. Some sold jade or precious stones, but almost everything seemed available, from washing machines to photocopiers to children's toys. I was there on a weekday afternoon and the square was very crowded. Some people were in Burmese dress, in *longyis*, but I also heard Burmese spoken by many in Western clothes. Chinese tourists posed for photographs in the middle of the square, with the big sign saying 'Welcome to Myanmar' in the background. More than two-thirds of Yunnan's international trade passes through Ruili. It is where Yunnan makes money.

A group of Burmese transvestites, tall and glamorously dressed, in tight blouses, mini-skirts and high heels, were milling around. In Mongla there had been a well-known cabaret of Burmese 'lady boys' and I wondered if, after the recent casino crackdowns in Mongla, some of the transvestites had drifted north to Ruili looking for new work. Many billboards advertised KTV which I later found out stood for Karaoke TV. Taxis and handsome saloons and four-wheel drives competed for space with giant air-conditioned coaches in the main car park. Here and there I saw ragged-looking Burmese, in worn *longyis*, looking lost. For some it was their first time outside the country and China must have seemed like a vision of the future.

At first glance, Ruili seemed to be solidly part of the new, affluent China. Property prices here were said to be equal to those of Shanghai or Beijing. But the town was still fairly compact and after about an hour of walking I felt I had covered nearly the entire downtown area. There were smiling kids bicycling around in their school uniforms, navy and white with red scarves tied around their necks, and on the side streets old men and women were playing mah-jong. People seemed relaxed, drinking green tea and eating sunflower seeds. Under a warm tropical sun, Ruili appeared prosperous and sedate.

There were also many Burmese, less relaxed. Some were easy to spot, poor dishevelled Burmese who seemed uncomfortable and misplaced. That first day, I saw two men at a road junction, carrying their clothes in rubbish bags, looking at a little piece of paper, scratching their heads, and wondering which way to turn. There were Burmese ruffians, with sunburnt faces, looking wild and uncertain. One evening, under a bright street light, waiting to cross the street, I found myself next to a young couple, in Burmese village clothes, arguing loudly about what to do next, whether to return to the house they were at or find a new contact. Other Burmese seemed more well-to-do, strolling around, happily searching for a DVD player or a new set of golf clubs.

Some Burmese were hard to detect. Walking amongst what I thought was a Chinese crowd down a Ruili street, I was often astonished to discover, after overhearing their conversations, that the men in front and behind me were actually Burmese. It was as if they were in disguise, making themselves indistinguishable from the locals, wearing trousers and shoes and polo shirts. But then, I suppose, so was I.

Others from Burma were of an Indian or Pakistani or Bangladeshi appearance. In the early 1990s, harsh repression had driven hundreds of thousands of Rohingya people, Muslims in western Burma of primarily Bengali descent, into Bangladesh. A few hundred trekked in the opposite direction and wound up in Ruili where they have stayed ever since, even establishing their own mosque. Others were simply Burmese of south Asian ancestry, perhaps from Rangoon or Mandalay, who had come to make money, like everyone else. On my second afternoon, I was eating at a halal restaurant, and spoke to the man at the next table, who told me his family were Punjabis (from what is now Pakistan) but that he had been born in Mandalay. He had a narrow face and longish hair and was working through a big plate of kebabs. He told me that he was here for just a couple of days, to buy a motorcycle and visit some friends.

I was trained as a zoologist, can you believe it? But what am I supposed to do with a zoology degree? My family owns some businesses, small businesses, you know. We work with the Chinese, importing things, and we've managed to get by. I was the one who thought of trying to make connections here, inside China. This time, though, it's really just the motorcycle, then I go back.

I asked him what he thought of Ruili and China in general:

I guess it's more developed and all that. But it's boring too. I prefer Mandalay. I wish Mandalay were just a little better off. For me, it would be great if there were also a zoo as well. Or if my family could set up one of those safari parks I've read about, the ones where all the animals can wander around and we could charge for people to drive their car right through.

He finished his last kebab and motioned to the waiter for more tea. 'That's my dream.'

Ruili was once infamous for drugs and prostitution. Though opium had been grown nearby for decades, up until the 1990s, the opium had to be transported all the way down to the Thai border, to be made into heroin, and then shipped out to Western markets via Bangkok. From the early 1990s, however, Burmese militia groups just on the other side of the border started manufacturing heroin themselves, cutting out the Thai middlemen, and taking advantage of China's growing links with the rest of the world. Ruili became a key hub. The penalty for drug-running in China is death but this did not deter Burmese drug runners who could earn two years' wages over just a few days for carrying the contraband to Kunming. And with heroin and hookers came AIDS. Some time in the thirteenth century, Mongol horsemen had carried the Black Death from the Burma–Yunnan frontier (where it had been endemic for centuries) to cities in the interior of China, from which it spread, first across the steppe, and then to Europe, where it would kill tens of millions. And in the 1990s, it was this same region, and Ruili in particular, that became the source of the HIV/AIDS problem in China. The disease had entered from Burma, where infection rates were already climbing steadily. In 1989 local officials discovered that 150 heroin users here were HIV-positive. They were the first confirmed cases in China.

For a while, Ruili had a deservedly wild and dangerous image, but there was little sign of this when I was there, even at night. A couple of years earlier, a nationwide crackdown on casinos had led police to shut down a lot of the town's nightlife. And other crackdowns, on prostitution and drugs, together with the town's rising wealth from other licit and illicit trade – jade, timber – gave Ruili a more respectable veneer. The sale of jade alone, the 'imperial jade' found only in Burma and much sought after in Chinese markets, is worth well over a billion US dollars a year. Heroin production has gone down and addicts no longer openly shoot up in the middle of town. On the wall of one building was a huge poster advertising the Cutie Club and showing a bikini-clad woman with a snake wrapped around her. Next door, a big building that looked like it could have been a nightclub – perhaps the Cutie Club – was being torn down.

Ruili itself had become fairly well-off, but the countryside nearby was still far from prosperous. Though Yunnan's per capita income was now at least twice as high as Burma's, it was still one of the poorest provinces in all of China, and islands of development, like the centre of Ruili, were surrounded by impoverished rural areas. Walk less than an hour out of town and the fall-off in living standards is apparent, as the big houses and walled compounds, some with badminton courts and all with expensive-looking cars out front, quickly give way to hamlets, where water is in short supply and where the farmers seem little better off than in Burma.

The Chinese government began its 'Go West' strategy in 2000 and has since spent enormous amounts of money trying to develop infrastructure in these poorer interior regions. Yunnan's economy has benefited considerably, quadrupling in size from approximately $24 billion at the beginning of the decade to $91 billion in 2009. In Kunming ambitions are soaring. A few months after I was in Ruili, in July 2009, Yunnan's governor, Jin Guangrong, suggested the creation of a 'Eurasian Land Bridge', an ultra-modern train line that would run from the Pearl River Delta (near Hong Kong and Guangzhou), through Yunnan and Burma, all the way to Rotterdam. China had growing export markets in Africa, he explained, and this would cut no less than 6,000 kilometres off the current Guangdong to Cairo sea-route.

Perhaps one day soon freight trains bound for Holland will indeed run right past Ruili. For now, Ruili's interests and concerns are much more parochial. Here development means first and foremost the Burma market. Ruili is not so much an indication of general development in this frontier region, as an outpost of China's east coast prosperity, and a bridgehead towards Burma. Over the past two decades or so, relentless logging has denuded the once lush mountain scenery, and intensive irrigation and big hydropower projects have brought drought and environmental destruction. A growing popular reaction is forcing Chinese companies to look across the border, to Burma, for more forests to cut down, and more rivers to dam, and Ruili is becoming wealthier from this hunger for new resources.

However, reaching into Burma presents special challenges – drugs and disease, not only HIV/AIDS but also malaria, are rampant along parts of the frontier. There is also the huge Chinese migrant population in Burma. The Burmese tend to see them as Chinese colonists. For the Chinese authorities, however, they are also a worry. In this age of Chinese nationalism, any threat to their safety would have country-wide repercussions. A few Chinese were kidnapped by criminals in Burma in late 2009 and held for ransom; this made national headlines. Anti-Chinese riots would be a disaster for Beijing. In a normal situation, all these challenges would be managed together with the government on the other side of the border. But Burma is a special case. There is a Burmese government. But there are also all the many non-government armies, independent of any state's control.

The Ruili River valley has been seen for a long time as a natural border between Burma and China. It has been said to mark the limit of Burmese royal authority on the one side and the beginning of the Chinese empire on the other. But this was more a conceit in the minds of Burmese courtiers and Chinese mandarins than a reality for the people of the area themselves. Both sides of what is today the border were within the realm of the Shan peoples, here called the Dai, governed by their own hereditary chiefs, with no obvious cultural or linguistic frontier dividing them. Further to the southwest, towards Mandalay, the influence and power of the Burmese kings and Burmese court culture increased, whilst to the northeast, successive Beijing-based dynasties – Mongol, Chinese and Manchu – attempted to extend and consolidate their direct administration.

The Dai are today categorized as yet another official nationality of the People's Republic and over a million of them live in Yunnan, in this area as well as further south, closer to the Laos and Thai borders, where their dialect and customs are almost indistinguishable from those of their cousins next door. On the Chinese side, consolidating Beijing's hold over these messy borderlands was only half-finished when the communist revolution brought along a much more determined and often violent integrationist campaign.

Up to the 1950s there was still a Shan *sawbwa* governing the area, a man by the name of Fang Yu-chih, who would have been forgotten by history if it were not for his inspired appointment, in 1942, of C. Y. Lee as his private secretary. C. Y. Lee was born in 1917 in Hunan province and belonged to a family of distinguished scholars. He earned a bachelor's degree from China's Southwest University and emigrated in 1943 to the United States, earning a Masters in Fine Arts from Yale University, and then writing a bestselling novel, *The Flower Drum Song*, adapted in 1958 for a Rodgers and Hammerstein musical. In the period between his graduation from university in 1940 and his emigration to America, C. Y. Lee lived in Mangshih (the town adjoining Ruili) as private secretary to the local prince, *sawbwa* Fang.

On his arrival, the new Secretary Lee wrote:

To my pleasant surprise, Mangshih is not a poverty-stricken wilderness as I had pictured it: it is a small utopia of some two thousand square miles, endowed with rich valleys and rolling hills, its little villages surrounded by bamboo clusters. The rice fields extend for miles like soft green velvet carpets, dotted here and there by huge banyans and tall and slender papaya trees; beyond the hills, mountains rise into strips of haze in the deep blue semi-tropical sky. The red Buddhist temples peek from behind clusters of bamboos. Mangshih is like an art gallery full of oriental water colours.

The *sawbwa* was then forty-one and saw the Burmese and Chinese worlds closing in around him. He believed that the key to Mangshih's future was to modernize itself and make itself into a bridge between the two countries. With this thinking in mind he turned his little town into an appealing stopover on the new road from Mandalay to Kunming, with cafés and public bathhouses owned by Shanghai merchants. He also conducted his inspection tours in a new Buick, before returning home to meals of roast beef and fried chicken, all part of the 'modernization drive'.

The *sawbwa* decided as well that the time was right to take his first concubine (he was already married), and for this important mission he had Secretary Lee accompany him on a pleasure trip to Rangoon. They journeyed by car, down the Burma Road to Mandalay, and then by rail. High-class pimps in Rangoon were happy to see him. He was invited to parties and made the rounds at the clubs and racecourses. 'Being a *Sawbwa* has this advantage in Burma,' he told Secretary Lee. 'You attract a lot of women, like a piece of rotten meat attracting horseflies.' He met and settled on a beautiful wavy-haired Eurasian named Ida. She was the daughter of an Irish seaman and a Chinese dancing girl, but feeling that this wasn't quite the right pair of pedigrees for a future royal wife he turned her parents into an English colonel and a Mongolian princess. Ida played badminton and bridge and even spoke a little French which she had learned from the Hindu professional strongman who helped raise her. She wore khaki shorts and high heels and the *sawbwa* called her 'Ida darling', the only English he had learned as part of his modernization efforts.

This was a world that ended abruptly in 1953 when the Chinese communists, already four years in Beijing, marched in and then abolished the *sawbwa* system. Many local people as well as the entire court fled to Burma. Later, during the Cultural Revolution, all the palaces of the Shan or Dai rulers were torn down, scores of monasteries and pagodas demolished, monks defrocked and forced into hard labour. The Shan aristocrats who stayed were beaten up or killed. The old hereditary elites disappeared. But on the Burmese side, a new breed of local chiefs, warlords and middlemen emerged to take their place. And they are still there today.

Directly south of Ruili are the Wa Hills and the territory controlled by the United Wa State Army. In the 1970s and 1980s, Wa militia had been part of the forces controlled by the Burmese communist insurgents, backed by Beijing and fighting Rangoon. When the communist insurgency collapsed in 1989, the Wa militia regrouped to establish the UWSA, with Beijing's tacit support. The current Wa leaders speak Chinese fluently and enjoy a close relationship with Chinese officialdom. Several were born on the other side of the border, in the Wa autonomous prefecture in Yunnan. Their top military officers and business associates are ethnic Chinese. When they agreed to a ceasefire with the Burmese army in 1989, the Burmese promised development assistance and looked to Western governments and the United Nations for help. This never came and instead China has stepped into the breach, building roads and other infrastructure and encouraging trade and investment. Chinese rubber plantations have replaced some of the old opium fields. And the Chinese, aware that disease respects no international boundary, have facilitated trans-border health programmes. But big problems remain. The Wa are not only well armed but have started in recent years to produce arms as well, helped informally and perhaps illegally by ordnance factories in Yunnan. The degree of official complicity in Yunnan is not known, but there are allegations that arms manufactured by the Wa are making their way to India, to insurgent groups in India's far northeast. Han Chinese rule over Yunnan may now be well consolidated, but in expanding its reach into Burma, Beijing is having to deal with yet another, very similar but 'less cooked' array of barbarians, as well as a frontier mindset amongst its own, sometimes wayward local officials.

In the past, these marcher lords have been the cause of war. In the 1760s clashes between the Shan chiefs in this area, chiefs who owed nominal allegiance to both the king of Burma and the emperor of China, were quickly transformed into armed conflict between Burma and China itself. The trigger was the murder of a Chinese businessman, followed by Chinese demands for redress and Burmese support for a recalcitrant local ruler. Four massive Manchu Chinese armies would invade Burma over a four-year period, intent on imperial conquest. The Burmese emerged victorious in the end, but Sino-Burmese relations remained damaged for decades.

But frontier personalities have also been important bridge-builders and peacemakers. There is, for instance, the amazing case, only recently discovered, of a man named Wu Shangxian, nicknamed Ai-chiao-hu or 'The Short-Legged Tiger'. Wu was an ethnic Chinese, born into a poor family in the east of Yunnan. Sometime in the 1740s, he arrived in the Wa Hills in search of fortune, setting up a business at the one of the great silver mines in the area. He quickly became rich, and later became a trusted confidant of the governor of Yunnan, who appointed him a collector of taxes. This was a time when there wasn't much trade between the Burmese kingdom and China proper, and Wu and the Yunnan governor both reckoned that growth in trade would mean more money for them. As neither government seemed very interested in improving commercial ties, they decided to intervene, directly. Wu made his way to the Burmese court of Ava, pretending to be no less than an envoy from the emperor of China. The Burmese were flattered and pleased by this attention. When Wu went back to China, a Burmese embassy accompanied him, and together they went to Beijing where they were courteously received. In the end, not much came of the 'exchange' of embassies, but only because civil conflict in Burma made any proper follow-up impossible. Wu himself was eventually found out (by a new governor of Yunnan) and arrested.

What these incidents demonstrate is the role local people have long played in the evolution of the Burma–China frontier. Today, with a virtually open frontier, there has been more contact and commerce than at any time in recent history, and this has created new and dynamic networks far from any state control. They include local ethnic Chinese networks, running from overseas communities in Taiwan or Hong Kong to towns along the border. But they also include networks of other, non-Chinese, people, like the Shan or Dai, who sometimes act as middlemen and run businesses linking the Burma–China border not only with Mandalay and Kunming, but also the Thai cities of Chiangmai and Bangkok. Inside Yunnan, the Shan/Dai are heavily influenced by Chinese culture, profess Chinese ways, and speak in a Dai dialect long influenced by Chinese. Closer to the border, their orientation is more towards Burma and Burmese culture. Further south, it's the connections with Thailand that are strong. Families may have relatives in all three countries, perfectly positioned to exploit expanding markets.

Local peoples and local dynamics are shaping the emerging landscape, as much as any directive from Beijing. And it's a landscape that is being pulled onto the global stage.

In the fifteenth century a colossal fleet of ships, under the command of the imperial eunuch Zheng He, sailed several times around the Indian Ocean, reaching the east coast of Africa, and possibly beyond. The fleet included huge vessels over 400 feet long and 150 feet in beam, twice the size of the biggest Spanish and Portuguese ships at the time, as well as water tankers and transports carrying nearly 30,000 soldiers. It was a dramatic projection not so much of Chinese power but Chinese prestige, meant to shock and awe the peoples of the Indian Ocean into grateful submission. Zheng He, a Muslim native of the Yunnan–Burma borderlands, brought back presents from Asian and African kings, including a giraffe for the emperor's menagerie, as well as news of the Western world. But unlike the European expeditions of a century later, which would lead to lasting trade and conquest, the Chinese expeditions were a one-off, like the American missions to the moon. The Chinese security establishment of the time wanted attention instead to be focused towards the empire's inland frontiers, where they were facing irksome enemies like the Oirat Mongols and the Uighur kingdom of Turpan, and China never tried again to develop a blue-water navy.

Until now. Over the past twenty years, China's navy has been growing. China still doesn't have an aircraft carrier, the mark of a true global naval power, but it does have an expanding fleet of destroyers (bought from the Russians) and submarines, including nuclear ones, and China is said to be testing the world's first anti-ship ballistic missile, one capable of threatening America's Pacific Fleet. In late 2008, the Chinese decided to flex some of their new muscles and joined the international task force that was fighting pirates off the Somali coast, sending some of their best ships as well as commandos expert in martial arts. A year later, a retired Chinese admiral proposed the establishment of a permanent naval base in the western Indian Ocean. The fight against the pirates is meant as a sign of things to come.

In 1793, China's Qianlong Emperor told visiting British envoy Sir George Macartney that the Middle Kingdom desired little from the outside world. But the Middle Kingdom today desperately desires the raw materials needed to bring further power to its industrial revolution, in particular oil and gas. China has oil but consumes more than it produces. It was an exporter of oil until 1993 but since then its imports have risen dramatically. It now imports more than 170 million tons a year and at present trends (an admittedly speculative projection), China could be importing five times this amount within twenty years. The Chinese also need copper, iron ore and rare earth minerals and easy access to export markets as well.

All these raw materials will come from the Middle East and Africa as well as Australia and the countries of the Pacific Rim, increasing significantly the importance of Indian Ocean shipping lanes for Beijing. From Ruili to the sea is now only about a 24-hour drive, over the road that passes through Mandalay and then over the Arakan hills, to a brand-new port that Chinese engineers have begun to build on the island of Ramree. The oil and gas pipelines will travel along the same route, as well as the railway lines and expressways that will follow. Within a few years, China and Chinese influence may be much more present on the Bay of Bengal than at any time in history.

At first glance, there seems little reason to doubt that all this will happen. Western sanctions on Burma have entered their third decade and are still going strong, removing any possible American or European competition. The Burmese regularly affirm their appreciation of Chinese friendship, and the Chinese in turn continue to provide key diplomatic support. Unlike Western governments, Beijing could not care less about the nature of Burma's own political system. China has good relations with regimes throughout southeast Asia – democratic, communist, authoritarian, or somewhere in between – and is happy doing business with them all. What China does care about is stability in Burma. Chinese government officials say this often and it is not just a mantra. Perhaps more than any other government, Beijing realizes that after decades of civil war, the fighting in Burma has almost entirely stopped. They saw the Burmese moving ahead towards a new constitution and new elections and were more than satisfied. They also felt that their economic projects – though motivated by self-interest – were helping the Burmese too, and that massive infrastructure development will do more for Burma in the long term than the humanitarian efforts undertaken by some Western countries. But by 2009 a certain nervousness was also creeping into the picture.

Then came the Kokang incident. Kokang is a small ethnic Chinese enclave just inside Burma, a few dozen miles to the east of Ruili. Its people, like many people on the Yunnan side of the border, are descended from pioneers and freebooters who drifted in from other parts of China over the centuries. They speak Mandarin with a particular accent and long supplied muleteers for the caravans that once travelled through the area. In more recent times, Kokang also supplied many of Burma's better-known drug barons, and in the 1970s and 1980s militia from Kokang were part of the insurgent army of the Communist Party of Burma. When the Communist Party of Burma collapsed in 1989, the Kokang militia broke away, restyling itself the Myanmar National Democratic Alliance Army. It was the first to agree to a ceasefire with the Burmese junta and by 2009 this ceasefire had lasted a full twenty years.

For the leaders in Beijing, the fighting that erupted in August 2009 came like a bolt out of the blue. The Kokang militia had long been involved in illegal narcotics trafficking and gun-running and even gun production, and the charge of illegal weapons production was used as a pretence for the Burmese army to move forcefully into the enclave and establish a new leadership. There had been a growing split in the top ranks of the militia, and the Burmese saw an opportunity they did not want to miss.

It was not particularly bloody, and was over in days, but it was the largest military operation undertaken by the Burmese army along the border since the early 1990s. Some 20,000 refugees – all ethnic Chinese – fled into China, creating the largest refugee crisis on China's border since the end of the Vietnam War. Beijing was caught off guard and was intensely upset.

The Kokang incident has weighed heavily on Beijing's thinking ever since. Kokang and the other areas controlled by ethnic-based militias had been seen as useful buffers. Yunnan officials and businessmen had turned them into mini-Chinas, and used them as footholds for their influence inside the Burma frontier. The Chinese tried to wish away the incongruity between their support for the Burmese junta and their chummy relations with these militias. 'The Chinese like to feed both sides, be the big brother to everyone,' a man in Ruili told me. But there was no clear thinking about what the end-game might be; Beijing had been content to leave the Yunnan provincial government to set the direction, allowing local security forces to maintain day-to-day contact with all the armed groups.

But the willingness of the Burmese army to use force meant that the borderlands were much more volatile than Beijing had suspected. It meant that the Burmese were unpredictable. And it also meant that subcontracting Burma to Yunnan was no longer an option. Yunnan authorities had given little or no warning that Kokang was about to be overrun. With billions of dollars being invested in the pipeline and other projects, a more proactive approach was now required. Added to the mix was a gnawing sense that the clear run Beijing had enjoyed for twenty years could shift quickly.

This was at the time when the Burmese junta and the Americans were trying to improve ties, under President Obama's new policy of 'engagement', and though this had not gone very far very fast, the mere possibility of a Burmese rapprochement with Washington was making the Chinese extremely anxious. In the Chinese journal *Contemporary International Relations*, two academics at Yunnan University, Luo Shengrong and Wang Aiping, argued that the Kokang attack was a carefully timed message from the Burmese generals not to take them for granted. 'It was done to show the West that Myanmar's military government is adjusting its foreign policy, from just facing China to starting to have frequent contact with the United States, India and other large nations,' they wrote in a December 2009 article. The Burmese believed Sino-American relations were increasingly confrontational, and they wanted to demonstrate to Washington 'what a useful ally' Burma could be. The Kokang militia were known drug-traffickers and the Burmese were also calculating that the Americans still cared about reducing drug production in the region. There is actually little sign that Washington took notice. But not according to the Chinese academics, who seized on a meeting just weeks later between American diplomats and Burmese Prime Minister Thein Sein on the side of the United Nations General Assembly debate in New York. At a regional summit in Singapore in November, President Obama himself shook Prime Minister Thein Sein's hand, the first such gesture since the 1980s. The Chinese were suspicious. There is a well-known saying in China, *Yelang zi da*, meaning roughly 'Yelang thinks too highly of itself', that is used to refer to anyone arrogant or conceited. Yelang was an ancient kingdom on China's southwestern border, that had straddled the trade routes to India and the Indian Ocean, whose kings had seen themselves as equals of the Han emperor. This was laughable in Chinese eyes. Was Burma the Yelang of the early twenty-first century, daring to play off Beijing, New Delhi and Washington? China's leaders felt they now had too much at stake. In late 2009 and 2010 they began to move, fast.

And so, in those years, Beijing began to move its Burma policy into high gear. Close attention was focused on the situation between the Burmese army and their biggest battlefield rivals the United Wa State Army. The Wa were balking at Burmese demands to accept the new constitutional order and become a Border Guard Force and Beijing, fearing all-out war between the two sides, stepped in quietly to mediate and pressure both to maintain the existing ceasefire. A war between the Burmese and the Wa would be a first-class catastrophe for the Chinese. There could easily be a wave of tens, perhaps even hundreds of thousands of Chinese-speaking refugees flooding across into Yunnan, their pictures beamed into television sets in Beijing and

Shanghai. If the fighting carried on, who would China support? More importantly, would Washington take advantage of the situation, lending a helpful hand to the Burmese generals and in the process winning them over? Beijing would take no chances.

Soon, the Chinese were sending a wave of top leaders to cement ties with the junta and make sure that any tentative contacts with the Americans remained just that – tentative. Powerful Chinese Communist Party politburo member and likely future president Xi Jinping came in December 2009. Chinese premier Wen Jiabao followed in June 2010. There were other visits, too, by other politburo members, provincial governors and party secretaries. Dozens of economic agreements were signed and promises made of further cooperation.

Chinese support for the Burmese military regime is sometimes lumped together with its support for other countries inimical to the West, like Sudan or Zimbabwe, and its growing commercial presence there viewed as comparable to its quickly expanding relations with many other poorer countries, especially in Africa. These too were countries that were able to provide raw materials and where Chinese economic interests appeared to be trumping any other consideration.

Burma was something qualitatively different as it was alone in sitting right next to a newly invigorated Chinese hinterland. There has been an unprecedented migration of ethnic Chinese into Burma, one of the largest waves of Chinese emigration in history, with estimates now running in the millions. The border has become blurred. And between the two countries there is a long and convoluted history, not always friendly by any means. The Chinese are not in a position to tell the Burmese what to do and are keenly aware that Burmese nationalism has often had China in its sights. And any backlash in Burma or violence along the border would have serious consequences for Beijing. Burma sits on top of the Bay of Bengal and will soon be southwestern China's access to the sea as well as a conduit for its twenty-first-century energy needs. The stakes will only climb higher.

In late 2010, as the Burmese elections approached, and with the remaining ceasefires still holding, Burma, under the increasingly watchful eye of Beijing, appeared to be lurching firmly towards China. In August, Chinese warships made their first ever call at Rangoon. A week later Burmese supremo, General Than Shwe himself, travelled to China and was received with great honours. China's President Hu Jintao called for stability along the frontier and declared that maintaining good relations with Burma was 'the unswerving policy' of his country.

But there is another Asian giant, also waiting in the wings. Less than two months before travelling to Beijing, General Than Shwe made another rare foreign visit, to New Delhi, and was received there with equally open arms. The symbolism on both sides was clear: for the Burmese, the visit was a demonstration that it would seek to balance China with India. And for the Indians it was a signal that Burma was of increasing strategic significance, and that Delhi would not sit idly by and allow China to cement its economic hold over the country. A slew of economic agreements were signed here too and plans for new overland connections between Burma and India were finalized and set into motion. India's historic ties to Burma are even deeper than China's and indeed, for most of the late nineteenth and early twentieth centuries, India and Burma were both part of British India. Just after Than Shwe visited New Delhi, and before he travelled to Beijing, *The Economist* ran the cover story 'China and India: Contest of the Century', arguing that the relationship between the new powers was destined to shape world politics. India was another and critical piece of the emerging puzzle.

From afar, China's push across Burma seemed straightforward, but close up what is unfolding is incredibly complex, involving not only the two governments, but many other peoples, histories and relationships in between. And in India, too, as we will see, the region across the border from Burma is at least as complex, with its own once independent kingdoms, highland communities, conflicting nationalist narratives, and ongoing insurgencies. More than a thousand years ago, the emperor of China sought, in vain, to find a southwestern passage to India. But in just these few decades, once insurmountable geographical and political barriers are being overcome. A millennia-old frontier has reached the hills and valleys between Burma and Yunnan and is sliding over into a world of unfinished civil war and uncertain political futures. China and India are now also closer to one another than at any time before.

Part Three

THE EDGE OF HINDUSTAN

Looking East

Whilst visiting China in 1938, Pandit Jawaharlal Nehru told Chiang Kai-shek: 'More and more, I think of India and China pulling together in the future.' Nehru was at the time a leader of the Indian National Congress and would go on to become the country's first prime minister. He saw China as a friend and as a natural partner in leading post-colonial Asia. And even after the communist take-over of China, his vision of close Sino-Indian cooperation remained strong. Under Nehru's leadership, independent India remained formally neutral in the new Cold War and focused its attentions on building up the Non-Aligned Movement, the grouping largely of Asian and African countries that vowed to steer clear of American or Soviet military alliances. Nehru wanted both India and China to have major roles in this new 'developing world' and made it possible for Chinese premier Zhou Enlai to take part in its inaugural meeting, even though communist Beijing was clearly an ally of Moscow. Not long before, Nehru even turned down an American offer of a permanent seat on the UN Security Council (now much coveted by New Delhi) in protest against Washington's refusal to offer the same to the Chinese communist regime. Pandit Nehru had spent much of his life as a leader of India's non-violent campaign against British rule, alongside and as a student of Mahatma Gandhi. He saw India's foreign policy in an idealistic light.

China's leadership saw things differently. They had come to power in a blood-soaked civil war and would go on to fight the Americans to a standstill in Korea. They adopted an expansive view of China's geography and aggressively sought to resurrect the boundaries of the Manchu Empire. By 1951 they were on India's doorstep. That year, the Chinese People's Liberation Army invaded Tibet, and eight years later crushed a Tibetan uprising, forcing the Dalai Lama to flee to India, where he was warmly welcomed and has lived ever since. China and India now shared a 1,240-mile-long border and by the late 1950s disputes over the border had led to mutual recriminations and increasing tensions. Pandit Nehru's dream of Sino-Indian cooperation withered and then collapsed entirely in 1962 with a war that has coloured perceptions on both sides ever since.

The origins of the 1962 Sino-Indian War, like so many conflicts of the past half century, actually go back to colonial times and the drawing up of the border between what was then British India and Beijing's Manchu rulers. In 1825, the British East India Company gained control over the erstwhile Burmese possession of Assam. Assam is today a state in India's northeast, but had been an independent country for centuries before coming first under Burmese occupation in the early nineteenth century and then under British colonial rule. To the north of Assam was Tibet, at the time part of the Manchu Empire, but the boundaries were unclear. This had not mattered much at first. For a while colonial policy-makers were not even sure what to do with Assam, but soon Assam grew in significance once it was discovered that its upland plains were an ideal place to grow Britain's new favourite drink – tea. An obvious and natural boundary between Assam and Tibet were the Himalayas. Colonial agents, however, learned that in the foothills south of the Himalayas were people who spoke Tibetan as well as others who practised Tibetan Buddhism. At Tawang, in the foothills, there was even an important Tibetan monastery that had been the birthplace of the Sixth Dalai Lama. The British would have either to risk a foreign presence dangerously close to their new tea-rich possessions or come up with a fudge.

The British then 'discovered' a distinction between what they called 'Outer Tibet' (the main part of Tibet north of the Himalayas and including the capital Lhasa) and the foothills that were to the south of the Himalayas but north of the Assam valley. The foothills would be incorporated into British India, though only lightly administered, if at all. Tibet itself was not particularly important, but from the 1830s the British were concerned about growing Russian influence throughout Central Asia. Russia was Britain's competitor in the 'Great Game', and British Indian strategists worried about Russian intrigue in Lhasa. The British also had no desire to see Manchu Chinese forces too close to their Indian territories.

In 1905, an expeditionary force under Francis Younghusband had somewhat cavalierly invaded Tibet, killing many lightly armed Tibetan defenders, before withdrawing, not having achieved very much. A few year later however, when the Manchu Empire collapsed and the Dalai Lama's regime declared itself fully independent, British diplomats were able swiftly to take advantage of the new environment. A separate boundary agreement was soon concluded with Lhasa. The 'McMahon Line' (named after the British diplomat Henry McMahon who negotiated the agreement in 1914) recognized the highest ridges of the Himalayas as the border between Tibet and British India, leaving the Tibetan-speaking foothills on the British side. The government of China protested but couldn't do anything about it. From the 1910s until the 1951 invasion, Tibet proper was isolated and independent, whilst the British in India continued to govern, lightly, the Tibetan-speaking areas just north of Assam. When the British left India in 1948, these Tibetan and culturally related areas became part of the new Indian dominion as the 'Northeast Frontier Agency'.

Independent India and communist China thus inherited a border that could easily be disputed. Pandit Nehru's government, though espousing eternal friendship with Beijing, was adamant that the McMahon Line remain the international frontier. The Chinese rejected the McMahon Line as a colonial artifice. Of course the Chinese claim rested in turn on the Chinese claim to Tibet, and their vision of Beijing as the inheritor of all areas that had once been under Manchu suzerainty, however tenuous or fleeting. For a while, no one complained too much. But the arrival of the Dalai Lama in India in 1959 created new pressures. Beijing began insisting that all the foothills below the McMahon Line were part of China.

The Chinese army had also started building a road through a remote wind-swept desert far to the west, near Kashmir. It was on the other end of the Himalayan range, at a place called Aksai Chin. The Chinese had no historical claim at all to Aksai Chin but this did not deter them. Aksai Chin would be another area of contention. In those days, Beijing had road access to its far-western possessions in Xinjiang; Aksai Chin was the critical link that would allow this road to continue on to Tibet. There was as yet no direct road (as now exists) from China proper to Tibet. China and India had talks on both issues, the McMahon Line and Aksai Chin, but diplomacy went nowhere. There were clashes along the border. Pandit Nehru apparently believed that the Chinese would eventually back down and, despite objections from senior military officers, he pursued a 'Forward Policy', establishing Indian outposts along or even beyond the McMahon Line in the frozen Himalayan peaks. Nationalist feelings ran high on both sides.

In December 1961 the Indian army invaded the Portuguese-controlled enclave of Goa in the south of the country and incorporated Goa into the Indian republic. This act, together with India's 'Forward Policy' and its very public support for the Dalai Lama, fuelled Chinese anxieties. The Chinese also feared potential Indian ties to the Americans, who were busy funding and equipping Tibetan insurgents (as well as the Chinese Nationalist fighters based in Burma). In a late round of negotiations, Beijing essentially offered to let India keep the disputed territory in the northeast in return for recognition of its annexation of Aksai Chin, which it viewed at the time as being of greater strategic importance. The offer was rejected.

Then, in October 1962, the Chinese launched a massive two-front assault. This was during the Cuban Missile Crisis, when Beijing knew high-level international attention was firmly fixed elsewhere. Two Chinese divisions attacked in waves, supported with machine guns and heavy mortars. In the western theatre (around Aksai Chin), the Chinese overran key Indian positions, despite a spirited defence, and then marched towards Leh, the capital of the erstwhile kingdom of Ladakh, and in 1963 part of Indian-administered Kashmir. In the east, Chinese troops advanced along a 500-mile front, descending from the Himalayan passes, and seizing Tawang on 24 October. The Indians were woefully unprepared and were outnumbered five to one. The Indian army was trained for tank battles on the plains and deserts along the border with Pakistan, and not for fighting in frozen mountain conditions. The Chinese for their part had been fighting not only in Korea against the Americans but in Tibet itself and could be much more easily resupplied from their high-altitude positions.

Reinforcements including light tanks were rushed in from Calcutta, the Punjab and elsewhere. But it was to no avail. By mid-November, the Chinese had wiped out nearly all Indian positions in the east and were on the outskirts of the major town of Tezpur in the heart of Assam. The local government soon fled, after burning all the cash in the local bank and freeing all the inmates from the mental asylum. After the Indian 48th Brigade collapsed on 20 November, there was no organized Indian military force left on either front. The rout was complete. The next day, the Chinese ordered a ceasefire and retreated back to the McMahon Line.

The Chinese got what they wanted – control over the road from Xinjiang to Tibet, and the removal of any Indian threat, real or imagined, beyond the McMahon Line. Beijing had also humiliated New Delhi. India was left in shock and with a dread of China as a mortal threat. In the decades that followed, however, both countries had other preoccupations and the border dispute was left on the back burner. China was soon convulsed by its own Cultural Revolution. And India was again distracted by its wars with Pakistan. Both were also in their very different ways trying to hold together their gigantic new nations. To the extent that China focused on the rest of Asia, it was to export its brand of communism through local communist movements in places like Indonesia, Thailand and Burma, and to support North Vietnam's war against the South and later the Khmer Rouge against the American-backed government in Phnom Penh. In all these places, India didn't bother to have much influence at all.

Neither Beijing nor New Delhi was then thinking about economic opportunities abroad. And southeast Asia in the 1960s and 1970s did not present an especially enticing market. The end of colonial rule had often proved a violent process and the region was wracked by bloody conflicts and civil unrest. There were wars in Indochina leaving millions dead and entire countries in ruins. In Indonesia, mass killings followed the military coup of 1966. There would be a long-running insurgency in Aceh and in 1975 the Indonesian army invaded East Timor, until then a Portuguese colonial possession. The Burmese communist rebellion was at its height. In 1978 Vietnam invaded genocidal Cambodia and the entire region was divided between Vietnam and its ally Laos on the one side, and those countries, like Thailand and Indonesia, who opposed the Vietnamese-installed regime. Poverty remained endemic, except in a few small places like the island-state of Singapore.

The two Asian giants only began to improve relations in the 1980s. Indian prime minister Rajiv Gandhi, grandson of Pandit Nehru, travelled to China in 1988, and was the first prime minister to do so since his grandfather went in 1954. China's elder statesman Deng Xiaoping met with Rajiv Gandhi and told him, 'If there should be an Asian Age in the next century, then it can only be realized after both India and China become developed economies.' Many more high-level trips followed, in both directions. In 2005, during a visit of Chinese prime minister Wen Jiabao to New Delhi, his Indian counterpart Manmohan Singh said, 'India and China can together reshape the world order.' There were shades of an old ambition, of India and China taking their places as global powers, but in the contest for regional economic influence China was already far ahead.

India for me was never quite a foreign country. My parents were born in the 1930s, at a time when Burma was still part of the Indian Empire; my great-grandfather had studied at Calcutta University in the late nineteenth century and I remember seeing when I was a small child the portraits of Mahatma Gandhi and Pandit Nehru in my grandfather's study. I was drawn to Burma's part in the British India story and this led me to graduate work at Cambridge where I studied under historians of the British Raj. On trips back to Rangoon, I sought out people of the older generation, including in my own family, who were, from the way they spoke English and in their learning more generally, very much products of the Empire. It was a colonial legacy that was still very present in the 1980s.

In 1995 I spent two months travelling through parts of India, from Dharamsala in the Himalayan foothills (where I was very graciously given an audience with His Holiness the Dalai Lama), down through Rajasthan to Bombay and then around south India. And over the years, I made other, much shorter trips to New Delhi, mainly for work but also to see old friends. When I went back in 2008 and 2009, reports about India's 'rise' in the world were everywhere in the news, in the West and in India too. There seemed an endless stream of books and articles celebrating India's economic success as well as others warning Americans and Europeans of the dangers that the rise of India was posing to present and future jobs. India was now a nuclear power, its military modernizing fast, and its IT companies amongst the best in the world. Over the first decade of the new millennium, India's stock market had been yielding returns for investors of up to 350 per cent a year. Indian millionaires and billionaires were more visible at fashionable events in the West than at any time since the heyday of the maharajas during the British Raj,

Indian writer Aravind Adiga had just won the Booker prize for *The White Tiger*, and even India's space agency was sending its Chandrayaan rocket on an unmanned mission to the moon. And while lifting millions from poverty, India had remained a democracy and a free if at times tumultuous society.

Back in Delhi, though, I could see little that had changed since I was last there in the 1990s, at least on the surface. The airport was singularly unimpressive, with mouldy walls and long queues (though a new terminal has since been built), and the road into town was as slow, chaotic and noisy as ever. Monkeys wandered around freely, both individually and in small groups. And though there were several smart hotels, they were all hugely overpriced, and still nothing very special by the standards of Asia's ultra-luxurious tourist industry. A few stylish bars and clubs had cropped up in recent years and away from the centre of the city were new shopping malls and office and apartment complexes. And there was as well a very new subway, as good as any in the world, with punctual trains and immaculate stations. But there was nothing like the transformations further east, in Beijing and elsewhere. Instead, in Delhi, the past still seemed all around.

Unlike Beijing which had torn down its architectural heritage and replaced its old buildings with the anonymous skyscrapers of the early twenty-first century, Delhi's Islamic and British legacies confidently dominated the centre of the capital. Delhi had been the capital of a series of short-lived Turkish sultanates in medieval times, before being annexed by the Central Asian conqueror Timur Lang in 1526, and then by Babur, the founder of the great Mughal dynasty. There is still the mammoth Mughal-era Red Fort, with its ornamental pavilions and crowded market stalls out front, and the beautiful garden burial complexes of the sixteenth-century emperor Humayun and Safdarjung, the eighteenth-century Nawab of Oudh. When the British built 'New Delhi' in the environs of the old city in the 1910s and 1920s, they drew on these earlier styles, using the rose-pink and yellow sandstone of the region, and decorating their imperial buildings with domes and wall-railings and sculptures of lions, snakes and elephants. Many of the buildings stand along Rajpath or the King's Way, exactly as they had a century ago, stretching from India Gate, past Parliament House and the Secretariat, to Rashtrapati Bhawan, once the home of British viceroys, and today the residence of the president of India.

A much more human scale to things remained intact. I went several times to Khan Market. It was a warren of shops, including some very good if small bookstores, with a McDonald's in one corner, small boutiques selling fabrics and imported men's shirts, a fruit seller and a pharmacist, a few cafés, an Italian restaurant called Big Chilli and a Subway sandwich place. In one small passageway there was a wall of local and foreign magazines for sale, and very close by were two young women, one with luminous green eyes, sitting, rather than standing guard, in khaki-coloured uniforms, holding their Lee-Enfield rifles against the dusty ground. There was overgrown grass in the lots to the side, open drainage and cable wires dangling overhead, a few stray dogs and an ancient-looking petrol station. Chauffeur-driven cars, many of them the white Hindustan Ambassadors that have plied Delhi's roads for generations, dropped off and collected elegantly dressed women and less elegantly dressed men. Property prices at Khan Market were, apparently, the twenty-fourth most expensive in the world (according to Cushman and Wakefield, a global estate agency). It was a list headed by Fifth Avenue and New Bond Street, and Khan Market, which appeared more like a village centre, was positioned between Orchard Road in Singapore and Beijing's Wangfujing, with their huge and ultra-modern shopping malls. In China the sense was of everything being remade, the new overwhelming the old. Here the pace and manner of change suggested accretion – slower, but perhaps steadier change.

There are, however, grand predictions. Sometime over the next thirty years, India will in all likelihood overtake China as the most populous country in the world. And some believe that its economy will become the third biggest, after both China and the United States. The US investment bank Goldman Sachs, for example, has speculated that India's economy may grow faster than any other over the coming decades, expanding to forty times its present-day size. And in India as in China there is a great confidence in the future, not universal, but amongst the young middle classes in particular. 'Our parents' generation was the most boring in history,' said a university student I met. 'Our grandparents' generation was amazing: they were freedom-fighters and many went to jail to win independence. But then our parents just accepted the status quo and became salary-men and bureaucrats.' Tall and lean, with a receding chin and thick black hair, he was studying at business school and said he wanted to be an entrepreneur. He felt India now had boundless possibilities and had moved past older, conservative mentalities. There was a great pride in being Indian and a strong feeling that the problems of today will without a doubt be overcome.

These problems are, however, severe. There is still very little in the way of modern infrastructure in nearly all parts of the country, and the economy is crippled by a lack of everything from highways to ports to running water. More than 400 million people have no access to electricity. The airports nearly everywhere are far worse than those in eastern Asia, including in Burma. There are the problems of endemic corruption, stultifying red tape, and bureaucratic structures that resist any attempt at quick and decisive action.

There is also a widening gap between the India that has benefited from the growth of recent years and the India that lags far behind. Nobel prize-winning economist Amartya Sen once warned that India risked becoming a country where half enjoyed the living standards of California and the other half of sub-Saharan Africa. In China there is an east to west slide in income. In India it's the other way around. India is currently planning for two mega-industrial corridors, one linking Delhi in the north to Bombay on the west coast, another between

Madras and Bangalore in the south, with projected investments of $150 billion in total. Already states (in the west) like Gujarat and Maharashtra (around Bombay) are industrializing fast and others (like the Punjab) benefiting from an agricultural sector that has become more profitable in recent years. Bangalore and Hyderabad are world-class centres in information technology.

Move eastward, however, and the picture is very different. It is as if there is an invisible line running through the middle of the country (say just east of Bangalore) where the economic juggernaut runs out of steam and a different subcontinent is revealed. This is not to say that there are not extreme income inequalities in every part of the country; there are, as in China. But there is also a very real geographical gradient: in Gujarat, for example, growth rates have run at about 12–14 per cent through most of the 2000s, while in the east, in Bihar and Orissa, growth has generally remained below 4 per cent. Not surprisingly, it is in this part of the country where the Indian state is confronting a newly invigorated Maoist insurgency. The Maoists, or Naxalites as they are often called (after the site of an early rebellion), are now active in no less than a third of all of India's administrative districts, overwhelmingly those located in the east of the country, along a spine that runs south from Nepal and through West Bengal. They control large swathes of dense forest and have mobilized support from the aboriginal tribal peoples there – people whose lives are about as far away from the bright lights of Bombay and Bangalore as possible.

Further to the east are yet more problems, an even more different India. These are the states of the 'Northeast', up against the Burma frontier, also amongst the poorest in the country and wracked by insurgencies decades older than that of the Maoists. The Northeast, home to around forty million people, has long been a policy headache for New Delhi, and a linking up of militant groups from this region with the Maoists is seen as a potential security disaster. Whereas in other sections of the country ethnic differences, to a large extent, have been channelled into electoral politics, in the Northeast violent ethnic-based militias and separatist insurgencies are entrenched in the local scene.

There was thus an almost exact mirror of China's situation. Whereas in China the poorer provinces and 'autonomous regions' were to the west and southwest, in India the poorer states were to the east and northeast. And for both China and India there was Burma, hovering along the edge, a potential crossroads, and building block for future economic growth. But the parallels end there, as we will see.

In the early 1990s, the government of India embarked on what was called its 'Look East' policy. The hope was to connect India better to the increasingly prosperous nations of the Far East, and there find new markets and new friends. Narasimha Rao was prime minister at the time and India was just starting off the process of economic reform that would soon boost the country into the top ranks of the world's emerging economies. For decades the economy had been growing at just a few per cent a year, but this was now changing, and under Prime Minister Rao and his finance minister, Dr Manmohan Singh, many of the state controls that had long hobbled commerce and industry were being undone and the stage was being set for what would be two decades of unparalleled growth. New economic vigour called for new international relations.

To the west of India was its old foe Pakistan against whom it had fought three wars. Beyond Pakistan was Afghanistan, soon to fall under the Taliban, and Iran, under the ayatollahs. These were all places with deep historical and cultural connections to India, but an economically vibrant India would need to look for fresh partnerships in new directions.

India's ties to eastern Asia were at the time extremely limited and India's policy-makers believed that it was important to strengthen them. Countries like South Korea, Taiwan and Singapore were fast reaching first-world levels of income, and others like Malaysia and even Thailand appeared not far behind.

Armed violence was abating throughout this region and a new era of prosperity seemed (almost) everywhere on the rise. In a near miraculous transformation, southeast Asia, which had been a byword for war and suffering in the 1960s and 1970s, turned itself into one of the most peaceful and economically dynamic parts of the world. The Association of Southeast Asian Nations, originally founded as a non-communist block, had by 1997 come to include all ten countries of the region, including the association's one-time foe Vietnam. Tourism, trade and satellite television drew the peoples of the region together as never before. For tens of millions in the emerging southeast Asian middle class, consumerism replaced ideology. As India's own economy opened up and grew rapidly, closer links eastward seemed a natural next step.

A natural partnership was with China. India's and China's economies were in a sense complementary. China's strengths were in manufacturing and infrastructure, India's in information technology and financial services. Current Environment Minister Jairam Ramesh has even coined the term 'Chindia' to describe his vision of a China and India that would cooperate closely and reinforce one another's economic development. He has argued in many essays and speeches for a changed mindset, one that would overcome old suspicions and embrace more open borders. And since the early 1990s, trade has grown enormously, from practically nothing to nearly $60 billion a year in 2010. As there are calls in Yunnan for major investments in new trading ties with India, in India too there are those who are optimistic about the future for Sino-Indian business.

Many in India, though, are more cautious. There is a worry, for example, that with improved transport links will come a flood of cheap Chinese goods, overwhelming local industry. China is today the biggest trading power and the biggest exporter in the world, having overtaken Germany in 2009, with exports worth $1.2 trillion a year. India is still in a lowly twenty-first place and runs a trade deficit of $114 billion a year, $20 billion alone with China. Chinese businesses are already doing well in India's consumer market but India has not had anything like the same success in China. What India exports to China is mainly iron-ore (about half the total) and other basic commodities.

But a more primal fear is a security one. Half a century after the Sino-Indian war, suspicions of China's intent remain high in many quarters. Trade is increasing and there have been high-level visits between top leaders. But the border issues are still unresolved; there are differences of feeling over Tibet; concerns about China's ties around the Indian Ocean; and very generally a shared sense of the two countries as rivals, now and for the rest of the twenty-first century.

It's useful to take a step back and consider the very different international positions these two old civilizations are in. The People's Republic of China includes within its boundaries all of Chinese-speaking 'China proper' (with the disputed exception of Taiwan). Hong Kong and Macau were returned by the British and Portuguese respectively in 1997 and 1999. But Communist China also includes all the areas Beijing sees as having once belonged to the Manchu or Qing Empire, including Tibet and Xinjiang in the west, as well as Manchuria and Inner Mongolia in the north. Yunnan, as we have seen, has also been brought under greater central control than ever before. With the exception of northern Vietnam and northern Korea (which were under Han dynasty domination 2,000 years ago), and some of the oasis states of Central Asia (which briefly came under Chinese domination during the Tang dynasty in early medieval times), China now controls everything it has ever controlled in the past, and then some.

India is in a very different situation. In its heyday, the British Indian Empire stretched all the way from the Khyber Pass to the Malay peninsula, including all of what is today Pakistan, India, Bangladesh and Burma. In 1937 Burma was separated from the rest, and then, at independence, the new nation of Pakistan was carved out of what was left. True, a colonial power had created the pre-1937 boundaries, but even under the Mughal emperors (and the Mauryans and Guptas in ancient times), 'India' included much of what is today Pakistan, India and Bangladesh together. And over the past half century, modern India's relations with countries on its immediate periphery have drawn in nearly all of New Delhi's foreign policy energy.

China is also a far more dominant economic power among the nations of southeast Asia, a region of ten nations that has a population of 600 million, twice that of the United States. China's relations with many southeast Asian governments were frosty to non-existent during the Cold War, but by the 1990s relations had warmed considerably. It is now the region's top trading partner (displacing the US in recent years), with total two-way trade approaching $200 billion in 2010. And in southeast Asia, China has a big advantage. For centuries, Chinese entrepreneurs and others just looking for a better life had migrated all across the region, and many had become rich and successful. They had come from China's southeast coast, like the immigrants who ventured across the Pacific to America, and were famously good businessmen. In cities like Bangkok, Jakarta and Manila they became the merchant elite. And they formed the overwhelming majority of the population in Singapore, which had emerged as the financial capital of southeast Asia.

Post-Mao China formed links with overseas Chinese business-men and they in turn became a critical part of China's own economic rise, investing in their ancestral homeland and facilitating contacts abroad. A southeast Asia so dominated by ethnic Chinese business gravitated naturally towards the rapidly expanding Chinese economy; since the early 1990s, nearly 60 per cent of all the foreign investments made in China have been by overseas Chinese (including from Taiwan, Hong Kong and Singapore). By the 2000s, the economies of the region were strongly tied to China's success. Component parts for products, from cars to iPods, could be manufactured in several different countries before being assembled in China and then shipped to

Western and other markets. Political as well as business elites visited Shanghai and the big Chinese industrial cities and were impressed with what they saw. As the global recession rolled around, the West appeared in crisis and the Chinese way of doing things seemed to be shining more brightly than ever. Twenty years into India's Look East policy, ties between southeast Asia and India were on firm and friendly footing, but it was the Chinese model that was clearly in the ascendancy.

It was not always this way. It is important to remember that for most of the past 2,000 years it was India, not China, that enjoyed the closest connections with southeast Asia and was by far the premier source of outside cultural and religious inspiration. And the effects of centuries of interaction with India in southeast Asia remain deep and enduring. There was a time, not long ago, when the countries of the region, from Burma to Bali, were known to Europeans as 'Farther India' and scholars referred to the 'Indianized states of southeast Asia'. The reasons were plain to see. For centuries this vast area was profoundly influenced by its connections with Indian civilizations, from notions of kingship to cosmology to literature.

Even today, the sway of these ancient interactions is everywhere apparent. The overwhelming majority of people in Burma, Thailand, Laos and Cambodia profess an Indian religion, Buddhism, and more than 90 per cent of people on the island of Bali, in Indonesia, are Hindu. Islam arrived in southeast Asia via India, as well as from the Arab world and Persia. Court Brahmans officiate at the royal courts in Bangkok and Phnom Penh, as they did before in palaces from Mandalay to Jogjakarta. The major languages of the region are still written in scripts derived from Indian alphabets, and nearly all have incorporated a vast Indian vocabulary. Words from the Indian liturgical languages, Sanskrit and Pali, are used to express everything from political ideas to modern inventions, and Indian classics such as the *Ramayana* are still seen as integral parts of local tradition. Southeast Asian art and architecture draw heavily from earlier Indian models, and it is impossible to visit the great archaeological sites of Pagan, Angkor or Borobadur and not appreciate the immense impact of the region's contacts with India.

No one knows how this influence originally developed. The older theory imagined Indian colonists sailing across the Bay of Bengal in ancient times to civilize a barbarian wilderness and establish the earliest kingdoms. It was a reasonable assumption. The rulers of the first recorded kingdoms of southeast Asia bore Sanskrit names and titles and often traced their ancestries back to semi-mythical Indian dynasties. They named their cities after Indian ones (the Siamese capital Ayuthaya, for example, was named after the legendary capital of the god Rama) and performed kingly rituals according to Indian Brahmanic tradition.

It is possible that Indians were first driven to southeast Asia in significant numbers by the ambition to find new sources of gold. From the late centuries BC to the first century AD trade between India and southeast Asia was largely restricted to the Bay of Bengal and the few scattered ports and peoples along the opposite shores. India's main trade in these ancient times was westward to Persia and the Red Sea. South Indian ports were thriving trading centres and Roman ships were using the monsoon winds to sail regularly from Aden to India. In all this India enjoyed a massive trade surplus, draining the Romans of their gold, and this led to a Roman response. The Emperor Nero first tried to reduce the gold content of Roman coins and in the late first century AD the Emperor Vespasian banned gold exports altogether. About a hundred years before, India had lost its principal source of gold in Siberia due to nomadic movements in Central Asia. After Vespasian's prohibition, the gold shortage in India became acute. Southeast Asia would become the answer. Before it became known as the land of spices, camphor and aromatic woods, the region was known to Indians for centuries as Suvarnabhumi or the 'Land of Gold'. It was India's earliest Look East policy.

Recent scholarship, though, also suggests that southeast Asia prior to its Indian contacts, far from being a barbarian wilderness, was already a dynamic place, with settled agriculture, complex systems of irrigation, and ships able to undertake long-distance voyages. Desires for trade were not just a one-way street. Ancient southeast Asian sailors doubtless roamed far and wide. The main language today of Madagascar, for example, off the east African coast, is Malagasy, a language closely related to the languages of Indonesia, a testament to these now forgotten but epic voyages.

What seems likely is not that Indians colonized southeast Asia, in search of gold or anything else, but that southeast Asians and Indians established mutually beneficial contacts, and that the peoples of southeast Asia, in particular their chiefs and ruling classes, were awed by what they came to know of the great nations across the bay. There was at the time also a degree of contact with China. India displaced this, in what the French scholar George Coedes in the last century called 'one of the outstanding events in the history of the world'. The first kingdoms of southeast Asia – for example in what is now Burma and Cambodia – emerged in the early centuries AD, during the time of the Guptas in India, and it is easy to understand why India became the place to look for ideas and inspiration.

The Guptas were then the ruling family of northern India at what was a time of great intellectual, religious and artistic ferment. Gupta society included astronomers like the fifth- and sixth-century Aryabhata, who penned numerous works on algebra and trigonometry and who for the first time calculated the earth's circumference with extreme precision, coming to within 0.2 per cent of what we know today. The system of numbers we use in the West, including the concept of 'zero', is derived from the Indian numerical system developed at this time, by Aryabhata and others. It would be exported to Europe, together with much other knowledge, via the Islamic world. This same system was exported eastward to southeast Asia, and this common ancestry is the reason why, with some imagination, one can see the similarities still between the 'Arabic' numerals used in Europe and the numerals used in, say, Burma and Thailand. There were many other achievements. A near contemporary of Aryabhata was the philosopher Vatsyayana who authored the *Kama Sutra*, the definitive treatise on human sexual behaviour. Even the game of chess is believed to have been first devised and played in the courts of the Gupta kings.

The Guptas patronized and revived Hinduism, but they also tolerated a Buddhist tradition that was then still vigorous, a millennium after the first teachings of its founder. Buddhism and Hinduism drew closer to each other. Within the Hindu fold, the new Saivite and Vaishnavite faiths and the Bhakti movement incorporated Buddhist elements, and many began to see the Buddha as an avatar of Vishnu. India, then as now, offered up an eclectic and exciting mix of spiritual ideas and practices.

Buddhism itself was undergoing many changes and adopting new forms. The northern parts of the Gupta domains were a stronghold of the new Mahayana school of Buddhism, which spread from there to Afghanistan, Central Asia, and along the Silk Routes to China and beyond. The Chinese pilgrim and monk Faxian travelled to India in the late fourth and early fifth centuries, visiting the Buddha's birthplace and then going on to Ceylon before returning to China by sea. At almost exactly the same time, the Indian monk Kumarajiva, travelling in the opposite direction, arrived in China and launched a project to translate Buddhist works. He had been born in the Central Asian oasis town of Kucha and educated in Kashmir, then a fabled centre of Buddhist learning. Together with his Kashmiri colleagues Yasa and Vimlaksha, and at the urging of the Chinese emperor himself, he would translate over 300 Buddhist works into the entirely dissimilar Chinese language, making Buddhism accessible for generations to come to the peoples of China, Korea and Japan.

One of the more important points of contact for southeast Asia, though, was the eastern coast of India, along the Bay of Bengal. Prime Minister Narasimha Rao, who ushered in the Look East policy in the early 1990s, was born in a village called Vangara, in what is today Andhra Pradesh, and in precisely the same area that 1,500 years before was southeast Asia's gateway to Indian civilization. The Satavahana dynasty were the early rulers of this region and were patrons of Buddhism as well as Hinduism. Burma's earliest Buddhist ties were probably to Satavahana-sponsored monasteries. And some say that Bodhidarma, the founder of what would be called the Chan school of Buddhism in China (called Zen in Japan), was a prince of the Pallava dynasty, another and slightly later regional dynasty in this part of India.

The connections were almost endless. What we need to remember is the relative position of these two lands. On the one side was India, with an estimated population even then of over a hundred million people, with cities that were amongst the biggest in the world, a towering economic and intellectual power. And then on the other side of the Bay of Bengal was southeast Asia, still heavily forested and with a population that was only a tiny fraction of India's. The little states there were advanced in their own ways, but the pull of Indian exemplars must have been strong. In Burma, the very first known kings along the Irrawaddy valley styled themselves 'Vikram' and 'Varman'. *Vikram*, meaning 'valour', was a title used by many contemporary Indian rulers, including the Guptas. And *Varman*, meaning 'protector', was the preferred title of the Pallavas, used not only in Burma, but by the kings of Cambodia as well. It was an epic effort at imitation and adaptation, designed not so much to flatter the Indian originals as to awe their countrymen and perhaps satisfy their own desire to feel a part of what was arguably the world's most impressive civilization.

Many in India have long been proud of this ancient link. 'To know my country,' wrote the great scholar and poet Rabindranath Tagore,

one has to travel to that age when she realized her soul and thus transcended her physical boundaries, when she revealed her being in a radiant magnanimity which illuminated the eastern horizon, making her recognized as their own by those in alien shores who were awakened into a surprise of life . . .

In Delhi, I stayed with a friend who lived in a gorgeously restored British-era home, one that had belonged before independence to a leading Indian barrister. There was a square central courtyard with a water fountain and an immense garden behind the house. The heat outside was oppressive, but inside the rooms were all quietly air-conditioned. My friend was the perfect host and his guests, charming and articulate, were from a mix of backgrounds – politicians, journalists, scholars, both Indian and foreign.

During the several days I was there, I gave talks on Burma, met old friends, made new ones, and engaged in discussions over many meals. I went to book launches and attended panel debates. Delhi's was an elite whose nature and orientation were fundamentally different from those further to the east. Many had studied in the UK or US and travelled there often. Some were only back in India for a holiday. Burma seemed far away. It was also a small elite. I felt I was socializing in a very small circle. People I met would mention a friend who turned out to be someone I had encountered at a lunch or dinner the day before. At Khan Market, I started seeing people I knew, in the bookshops or running an errand. I was in a leafy, expensive part of south Delhi, but it was as if I were in a small town, not the capital city of a nation of more than a billion people.

It was at a restaurant in Khan Market – the Side Wok – that I arranged to see an analyst of the region. We had met a few times before at academic conferences abroad and he had suggested the Side Wok, which offered dishes from across the Far East. It was a modern and stylish place, with lots of dark wood and dim lighting, an exposed brick wall, and a menu that identified different dishes as being Japanese, Chinese, Vietnamese, Thai or Indonesian. Little drawings of a chilli marked which dishes were especially hot.

We talked about India–China relations and he said he was moderately optimistic and that fears of a 'China threat' were understandable but overblown:

The media on both sides like to hype up the problems, which are there, but there is enough common sense as well. 1962 won't happen again. A problem is that there are not enough scholars of China, and the very few Indians who speak Mandarin go into the private sector, not into government or media. There's not much understanding of China today, the complexities. There's a huge contrast with India's ties with the US. There are challenges there too, but there is much more people-to-people interaction. There are hundreds of thousands of Indians living in America; many have relatives living there, children going to school. Everyone hears the success stories of Indian-Americans and can easily follow American politics. There is nothing like that with China.

There was also nothing like that with Burma. Many people I met in Delhi were curious about Burma. But Delhi was a city, once Turkish, Mughal and British, whose ruling classes were eager to assume a long-denied place on the world stage. Burma had no real place in the emerging narrative of India as a twenty-first-century power. Almost no one I knew in Delhi had even been to Burma and whereas in China I encountered several scholars who spoke at least some Burmese, I was told there were no Burmese-speaking experts in India. Instead, there were hints of a slightly forlorn connection: a relative who had been born in Burma, a recipe that had been kept in the family after a time spent long ago in Rangoon, a sense of an old religious or cultural affinity, an interest, but otherwise little knowledge, and little focus on the changes taking place.

In the sixteenth century, China and India together formed half the world's economy. Within a generation, this could be the case again. And no one in principle was against more trade, more economic interaction between the two rising giants. A very likely scenario is not war or heightened animosity, but growing commercial and people-to-people ties. In 2010, Burma and

China reached an agreement to rebuild the old Stilwell Road, originally built by African-American soldiers during the Second World War, linking Ruili to India's Northeast. Nearly all trade between China and India today is by sea. But it is unclear what will happen if and when Beijing's and Kunming's development plans materialize and China's southwest, with its new oil and gas pipelines, high-speed trains and mass tourism, becomes only a day's drive away from India's eastern edge. China is already transforming Burma. What will the effect of more open borders be on India? From Delhi I went first to Calcutta, almost a thousand miles away, and from there up to the far-away states of the Indian Northeast and the very fringes of the Indian republic.

Forgotten Partitions

Two hundred years ago, British India had a different kind of Look East policy. From its earliest coastal enclaves, the British East India Company had expanded its domains and was fast becoming the dominant power on the subcontinent, governing all of south India as well as Bengal. The capital was then Calcutta, which was in the process of becoming a great imperial metropolis, the second city of the British Empire, and a vibrant commercial and intellectual centre. And it was from Calcutta that the British would defeat the Maratha Confederacy and the Sikh kingdom of the Punjab, overthrow the last of the Mughal rulers, and establish a hold on all India that would last until just after World War Two.

India was the centrepiece of British imperial might. And keeping this prize possession safe meant guarding its frontiers. To the west the frontier was Afghanistan, never directly ruled by the British but kept in check through a series of (sometimes very messy) interventions. By the 1830s, a scheming and aggressive Russia was well entrenched in Central Asia, and blocking Russian moves southward, into Afghanistan, became a British imperial preoccupation. Further to the west were the sea lanes that connected India to England, and, once the Suez Canal was built in the 1860s, the protection of these sea lanes meant securing control of Aden (in today's Yemen) as well as Egypt, which was occupied in 1880. After World War One, British Indian forces even took over Mesopotamia, remaking that once Ottoman province into the Hashemite kingdom of Iraq.

And looking east meant control of the sea lanes and this meant control of the Straits of Malacca. Beyond were the lucrative markets of eastern China, with the British port of Hong Kong. At the end of the Napoleonic Wars the British had seized Singapore and they soon extended their rule up the Malay Peninsula, from Johore to Penang. Looking east also meant dealing with the troublesome kingdom of Burma. In the early part of the nineteenth century the last Burmese dynasty – the Konbaung – were at the peak of their power. They had crushed their Siamese foes and even successfully resisted four Manchu Chinese invasions. They were extremely self-assured, pushing westward, annexing the little kingdoms of Arakan and Manipur and then the much larger one of Assam, along the Brahmaputra River. The Burmese were hemming in Bengal. This was something the East India Company could not accept and three Anglo-Burmese Wars would follow. By 1860, only the British flag flew all round the Bay of Bengal. The Indian Ocean had become a British Indian lake.

This Indian Ocean world was centred on Calcutta, and its passing is perhaps the single most important development of twentieth-century Asia, rivalled only by the communist revolution in China and the emergence of America as a Pacific power. And with its passing there has surfaced a much more broken land-scape, strewn with many little wars and ethnic conflicts, a former empire that is today not one but four independent nations, adjacent to a China that is bigger than ever.

I had planned to go to Calcutta during my trip around India in the mid-1990s but never made it. I was exhausted from many weeks on the road (with a backpack and tight budget) and after studying bus maps and railway timetables (I was then in south India) and worried about the monsoon rains, hopped on a plane instead from Bangalore to Delhi, and flew back to England where I was then living. When I finally arrived more than twelve years later I was keen to see the city I had read and thought about for so long.

I had expected the grand British-era buildings, the crowds, the poverty, the few new office towers and modern hotels. What I hadn't expected, however, was how much Calcutta resembled

Rangoon. It wasn't just a slight resemblance. At times Calcutta seemed almost identical, not to Rangoon as a whole, but to downtown Rangoon, the part of Rangoon that had been built during the Raj. The street life was the same down to the smallest details: the little shops selling cheap clothes and tattered books, the vendors hawking single cigarettes and cut fruit, the ill-nourished-looking men in their light blue checked cotton *lungis* (just like the one I am wearing now as I write this), the vats of steaming curry and rice, the potholes, the dirt and humidity, the crumbling yellowish façades, ill-made signs in both English and in a squiggly local alphabet, here and there verandas with flowering plants. Whereas Delhi and nearby cities in Rajasthan and the Punjab were alien to me, Calcutta was instantly familiar. The faces were different, but not entirely, as there were so many people of Bengali descent or mixed Indian descent in Rangoon. Calcutta, I realized, had clearly been the 'mother ship', the model on which downtown Rangoon was based. I felt very much at home.

There was little in the way of recent construction. There was the hotel where I was staying, a cavernous business hotel on the outskirts of town, and towards the centre there was the new 'South City Shopping Mall', with a state-of-the-art multiplex cinema, international chains like Marks and Spencer, Nike and Body Shop, and restaurants featuring Thai and Chinese food. But I saw few other China-style developments, only billboards overhead advertising housing estates, presumably in the suburbs, with immaculate homes and gardens, a Singapore-style life that seemed a world apart from the grimy street life below.

Calcutta is the capital of West Bengal, a densely populated state, about the size of Massachusetts, with over eighty million people (including fifteen million in and around Calcutta). The city spreads south to north along the Hooghly River and the sea is not far away. Arakan in Burma, where the Chinese pipeline to Yunnan will originate, is less than 400 miles down the coast.

Calcutta ceased being the capital of British India in 1912, but for decades afterwards still remained a key Asian hub for business and education. Even in the 1950s and early 1960s West Bengal was second only to Bombay as the country's most industrialized region. But by the 1970s Calcutta was clearly in decline. There was little new investment, services were strained, and many middle-class professionals began leaving for other cities in India, or overseas, including and especially to the US. Around the same time, there was a mass influx of poor people from newly independent Bangladesh next door, also extremely densely populated. Calcutta was plagued by power shortages and labour unrest. The 'Left Front', led by the Communist Party of India (Marxist), came to power and has been in office ever since, making it the longest-running democratically elected communist government in the world. It has not been a particularly radical communist government, but it has also not been particularly pro-business. In 1985 Rajiv Gandhi referred to Calcutta as a 'dying city'. More recently, there have been efforts at reform, but in general West Bengal has not experienced anything like the economic growth and dynamism of states further west. Its infrastructure is poor and few companies see the investment climate as very friendly. In October 2008 the industrial giant Tata withdrew plans for a $350 million plant near Calcutta following agitation by the opposition parties claiming to represent the interests of farmers in the area.

There is also the threat of the Maoists, stronger in the states just to the west of Bengal, but increasingly active within West Bengal itself. In June 2009, Prime Minister Manmohan Singh called the Maoists the 'greatest threat to India's internal security'. And in February 2010, the Maoists brazenly attacked a police camp in West Bengal's West Midnapore district, leaving twenty-four officers dead. In May the same year the Maoists derailed a Bombay-bound train outside Calcutta, which was then hit by a freight train; seventy-six people were killed and over 200 injured.

These stories briefly made the international headlines, but in general, for one of the biggest cities on the planet, Calcutta is not that much in the news. Looking through the *New York Times*, one of the very few recent articles I could find was a story from 2006, reporting on the death of a tortoise at the Calcutta Zoo. This giant Aldabra tortoise was believed, amazingly, to be no less than 255 years old. It was one of four brought by British seamen from the Seychelles islands in the mid-eighteenth century, and had been presented as a gift to Lord Robert Clive of the East India Company. Clive had died in 1774 but the tortoise had lived on, for a very long time.

During my few days there I took many long walks and was able to enjoy several meals of delicious Bengali food – fish and prawn dishes and rice – eaten, as in Burma, with one's right hand. And during these meals there were discussions about the old British-era Zamindari mansions in the north of the city, 1950s politicians like U Nu and Krishna Menon, tiger conservation, Oxbridge historians, and the year's monsoon. This was all very familiar. The homes I was invited to reminded me exactly of the slightly mildewed homes of the upper middle class in Rangoon, with the overhead punkahs and attentive servants, the overstuffed book-cases and black and white photographs, and curry-smells from unseen kitchens.

And in remembering Rangoon, I thought of Calcutta as the path not taken. Calcutta was a centre of a democracy, its politics untidy and hotly contested, with an elite still connected to its past. It was not much more prosperous materially than Rangoon, but far richer intellectually, and enjoyed a political freedom long denied its smaller sister city. When I was there a rally of the Communist Party of India (Marxist) was making its way through one of the main streets, with busloads of men and women from the countryside waving red hammer and sickle flags heading to the *maidan* to hear speeches, air their grievances and chant slogans.

I imagined the Pegu Club in Rangoon (once a colonial bastion, long derelict and on the verge of being demolished) like the Bengal Club today, a somewhat shabby watering-hole offering not-very-expensive rooms for the night, a library and a barber-shop, a place for the visiting Vice Chancellor of Cambridge to give a speech and meet with local alumni. Whereas the Burma Research Society, founded by the former Indian Civil Servant and later Cambridge sociologist J. S. Furnivall, is long gone, the Asiatic Society, founded by the linguist William Jones (and once home to the only museum in Asia), is still there, with a modern wing recently added. The buildings of the Raj were maintained and beautiful. Government House, now Raj Bhawan and the residence and office of the West Bengal governor, is modelled on Kedleston Hall, the ancestral home of Marquess Curzon. Government House in Rangoon has been torn down. The Writer's Building, once the headquarters of the East India Company, is now the seat of the West Bengal government. The similarly grand Secretariat in Rangoon is empty and forlorn, in 2010 up for sale to the highest bidder. In Calcutta there is the Victoria Memorial, really an enormous white marble museum to the British Empire, complete with a giant statue of the queen, whilst in Rangoon every street name has been scrubbed of any possible colonial legacy. I had no sense that the people of Calcutta were any more enamoured of British times than those in Rangoon, but with democracy had maintained a certain confidence that allowed them to accept and build on the past.

Calcutta was also a place with old family ties. The exact history is a little obscure but one of my great-grandfathers studied in Calcutta as a young man in the 1880s. Some in my family say that he was partly of Indian descent himself, and that his grandfather had arrived in Burma's Irrawaddy delta thirty years or so before from Arakan, the part of Burma closest to Bengal. He was a Muslim and his family were then prominent land-owners; after university he spent some time working as a colonial civil servant, before returning to the delta to help run the family business. In those days Calcutta was not very far away from Rangoon. A steamer service (the Calcutta and Burmah Steam Navigation Company) ran from Calcutta through the Irrawaddy delta to Rangoon and then on to Penang and Singapore, and this was his intellectual life-line to the world. He could order books from Calcutta bookshops and subscribe to newspapers and magazines. And when he married my great-grandmother in 1905, it was to the capital of the British Raj that he took her on their honeymoon.

My great-grandfather was far from unusual in his ties to Calcutta. Both Burma and Bengal were provinces of British India and Bengal was the province closest to Burma geographically and the province with which Burma had the closest relationship. Hundreds of Burmese students studied at schools in Calcutta and in the nearby hill station of Darjeeling, and many stayed on for university. More importantly, there was a significant migration of Bengalis to Burma in the late nineteenth and early twentieth centuries. Some were casual labourers, especially in the area near the present-day Burma–Bangladesh border, but a large number were businessmen, civil servants and professionals. There were many Bengali teachers in Burma as well as lecturers and professors at Rangoon University and several generations of Burmese grew up speaking English with a Bengali-influenced accent. Calcutta was also the place from which many other communities established themselves in British Burma, including those of the Marwari and Jewish merchants who prospered in Rangoon. And there were journalists and writers, like Sarat Chandra Chattopadhyay, one of the most popular Bengali novelists of the early twentieth century, who lived in Rangoon in the 1930s, worked as a clerk in the Public Works Department, and there began writing the books that are unknown today in Burma but are still favourites in Bengal.

This was a time when important political figures routinely travelled from India to Burma. Mahatma Gandhi was a repeat visitor. He first came to Rangoon in 1902 (when he was living in Cape Town), writing afterwards of his sadness at seeing Indians teaming up with British merchants at the expense of the Burmese. (He also remarked: 'The freedom and energy of the Burmese women charmed just as the indolence of the men pained me.')

He came again in 1915 and in 1929, and on both these occasions stayed with an old friend from London student days, Dr P. J. Mehta, the scion of a rich diamond-trading family, then settled in Rangoon, who had founded the Burma Provincial Congress Committee, the first overtly political organization in Burma. Gandhi toured the country and gave speeches to big crowds wherever he went. Burmese nationalists had been very influenced by the rise of Indian nationalism and Burmese students and activists, especially those on the radical fringe of anti-colonial politics, joined resident Indians in cheering the visiting Congress leader. In Mandalay he reminded people of Lokmanya Tilak's incarceration in Mandalay jail twenty years before. Tilak had been a hard-line political figure (and the author of a wonderful book called *The Arctic Home of the Vedas*, postulating that the Aryan people originated at the North Pole 10,000 years ago), locked up by the British for sedition. 'It was Tilak who gave India the mantra of *swaraj* [self-rule],' Gandhi told the mixed Burmese–Indian crowd. 'In India it is a common saying that the way to *swaraj* passes through Mandalay.'

Mahatma Gandhi was originally from Gujarat, on the western coast of India. But many other regular and distinguished visitors to Burma were from Bengal itself. The great poet and philosopher Rabindranath Tagore came in 1916, three years after he had won the Nobel Prize for Literature. The editor of the *Rangoon Mail* at the time was also a Bengali, Nripendra Chandra Banerjee, and he acted as Rabindranath Tagore's host in Burma, organizing meetings for the visiting dignitary with Burmese *swaraj* activists and many other city notables, Burmese, British, Indian and Chinese. Tagore too would come back, in 1924, on his way to China, and came to see Burma as a bridge between India and China. On both occasions there were discussions on Buddhism, and more generally on religion and philosophy, and on the very old ties that once linked India and Burma, and India, through Burma, to the Far East.

*

Aeons ago, most of what is today India was part of a super-continent called Gondwana, separated from Eurasia by an immense sea called the Tethys Sea. And over millions of years, what became India gradually peeled itself away from the rest of Gondwana, then slid northwards, eventually colliding into Asia, lifting up the shoreline into the Himalayas and creating the Tibetan plateau. What was the Tethys Sea disappeared and in its place below the Himalayas is the vast floodplain of the Indus and Ganges Rivers. This was once grassland, much like the African savannah, home to elephants, lions and hippos; it is now a mix of urban and rural areas, a little bigger than Burma or Texas, incorporating parts of modern-day Pakistan, northern India and Bangladesh, and home to a billion people or more. Other than China's eastern provinces, the greatest concentration of people in the world lives in the Indus–Ganges floodplain.

Though there were times of imperial consolidation, for most of its history this great floodplain was divided up into several kingdoms. Bengal was one of them. And Bengal's geographical position – at the end of the Ganges as well as at the top of the Bay of Bengal – meant that it was connected westward to the regions around Delhi that had come under successive foreign invaders, Greek, Turkish, Afghan and Mughal, and in other directions to the rest of Asia.

In ancient times, people speaking an Indo-European language (very distantly related to most European languages) lived at the other end of the Ganges and along the Indus River. This language would give rise to modern Hindi, Punjabi, Bengali, and the many other languages of the north and west of the subcontinent as well as Singhalese on the island of Ceylon. The more refined version of this language was developed by ancient grammarians as Sanskrit, which became the liturgical language of Hinduism as well as some schools of Buddhism. The relationship between Sanskrit, the vernacular tongues on which it was based, and modern Indian languages like Hindi or Bengali, is very similar to the relationship between Latin, vulgar Latin and modern French or Italian. They are all often referred to as the Aryan or 'noble' languages, after the self-style of the people who first spoke them millennia ago.

It was the eighteenth-century polymath Sir William Jones, founder of Bengal's Asiatic Society, who first concluded that these Aryan languages were (ultimately) related to Greek and Latin and postulated the existence of an 'Indo-European' family of languages, giving rise to the science of comparative linguistics. These ideas, now well established, were followed by theories of ancient invasions and of heroic migrations by Aryan-speaking peoples from some more northerly realm, with their Vedic gods (so similar to the gods of Greece and Rome), defeating and over-whelming the darker-skinned natives of the subcontinent. The caste system of India, it was said, was born from this primeval conflict, with the Aryan invaders organizing themselves into the top castes, and the darker natives finding themselves locked into lower-caste servitude or forced into separation as 'untouchables'. Colonial-era racial theorists were not unhappy to discover an ancient system of race- and colour-based discrimination.

More recent scholarship challenges some of this. There is little evidence of an actual migration of people from a purer Aryan homeland to the north. As in Europe, the spread of Indo-European languages (which in Europe displaced all but outliers like Basque and Finnish) may have been as much the result of cultural changes linked to the spread of farming as a physical movement of people. The caste system is now considered less fixed through time than previously thought, and in general there is now a more complex understanding of the interplay of genes, language and culture through history.

What we do know is that, from about 3,000 years ago, a society speaking the earliest Aryan languages and worshipping the Vedic gods began to spread eastward along the Ganges, into what is now the state of Uttar Pradesh and then to Bihar. It was clearly a hierarchical society, with a priesthood near the top and a belief in ritual purity and pollution. The Aryans and

Aryan society of the northwest was pure, whilst the new peoples discovered towards the east were stigmatized.

There were gradations, including areas seen as mixed as well as those that were clearly beyond the pale. But despite these restrictions, people and ideas continued to move eastward, towards the lower Ganges, retroactively shifting forward the frontier between the 'clean' and 'unclean', perhaps absorbing, perhaps displacing earlier inhabitants. By the late first millennium BC, Aryan-speaking civilization had diversified: what was originally a mixed society of pastoralists and farmers of wheat and barley, led by patrilineal chiefs and Vedic priests, was transformed in the east into a society of rice farmers, organized into kingdoms and republics. It was in one of these little republics, Kapilavastu, that Siddhartha Gautama was born and it was in this region that he, as the Buddha, would teach his path to Enlightenment.

In the centuries that followed, Bengal, at the edge of the Indian world, grew into a great centre of Buddhism, with an influence that swept across a considerable part of Asia, from Tibet and Yunnan to Java. Buddhism likely arrived in Bengal at a very early date. The kingdom of Magadha, where the Buddha had lived and taught, was just to the west of Bengal. The Chinese pilgrim Xuanzang, who travelled around India in the seventh century AD, noted that nearly a millennium earlier, the Emperor Asoka had erected stupas in Bengal to commemorate the Buddha's visits there, noting the monasteries he saw, monasteries that were home to thousands of Buddhist monks.

Bengal remained a stronghold of Buddhism at a time when the religion was losing ground further to the west, first to revived and new Hindu faiths, and later to Islam. The Pala kings, who ruled Bengal from the eighth to the twelfth centuries, were devout Buddhists who routinely invoked the Buddha and his teachings at the beginning of their official records. At a time when Buddhism was dying in other parts of India, in Bengal it not only survived for hundreds of years longer but gave rise to a new and enduring interpretation of the original teachings. It is known alternatively as Vajrayana or Tantric Buddhism and emphasizes esoteric rituals and practices. Its various schools spread from Bengal throughout the Far East, including from Burma to Yunnan in China, where it was long entrenched.

The great Buddhist universities of this part of India, the universities of Nalanda and Vikramshila, were famous throughout the east. Nalanda was a very old university, founded in the fifth century, and was actively patronized by the Pala court. At its peak, it attracted scholars and students from as far afield as China, Japan, Persia and the eastern Mediterranean, and was one of the world's first residential universities, with more than 10,000 students and 2,000 teachers living in its vast thirty-acre campus, complete with dormitories, classrooms and meditation halls, Buddhist temples and carefully designed gardens and artificial lakes. Xuanzang wrote that its 'observatories seem to be lost in the vapour of the morning and the upper rooms tower above the sky'. Nalanda was said to have been an architectural masterpiece. Its library, filled with Tantric texts, was nine storeys high and served as well as a scriptorium where ancient texts were carefully copied. The curriculum covered every field of learning, from Sanskrit grammar to mathematics, and much of what today comprises Tibetan Buddhism derives from the teachings and traditions first conceived at Nalanda.

Bengal's links to Tibet and nearby Nepal were extensive during this heyday of Tantric Buddhism. They also stretched across the sea to the empire of Sri Vijaya whose kings ruled over much of Sumatra and Java as well as the Malay Peninsula, dominating the Straits of Malacca and the trade in spices from east to west. For hundreds of years this maritime kingdom was the hub of Bengal-derived Buddhism, hosting Chinese pilgrims on their way to Nalanda, as well as scholars from India, like Atisha, who afterwards played a decisive role in the spread of Buddhism in Tibet.

At the same time, control by Bengal's Pala kings over Magadha, the birthplace of Buddhism, served to enhance that dynasty's prestige as the supreme patron of the Buddhist religion. They were the gatekeepers of the sacred land. Envoys came from Burma and Sri Vijaya and elsewhere to seek permission to endow monasteries, sending jewelled treasures by ship to help restore the ancient temples.

With the decline of the Palas, Buddhism declined as well, since the new dynasty, the Senas, were orthodox Hindus. Then came the advent of Islam. In the twelfth century, bands of Turkish and Afghan cavalry, already masters of northwest India, galloped their way across the rich Ganges plain. One of these bands was commanded by the Turkish warlord Muhammad Bakhtiyar and raided and plundered many towns and cities all the way to Bengal, ransacking the Buddhist universities they encountered. Bakhtiyar's conquest was a blitzkrieg and his 10,000 horsemen utterly overwhelmed local kings and communities unaccustomed to mounted warfare. The invaders were apparently unaware of the heritage they were destroying. After one victory, Bakhtiyar's men put to death many men with shaven heads and found amongst their spoils great libraries of books. According to the distinguished Afghan scholar Minhaju-Siraj, 'It was discovered that the whole fort and city was a place of study.' It was in fact the renowned Buddhist university of Odantapuri, reduced to ruins.

For centuries after this conquest, Bengal remained an independent country, but with a Turkish-derived Muslim elite, ruling over a population still mainly Hindu, with perhaps a few pockets of Buddhists remaining. In the late thirteenth century, Marco Polo wrote of Bengal as a region 'tolerably close' but distinct from India, and its people not as Muslims but as 'wretched idolaters' who spoke a 'particular language'. The Turkish upper crust came to depend heavily on the existing Bengali Hindu nobility. Even if they had wanted to recruit more people from their original Central Asian base, the option did not really exist as Bengal was too far away. A unique mix of Turkish, Persian and indigenous Bengali and Hindu influences evolved. There were even Abyssinians, slaves imported from East Africa, who managed, briefly during a period of intense intrigue, to seize the throne in the late 1400s.

Bengal remained politically apart from the rest of India, living on its own terms. Islam spread gradually, especially in the swampy eastern areas where the writ of the old Hindu kings was never strong, and eventually became the majority religion. The sultans of Bengal also became regional powers. The nearby kingdoms of Kuch Behar and Kamarupa were annexed, and Orissa and Tripura were at times tributaries. A close relationship developed as well with the kingdom of Arakan. Arakan is today a state on Burma's western coast, but in the fifteenth and sixteenth centuries it was independent and a significant force in its own right, with a cosmopolitan court of Buddhists and Muslims, as well as buccaneers and adventurers from as far afield as Lisbon and Nagasaki. Bengal is an integral part of Indian civilization. But it has also had a long and special history, one linked in a multitude of ways across a vast region, from the Horn of Africa to the Sea of Java and beyond.

With independence from Britain in 1947 and the ending of colonial empires across Asia, there could have been a restoration of old ties, cultural and economic, to Tibet, Burma and Yunnan, and across the Bay of Bengal. But instead there has only been the severing of the links that existed. Three independent countries came into being where there had been a single British empire, the frontiers with Tibet and Yunnan were closed off, and a uniquely tenuous region known today as Northeast India was created, barely connected to anywhere else. It is only now that this separation, an unnatural and unprecedented separation, is beginning to be overcome.

The first slice occurred in 1937 when the British government formally separated Burma from the rest of British India, granting the former province its own constitution and semi-elected government. The days of uncontrolled immigration from India were over. A little over four years later came the Japanese onslaught across southeast Asia and the flight of hundreds of thousands of ethnic Indians over the mountains into Assam, the Japanese army following swiftly behind. At the end of the war, many chose not to return, seeing which way the wind was blowing and hearing the nationalist rhetoric of the young Burmese politicians who were about to come into power. Tens of thousands more ethnic Indians left at independence and approximately 400,000 others were compelled to leave in 1964, after the ultra-nationalist army regime had come to power in 1962. The steamer service that had bound Rangoon to Calcutta was by then long defunct, and few if any Burmese students remained in India's private schools and universities. The days when Burma was seen by young and adventurous Indians as a land of opportunity were gone, probably forever.

In August 1947, Bengal was partitioned. In the early 1940s as the British began seriously to contemplate withdrawal from India, the contest between the India National Congress, long the main nationalist force, and the Muslim League, which claimed to represent the country's biggest minority, heated up, and the Muslim League veered towards demands for an entirely separate Muslim homeland or 'Pakistan'. In 1946, Hindu–Muslim riots in Calcutta left approximately 4,000 dead and 100,000 injured, as the Muslim League's leader Mohammed Ali Jinnah called for a day of 'Direct Action' and as Hindu feeling rallied around anti-Pakistan slogans. Different schemes were produced by the British, including ones that would have created a very loose federal system, but in the end the British agreed to break up the empire, with the new Pakistan incorporating Muslim-majority areas on two different sides of the subcontinent. In the west, nearly fifteen million people – Muslims, Hindus and Sikhs – were uprooted and well over a million died in the ensuing confusion and mass violence. In Bengal, the partition was less traumatic, with far less violence, but the consequences were dramatic and enduring nonetheless. Calcutta was granted to India and made the capital of the new state of West Bengal, whilst a big part of the countryside that depended on Calcutta's factories and ports was made East Pakistan with its new capital at Dacca (now spelled Dhaka).

The British partitioned the country along demographic lines, between Muslim- and Hindu-majority districts, meaning that little thought was given to the economic or future security ramifications of the new border. Colonial policy-makers assumed that the newly independent India and Pakistan would get along rather well and that commerce would carry on as before. But with conflict and war ensuing straight away, the ferries and barges that had carried people and cargo every day back and forth from Calcutta to its rural hinterland, now East Pakistan, were halted, the trains and buses stopped running, and millennia-old contacts came to an end. In their place came new animosities and lasting security headaches, and an entirely artificial border (which is today being fenced) snaking across what had been the province of Bengal.

Within a quarter of a century Pakistan was itself then torn in half, and its eastern wing became independent, as Bangladesh. The catalyst was the 1970 general election in Pakistan that had led to a victory for the Bengali National Awami League of Sheikh Mujibur Rahman. In the years since independence, the relationship between the two halves of Pakistan had developed into a very unbalanced one. The West dominated the East. The Awami League's campaign was based on Bengali East Pakistan's sense of victimhood, its anger at the suppression of the Bengali language and the exploitation of its resources by the military rulers based in the other half of the country.

The results shocked the Pakistani establishment. There were worries that the Awami League would insist on a federal arrangement where the central government would be left with responsibility for defence and foreign policy only. And, for many in West Pakistan, the idea of coming under a Bengali prime minister was difficult to accept. The East also had a large Hindu minority (nearly ten million people, including many professionals) and some West Pakistanis seemed to think that these Hindus would also soon be lording it over them.

President Yahya Khan, the army commander-in-chief, postponed seating the new National Assembly. But soon in East Pakistan there were strikes and protests, shutting down the railways and airports. Clashes erupted daily between police and demonstrators and before long the army was called in, arriving both by air and by ship, attacking the university, a hotbed of agitation, and arresting leading politicians. The Pakistani army then fanned out into the countryside. Ethnic Bengali troops mutinied in several places. Foreign journalists were expelled and the Hindu minority in particular came in for violent harassment. There was a panicked flight from Dacca. Millions of refugees streamed into India.

India did not miss the strategic opportunity, and began hosting training camps for Bengali guerrillas, known as the Mukti Bahini, about 20,000 in all, including former officers of the Pakistani army. The United States, under President Richard Nixon, was sympathetic to the Pakistani side. 'The Indians are no Goddamn good,' Nixon had told his national security advisor Henry Kissinger. Yahya Khan was helping Nixon and Kissinger in their secret diplomacy with Mao, Pakistan's friend. At the same time, New Delhi was entering into closer military and economic relations with Moscow.

By October 1971 the conflict had escalated, with shelling along the border. Twelve Indian divisions were now massed near East Pakistan. The Pakistanis decided to strike first, attacking Indian positions in Kashmir. The Indians responded with massive air strikes. The Indian navy shelled Karachi. The end result – an Indian victory – was a foregone conclusion and took only took weeks to reach. The Indian army was much bigger than the Pakistani army and better equipped. The Indians rolled towards Dacca from four different directions, helped by the Mukti Bahini. The timing was advantageous. With the onset of winter, it was impossible for the Chinese to intervene across the Himalayas, something the Pakistanis may have been hoping for, whilst the terrain in East Pakistan itself was excellent for a mechanized push. On 6 December the government of India formally recognized 'The Provisional Government of the People's Republic of Bangladesh'.

Given this background, one would think that the new Bangla-desh would have enjoyed excellent relations with India ever since, but instead the two states have had only the frostiest of dealings. Ties were reasonably cordial to begin with, but soon resentment by the smaller neighbour set in. Many Bangladeshis point to India's Farakka Barrage, a giant dam on the Ganges River, as a special cause of animosity, saying that this dam, which was completed in 1974 and which diverts water from the Ganges, has dramatically and negatively affected their water supply. With the onset of military rule in Bangladesh in the late 1970s, relations soured further and Bangladeshi nationalism took a decisively anti-Indian turn. Links between the Bangladeshi and Pakistani armies and intelligence services grew closer and over the past twenty years Bangladesh has even provided support and sanctuary to Indian insurgent groups such as the United Liberation Front of Assam. In 2004, Indian Foreign Minister Yashwant Sinha described relations with Bangladesh as being at their lowest ebb ever, and even worse than with Pakistan.

Partition and its aftermath have thus left a troublesome and enduring legacy in this part of Asia. From Burma, I had seen the approach of Chinese power and influence and wondered why from India there was not a similar energy, a similar dynamic. The unique geography that was created to the east of Calcutta, the unfinished ethnic conflicts and Maoist insurgency, and the fraught relationship between Delhi and Dacca were certainly among the reasons. In this region at least, India's posture was mainly a defensive one, its strategists and security officials eyeing Chinese moves, especially into Burma, with unease.

In the middle of Calcutta, along the Hooghly River and across the *maidan* from the Victoria Memorial, sits Fort William, an imposing star-shaped complex built by Robert Clive in 1781 and for over a century a symbol of British power in the East, the Pentagon of its time. Today it is the headquarters of the Indian army's Eastern Command, responsible for eight of the army's thirty-four divisions and nearly a quarter of its more than one million men and women under arms. From Fort William British strategists plotted their wars against an array of foes from the Emir Dost Mohammed of Afghanistan, to the Maharaja Ranjit Singh of the Punjab, to King Thibaw of Burma. Present-day security preoccupations are perhaps not nearly as colourful as those of the Raj, but equally complex. And though the old British fixation on tsarist intrigues is long gone, there is in its place a not altogether dissimilar anxiety about China's intentions and China's reach for the warm waters of the Indian Ocean.

Whereas the British worried about a possible Russian presence in Tibet, Beijing is now firmly ensconced across the entire Tibetan Plateau, from the borders of Kashmir in the west to Yunnan in the east. China also maintains a very good relationship with Pakistan, and since the early 2000s Chinese state companies have been building a big new port at Gwadar, not far from Karachi, that will be linked over the Karakoram mountains to China's far west. China has also worked to deepen ties with Bangladesh and over the past few years has agreed in principle on a highway that will eventually tie Kunming to Chittagong, Bangladesh's main port. Beijing has even reached out across the Bay of Bengal to Sri Lanka, building a port there too, and started discussions with Nepal on the idea of a Lhasa to Kathmandu train.

What from one perspective is a welcome increase in intra-Asian ties is from another a harbinger of more aggressive Chinese designs to come. A US Army War College paper in 2006, entitled 'A String of Pearls: Meeting the Challenge of China's Rising Power Along the Asian Littoral', questioned whether China's attempt to secure its sea lanes, from the Straits of Malacca to the Arabian Gulf, would soon translate into a bid for regional supremacy across the Indian Ocean. Indian analysts too began to worry that China's rapidly expanding trade ties and civilian infrastructure projects could very soon become military ones as well, directly threatening India's security.

In an essay posted on the website of the China International Institute for Strategic Studies, a writer using the pseudonym Zhan Lue (or 'Strategy') argued that Beijing should work to break up India into twenty or thirty independent states, with the help of 'friendly countries' such as Pakistan and Bangladesh. Written in Chinese, the article says, 'If China takes a little action, the so-called Great Indian Federation can be broken up.' China should, he contends, join forces with 'different nationalities' like Assamese, Tamils and Kashmiris and support them in establishing independent nation-states of their own. In particular, the article asks Beijing to support the United Liberation Front of Asom (ULFA), a militant separatist group in the Indian northeast, in its efforts to achieve independence for Assam from India. Bangladesh, says Zhan Lue, should be given support to unite with West Bengal into one Bengali nation. The article was dismissed by many as representing a lone voice; others, though, had a nagging sense that it echoed more widespread if still marginal thinking.

And it is partly from a common mistrust of Chinese power and Chinese intentions that New Delhi and Washington have drawn closer together, burying Cold War animosities. The administration of President George W. Bush saw India as a potential bulwark of democracy against China and pushed hard for an agreement on nuclear cooperation, signed in 2006 and ratified by Congress two years later. In 2007, India, the US, Singapore, Japan and Australia joined together in what was the biggest ever wargame in the Bay of Bengal. Code-named Malabar 07 it was a five-day exercise that saw seven Indian warships in action alongside thirteen from the US, including the nuclear-powered aircraft carrier the USS *Nimitz*, another aircraft carrier, the USS *Kitty Hawk*, and the nuclear submarine USS *Chicago*.

And as China beefed up its own armed forces, India was doing the same, with heightened attention to its eastern flank. By 2010, India had stationed no fewer than three army corps or a hundred thousand soldiers in Assam, together with a full squadron of advanced Sukhoi 30 fighter planes, and was building up its naval capacity in the Andamans, the little islands south of Burma that Delhi had inherited from British India.

China's nightmare scenario is of the US or India blocking the Malacca Straits. But India's nightmare is Chinese naval supremacy across the Indian Ocean. And as thoughts of China grow, Burma veers towards centre stage.

Sixty years ago, India's Home Minister and Congress leader Sardar Vallabhbhai Patel in a letter to Prime Minister Nehru wondered whether India should not 'enter into closer relations with Burma in order to strengthen the latter in its dealings with China'. A similar feeling motivated India's policy-makers in the 1990s as they watched their smaller eastern neighbour being drawn fast into the Chinese orbit.

In the years immediately following the failed 1988 uprising in Burma, the Indian government took a very hard-line position against the Burmese military government, perhaps the hardest line anywhere in the world. The West was then just starting to impose sanctions, but India was already actively financing Burmese opposition groups, including exiles and militant groups based along the Thailand–Burma border. This was during the government of Prime Minister Rajiv Gandhi, grandson of Pandit Nehru, and there were generations-old personal ties that linked the Nehru family to Burma and to two of its most prominent families: the family of independence hero General Aung San and the family of 1950s Prime Minister U Nu. Pandit Nehru had known Aung San and had travelled many times to Burma as a guest and friend of U Nu. Aung San's daughter Aung San Suu Kyi had gone to school in India (when her mother was the Burmese ambassador to New Delhi) and she had just emerged as a key leader in the nascent pro-democracy movement. Rajiv Gandhi wanted to be seen on the right side of history and sincerely believed that India should assist the Burmese in the fight for democracy. Declarations of support were coupled with more clandestine efforts at political change.

By the mid-1990s, however, this hard-line approach had been replaced by an all-out effort to cosy up to the Rangoon government. There were many reasons for this, but perhaps the most important was a very simple one: the old policy had failed. The Burmese junta had recovered from its near overthrow in 1988 and Indian support for pro-democracy activists was doing little or nothing to move the country in a liberalizing direction. What the policy had done instead was leave the field entirely open to the Chinese, who were quickly becoming the military government's best friend and ally. Delhi's Look East policy had originally meant improved commercial ties between a liberalizing Indian economy and the 'Asian Tigers'. But by the mid-1990s, the Indian government was increasingly mindful of China and eager to solidify relations in the Far East. An all-out rupture in relations with Rangoon, and the emergence of a Burma dominated by China, seemed intolerable.

There is no doubt that many in the Indian government, then and now, would prefer a democratic regime in Burma. In the world's biggest democracy, supporting and being seen to support a popular movement for democracy would have been an easy sell, both at home and abroad. Many journalists and scholars I have met in India have appeared genuinely concerned by the stories of political repression in Burma and want to know how best India can help. There were Indian politicians like George Fernandez, who served as a defence minister in the late 1990s and early 2000s, and who remained a staunch advocate for democratic change in Burma, for many years even providing shelter to Burmese dissidents at his own south Delhi home. But few believed that India could simply follow an idealistic policy that produced no results, at least not in its immediate neighbourhood. In India, as in China, analysts were often scathing in their assessment of Western government policies towards Burma, seeing them as hypocritical at best and deeply damaging to the Burmese people at worst.

There was apprehension about China but there were other concerns as well. With India's economic rise, access to foreign markets and future energy security were much higher on the agenda than before. Burma was a potential trading partner and the country's economic importance had increased with the discovery of offshore natural gas fields in the 1990s. But perhaps much more important than this were concerns related to the long common border and the situation of the country's Northeast. This region has been the site of violent unrest for decades and rebel militias, many demanding secession from the Indian union, have found sanctuary within Burma's western forests. For Indian security officials, there was not only the distant threat of a Chinese-dominated Burma, but a more immediate need to secure the Burmese army's cooperation against these insurgent hide-outs. In 1993 the Indian government had seen fit to bestow on Aung San Suu Kyi the prestigious Nehru Award for International Understanding. But by 1995, after a two-year policy U-turn, the Burmese and Indian armies were mounting a joint military operation, Operation Golden Bird, against the border insurgencies.

Since then relations have warmed still further, with visits by top leaders, rising trade, and major Indian investments in Burma's developing energy sector. India has decided to move closer to Burma in part to offset China, but the Burmese regime too wants better ties with Delhi to balance Beijing.

In July 2010, Burmese supremo General Than Shwe made a high-profile visit to India and was welcomed with open arms. He travelled first to Bodh Gaya, the place of the Buddha's Enlightenment, and Sarnath, where the Buddha preached his first sermon, went on to Delhi to meet the President and Prime Minister Manmohan Singh, and then toured an IT centre and high-tech pharmaceutical plant in Hyderabad and a Tata car factory near Calcutta. Both sides declared the importance of strengthening ties, and settled on several new economic deals. India's long-standing project to rebuild the port at Akyab, or Sittwe, on Burma's western coast, was now moving ahead. So too were plans to build a system of roads and waterways linking the port to the Northeast. Tata Motors would start a factory in Burma to build its new ultra-cheap Nano cars. A project was even begun to jointly renovate the medieval Ananda temple at Pagan. All this did not, however, mean a new tilt towards India. General Than Shwe had recently hosted Chinese Prime Minister Wen Jiabao and two months later would travel himself to China. Burma's army chiefs were clearly attempting to balance their relationship with the two Asian giants and in this way gain maximum leverage and maximum benefit.

In 1958, Pandit Nehru had told American journalist Edgar Snow that 'the basic reason' for the Sino-Indian dispute was that they were both 'new nations', in that both were newly independent and under dynamic nationalistic leaderships, and 'in a sense were meeting at their frontiers for the first time in history'. In the past 'there were buffer zones between the two countries; both sides were remote from the border'. He was referring primarily to Tibet, lost as a buffer zone to the People's Liberation Army. But Burma too has long been a buffer zone and a clear-cut Chinese domination of Burma in the future could well lead to far greater tensions between Delhi and Beijing. In 2010, it was still uncertain whether Indian influence in Burma could even come close to matching what the Chinese had on offer. Much would depend not only on Delhi, but also on people and events in India's melancholy Northeast.

Inner Lines

On a map, Northeast India looks like a nearly severed hand, reaching eastward from the rest of the country. 'Northeast India' is a relatively new term. It normally refers to Assam as well as to the other six of the 'seven sister' states: Meghalaya, Arunachal Pradesh, Nagaland, Manipur, Mizoram and Tripura. These are places few people outside India even know exist and, indeed, it's hard to think of a part of Asia less well-known than Northeast India.

The region is far from insignificant in size and population, being about as big as England and Scotland combined, with over forty million people. And it's a place of remarkable ethnic and linguistic diversity, with at least twice as many distinct languages as all of Europe, with Hindu, Christian, Muslim, Animist, and Buddhist peoples, peoples who by appearance could be mistaken for anything from Spanish to Siberian. There are the Meitheis, the Nagas, the Abors, the Miris, the Bodos, the Garos, the Kukis, and dozens of other communities. Areas of Northeast India are also incredibly remote, not unlike adjacent areas of Burma. Just recently, in October 2010, a team of linguists working for *National Geographic*'s 'Enduring Voices' project 'discovered' an entirely unique language, Koro, spoken by only 800 people in a valley in the foothills of the Himalayas, as distinct from the languages around them as Persian from Portuguese.

The Northeast is essentially landlocked. Partition in 1947 and the creation of East Pakistan cut this region off from its natural access to the sea and also from the major cities such as Dacca and Sylhet with which the region had traded for centuries. Only a long thin corridor, less than twenty miles wide in places, known as the 'Chicken's Neck' connects the Northeast to the rest of India. And the region is not in a particularly enviable neighbourhood. Bangladesh, poor and densely populated, is to the south and west. To the north are the Himalayas, and to the east is Burma, poor as well, and isolated internationally for decades. And at the other side of the Chicken's Neck is not the India of software companies and call centres and Bollywood blockbusters but rural West Bengal and then Bihar, the poorest and arguably most lawless backwater in the country. Few Indian and fewer foreign tourists visit; a special 'Inner Lines' permit is needed even for Indian citizens to visit certain areas. And because international journalists are only very rarely allowed, Northeast India is almost never in the news

The Northeast is a mix of valleys and highlands. Millions of years ago, before what became India smashed into Asia, the ancient Brahmaputra River ran straight southward from Tibet into the Tethys Sea. But with the rise of the Himalayas, the great river, one of the longest in the world, was forced to make a dramatic U-turn, first heading east and then bending west, skirting around the edge of 15,000-foot-high mountains, finally rushing down through steep jungle gorges, and then emptying into the Bay of Bengal.

Before reaching its delta, the river flows through a long valley. This valley, about the same size as all of Ireland, is Assam, the main state of the Northeast, a low-lying landscape of rice fields and tea plantations, with little towns and villages, a countryside very similar to that of Upper Burma, but with the added splendour of the Kaziranga National Park, home to two-thirds of the world's great one-horned rhinos and with the largest density of wild tigers anywhere in the world. And in the way that Burma's Irrawaddy valley is surrounded by a horseshoe of hills and mountains, Assam's Brahmaputra valley is similarly encircled by upland areas. In both places the majority people of the plains (the Burmese Buddhists and the Assamese Hindus) are distinct from the largely Christian peoples of the hills.

Gauhati (also spelled Guwahati) is the capital of Assam and with a little under a million people, it's the largest (and more or less only) Indian city east of Calcutta, about 400 miles away in a straight line. In China, an equivalent trip on a newly tarred expressway or air-conditioned train might take only a few hours, but from Calcutta to Gauhati such as trip is not possible as it would mean crossing Bangladesh. Instead, the journey overland today involves a very circuitous route, taking no less than eighteen hours by train, and even longer by car or bus, first heading north and then through the Chicken's Neck, before heading east, parallel to the Brahmaputra River.

The trains are often delayed, and sometimes attacked by bandits and militant outfits of various stripes. Not long before I was there, a Rajdhani Express train had been ripped apart by a bomb blast on the approach to Gauhati. It was the handiwork of an obscure group known as the 'Adivasi National Liberation Army'. In September 2010, a train travelling through the Chicken's Neck rammed into a herd of elephants trying to cross the tracks, killing seven. There are also frequent landslides. And so, after studying my options, I chose to fly. In Calcutta I purchased a ticket on Jet Airways, a relatively new private airline. Their in-flight magazine offered pictures of lavish first-class service to New York: each passenger had his or her own little cabin, with a proper bed, endless food and drink, a flat-screen TV, and hundreds of movies to choose from. My flight from Calcutta to Gauhati had none of these things but was comfortable nonetheless. Half the people in the cabin looked as if they could be from Burma. But I knew that they were almost certainly not Burmese, but people from Assam or the states beyond. I doubt anyone took me for anything other than a local.

Assam was a place I had read about and thought about for many years. For most people, India first means Delhi or Bombay, the Taj Mahal or the desert cities of Rajasthan. But for me, as a student of Burmese history, I learned first about this very different piece of India. In the early nineteenth century, the Burmese general Thado Maha Bandula had led his armies over treacherous passes and vanquished the once mighty kingdom of Assam. Members of the Assam royal family, their officials and retainers were then marched back as captives to the Burmese court of Ava; an Assamese princess was made a consort of the Burmese king and her brother a minister. The Burmese were curious about their different ways and their knowledge of Hindu ritual, and in this way the arrival of the Assamese captives prompted fresh interest in Sanskrit tradition. But within a couple of decades came war with the British, and with the Burmese defeat and the British annexation of Assam, Assam disappeared from Burmese history. Burmese schoolchildren are taught about Bandula's conquest of Assam, but only in a summary way, as part of a listing of past victories. Nothing is taught about Assam itself or its people, and certainly nothing about the devastation wrought by the Burmese conquerors. Even in the colonial histories of Burma, Assam comes in and out of the picture over a few pages, a supporting actor in a single scene.

No Burmese I knew had ever been to Assam. But would this now change? India's Look East policy means different things to different people, but to the extent that it means a new overland connection between India and China or from India across Burma to southeast Asia, Assam is critical for its success. Together with Burma and Yunnan, Assam and the other Northeastern states sit between the great population centres of India and China. Once a cul-de-sac, Assam, like Burma, could be at the crossroads of a new Asia.

My first impressions of Gauhati were of a rural rather than urban setting, with the big trees and dirt roads that could have been anywhere around Rangoon, little wooden shacks with corrugated iron roofs, stray dogs and light but chaotic traffic, scooters and motorized rickshaws zigzagging around ramshackle lorries and white Hindustan Ambassador saloons. I checked in to one of the nicer hotels in Gauhati, the Brahmaputra Ashok, and was shown to a pleasant if somewhat musty room, with a balcony looking out onto a vacant lot. Outside, boys in shorts were kicking around a football, creating little clouds of dust, whilst a brown cow munched on a few tufts of grass to the side. And beyond was the Brahmaputra River itself, very wide and majestic, with sandy beaches and a ridge of low blue-green hills lining the far shore.

The hotel room service menu was not very appetizing. One of the large sections was titled 'Fluid Starters' and offered a choice of 'Noodle Soup', 'Cream Soup' and 'Canadian Cheese Soup'. A folder with facts about the hotel explained that downstairs there was also the Ushaban, a 'restaurant cum coffee shop' where one could enjoy 'the choicest & mouth watering dishes from Indian, Chinese & Continental Cuisines ... widely known in the city for offering the best "SIZZLERS" in town'. I put that down as a possible evening option, together with 'Silver Streak: The First Lounge Bar of the entire North East India'. On television was a news report on the visit of a government minister from Thailand and a programme about local sweets that took many days to cook. Other channels showed people in tribal costumes dancing in a studio.

Most of Gauhati is on one side of the river and along the waterfront is the older part of town, with a few colonial-era bungalows, now belonging to high officials. The British had made Shillong, a hill station several hours' drive away, their administrative seat in the region, and so there were few (if any) of the big Anglican churches and Victorian or Edwardian office buildings one associates with the more important centres of the Raj. Instead, there was a more recent and unattractive urban sprawl, with many new and shoddy-looking concrete buildings, interspersed here and there with green areas. There were also several Hindu temples in the distinctive style of Assam, oblong structures with peculiar lemon-squeezer-shaped tops.

Not far from the hotel was the Pan Bazaar, with heaps of open rubbish and great masses of tangled electrical lines overhead, like a great spider's web waiting to catch the unsuspecting people below. There were some mobile phone sellers and service providers and shops selling second-hand clothes. Later, I strolled back towards the river and around the Nehru Park close by where there were several statues of people dancing. The people in the statues seemed to wearing some sort of tribal costume, and I thought of Kunming and the statues there showing dancing 'minority nationalities'. It was a holiday and at the park and along the promenade by the river there were couples holding hands and middle-class families strolling around with their children. More children were running around a playground nearby. Across the street, a sign read 'Dr Q – First Sexology Therapy in the Northeast'.

Here in the town centre was also Cotton College. It had been founded at the start of the twentieth century and named after the chief commissioner at the time, Sir Henry Cotton. It must have been a fairly modest place then, as Gauhati was a small provincial town. The archway leading into the university read 'Cotton College: 100 Years of Excellence' and the campus itself was made up of many small buildings in a British-Indian style. I read later that the university now offered postgraduate courses in a range of disciplines from Persian to physics.

Across the way was an archaeological site. Recent excavations had found remains of settlements dating back to the sixth century. A small house stood by the entrance and when I peered in I saw three or four men watching the Australian Open tennis on a little television set. No one asked me to pay a fee. I walked around the ruins, the sound of tennis balls being thwacked in the background, tracing the old brick foundations that were still visible across the site. There was no one else there. A board explained that the ancient city of Pragjyotishpura stood where Gauhati is today.

In the evening I had dinner on the outskirts of town and on my way back passed by a little Baskin-Robbins ice-cream shop, all lit up along an otherwise dark and poorly paved road. A single car was parked in front and I could see a family inside, a man in a polo shirt, his kids in shorts, in a sort of facsimile of American suburban life. I imagined a middle-class life here in Gauhati, a house beyond the squalor, children at one of the church-run English-speaking schools, with occasional visits to Delhi or Calcutta or perhaps even Singapore or London to shop, bringing back books and clothes and toys, a generator helping at home when the electricity failed, the television and DVDs providing a continuous glimpse of the wider world, and here, an occasional treat at the Baskin-Robbins. It was a life not unfamiliar to me.

In ancient times, western Assam, including the area around Gauhati, was known as Kamarupa, the land 'Where love regained his form'. The story goes something like this. The god Daksha had a daughter who married another god, Shiva. Daksha hated Shiva and disapproved of the marriage. One day Daksha hosted a great sacrifice, and invited everyone but Shiva. His daughter attended, but was so distraught with her father's treatment of her husband that she killed herself. Shiva then became mad with grief and anger, dancing a terrible dance around the world while clutching his dead consort's body, which then fell to the earth in fifty-one pieces.

The other gods became worried and finally sent Kamdeva, the Cupid of India, to make Shiva fall in love again, forget his wife, and end his dance of death. The plan worked. But Shiva then became so angry at Kamdeva that he turned him to ashes with a fiery glance of his eyes. Kamdeva eventually regained his life and form. The place where this happened was called Kamarupa.

Many believe that one of the pieces of Shiva's consort's dead body – her *yoni* or genitalia – fell to the earth just outside Gauhati at a hill-top where there is a temple to the goddess Kamakhya. All the fifty-one places where the pieces fell, spread over India, Nepal and Bangladesh, are places of pilgrimage and worship; Kamakhya is one of the more important, a powerful centre of Tantric practice. On my third day in Gauhati, I went with a friend to the Kamakhya temple, taking a taxi up a winding road and then walking across a big car park full of buses to the late medieval complex. There had been human sacrifices here in the past, and these days there are still goat sacrifices as well as the occasional sacrifice of a monkey. I saw people leading in goats on a leash as well as a little boy carrying a live chicken. A facilitator first took us to perform a *puja* for the god Ganesh. As a Buddhist, I'm not entirely unacquainted with Hindu rituals but I needed a little guidance. Hundreds of the faithful were making their way towards the centre of the temple, ready with flowers and butter and incense, their foreheads smeared with red powder. Signs read 'No Not Offer Coconut Inside Temple', 'No Mobile Phones' and 'Electric Control Room'. There was a long queue and I was told this was to descend into the temple body itself. We paid some extra money to join 'Special Queue No. 5' but for twenty minutes the line barely moved. We politely complained, and after some discussion we paid 500 rupees more and went straight in through the VIP entrance.

The inside was dark and the humidity must have been close to a hundred per cent. We were pressed up in what can only be described as a throng of people, luckily all patient and good-natured. There was a very dank smell in the air, cut through with the odour of human sweat. A few feet away were strange sculptures, including one of what seemed to be a pregnant woman, bent over and holding a bow and arrow. We shuffled past two great silver doors, each adorned with the image of a lion. The walls were made of stone and utterly smooth from the centuries of people who must have pressed against them as we were doing now. The corridor became narrower and narrower until at the very bottom, with a crush of people behind, and the walls seeming to close in, the only light coming from a few flickering candles, we came to a moist cleft in an exposed part of the bedrock, an almost imperceptible spray of water coming from what must have once been a natural spring. We knelt down and sipped the water and then began our ascent, happy to have had the privilege.

No one knows when the Kamakhya hill and the little spring were first worshipped as a sacred site, and the very early history of the area is hazy at best. Ptolemy, writing from Alexandria in his second-century *Geography*, referred to an 'India Beyond the Ganges', perhaps meaning not only Assam but also Burma. The accounts are not particularly flattering. He said that the people of this area were 'white, with flat noses', 'stooping, ignorant, uncultivated, and with a broad forehead'. It was, he said, a place rich in gold, with tigers and elephants and the best cinnamon in the world, with robbers and wild men living in caves, with skin like hippopotamuses, able to hurl darts with ease.

Today there remain people spread in pockets around central and eastern India who speak different Austro-Asiatic languages, such as Munda, that are distantly related to Vietnamese and Cambodian, as well as lesser-known languages such as Mon and Wa in Burma. Scholars believe that in ancient times Austro-Asiatic speakers may have been much more widespread, the arrival of later migrants leaving them in their present scattered locations. Their societies, now forgotten, may have been fairly advanced. Their words for rice farming, for example, have found their way into the eastern Indo-Aryan tongues that arrived later, like Assamese and Bengali, and this suggests it was these Austro-Asiatic speakers who were the agricultural pioneers of the region.

What we do know for certain is that Kamarupa and the western areas of present-day Assam became home to a hybrid of Buddhist and Hindu dynasties, from at least the fourth century AD. The centre of the Indian world was then not far to the west, along the middle and lower Ganges, and the kings of Kamarupa were doubtless influenced by the more powerful monarchs and imperial courts next door. And it was from middle India that the great Chinese traveller and Buddhist pilgrim Xuanzang came to Assam in the early seventh century, as a guest of the Kamarupa king, Bhaskaravarman, a devout Buddhist himself, who had heard of Xuanzang's learning and piety. Xuanzang had come to India the long way around – across the deserts of Central Asia and Afghanistan. When he was in Assam, he had been away from home for more than ten years and reflected wistfully on how close he was again to China. But he also felt that it was too difficult and too dangerous to attempt to travel onwards via Assam and Burma to China, and would later return the way he had come. This was at the time when there were already the first little Buddhist and Hindu states along the Irrawaddy River, and just before the emergence of the Nanzhao kingdom in Yunnan. The route eastward from Assam was dangerous, but not closed, and for those living throughout this region, from Bengal to Dali, there was regular if limited contact and commerce. Six hundred years later, Assam would be conquered from the east, by a people known as the Ahom, who would then rule the valley, until they themselves were conquered, first by the Burmese in the nineteenth century, and then by the British East India Company.

The Ahoms had come over the mountains from present-day Burma. Ahom is also pronounced 'Asom'. It is the same word as 'Assam'. It is also the same word as 'Shan' in Burmese and 'Siam', the old name for Thailand. These different names sometimes obscure the fact that in the thirteenth and fourteenth centuries there was a vast expansion of people speaking very closely related Shan dialects, from a core region along what is now the Burma–China border, reaching south to form the Thai kingdoms of Sukhothai and later Ayuthaya, east to found Vientiane, and west to conquer Kamarupa. Much of what is today Assam, northern Burma, western Yunnan, Laos and Thailand came under a medley of closely related ruling elites.

The first Ahom king was Sukaphaa and for centuries to come, until the final extinction of the monarchy in the mid-nineteenth century, he and his heirs styled themselves as the *swargadeos* or 'gods of heaven' of Assam. Slowly, they and their court came under Hindu and other Indian influences; within 200 years Ahom ceased being the court language and was replaced by Assamese, an Aryan language related to Bengali and Hindi. But memory of their eastern origin was never forgotten and in the upper Brahmaputra valley Ahom villagers lived much as their not very distant Shan cousins in Burma and elsewhere. Their court maintained systems of government, including the *paik* system of corvée labour, they had brought with them from across the mountains. And they fought little wars against their immediate neighbours, like the hill principalities of Jaintia and Cachar. The zenith of Ahom rule in the seventeenth century was also a period of Burmese imperial expansion, but the Burmese were then focused east towards Laos and Siam. Instead, the threat to Assam when it came, an existential threat, was from the west, from the Mughals who from Delhi had snuffed out the old Bengal sultanate and were moving up the Brahmaputra.

At the time, the Mughals were perhaps second only to China as the greatest power on earth. The founder of Mughal rule in India, Babur, claimed descent from both Genghis Khan and Timur Lang (the Tamerlane of Christopher Marlowe) and had conquered Delhi from Afghanistan. His successors would expand Mughal rule across the subcontinent but failed to take Assam. The Ahoms shaped the limits of Mughal power. The Mughals were used to fighting Hindu kingdoms that had been ground down by decades or centuries of struggle against other Muslim invaders. The Ahoms, however, were fresh and at the pinnacle of their power and presented the Mughals with a very different type of warfare. As in many political systems to the east (such as Burma) the focus of Ahom administration was on the organization of manpower rather than the control of land; this meant they were able thus to mobilize quickly and move entire communities as necessary during conflict. It was something the Mughals had never seen.

From the beginning relations between the Mughals and the Ahoms were hostile. From their strongholds in Bengal, the Mughals quickly moved into what is now western Assam, stationing their forces near Gauhati, then probing and pushing further up the Brahmaputra valley. During the reign of the Mughal emperor Jahangir in the early 1600s, the two sides battled almost every year in thick jungle and along the sandbanks of the great river. The Ahoms deployed guerrilla tactics, much like those the Burmese would deploy against the British 200 years later, building makeshift bamboo stockades, setting traps, and launching surprise night-time attacks with their experienced musketeers. They demoralized the Mughals, who referred to the Assamese as 'black and loathsome in appearance' and Assam as a land of witches and magic. And, as they moved their cannon and cavalry up the swampy river tracts, the Mughals, more used to the open deserts of western India, blamed the magic of these infidels for their troubles.

The last war came in 1661. The Mughal emperor Aurangzeb had appointed Muhammad Said Mir Jumla, the son of a Persian oil merchant and a veteran of the Deccan wars, to be his governor of Bengal. With 12,000 cavalry, 30,000 foot soldiers and hundreds of armed ships, Mir Jumla soon marched north, annexing the nearby kingdom of Cooch Behar, then capturing Gauhati before routing the Ahoms in a big river battle. Within a year he was in possession of the then Ahom capital of Garhgaon, forcing the king and court to flee. He vowed to open 'the road to China'. The Ahoms then attempted to counter-attack, harassing Mughal lines during the heavy rains, but by early 1663 the *swargadeo* of Assam was forced to sue for peace. His daughter Ramani Gabharu joined the harem of the Mughal emperor (she would later wed prince Azamtara, governor of Bengal), and he was forced to surrender his western districts, as well as elephants and treasure, and become an imperial vassal.

It seemed the end of hostilities, but then suddenly Mir Jumla died of sickness and the Mughals never really followed up with another appointment of similar stature. When the inevitable disputes arose over the treaty and hostilities followed, the Ahoms emerged victorious. Gauhati was retaken. And in 1667, after what was a century and a half of on-and-off warfare, the Ahoms, under their supreme commander Lachit Borphukan, decisively routed a Mughal force under the Raja Ram Singh of Amber.

The Ahoms set the frontiers of Mughal power. From a Delhi and even a Calcutta perspective, power in India is normally seen as shaped from the west, by armies invading across the Hindu Kush. But here the map was being drawn from the east. A hundred years later, in the 1760s, the Burmese at Ava were setting the south-western frontiers of the Manchu empire, defeating four successive attempts to invade and annex their countries. In this way, these two middle kingdoms – Assam and Burma – prevented, for better or worse, what might otherwise have been a historic meeting-up of Mughal India and Qing China. And when collapse for the Ahoms finally came in the early nineteenth century, it was not at the hands of any Indian power, but from the king of Burma, who had set his sights on the plunder of the Brahmaputra valley.

The eighteenth and early nineteenth centuries were a period when the Burmese kingdom was relishing one military success after another, and Burmese generals, aided by levies of Kachin tribesmen, had marched over the frozen mountains that separated the two countries and then down into the Brahmaputra valley, smashing Ahom defences. After one early invasion, tens of thousands of ordinary Assamese were allowed to be carted away and resettled very close to present-day Ruili on the Burmese–Chinese border. In desperation, the besieged *swargadeo* of Assam, Chandra Kanta Singh, sent his sister Princess Hemo as a gift to the Burmese ruler, to become his concubine, together with a large retinue and fifty war elephants.

The Burmese accepted the gifts but continued their aggression. Burmese royal strategists dreamed of a permanent annexation of Assam and perhaps a drive further west, into the heartland of India. It was at this point that the British East India Company stepped in, declared war on Burma and, after a bloody two-year campaign, sailed up the Irrawaddy and forced a Burmese surrender. Under the Treaty of Yandabo that ended the war, the chastened Burmese were forced to surrender Assam, which then became part of the expanding British Empire.

At first, the British were uncertain about what to do with their new Assamese possession. They had gone around distributing pamphlets stating: 'We are not led into your country by the thirst of conquest, only by our desire to deprive our enemy of the means of annoying us', and promised 'a government adapted to your wants and calculated to promote the happiness of people of all classes'. But then they decided to stay, and when this was followed by resistance, there were violent reprisals. The last king of Assam, Purandar Singh, had initially been kept on as a 'protected prince' of 'Upper Assam', and given a budget of 50,000 rupees a year. When he went bankrupt, the British launched an investigation, found his court to be a 'hotbed of corruption and malfeasance', and in 1838 packed him off into obscurity. In this way the 600-year-old monarchy of Assam came to an end.

The earliest colonial administrators did not have a very favourable impression of many of the people they first met in Assam, especially in the more remote tracts. In 1857 a British soldier wrote about Assam, 'Though being used lately to see such large tracts of country without dwellings or inhabitants one almost feels disposed to fraternize with the first savage that turns up; and so far as looks go, such of the natives as I saw today, are perfect savages indeed.' Then they discovered tea.

The belt of territory from Assam to northern Burma to southern China is the only area in the world where tea is a native crop. In the 1820s, Robert Bruce, an employee of the East India Company, saw the plant growing wild not far from Gauhati and enjoyed a cup of tea with some local villagers. This was when tea was already popular in Britain and tea imports from China were weighing heavily on the Company's exchequers. Specimens of Assamese tea were sent off to the Calcutta Botanical Gardens and by 1835 the Assam Tea Company was established, with big hopes for the future. Soon, Europeans were encouraged to set up vast new tea plantations, and to bring in cheap labour from Bengal and elsewhere in India. It wasn't easy in the beginning to clear the dense jungle tracts whilst also fending off wild tigers and jungle disease. But soon the industry proved extremely profitable, and the strong and malty tea of Assam (and later of Darjeeling next door) made its way into homes across the British Isles.

Tea was to Assam what rice was to Burma. It was the British Empire's cash crop and the focus of its official and commercial attention. Other profitable businesses were later identified, notably oil and coal, but more than anything it was tea that drove British interests in Assam. There were few security concerns other than those on the borders with Tibet, and even these were minor compared with those on the Afghan frontier. Colonial policy-makers cared little about Assam's past or the preservation of its diverse languages or ways of life. Instead they saw an under-populated but potentially lucrative place, lacking people not only through the ravages of the Burmese invaders but also by a string of other little wars against smaller neighbours like Cachar and as a result of earlier nineteenth-century rebellions. Under-population, however, was easy to fix in India. And so, as in Burma, the British encouraged an influx of people from elsewhere on the subcontinent. In Burma the consequences of this demographic change would dominate politics for decades, culminating in the Buddhist–Muslim riots of 1938, the flight of ethnic Indians in the 1940s, and the expulsion of people of Indian descent in the 1960s. In Assam, the politics around demographic change remain central to this day.

Huge numbers of workers were brought in from other provinces, beginning around the 1870s. By the turn of the century, the number of people in Assam born elsewhere had risen from 100,000 to 600,000 out of a total population of two million. Initially, most came from tribal areas in Bihar that had been stricken by widespread famine. They included Mundas, Santhals and Oraons, peoples who had long existed on the margins of Indian civilization; many were now forcibly brought to Assam, in what was one of the largest organized forced migrations in history. The tea planters were almost all Scotsmen.

In the scramble for land that followed, literally nothing was kept sacred as even the burial mounds of the *swargadeos* and other high-ranking Ahoms, as well as those of defeated Mughal generals, were appropriated as especially good for cultivation.

Poor and landless Bengali Muslim villagers were also encouraged to migrate to Assam, and for decades they would toil away, their back-breaking labour transforming forest and wasteland into rich farming land. In the 1920s, 200,000 Bengali immigrants had settled in one district alone (Nagaon). Others came as well. British-educated Bengalis helped to run the tea plantations and held middle- and lower-ranking civil service positions and (as in Burma too) became local teachers, lawyers and doctors. In 1905, Bengal was briefly partitioned into a Hindu-majority West Bengal and a Muslim-majority East Bengal. It was part of a ploy by Lord Curzon to 'divide and rule' and thereby tamp down growing nationalist dissent. The effect, though, would be the opposite; the outburst of anti-colonial sentiment that followed soon forced a British about-turn. As part of this scheme, Assam had been casually merged with East Bengal. This stirred local feelings and anxiety about the future existence of a distinct Assamese identity.

And, as in Burma, the later decades of British rule in Assam would witness the emergence of complex and sometimes contradictory opinions about ethnic belonging and nationalism amongst the array of peoples that called Assam home.

Not long after I was there, on 30 October 2009, a series of coordinated bomb blasts shook Gauhati and three other towns in Assam, killing sixty-one people and wounding at least another 300. The culprits were later believed to be a splinter wing of the National Democratic Front of Bodoland (or NDFB), which had been formed in 1986 with the stated objective of securing a sovereign 'Bodoland' along the north bank of the Brahmaputra River. The Bodos are one of Assam's many different peoples and their language, related to several others in the Northeast, is ultimately related to Tibetan and Burmese as well. The NDFB see themselves as heirs to an ancient and indigenous tradition. They are also more than willing to kill innocent civilians in order to push forward their agenda.

The decades after independence have not been very good for Assam. Wartime links to Burma and China dissipated with the end of fighting. And ancient trade and transport routes to Bengal, over the lower reaches of the Brahmaputra River, were snapped by Partition. For a year after Partition, even the narrow rail link across the Chicken's Neck was severed. A long period of neglect by the central government was followed by the Chinese invasion of 1962. Isolation led to growing poverty and a sense that policy-makers in Delhi and the general public in other parts of the country cared little for Assam's plight. Assam's per capita GDP had been slightly over the national average at independence; today it is one of the lowest of any Indian state. And since independence, both the Brahmaputra valley and the adjacent upland areas have been rocked by tribal rebellions.

There has also been a large and continuous (and illegal) migration of people from what was first East Pakistan and then Bangladesh, the continuation of trends that existed for centuries and then accelerated in colonial times. East Pakistan/Bangladesh has experienced one of the highest rates of population growth anywhere in the world, and its population has soared from around 40 million in the 1940s to over 150 million today, placing tremendous pressure on land and other resources. And as there are no natural barriers between Bangladesh and India, millions of people have moved there in search of opportunity, as others had during British times. In Assam, many were registered on the voter rolls by political parties looking for new sources of support and this sapped local confidence in democratic institutions. The All Assam Students' Union came to prominence in 1979 with an 'Assam Agitation' campaign aimed at purging illegal immigrants from the voter rolls and deporting them. The old struggle against the Mughals was explicitly evoked.

An armed group – the United Liberation Front of Asom (or ULFA) – was formed around the same time with the declared intent of ending what its members termed the Indian 'colonial occupation of Assam' and establishing a 'sovereign socialist state'. In the 1980s contact was established between ULFA and other rebel outfits further east including the Kachin Independence Army in Burma, who sold arms and helped with training. Links were also established with intelligence services in Pakistan, keen to exploit weakness on India's eastern flank, and, ironically, with Bangladesh, despite the group's origins as a movement against Bangladeshi illegal immigration. ULFA set up bases in Bangladesh and in the western forests of Burma, in areas beyond the government's control. ULFA even maintained bases for many years in Bhutan, the Himalayan kingdom to the north of Assam, until 2003 when the Bhutanese army, in Operation Clear Out, forcibly expelled them.

By then, long-standing grievances, coupled with opportunities for money-making, had spawned dozens of armed groups of varying size. There was not only ULFA and the NDFB, but also the United Liberation Front of the Barak Valley, the Karbi Longri North Cachar Hills Liberation Front, the Bodo Liberation Tigers, and many more that have waxed and waned over the years, some agreeing to ceasefires with Delhi, often only to see break-away groups continuing attacks on their own. Thousands of innocent people have been caught up in the violence. And many of the militant groups, however heartfelt their initial grievances, have tended to become extortion rackets and have often resorted to terrorist tactics as well.

Several of ULFA's bases are presently in Burma, approximately 250 miles northwest of Mandalay, in the hill areas away from the Burmese army's control. The thousand-mile-long border between India and Burma is extremely porous and practically unguarded. A shadowy network of Chinese, Wa and other arms dealers and brokers, conniving with corrupt local officials, bring in arms, either from Yunnan or from the areas of Burma controlled by the

United Wa State Army. They include old AK-series and Type 56 rifles, discarded by the Chinese army as part of its modernization drive, but then sold illicitly to various middlemen, and then finally to ULFA and other militant groups in northeast India.

For many years, ULFA also had bases in Bangladesh, where its leadership was headquartered. This changed soon after the Bangladeshi elections of December 2008 and the coming to power of Sheikh Hasina and her Awami league. Sheik Hasina was keen to improve long-strained ties with India and in January 2009 she and Indian prime minister Manmohan Singh signed a broad-ranging communiqué on trade relations and improved transport links. More dramatically, she cracked down on ULFA militants operating from within Bangladesh. In December 2009 her government 'facilitated' the arrest of ULFA leader Arabinda Rajkhowa, who had been living in Bangladesh, and in May the following year, top Bodo separatist Rajan Daimary was similarly turned over. Both were sent to jail in Gauhati. ULFA's 'commander-in-chief' Paresh Barua, however, is still at large and almost certainly somewhere along the Burma–Yunnan border, possibly in Ruili.

Governments in India, Bangladesh, Burma and China now routinely talk about the need for improved 'connectivity' between their countries and sign agreements pledging new roads and more open borders. But there is already a connectivity of a different sort, of violence and criminality, which in the future may only grow.

It's hard not to compare the situation of Assam with that of Yunnan in China. There are similarities. Both are on the periphery of their respective countries and far from the main population centres. Both border on Burma and are landlocked and have traditionally been home to peoples somewhat or entirely distinct from the mainstream. And both are poor relative to the rest of India and China. But whereas Yunnan has seen significant development in recent decades and has become an engine of economic expansion into Burma and elsewhere in southeast Asia, Assam remains a troubled place, with continuing violence and an uncertain future. In Yunnan, the Chinese Communist Party and the People's Liberation Army deployed ruthless means forcefully to integrate the province and stamp out any dissent. And though the Indian army has countered insurgencies with a heavy hand, India is a democracy, has created or maintained representative institutions as well as a free media, and has at times engaged in dialogue with its armed opponents in a way entirely alien to Beijing.

For China, all roads have led to Burma. The opening up of trade between Yunnan and Burma and the strengthening of ties more generally is seen in China as a strategic hedge against over-dependence on the Straits of Malacca, as well as a way of developing a new outlet to the sea for its landlocked interior. There is no downside to a policy of maximum economic engagement. But in Assam and India's Northeast states more generally, security calculations have remained paramount and this has steered thinking as much towards a closing down as an opening up.

And whereas tourism has been a big part of Yunnan's development, tourism in Assam, whether international or domestic, remains a negligible part of the economy. Some argue for an emulation of the Yunnan approach. An acquaintance in Gauhati said:

A more confident Delhi should allow the Northeast to become a regional hub, like Yunnan is trying to be. Only this will lead to positive change and real development. But there is a fear of letting go, a fear that greater openness, greater trade with China, a road to China through Burma, will be to China's advantage.

The wife of a senior politician had made a similar point more prosaically:

Senior army chaps complained that if they allowed a road to China, Chinese forces might one day come down. I asked them – why is it always about the Chinese coming down, why can't you go up?

From afar, the reports of new roads and new connections across Burma and between India and China seemed straightforward. Perhaps it was a new Silk Road in the making, perhaps the beginning of a twenty-first century Great Game. But an additional element was generally overlooked: Burma would not be connecting the parts of India and China most familiar in the West, the maritime Asia, that runs from Bombay to Shanghai and Tokyo, via the beaches of Thailand and Bali, Singapore and Hong Kong – the Asia that is developing fast, the Asia of high-tech manufacturing, glittering fashion shows and luxury tourism. Instead, Burma would be connecting the vast hinterlands of India and China, much less visible to the outside, poor and with a spine of violent conflict running right through.

'Burma was for me the missing piece,' a journalist had told me. He was from Assam and though he had lived overseas and travelled extensively, around Asia and the world, he had only gone to Burma for the first time a couple of years ago. We were in the living room of a small bungalow in Gauhati, the bookshelves slightly bent from the weight of books and papers, the windows open to the cool breeze outside, sitting around a wobbly wooden table and drinking glasses of Johnny Walker Red Label whisky. I understood exactly what he meant, because for me, Northeast India was my 'missing piece', together with Yunnan. Though I knew a little about Northeast India and Yunnan's history before, it was not until the past few years that I had tried to learn more about these regions, regions intimately tied to Burma's past, present and future.

Part of my time in Gauhati was spent at a conference attended by scholars, students and activists from around Northeast India. I had probably met no more than two or three people from Northeast India until this time, and what struck me immediately was how similar they seemed, in appearance and manner, to people in Burma. At the conference, there was discussion of China and China's plans, in Burma and towards India. There were mixed views and many arguments. Some believed it could be a good thing if properly managed. Others believed the oppo-site. There were heated debates on the future of Northeast India generally, its place within the Indian Union, Indo-Burmese relations, and the future of ethnic minority rights. 'I bet the Chinese are not having a seminar like this and just debating endlessly,' said one participant. All agreed on the speed with which China was changing the landscape next door and that Northeast India itself was fast approaching a watershed.

In Assam I felt there was a degree of interest in Burma I had not felt anywhere else in India. People followed the politics closely, and there was sympathy both for the democracy movement and for the efforts of ethnic minorities to find some measure of self-determination. It wasn't a memory of Burma, as in Calcutta, but an intuition that Burma's future and Assam's future were intertwined.

The feeling of shared connections would be even stronger in Imphal, at the very edge of the republic.

Instruments of Accession

Imphal is the capital of Manipur, India's easternmost state, and both Imphal and Manipur have a bad reputation. A 'Protected Areas Permit', not easy to get, is required for any foreigner to visit, and few bother because of the area's history of violence and instability. 'When I went I had to have a company of Indian soldiers protecting me,' a Western diplomat had remarked by way of warning. I would have liked to have travelled by road from Gauhati. It would have meant a day by bus going over the Khasi and Jaintia Hills, past the old British hill station at Shillong, and then through Cachar, once a small independent kingdom. These names will mean nothing to most foreigners and little even to people in India, but they are names of places deeply associated with Burmese history. But I learned that foreigners were not allowed anywhere in Manipur other than Imphal itself. And so I flew, again on Jet Airways.

The outskirts of Imphal looked pleasant, with tall trees and well-maintained asphalt roads, the forested mountains visible in the distance. From the airport, I passed a sign advertising an 'International Tent Pegging Championship' that had just taken place, with a picture of men on horseback galloping across a green field. Further on was a small amusement part with a Ferris wheel and, at a couple of roundabouts, were billboards with posters for local films. Little houses alternated with open green space. The traffic was light, the sky was blue, and the air was cool and fresh.

Closer to the downtown area, though, the scene was less bucolic. Every couple of hundred yards were soldiers with slung rifles manning checkpoints. Some were in WWI-style steel helmets and surrounded by sandbags, as if expecting an imminent assault along the Somme. There was also rubble everywhere, which made some streets look like a war zone. I was later told that this wasn't the result of conflict, only that elections were approaching and local authorities were trying to make good on their earlier promises of repairing the sewers, but the overall effect was still disconcerting. The buildings were mainly ugly concrete or brick piles, rudely made, and many seemed to be unfinished. Through the chaotic traffic, cars, old buses and many scooters, I could see skinny men dragging piles of boxes on rickshaws. On top of one tiny shop was a sign that said 'Fast Food', another said 'Pharmacy'.

Stories about Manipur in the Indian media were almost always about violence. In late 2008, the Cobra Task Force of the People's Revolutionary Party of Kangleipak had attacked the local parliament with a hand grenade. Another grenade had exploded closer to the residence of the governor himself, in what was meant to be one of the most secure parts of the city. Not long after, a different armed outfit, the Kangleipak Communist Party (Military Council), had attached an improvised bomb to a scooter and detonated it in a posh residential area.

On the first night at my guest-house, a spartan but clean place in the middle of town, I could occasionally hear a distant pop-pop-pop of gunfire. On television, the local news featured a story about the police killing some militants. There were interviews with family members who disputed the police story, arguing emotionally that the men had not been killed in a fire-fight but had instead been shot after being apprehended and taken outside. Other killings were shown. The television pictures included close-ups of dead bodies as they were found, with the eyes wide open.

Any nervousness on my part about being in Imphal quickly disappeared, however, after I changed the channel and began watching *Most Shocking* on the StarWorld satellite station. It was an American programme that featured 'wild riots' and 'bedlam and brawls'. There was footage of furious gun battles in suburban California, a brutal no-holds-barred fight in Texas between several escaped convicts and highway police, and a riot at a heavy metal concert that left dozens bloodied. Imphal didn't seem the safest place in the world, but I doubted I would come across anything even remotely as scary.

Manipur was an independent kingdom for centuries. The core of the kingdom was the little bowl-shaped valley right around Imphal. At times the rulers or rajas of Manipur had not controlled much else; other times their rule had reached further, sometimes as far as the Irrawaddy River, hundreds of miles away. South of Manipur was the rival kingdom of Tripura, today another state in the Indian republic. To the west were even smaller kingdoms, like Cachar, now long gone from the map, and then Assam, the big power in the neighbourhood. And all around were tribal peoples up on the sides of the mountains, such as the Nagas and Mizos, who lived under their own chiefs and were normally beyond the writ of any king. Up until the middle years of the nineteenth century, the region was a patchwork of these modest polities interspersed with highland areas of tribal autonomy; the languages of the different valleys and hills were sometimes as distinct from one another as English from Japanese.

The Manipur kingdom was at the height of its power in the early eighteenth century. Around the time of Louis XV in France and the War of the Austrian Succession, from here in Imphal Garib Newaz had conquered his tribal neighbours and defeated the rival kings of Cachar and Tippera. The valley was then under growing Indian influence and Garib Newaz had become a devout and proselytizing Hindu. With his newly found religious fervour came an interest in all aspects of Indian culture, so pundits from north India were invited to teach the Manipuri ruling elite the proper ways of a Hindu court. New ceremonies were adopted, together with imported caste rules and Indian titles, and Sanskrit texts were eagerly translated into the local language, Meithei (related distantly to Burmese and Tibetan and more closely to the hill dialects nearby). Emboldened by his new faith and early victories, Garib Newaz then led daring cavalry raids deep into Burmese territory, reaching the banks of the Irrawaddy in the

1740s and helping bring about the collapse of Burma's tottering Ava dynasty.

A few decades later the tables would be turned and the Burmese, under an invigorated and vengeful new dynasty, invaded Manipur, not once but several times, wreaking havoc on the Imphal valley and bringing back several thousand captives. Some were the court pundits and Hindu ritualists and scholars of Sanskrit, and their descendants still live around Mandalay today.

And after the Burmese came the British. Together with Assam, Manipur was one of the prizes of British victory over the Burmese after the war in 1824–6. The British had no real interest in Manipur except for a time as a frontier state against their Burmese foes. When the remnants of the Burmese kingdom were annexed after a final Anglo-Burmese war in 1886, even that minor strategic interest disappeared. Unlike Assam, with its new-found value as a giant tea plantation, Manipur offered little profit-making opportunity.

This did not mean, however, that the colonial rulers in Calcutta would leave Manipur alone and an agent was sent to watch over the local court. In 1891, when the king was overthrown in a palace coup, the British intervened and tried to arrest the offenders. In the ensuing drama, the chief commissioner of Assam, James Quinton (who was visiting and trying to sort things out), was speared to death and the political agent, Frank Grimwood, was beheaded, together with several other British officers. Only Mrs Grimwood (who had trekked out to this lonely outpost of the Raj to be with her husband) managed to escape, protected by an escort of Gurkhas. She would later write an exciting book about her ordeal. The British counter-attacked and the result was a foregone conclusion. The coup leader was hanged on the Imphal polo ground. A new prince was raised to the throne and in this way the British entrenched their presence.

For the next four decades Manipur was an Indian 'princely state', not one of the most important like Kashmir or Hyderabad, but on the rung just below. The maharaja of Manipur was allowed to build a big palace, invited to Calcutta and New Delhi for imperial assemblies and coronations, and assured of receiving the appropriate gun salute and place at the viceregal table. There was little unrest and no real development.

Then came the Second World War and Manipur suddenly found itself on the front line between the Allies and the empire of Japan.

The Japanese invaded Burma in early 1942, driving the British up in into the Kachin Hills and then over the jungle passes into Assam. It was the longest retreat in British history. A year of stalemate followed with the front line more or less the current India–Bangladesh–Burma border. But in 1944, as the tide was turning against the Axis powers, the Japanese high command decided for a make-or-break assault on India, through Manipur. No fewer than five divisions were placed under General Renya Mutaguchi and these were joined by the forces of the Indian National Army or Azad Hind Fauj, troops loyal to the politician and independence fighter Subhas Chandra Bose.

Bose was a graduate of Cambridge University and a former president of the Indian National Congress, alongside Mahatma Gandhi and Pandit Nehru. But he had little time for constitutional politics or the sort of non-violent campaigns led by Gandhi. He had spent time as a prisoner in Mandalay jail and later sought help, first from Nazi Germany and then from Japan, forming his army in Singapore and then going to Rangoon in the wake of the Japanese invasion. He hoped Manipur would be the first step towards the liberation of all India.

The speed and intensity of the initial attacks surprised the British, who were led by the immensely capable General (later Viscount) William Slim. A mammoth Allied presence had been built up in Assam and the hills between India and Burma over the past year, with new roads linking Calcutta and the tea plantations along the Brahmaputra to the little hill towns along what was now the front line of the war. With the Japanese attack, two British-Indian divisions, the 20th and the 17th, were ordered to retreat from their positions further to the south and back towards Imphal, but whereas the 20th reached Imphal safely, the 17th was cut off and had to fight its way back into the valley. Another division with artillery was quickly flown in from the Arakan sector on the Burma coast.

Weeks of heavy fighting followed. North of Imphal the battle of Kohima would prove decisive. Troops from the Assam Rifles and the 4th Royal West Kents were supplied by air as they engaged in grim and often hand-to-hand fighting against Japanese attacks. Through much of April, the grounds around the bungalow of Kohima Deputy Commissioner Charles Pawsey, including his tennis court, became the scene of some of the most ferocious combat. It would be remembered as the 'Battle of the Tennis Court'. Meanwhile, despite determined Japanese attacks, the British were able to hold on to the hills around Imphal and by late June Allied forces were able to reopen the road between Imphal and Kohima, effectively breaking the siege of Imphal. It was clear that the back of the Japanese assault had been broken. General Slim's strategy all along had been to lure the Japanese into a trap, crush them, and then counter-attack. It worked. The Japanese had lost tens of thousands of men and were now compelled to retreat back towards the Irrawaddy, with General Slim's battalions in hot pursuit. Mandalay would fall to the Allies in early 1945. By May 1945 Rangoon was again in British hands.

I visited the Allied war cemetery in Imphal. About 1,500 soldiers, mainly British, were buried here. Many were men of the West Yorkshire and North Staffordshire Regiments. Some had anonymous tombstones, that had 'A Soldier of the 1939–45 War' or 'Known Unto God' inscribed. Others were hauntingly personal. One said 'Treasured Memories of My Husband Reg, Until We Meet Again, Darling, Doris'. On another was written 'Thinking of you, dear, Mum and Dad. Age 22'. Other tombs belonged to Canadians, Australians, Indians and even a few

Africans, like the one of 'Pvt Sudi Mirazi Chingamba, East African Army Corps (Service Unknown)'. The garden around the cemetery was beautifully attended, like all the Allied war graves I have seen in Burma. There were little kids playing along the far wall and dark grey piglets were squealing just outside. Next door was the KBC or Kuki Baptist Church, the Kukis being a tribal people who were now almost all Christian. There was a service under way and I could hear singing. I saw no other monuments to the war in Imphal, no other sign that for a brief moment Manipur was at the centre of the global stage, the 'Stalingrad of Asia'. With the end of the war, the spotlight was gone, and the roads that had carried Allied and Axis armies were soon again dirt tracks, the connection again severed between this part of India and Burma and the Far East.

As 1948 approached, Manipur was at a historical crossroads. In August 1947 the British had pulled out of India, dividing the empire into India and Pakistan. As part of an implicit deal with India's new rulers, the departing Raj had agreed that all the princely states like Manipur would be forced to join one or the other of the new countries. There were hundreds of these states, some really just big landowner estates, others the size of European countries. Conservative voices in London, and within the British officialdom in India, had hoped for a while to retain ties with these princely states, and keep them separate from any newly independent India. There would be a three-way division – 'Pakistan', 'Hindustan', and 'Princestan' – with the last remaining loyal to the British crown. But as independence approached, the idea of a special deal for the princely states came to naught, not least because this arrangement was entirely unacceptable both to the Congress Party and to the Muslim League. But because in theory they each had their own treaty relationship with the British crown, the voluntary consent of their rulers was still necessary for their states to join India or Pakistan. Whichever they chose, the princes were told, they would still be guaranteed continued autonomy. Most were too small to be able to survive outside a bigger country and their rulers, knowing this, quickly signed the 'instrument of accession'. Some, though, imagined their states as viable independent nations – states like Hyderabad, as big as France, and ruled by its immensely rich nizam, or Travancore, along the Arabian Sea. Only maximum pressure compelled the princes of these states, so long coddled by the colonial regime, to sign. The ones that found themselves within the borders of the new Pakistan (very few) joined Pakistan, the rest joined the new Indian union. One state, Kashmir, with its Muslim majority but Hindu maharaja, was on the border between the two and was vigorously coveted by both; the dispute over its future would soon result in war, and is at the heart of the tense relationship that exists to this day between the two main successor states of British India.

The ruler of Manipur also came under maximum pressure. It was hard to imagine that Manipur could regain its independence but some people in Imphal certainly hoped that it was possible. There had also been discussion of the state becoming part of an independent Burma. In early 1947 the British had decided to quit Burma and an agreement was soon reached between Burmese nationalist leaders and the Shan princes or *sawbwas* and other more minor chiefs on a new union, in which a degree of local autonomy would be respected. Manipur was certainly much closer to Rangoon, both geographically and culturally, than New Delhi. There were unhappy historical ties, but ties nonetheless. But in the end this idea did not go very far, and Manipur was essentially given Hobson's choice: join India. And so, a few days after Indian independence, the last king of Manipur also signed away any thought of a separate future.

In some quarters, there was hope that accession to India would still mean only a very loose federal relationship. The king formally handed over political power to the first elected government ever in that state. A new constitution and a legislature of fifty members was established and some local politicians believed that these new representative institutions might strengthen Manipur's claims to self-rule. This was in 1948. Burma was already independent and at civil war. But the new Indian government saw little need to grant Manipur a special place in the new order and so, under considerable duress (the circumstances are still somewhat murky), the last maharaja of Manipur, Bodhachandra Singh, 'on behalf of himself, his heirs and successors' agreed as well to full 'merger' with the rest of India. Manipur would be ruled directly from Delhi as a 'Union Territory'. Only in 1972 would it become a full-fledged state of the Indian union.

Never before in history had the sovereignty of an indigenous government in Delhi extended so far east, well beyond the traditional limits of Hindustan, beyond the boundaries of Mauryan, Gupta and Mughal rulers, almost to the Irrawaddy valley and the frontiers of southwest China.

In addition to Manipur, Delhi also had to contend with the upland regions of the Northeast, home to a mix of dozens of different tribal peoples who felt they had little if any ties to 'India proper'. In British times their homelands were ruled as part of Assam, but, as with similar parts of Burma, the British had ruled these highlands indirectly, through local chiefs. This included the Naga Hills to the north of Imphal and the Lushai Hills to the south. And again as in the highlands of Burma, local peoples had converted overwhelmingly from earlier animist beliefs to Christianity and worried that, with independence, they would be swallowed up. Many lived in areas that had been heavily militarized by the Second World War and were awash in guns. They had also no connection to the anti-colonial movement and the now ruling Congress Party. In January 1948 Robert Reid, ex-governor of Assam, was touring Nagaland when he received news of Gandhi's assassination. Writing that he felt a great 'shock of pain' he shared his grief with his host, Changrai, chief of the Konyak Nagas, only to find that Changrai had no idea who Gandhi was. Reid replied that he was the man 'responsible for

the British leaving India. It is he who got India its independence.'
'I see,' said Changrai, 'it is he who has caused all this trouble for
the Nagas.'

The Nagas would soon rebel, refusing to recognize New Delhi's
authority, and in the sixty years that have followed, literally
dozens of tribal insurgent groups have followed suit, battling the
Indian army and police. Other rebellions against the Indian state
since independence (most notably by the Sikhs in the Punjab in
the 1980s), as well as the continuing violence in Kashmir, have
attracted far more attention. The armed conflicts of India's
Northeast are little known and even less understood, not only
internationally but even in 'India proper'. The consequences,
however, have been devastating.

A Naga National Council had actually been formed prior
to independence, in 1946, and this grouping had urged the
departing colonial authorities not to include the Naga Hills in
the soon-to-be-partitioned India. Some Naga leaders accepted
the idea of full autonomy, with Delhi managing only defence,
foreign affairs and perhaps a few other select issues. But militant
Nagas wanted nothing to do with India and their voices became
the loudest. Their leader, Angami Zaipu Phizo, travelled to
Delhi for discussions with the government of Pandit Nehru, but
these failed to produce any agreement. The Indian government
was not willing to negotiate actual independence and with the
monumental choices and challenges then facing its leaders, the
destiny of these remote highlands must have seemed an irritant
at best. But, by the early 1950s, an armed Naga rebellion was in
full swing. Phizo declared a 'People's Sovereign Republic of Free
Nagaland' and soon escaped to London, where he launched a
successful public relations campaign, claiming widespread Indian
atrocities and deeply embarrassing the Nehru government. It
would be the first of many rebellions along the Burmese–Indian
border.

The conflict soon ravaged entire communities, with whole
villages displaced and thousands killed or injured. Prime Minster

Nehru intensified talks with more moderate Naga leaders and these discussions eventually led to the creation of a separate state of Nagaland, with its own elected government. This was a not insignificant concession as there were only half a million people within the borders of the new state, compared with the tens of millions in nearly all others in India at the time. Over the following years, other small tribal states would also be carved out of the hill areas of Assam, at times satisfying local feeling, at other times leading to more demands and the militarization of new, even smaller tribal communities aspiring for recognition and self-rule.

The Naga rebellion has continued up to the present, though at the time of writing there is a ceasefire between the main armed group, the Nagaland National Socialist Council (Isaac–Muivah faction), and the Indian government. And over the past few decades, the Naga insurgency has been joined by a host of others. In some places the insurgents have been quelled or peace agreements reached, but usually only for new conflicts to appear or old ones reignite. In Manipur itself there are dozens of competing armed groups, and Indian security forces barely control more than the capital city of Imphal and the road leading to Tamu on the Burmese border. As in Kashmir, the Indian army and paramilitary Assam Rifles operate under what is called the Armed Forces Special Powers Act of 1958, a much condemned and draconian law that provides Indian soldiers immunity from prosecution, and allows them to 'shoot to kill' on mere suspicion, and search homes without a warrant. The Northeast of India today is far from being a war zone, and many areas are entirely free from insurgency, governing themselves through elected institutions, with local people enjoying the rights and freedoms of any Indian citizen. But lawlessness and the rule of the gun remain widespread, much worse in some places (like Manipur) than others, driving away prospective investment and tourism, and branding the Northeast with an image of violent unrest.

The underlying reasons for all this are complicated. It's important as well to remember that the peoples of the Northeast of India have what many minority peoples in Burma still long for (and some still take up arms for), a considerable degree of local self-government within a federal and democratic state. The press is free in a way unimaginable in Burma. To watch the news in Imphal was to be alarmed by the violence shown, but at least here the violence was in full view, and official responsibility hotly debated. Yet there is still the continuing feeling by many local people, whether in Nagaland or Manipur or elsewhere, that India is an alien power and that they are aliens within the larger Indian union. The Indian independence leader and politician Jayaprakash Narayan, who travelled extensively in the Naga Hills in the 1960s, echoed this idea when he later wrote that India was not simply a state but a civilization, and that this civilization, whilst including Pakistan, did not necessarily include these frontier areas in the far Northeast, which had no historic or cultural ties with other parts of the country, their recent conversion to Christianity only under-lining a feeling of difference. It is an argument made time and again. Naga students I met talked hopefully about oil fields that they had heard might soon be discovered in Nagaland and how this might provide an economic base for independence. I asked if they meant full independence, as a sovereign country, and they unhesitatingly said yes.

Poverty is part of the problem. Per capita income in the Northeast was higher than the national average at independence. The region is rich in natural resources, including oil and gas, and the valley of the Brahmaputra is one of the most fertile anywhere. But today it lags far behind and is a world away from the new centres of economic dynamism like Bombay or Bangalore. Money itself is not an issue. The Indian central government spends far more per capita in this region than in any other part of the country; with just forty million people, or 4 per cent of the population, the northeastern states receive 10 per cent of federal funds. But the money is channelled through vast and often corrupt and unresponsive bureaucracies that have done little to create jobs or stimulate development.

Related to this is the problem of access. As we have seen, the only overland connection between 'India proper' and Assam is the 'Chicken's Neck'. But these hill states further east are even more isolated, as their only overland access is via Assam. The British built railways across India, but not here. There has never been a train line anywhere between upper Assam and upper Burma. And though these states are with a few hundred miles of China, there is virtually no trade. The Look East policy originally meant a strengthening of India's trading links eastward, but for some it has also come to mean the reorientation of Northeast India as a bridge to Burma and China and a solution to the Northeast's long decades of economic isolation.

With an improvement in New Delhi's ties with Bangladesh since late 2008, there came a possibility that Bangladesh would again provide a conduit for Northeast India to the Bay of Bengal. In the meantime, both Delhi and state-level governments saw Burma as the key. As Burma had been the solution to Yunnan's landlocked position, so too could it be for Northeast India and in particular for the states closest to Burma: Tripura, Mizoram, Manipur and Nagaland. In 2008 the Burmese and Indian governments signed an agreement to rebuild the old port at Akyab (also known as Sittwe) on Burma's western shoreline and link this port to the Northeast. The Kaladan River would be developed as an inland waterway, and from the upper reaches of the Kaladan a new road would be constructed, one that would merge with India's National Highway 54. In this way, Manipur and these most remote parts of the Northeast would soon enjoy a much shorter connection to the sea.

It all sounded good on paper, but as of late 2010, the 'Kaladan Multi-Modal Transit Transport Project' was only slowly moving ahead. It was also unclear how useful this new link would be without an overall improvement in infrastructure in the Northeast. National Highway 54 runs several hundred miles to

Assam, almost to Gauhati (and has many useful signs along the way like 'After Whisky – Driving Risky'), but has only a single lane and is hardly an important commercial artery.

There is also the prospect of trade directly with Burma, from Manipur to Mandalay and then onwards south to Rangoon or north to Yunnan. Northeast India and Burma combined make up a market of over 100 million people, poor now, but not necessarily for ever. It has not helped Northeast India to have an internationally isolated, economically mismanaged, military dictatorship next door. But neither has it helped Burma to be adjacent to one of the most conflict-ridden and neglected parts of India. Gun-running and illicit trade in everything from narcotics to tiger parts are major components of the border economy. And there has been nothing like the same investment in new roads and infrastructure. Yunnan may soon have a high-speed train to Mandalay. From Imphal to Mandalay what exists is little more than a country road. In a way Northeast India and Burma have long reinforced one another's problems. As borders begin to open, the question is whether they can now support each other's progress instead.

Imphal reminded me of Mandalay. It was early in the year and though the afternoons were warm and sunny, in the early mornings people were bundled up in sweaters and nylon jackets, some with heavy scarves and even woollen hats. It was dry and dusty and the air smelled of wood smoke and diesel. There were constant blackouts. And as in Mandalay, the palace was in the middle of the city, surrounded by a big square wall and moat.

I met with a writer in Imphal and after lunch at a restaurant near my guest-house, we drove around town to see the sites. The palace itself is now in ruins, really just a pile of bricks over perhaps half an acre, the original architecture impossible to make out. The site had been used by the British as a fort (Fort Kangla here, Fort Dufferin in Mandalay), and there was still a neat row of colonial-era bungalows, including the one used by General Slim as commander of the British Fourteenth Army. In the early 1940s there had been thousands of British and other Allied soldiers and officers living in and around Imphal, during that brief period when much of the world's future quite literally hinged on what happened over these few square miles. But before that Imphal was a place of scant importance, perhaps the equivalent of one of the larger Upper Burma towns (like Katha where George Orwell had lived), home to thirteen 'Europeans' (the British colonial term for any white person) in the 1930s. There was a tennis club but no golf course, a clear sign that Scottish commerce had not penetrated into this remote corner of the Raj.

On my second day in Imphal, we also drove around the local university, which was home to India's only 'Burma Studies Centre'. It was the second Burma Studies Centre I had ever been to in my life. The first was at Northern Illinois University, a two-hour drive from Chicago past innumerable cornfields, McDonald's and Dunkin' Donuts outlets. The centre in Imphal had published a few papers and was a reminder that for Manipur, if for nowhere else in India, Burma really mattered, not as a distant or abstract place, but as the big country next door, with a shared past, and almost certainly a shared future.

After a couple of weeks elsewhere in India, I felt in Manipur that I was back in southeast Asia. Other than the traditional saris that many women wore, there was really nothing in the scenery or in the appearance of the people on the streets that was different at all from most places in Burma, Laos or northern Thailand. Imphal was a thousand miles from Delhi, but only about 400 from Mandalay. An acquaintance said:

If you dropped a chap from here in the middle of Mandalay he could learn his way around within a few days. Everything works in the same way. If you dropped the same chap in a town in Uttar Pradesh [India's biggest state, near Delhi], it would take him months.

What was different were the heavily armed police and army patrols; the soldiers, who were drawn from the Punjab and other faraway places in India, with their different complexions and aquiline faces, looked alien, swirling around in their armoured personnel carriers, automatic weapons on display. Another difference was the fluency in English of nearly everyone I came across, including ordinary shopkeepers and restaurant staff, a testament to the excellent Christian-run schools throughout the Northeast. Indeed, the only Western-looking people I saw in Imphal were an American family I saw at a restaurant, clean-cut and led by a white-haired patriarch, who I assumed was a missionary, as he had with him a loose-leaf binder with the words 'Faith Walk' on the cover, and a big hardcover book entitled *Lead Like Jesus*.

The violence in Manipur may have had its roots in a local patriotism against New Delhi, but in the decades since independence it has changed into something much messier, blurring the line between political violence and mafia-style racketeering, and setting one local ethnic group against another. Only a little more than half of the people of Manipur are Hindus speaking Meithei, the traditional language of the Imphal valley. In the hills are other peoples, mainly Nagas (who, as noted, now also have their own state, Nagaland, further north) and Kukis (closely related to the people of Mizoram state to the south as well as the people of the adjacent Chin Hills in Burma). These hill people are almost all Christians and are divided into innumerable tribal groups and sub-groups, each with their own dialects. There are also the Muslims, called the Pangals, who are about 7 per cent of the population and live mainly in and around Imphal. It's an ethnic complexity that only a courageous newspaper editor elsewhere would want to explain.

It was like a mini-Burma. The Meithei have always felt superior to the hill peoples, in the same way that the lowland Burmans and Shans have felt superior to the upland Karens or the Kachins. Between the different groups in Manipur there are rival visions of the future. None were happy with their place in India, but this shared feeling did not lead to common action. Instead, many different militant groups sprouted up and began fighting with each other as well as with the state authorities. Many Nagas, for example, would like to see independence from India not only for what is now Nagaland, but for a 'Greater Nagaland' incorporating parts of Manipur. This notion is hotly resisted by others. In early 2010, the Manipur government decided not to allow a visit by the Naga separatist leader Thuingaleng Muivah to his birthplace in Manipur, for fear this would serve only to underline Naga claims to part of their state. In protest, Naga groups blockaded roads to Imphal bringing the economy to a standstill. The blockade was only ended weeks later after New Delhi intervened and sent in paramilitary units. To make a long and complex story short, in this little corner of the republic, with only about two and a half million people, there are no fewer than forty different insurgent militias. Some fight the Indian state; nearly all fight each other.

There are several checkpoints along the way, but people in Imphal can cross the border to the town of Tamu in Burma, about fifty miles away. And some have received permission to travel onwards, through the Kabaw valley, all the way to Mandalay. This is a recent thing. I spoke to a man in Imphal who had recently gone as part of a group tour, sightseeing, visiting all the places in and around Mandalay linked historically to Manipur, and meeting members of the Manipuri communities that still exist in the area, descendants of eighteenth- and early nineteenth-century captives and immigrants. He and his tour companions dressed up and took photographs of themselves in the costumes of *ponnas* or ritualists of the Burmese court, the majority of whom had originally been from Manipur. He said he was happy in this way to reclaim a lost heritage.

The interest in Burma is considerable. On the morning of my third and last day in Imphal, I received a telephone call in my hotel room. The voice on the other side asked to see me, introducing himself as an avid historian of Burma. 'I have read your books and would like to meet you, to discuss Burmese history and share with you some of my writing,' he said. I thought he might have been someone from the Burma Studies Centre. I was packed up and ready to head for the airport and so at first declined. He phoned a second and then a third time, each time very polite but more persistent. 'I would really like to see you! I am now only a few minutes away from your hotel!' I finally agreed and walked downstairs and waited on the front steps.

Just then, a big convoy of armoured personnel carriers pulled up, heavily armed soldiers in full armour jumping out and taking position around the hotel. An officer and a few men walked briskly past me through the entrance and then up the flight of stairs. I thought there was going to be a raid on the hotel; perhaps a militant was holed up inside. But the officer, a small wiry man in green fatigues, suddenly reappeared and reintroduced himself. 'I'm sorry I didn't recognize you right away! Thank you so much for agreeing to see me!' It was the man on the phone. He was, he said, a colonel in the security forces but also an amateur Burma historian and head of the local Manipur–Burma history association. Over the next half hour we sat down over tea, looking at the papers he had written, and talking about the importance of renewing links between our two countries. He then apologized for having to leave, saying he had to join an anti-insurgent operation on the outskirts of town, and jumped happily into his waiting jeep, before his convoy of APCs raced off in a cloud of dust.

I had noticed the billboards advertising Manipuri films when I was coming in from the airport and saw them as well all around Imphal. The men and women on the billboards looked like Burmese actors, with their slightly plump faces and elaborate hairdos. One evening on TV I saw a Manipuri film awards ceremony, and later learned that Imphal actually had a long tradition of local cinema, going back to the 1930s. In 2000, a rebel group called the Revolutionary People's Front had banned the screening of Hindi-language films as well as the distribution of all Hindi satellite channels (rebel groups in Manipur can make and enforce these kinds of edicts), saying that these Bollywood imports were a corruption of local culture, obscene, and a vehicle for the 'feudal values' of India (rebel groups in the Northeast tend to have a left-wing and puritanical bent, as in Burma). They had already banned pornography, recreational drugs and alcohol and threatened to bomb any cinema screening these wicked imports.

This has had a curious if unintended consequence: a craze for Korean soap operas. The Korean satellite channel Arirang TV is widely available and I was told thousands of people in Imphal are glued every night to the screen. People say the Koreans resemble them (the Manipuris) in appearance and that they see cultural bonds not present with 'India proper'. This may be fanciful, but these shows have become a cultural phenomenon, with young people looking up to the Korean actors and actresses, listening to Korean pop songs, and copying the latest Seoul fashions.

There is no similar trend towards aping fashions from the Indian heartland. And people not just in Manipur but in other parts of the Northeast, especially these most eastern areas, complain bitterly about what they see as discrimination when travelling to Delhi, Bombay and cities further west. India is an incredibly diverse country, with the differences between north and south India, for example, being as great as between any two parts of Europe, in culture, language, and even the appearance of the people. But people from north and south India will almost certainly be seen as 'looking Indian' by each other. People from the Northeast, though, are routinely mistaken for foreigners, as visitors from China or Japan; others say they have found themselves the target of everything from racist jokes to unprovoked violence. Here looking east wasn't only about economic policy and political strategy, but related as well to issues of identity and a search for fresh connections.

Others looked for connections in another direction. There is a group of people, nearly 10,000 strong, called the Bnei Menashe, from the hills south of Imphal, who claim descent from one of the Lost Tribes of Israel. They speak a local language called Mizo and are called the Bnei Menashe because they believe that their legendary ancestor Manmasi is none other than Manasseh, son of Joseph. They also point to a traditional harvest song, in which their enemies chase them across a red-coloured sea, as clear evidence of their Israelite ancestry. They say that their fore-fathers escaped Assyrian captivity 3,000 years ago and began a long trek to Persia, Afghanistan, Tibet and China, and from there to the Northeast of India. The idea may have started under the tutelage of Christian missionaries, some of whom had millenarian leanings. Many Mizo converted to Welsh Pres-byterianism and many others were Pentecostals. There may have also been earlier, forgotten influences, as Christianity and Judaism are not newcomers in Asia.

As early as the 1950s, some Bnei Menashe were set on what they saw as a God-directed reversion to Judaism as well as a return to Israel. They began petitioning the Israeli embassy in Burma for help. Though many in Israel were dismissive of their 'Lost Tribe' beliefs others were keen to facilitate their immigration. In recent years, nearly 2,000 have been allowed to emigrate to Israel and undergo Orthodox conversions; 7,000 more are waiting to go. Most have wound up in the West Bank and (prior to the Israeli pull-out) in settlements in the Gaza strip; and during the 2006 Lebanon war at least a dozen of these men from the India–Burma borderlands even found themselves fighting against Hezbollah.

As along the Yunnan–Burma borderland, local peoples were not just pawns on a map, but actively shaping the landscape, identifying their own interests and, as in this case, looking beyond their immediate neighbourhoods for ideas about who they were and what they wanted to be.

In November 1950, Sardar Vallabhbhai Patel, then home minister, sent a letter to Prime Minister Nehru warning of the risks posed by China via the Northeast:

We have to consider what new situation now faces us as a result of the disappearance of Tibet, as we knew it, and the expansion of China almost up to our gates. Throughout history we have seldom been worried about our north-east frontier. The Himalayas have been regarded as an impenetrable barrier against any threat from the north. We had a friendly Tibet which gave us no trouble. The Chinese were divided. They had their own domestic problems and never bothered us about frontiers.

China is no longer divided. It is united and strong . . . All along the Himalayas in the north and north-east, we have on our side of the frontier a population ethnologically and culturally not different from Tibetans and Mongoloids. The undefined state of the frontier and the existence on our side of a population with its affinities to the Tibetans or Chinese have all the elements of potential trouble between China and ourselves . . . The people inhabiting these portions have no established loyalty or devotion to India.

Sixty years later, there is no indication that people in the Northeast have any desire to come under Chinese domination. Militant groups have received Chinese training and support, at least in the past, but this was done opportunistically and not out of any special affinity to Beijing. Indeed, in many of my conversations, there was more a sense of dread that, with China's growing stature and influence, the little nationalities caught between 'India proper' and China would find it harder, not easier, to maintain their separate identities and traditions.

The Chinese economic steamroller appeared unstoppable, drawing in natural resources, dominating everything in its path. If even rich and giant economies like the US were wary of China's growing might, what hope, people said, did places like Manipur have, when, in just a few years' time, the roads will be complete, and China just a day's drive away?

It is a line of thinking that is perhaps a little defeatist. After all, as we have seen, China has a raft of challenges of its own and Yunnan, though far more developed now than either Burma or Northeast India, is still poor. And the quiescence of Yunnan's many minority peoples is at least in part due to the country's phenomenal economic performance in recent years, something that is not guaranteed to continue. In early 2011, New Delhi began peace talks with both ULFA and the Isaac–Muivah faction of the National Socialist Council of Nagaland, two of the most powerful insurgent groups remaining in the Northeast. What if a peace actually comes to Northeast India, after six decades? The peaceful and democratic Northeast, with its ethnic and cultural diversity, would be a compelling example for others. China has been unmatched at building new infrastructure, and its roads through Burma may well bring an era of Chinese ascendancy. But roads go two ways, and in a slightly different world, it could well be India or even Burma that influences Yunnan's future, as much as the other way around.

The old frontiers that had long separated India and China were coming to an end and, in their place, a new crossroads was being made.

Epilogue

From Rangoon the road, a good two-lane metalled road, first curves around the Gulf of Martaban, past little towns and villages and seemingly endless fields of rice paddy, then crosses the mile-wide Salween River, before heading straight south, down the Tenasserim coastline. Burma is shaped like a kite and Tenasserim is its long and narrow tail, 670 miles long. On one side are the warm waters of the Andaman Sea and the Bay of Bengal. Madras is on the far shore. And on the other side of Tenasserim are the limestone mountains that separate Burma from Thailand, some with peaks over 5,000 feet high. There has been considerable commercial logging in recent years, but many of the mountains and the little valleys in between are still densely forested, with teak and bamboo, and remain home to herds of wild elephants, Malayan tapirs and perhaps even a few dozen Indochinese tigers, on the brink of extinction. During the monsoon, torrential rains soak the region. Most of the rest of the year it's sunny, hot and humid.

With a population of about half a million, Moulmein is the largest town along the coast, and a five-hour drive from Rangoon. Its setting is spectacular, with the land rising dramatically behind and big and small islands spread across the massive and gently rounded bay in front. In the early nineteenth century, it was briefly the capital of British Burma, a port of some significance, and a starting point for the American Baptist missionaries who set out to convert the Karen tribal peoples in the hills nearby. There are still many churches – Anglican, Roman Catholic, Methodist and Baptist – as well as a European cemetery that looks like a haunted graveyard from a Hollywood film, darkened from the shade of the overhanging trees, with broken tombstones and the statues of angels, their wings now covered in dirt and mould, peering out from the overgrown vegetation. One tombstone, its engravings barely readable, records the death of one Mary Eleanor Malcolm, who died in 1886, aged 48, as well as her daughter Lucy Harriette, aged 18, who died ten days later. Many others also record young deaths, likely from disease.

Rudyard Kipling stopped briefly in Moulmein in 1889 and it was Moulmein that inspired his poem 'The Road to Mandalay'. The town was also where George Orwell served as an imperial policeman, in the 1920s, and is the location for his essay 'Shooting an Elephant', which begins: 'In Moulmein, in Lower Burma, I was hated by large numbers of people – the only time in my life that I have been important enough for this to happen to me.' And it was to Moulmein that the Japanese army during World War Two built their notorious railway line, across the 'Bridge over the River Kwai', from Bangkok over the mountains, an effort that left 90,000 Burmese and Thai workers and over 16,000 Allied POWs dead.

Today it's a sleepy town, its wide streets, laid out in a grid pattern, lined with fruit trees and tall and slender palms. Several of the colonial-period buildings, with their gabled roofs and whitewashed and ornamented stucco façades, have been remade into government offices; one is a museum, with a few ancient and medieval artefacts and many more gorgeous eighteenth- and nineteenth-century statues of the Buddha. There is a new hotel, the Attran, and about a hundred yards away a tiny internet café, with half a dozen kids playing computer games. Along the waterfront, a recent fire destroyed many of the old shops but otherwise the town seems little changed from what I imagine it was like during Orwell's time. Golden-spired pagodas dominate the higher ground, and there is as well an exquisite nineteenth-century Buddhist monastery, built by an exiled Burmese princess in the 'Mandalay style', its teak walls slightly bent with age, its priceless murals fading away. The faces on Moulmein's streets are Indian as well as Burmese, a product of colonial times when many Indian immigrants made the town their home. At the covered market, fishmongers, all women, sell the day's catch from big wicker baskets.

Sleepier still is the town of Tavoy, 180 miles to the south. It's a little town, utterly dark at night from the lack of electricity, and shut off on three sides by high mountains. There are several British-era bungalows, all made of teak, including a fairly grand one, with orchids blooming in the garden, that was once the home of the British district commissioner. Nearby are small farms of cashews and mangoes. And then there is the sea, just a couple of miles to the west of the town centre, with picture-perfect beaches of white sand, the water as still and warm as a bath. Tiny wooden fishing boats float in the distance. About 450 miles to the south is the Thai island of Phuket, crammed with five million visitors a year, from international movie stars and European royalty to gap-year students and backpackers on $5 a day. But here, and in the dozens of islands offshore, the beaches, at least as beautiful, are virtually empty and pristine.

Perhaps not for long. In October 2010, the governments of Burma and Thailand revealed plans for the development of a massive industrial complex along the Tenasserim coast. Some $8.6 billion will be invested in the basic infrastructure. Another $58 billion in investments is meant to follow. The complex will include a deep-sea port, steel, fertilizer and petrochemical plants, and an oil refinery. A new highway will cut through the mountains to Bangkok. There would be tourist resorts as well, on a giant scale. Tavoy would be ground zero.

There are justifiable worries that all this will devastate the environment. And indeed, the Thai government has said that its prime motivation in supporting the project is to move environmentally damaging industries from Thailand to Burma. There are worries too about the fate of local people, especially the small farmers who stand to lose their land, for little or no compensation.

Its backers, though, say that the new Tavoy complex will create 'millions' of new jobs. Burmese officials and businessmen hope that it will emulate Shenzhen, China's first 'Special Economic Zone' that in the 1980s pioneered its epic industrialization. The plan is tied to Chinese schemes further east. Over the coming few years, Chinese companies hope to build new railway lines from Yunnan directly south to Laos, Thailand and Cambodia. A highway will then join these railway lines to Tavoy and the Indian Ocean. Container ships, piled high with goods from China's Pearl Delta, will be able to sail directly to Europe, making unnecessary the long route around the Straits of Malacca. Oil tankers from the Middle East will be able to dock here as well, the refined oil then transported over the mountains to Thailand and elsewhere. There is a link to India too: the highway will continue on from Tavoy to Moulmein, and then across central Burma to Manipur and Assam.

And as new plans are being made, older plans are being realized. Away to the north, off the Arakan coast at Ramree Island, the construction of another deep-sea port has begun, as well as of the oil and gas pipelines that are to run from there to China. Beginning in 2013, up to half a million barrels of oil a day, oil from Africa and the Persian Gulf, will be transported through this pipeline to Kunming. In December 2010, Chinese authorities announced that the Burmese government would be given 50,000 barrels of oil a day as a fee for the pipeline and that China and Burma together would build an oil refinery near Mandalay. By 2015 a high-speed railway line, long discussed, will finally be completed, and will allow people and cargo to travel from Ramree Island, via Mandalay, to Yunnan. Burma will be southwest China's back door to the Indian Ocean. The Chinese have also started work on repairing the old Stilwell Road, from the Chinese border through the Kachin Hills, right up to the Indian state of Arunachal Pradesh.

And India too is finally moving ahead with its plans, including the $400 million Kaladan 'multi-modal' project, that will link, by river and highway, an upgraded port at Akyab (just north of Ramree Island) to its state of Mizoram. By 2015, goods from Calcutta and India's other eastern ports, as well as from Indonesia, Malaysia and Singapore, will start to move via Akyab to India's hitherto landlocked Northeast. Talks have even progressed between China and Bangladesh. During a 2010 visit by Bangladeshi Prime Minister Sheikh Hasina to Kunming, it was agreed in principle that the new railway from Kunming to Ramree would be connected all the way to Chittagong in Bangladesh, joining up Yunnan and Bangladesh's 150 million people. With improved ties between India and Bangladesh, there is even the possibility that this new corridor will extend all the way to Calcutta.

What was barely discernible just a few years ago is now a readily visible fact: Burma, long a barrier between the great civilizations of the east, is becoming a new crossroads of Asia.

The hotel was full – the same hotel in downtown Rangoon where I had stayed two years earlier. Then, the only people staying there were UN officials and other aid workers, pulling up in Landcruisers, carrying laptops and folders, together with a scattering of Chinese and other businessmen. Now there were hundreds of holidaying tourists, mainly Asian, but also many Americans and Europeans. The glass counter on the side of the lobby that sold quiche, cakes and croissants had been remade into a sort of gingerbread house, with decorated pieces of cardboard making up the sides the new 'house', and the two women inside wore red Santa Claus hats, as did the waitresses at the adjacent café. There was a small Christmas tree next to the reception area, and a special Christmas dinner was offered at the main restaurant, featuring roast turkey and a selection of wines. A 'Merry Christmas' banner was draped over the main entrance.

I had checked in together with a coachload of young Spaniards, sunburned and spotty, and noticed later big tour groups of Koreans, Thais and Italians as well. And over the next few days, all around the city, I saw more tourists than I had ever seen before: a group of elderly Australians, the men in shorts, both the men and women in hats, examining the old colonial buildings along the Strand; linen-clad German and French shoppers bargaining for Burmese *longyis* and lacquerware at the Scott Market; and well-heeled Americans, often with their own private guides and cars. Not only were all the main hotels full, but so were the six flights a day from Bangkok. A friend who owned a small travel company said the 2010–11 'high season' was shaping up to be the best ever for Burmese tourism.

There were other signs of a sharp upturn in business. Several new shopping malls had just been completed, and along Prome Road, the main artery into the city, several large apartment complexes were being built. There was construction everywhere, and property prices were shooting up. In the more fashionable parts of town, four-bedroom houses were now selling for over $2 million and buyers were paying in cash. Electricity supplies were also more regular – close to twenty-four hours a day for the first time in decades – thanks to a newly built dam as well as a small natural gas pipeline that had just been completed. The streets downtown were crowded with billboards advertising movies, clothes, cosmetics and household appliances and even the cars on the street seemed slightly improved, with many new four-wheel drives and luxury saloons.

In the cool winter sunshine, with Christmas decorations all around, and New Year parties just around the corner, it was easy to conclude that Rangoon was better off than two years before, just after Cyclone Nargis. But Rangoon on the surface is not necessarily a good indicator of the more general Burmese economy. There was definitely a lot of new money. Some of this was down to just one source – the sale of jade to China, which through 2010 and early 2011 had netted over $4 billion, with some of the money going to the government in taxes, but most going to well-to-do businessmen, Burmese and Chinese, who had then invested the money in property or splurged on expensive new cars. But it was at best uncertain whether the lives of the vast majority of people, beyond say the top few hundred thousand, were improving at all. Income inequality was likely increasing, not decreasing, and by all accounts poverty in the countryside, and even for Rangoon's working classes, remained dire.

The country's first election in twenty years had been held on 7 November. It had been a carefully choreographed process, and so, as expected, the pro-junta Union Solidarity and Development Party, or USDP, won by a landslide, capturing approximately 80 per cent of the seats contested. A number of ethnic-minority based parties had done well in their own regions (one actually winning control of the regional legislature), but all the other independent parties had fared extremely poorly.

The USDP had entered the elections with an enormous financial and institutional advantage and had fielded candidates in every constituency, whilst high registration fees kept most independent parties from competing in more than a small minority. There were also widespread allegations of vote-rigging, especially in Rangoon, and no international monitoring except at a handful of polling stations. There were other factors as well. The leadership of the USDP were nearly all recently retired army men, but most of their candidates were drawn from small-town elites, businessmen and others, with their own money and bases of support. And the opposition itself was divided. Aung San Suu Kyi's National League for Democracy had split over the issue of whether or not to compete in the elections, with those in favour forming a new National Democratic Front and the rest supporting a boycott of the polls. Many who might have voted for the small number of opposition candidates chose instead to stay at home.

And then, on 17 November, just a week after the election, Aung San Suu Kyi was released after more than six years under house arrest. Over the next few weeks, she gave dozens of interviews to foreign media, repeating many of her old messages on the need for 'unity' and calling for a 'peaceful revolution' towards democracy. Western diplomats, one after another, went to see her to ask her advice on the way forward. But she was now more of a global icon, with an almost cult-like status, than the leader of a political movement within Burma. Her personality and her story of sacrifice, the inspiration she offered and the moral virtues she espoused, seemed to matter more to her supporters, at home and abroad, than did any ability to move facts on the ground. Three months later, she seemed to be still judging the new environment, waiting for the new government to form, undecided about what her strategy should be.

The breakaway National Democratic Front, now in parliament, appealed for an end to Western sanctions, saying they were hurting ordinary people more than anything, and this appeal was echoed by all of the independent and ethnic-based parties that had run in the elections. Aung San Suu Kyi's NLD, however, disagreed. They have argued that sanctions are the only card she has left to play in any future talks with the new government. They say that the new government was in any case little more than a façade for the continued rule of General Than Shwe, and that though there would be a new president and a parliament with some opposition parties represented, these new institutions would have little real authority. Others argue the opposite and say that the creation of a quasi-civilian government may still be the first step towards better government and better economic management. They argue as well that, in any case, the collateral damage wrought by sanctions on ordinary people has been tremendous, and far greater than any putative effect it has had on the regime itself. The new president, retired general Thein Sein, and his government were sworn into office in March 2011, and the president began by calling for urgent economic reforms, an end to corruption, and political reconciliation. This boosted the expectations of some. Others remained sceptical.

There was also much more talk about China, certainly more than two years before, a general uneasiness over China's economic grip on the country, and an awareness that a watershed was quickly approaching. But the future is impossible to predict. One only has to remember the self-assured predictions in the 1950s about Soviet economic might or in the 1980s about Japanese global economic domination, or the equally confident predictions a century back that Argentina and Austria-Hungary were destined to be world powers. It's not difficult to explain the present situation: Burma's anxieties regarding China, the impact of its unfinished civil war, the reasons for China's push southwest from Yunnan to the sea, India's preoccupation with security in the Northeast and its worries over China's presence in Burma. And it's not difficult to see why it is China, via Yunnan, and not India, via its Northeast, that is the bigger influence over Burma today. What is far less certain is what exactly will happen over the coming decades, when India, Burma and China begin to weave much more closely together. There is no historical precedent for the epic moves that are now unfolding.

And in the middle of this drama, Burma's rulers continue to play their balancing act, trying to secure the best possible deals from Beijing, whilst cultivating other potential partners and allies. But no one else can really compete with China, at least not for now. In addition to the new pipelines, roads and railway, Chinese government agencies and state firms have offered loans worth billions of dollars and help on everything from new IT and telecommunications infrastructure to a major expansion of the country's electricity grid. As part of this balancing act there remains the desire, by at least some in the Burmese government, to improve relations with the West, but the United States, together with the United Kingdom, have both tied their policies very closely to Aung San Suu Kyi, and have stood firm on sanctions, denouncing the recent elections as a sham and demanding further but only vaguely defined political reforms before any relaxation of sanctions can even be considered. In late 2010, just prior to the elections, General Than Shwe retired nearly the entire top brass of the Burmese army, replacing them with much younger men in their late forties and early fifties. They will be the first generation of army leaders never to have been to the West. China will undoubtedly roll out the red carpet for them soon. In October 2010, US Senator Jim Webb said that the US shouldn't allow Burma to become a 'Chinese province'. But many Western politicians have been happy to view Burma as a simple morality play and a useful issue on which to appear 'tough' on human rights. The actual consequences of a policy that has long failed to deliver results are not important.

So what of the future? Burma will probably see some sort of economic growth, whether Western sanctions remain in place or not. Democratic government itself is almost certainly a long way away, but there could be an improvement in economic policies, increased aid and investment, and perhaps even some success at reducing poverty, creating jobs, and training a new generation of skilled workers. Burma is naturally very rich in the very commodities that will be most valued in the twenty-first century, including food and energy, and China will likely bankroll any efforts to exploit these resources. What's unclear is whether the majority of Burmese people will benefit at all.

An even more important asset is the country's strategic location, between China and India, and this more than anything could provide tremendous opportunities going forward, for the entire country. But using this opportunity, to the benefit of ordinary people, will require a basic reorientation: an end to decades of armed conflict and a willingness by elites to see the country's ethnic and cultural diversity as an advantage, and not simply a problem to be managed; a new cosmopolitan spirit in place of the xenophobia that has dictated Burmese policy for generations; and perhaps more than anything, a strong and effective government that enjoys the trust and confidence of its people.

There are different scenarios for the future of Burma and the region. In one, Western sanctions stay in place, and they reduce the influence of Western democracies to near zero. Burma remains the only country in the region without access to Western markets and Western learning and grows economically, but mainly as a supplier of primary commodities to China and as China's corridor to the Indian Ocean. Chinese interests are served in the short term but in the longer term anti-Chinese sentiment increases; the opportunity for a friendly and mutually beneficial relationship, so important to Burma, is lost. At the same time, China's tightening hold over Burma alarms India and other states in the region, and this fuels new and old rivalries, even as trade increases. Conflicts in the area, in Northeast India and northern Burma, remain unresolved, and one or more of the Burmese ceasefires breaks down, leading to a new cycle of violent conflict, perhaps drawing in the big powers. Yunnan is not unaffected, and all cross-border problems, from gun-running to narcotics trafficking to the spread of infectious diseases, intensify. Burma is unable to manage its multiple political, economic and environmental challenges. A crossroads is established, but a dangerous one.

But there is another, happier scenario, one which sees real progress in Burma coupled with a quick end to Western sanctions. Development is more balanced, environmental destruction is minimized, efforts at reducing poverty win international support, and a rising middle class lays the foundations of more democratic government. The ceasefires are transformed into a sustainable peace and ethnic minority grievances are addressed. Peace comes to Northeast India as well, for the very first time since independence. Yunnan benefits from a more prosperous Burma, but as part of a more equal relationship, and this leads to a renewal of long-dormant cultural ties. Borders are opened and governments are able to cooperate and together address the challenges these open borders present. In Burma, where China meets India, a unique meeting place of cultures and peoples is created, at this new centre of the Asian world.

Progress in Burma would be a boon for the region. A peaceful, prosperous and democratic Burma would be a game-changer for all Asia.

Afterword

During the early morning of 19 August 2011, Daw Aung San Suu Kyi, accompanied by an aide and officials from the 'Special Branch' of the police, departed by car from her lakeside villa in Rangoon, heading first across the city's leafy and sprawling suburbs, then some 250 miles north along a concrete four-lane motorway, past endless dark green paddy fields, soaked in the monsoon rains. Her destination was the purpose-built capital Naypyitaw, and she had never been there before. Most probably she and her companions stopped about halfway at the 'Feel Restaurant', which offers strong coffee and savoury Burmese snacks, before continuing on for a couple of more hours, and finally veering right towards the new city, just before a big sign informing drivers that the way onwards was the road to Mandalay.

Her ostensible reason for going was to attend a workshop on 'rural development and poverty alleviation'. But the real motive was to see the new president, U Thein Sein, the meeting having been discreetly arranged over the preceding few days.

And so, after attending a session of the workshop and chatting over the coffee break with an assortment of business leaders, bureaucrats and ex-army officers, she was ushered across town to the gargantuan President's House, with its Corinthian columns and marble floors, for the first face-to-face meeting between a Burmese had of government and the world-renowned Nobel Laureate in well over a decade.

The photograph provided to the press afterwards showed the two together, each with a half smile, she wearing the green ID card of the poverty workshop, and behind both a prominent portrait of Aung San Suu Kyi's father, the nationalist hero General Aung San. After a long conversation, the two then walked together to the president's private apartments, where she was warmly greeted by his wife.

It was a turning point. The meeting had come after a tense couple of months, when no one could say for sure which way the wind was blowing. She had been planning a tour around the country, without official permission, and this would have risked arrest, and perhaps a new round of anti-government protests and repression. But the discussion had been a success. Speaking later to journalists, she offered the president public praise. And he would subsequently allow her party to organize as it pleased.

Other measures soon followed. The party registration law was amended to the satisfaction of the National League for Democracy and the party then duly registered. And in September and January, hundreds of political prisoners were released, including all prominent dissidents. This was all part of the understanding that President Thein Sein and Aung San Suu Kyi had reached. She repeated often in public that she felt he was 'genuine' in his commitment to a better future. More discreetly, she held back opposition activists who wanted to take to the streets.

The president was at the same time making one audacious move after another. All restrictions on a once heavily restricted internet were lifted. Media censorship was relaxed. Exiles were invited to return and a few even became advisers to the government. Perhaps most daringly, on 30 September, U Thein Sein sent a message to parliament, called the *Hluttaw* after the old daily conference of the king's ministers, to announce that he was suspending work on multi-billion-dollar Chinese dam project at Myitsone, in the far north. For years the local Kachin people had been complaining about the dam, which had displaced thousands from their homes.. And for months activists in Rangoon been issuing dire warnings about the dam's environmental impact. But few dared believe that the president would actually stop work on the dam, and risk Beijing's ire.

It turned out to be a master-stroke, at once confirming the

president as a man who listened to the people, and perhaps as importantly, signalling to the West that this was a government no longer comfortable with China's embrace. Not coincidentally, Burma's chairmanship of Asean in 2015, until recently a very controversial thing, was confirmed at a summit of leaders in Bali, Indonesia, in mid-November. President Obama had recently declared that with the winding down of the US presence in Iraq and Afghanistan, Asia would become the new 'top priority'. Less than a fortnight later, he dispatched Hilary Clinton, the first American Secretary of State to visit Burma since John Foster Dulles in 1955, partly as a mark of Washington's support for the reforms underway, but also as a sign of a heightening US engagement in China's backyard.

Secretary Clinton's trip was followed by an avalanche of other VIP visitors, from billionaire philanthropist George Soros to British Prime Minister David Cameron and UN Secretary-General Ban Ki-Moon. Tourist numbers shot up as well, and Condé Nast pronounced the country 'a destination to watch in 2012'.

There were important moves as well towards reforming the economy, such as a move in April to abolish the old and absurd exchange rate system and begin a managed float of the currency. Hundreds of businessmen were soon arriving, anticipating an end to Western sanctions, and scouting new opportunities. Flights and hotels were booked solid for weeks and house rental prices soared to well over $10,000 a month.

And it was discussion of the economy that dominated parliament, which, far from being a rubber-stamp, emerged as a dynamic new institution. Laws were passed legalizing trade unions and permitting freedom of assembly. Other legislation was hotly debated, including on land rights and local administration. Some had feared that the quarter of seats held by military appointees would be used to stymie reform, but the men in uniform did nothing of the sort. The only bill they themselves introduced was one on orthography, the responsible member calling for more disciplined spelling in the media. Many supported a motion calling for the release of all political prisoners. Ministers were grilled and the budget – the first national budget presented to a Burmese parliament in half a century – was carefully scrutinized, and then passed only after the government agreed to major amendments.

I remember that on the same day that week, a bespectacled old shopkeeper and a former general, now a government minister, both said to me the same thing: 'Now there is no going back.'

The armed conflicts also received attention. The ceasefires, most in place since the late 1980s and early 1990s had begun to unravel. President Thein Sein made clear that he wanted not only a new set of ceasefires but also a quick process towards a final peace settlement with all the ethnic armies. In the south, along the Thai border, there was considerable success. Not so however in the north, where the eighteen-year-old truce with the Kachin Independence Army crumbled, and bloody clashes forced tens of thousands to flee from their homes.

All told, however, there had been remarkable progress, far exceeding expectations. It was a process of reform from the top, perhaps more reminiscent of democratic transitions in Latin America in the 1980s than the colour-coded uprisings of more recent times. Many Western observers seemed caught entirely by surprise. A year before, they had been dismissing the new constitutional set-up as a 'sham' and railing against any notion that it might yet open the door to change. The new developments seemed to come out of the blue. Except, of course, they didn't.

The constitution had been in the works for years, as had preparations for the army to take a step back from government. General Than Shwe's decision to retire was well known, but so little were the inner workings of Naypyitaw understood that few gave this any weight, or appreciated the vacuum this would create. Growing diplomatic engagement had helped. So had the growth of the aid community and local non-governmental organizations since Cyclone Nargis, as well as the willingness of local media to constantly test the envelope of censorship.

There were new factors as well, not least the Arab Spring, which focused minds and taught two lessons. The first was that reform had to be real. The second was that reform had to be properly managed and well paced.

President Thein Sein made a enormous difference too. A former regional commander, he had risen up through the ranks as a loyalist, a hard worker, a quiet man who had little personal ambition. He was also seen as utterly clean, in a system not known for its lack of corruption. A different person facing the same set of strategic choices may well have taken the country in another direction. But he saw himself from the start as the architect of a unique political transition, one that would include reconciliation with the opposition.

The biggest reason though was the fact that Burma by 2011 was a far less isolated place, in spite of sanctions, than just twenty or even ten years before. Satellite television was present in nearly every village, and thousands of people were travelling each week to Bangkok or Singapore, for work or pleasure. The country's lowly position and the possibility of a very different future were plain for everyone to see.

On 1 April, by-elections were held for forty-five vacant seats in parliament. Aung San Suu Kyi campaigned hard, despite illness, and her star attraction was clear from the huge crowds that came out to hear her speak. The result was a landslide win. It was a testament to her personal popularity, as well as a vote of confidence in the process unfolding. And the willingness of the government to tolerate a major electoral loss was also seen a further mark of its reformist credentials.

The rewards were not long in coming. The European Union announced an end to all sanctions other than the arms embargo. Norway and Australia did the same. The US administration was hamstrung by its web of sanctions-related legislation, but promised to begin peeling away a number of key restrictions, including on assistance from the World Bank and other international financial institutions.

It was Japan, though, that moved most uncompromisingly. In late April 2012, President Thein Sein was welcomed to Tokyo, the first Burmese leader to visit in a quarter of a century. The Japanese agreed to write off more than $4 billion in past debt and announced fresh multi-billion-dollar loans. Big Japanese companies like Marubeni, Honda and Mitsubishi were quickly setting up shop in Burma, and Japan now schemed to build a giant industrial zone as a future home for their manufacturers, just to the south-east of Rangoon, at the port of Syriam, where in the early seventeenth century, the Portuguese adventurer Filipe de Brito briefly held sway, dominating trade along the Bay of Bengal littoral, until defeated by a rival Burmese prince and impaled on a nearby hill.

The happier scenario I sketched at the end of the last chapter is now not impossible. It is perhaps one critical step closer to reality. But it's still far from assured, and if I were honest, I would say it's still not likely.

There is now at last the political will to reform, but this reveals more clearly than ever what aid officials euphemistically term the lack of 'capacity', meaning educated and experienced people. This was underlined at a conference I attended in February, where a guest of honour was ninety-one-year-old Dr Hla Myint, a erstwhile acquaintance of John Maynard Keynes, a rector of Rangoon University in the early 1950s (when it was one of the best in Asia), and for three decades a leading professor at the London School of Economics. He had advocated export-led growth, long before it had become fashionable, and it must have been a cruel thing for him to see his country take an entirely different path and as a result become so impoverished. After the army takeover he had sworn never to return, but then did, a few months ago, wearing a tweed jacket in a sea of Burmese silk and cotton-clad officials, egging on the reformers in government, and warning in a now frail voice that this lack of 'capacity', was an Achilles heel that could still do much damage.

In the coming months and years there will probably be a

huge influx of aid and investment. But the ability to make good use of both these things may not exist. The Burmese economy is like a little plane, denied for decades any repair, that is now going to take off anyway. The key state institutions needed to manage development are critically weak. Rather than broad-based growth, there is the prospect of rising inequality, the displacement of small farmers from their land, and a new and more robust cronyism.

In a way, Burma has been denied the Asian model of a period of economic development preceding political liberalization as happened say in South Korea and Indonesia. The situation is perhaps more comparable to the former communist countries of Eastern Europe in the early 1990s, except with a dozen ethnic insurgencies thrown in.

In the short term, Japan may become more important as an economic partner, as might Burma's economic relations with several other Asian countries, like South Korea and Thailand, as well as with Europe and America (if sanctions are ever properly rolled back). And this comes at a time when China and especially India's rise seem a little less meteoric, with growth rates in both places slowing down, and signs in Beijing of possible political instability.

Over the long term however, the big picture remains the same. China and India's re-emergence as first-rank global powers are as sure as anything in the future can be, as are the historic processes of urbanization and industrialization, and the growing connections unfolding across the region. The old Burma, isolated in its mountain fastness has disappeared forever, and it can no longer avoid its place at the strategic heart of Asia.

And for now at least there is a new optimism, a new energy. If the country can forge a new path, end the civil war once and for all, rebuild its shattered education system, and channel this energy towards creating jobs and raising incomes for all its people, it won't be a moment too soon.

Rangoon, 25 April 2012

Notes

All current GDP and population figures are from *US Central Intelligence Agency World Factbook 2010* (https://www.cia.gov/library/publications/the-world-factbook/) and all historical GDP figures from the Angus Maddison databases (http://www.ggdc.net/databases/index.html) unless otherwise indicated.

Prologue

1 '*A few years before*': Bin Yang, *Between Winds and Clouds: The Making of Yunnan (Second Century BCE–Twentieth Century CE)* (New York: Columbia University Press, 2009), p. 76; Nicola di Cosmo, *Ancient China and its Enemies* (Cambridge: Cambridge University Press, 2002), chapter 5; Charles F. W. Hingham, *Encyclopedia of Ancient Asian Civilizations* (New York: Facts on File, 2004), p. 409.

3 '*noticing the news reports*': On plans in the mid-2000s, see for example David Fullbrook, 'China to Europe via a new Burma road', *Asia Times Online*, 23 September 2004; David Fullbrook 'Gas deal fuels China's plans for Myanmar', *Straits Times*, 2 February 2006; David Fullbrook, 'China paves way to Myanmar riches', *Asia Times Online*, 1 November 2006.

5 '*and Bombay*': Also known as Mumbai since 1995. Similarly, in 2001, the official English-language name of Calcutta was changed to Kolkata. I have used the older spellings for these and other Indian place names rather than the more recent versions, as the older spellings are still better known and to avoid using two different spellings depending on the historical period discussed.

5 '*Vietnam, Laos and Cambodia*': On the 'Great Asian War' of the mid-twentieth century, see Christopher Bayly and Tim Harper, *Forgotten Wars: The End of Britain's Asian Empire* (London: Allen Lane, 2007).

PART ONE The Back Door

Irrawaddy Dreaming

9 '*Before there was Rangoon, there was*': Elizabeth H. Moore et al., *Shwedagon: Golden Pagoda of Myanmar* (London: Thames & Hudson, 1999).

In 1989, the ruling junta 'changed' the name of Burma to Myanmar and Rangoon to Yangon. These are actually not new names but the Burmese-language versions of the same words. And in the same way that one would normally say 'Sweden' rather than 'Sverige' or 'Florence' rather than 'Firenze', and because the older spellings are still better known, I have used these older spellings rather than the now official Burmese-language versions.

10 *'rose superb, glistening'*: W. Somerset Maugham, *The Gentleman in the Parlour* (London: Vintage, 2001), p. 6.

14 *'Australia's Foreign Minister Alexander Downer'*: Mark Baker, 'Downer Warns ASEAN on Burma', *The Age*, 2 July 2004.

15 *'The lure of China'*: Archibald Colquhoun, *Across Chryse: Being A Journey of Exploration Through the South China Borderlands From Canton to Mandalay* (London: Scribner, Welford, 1883); *China in Transformation* (London: Harper and Brothers, 1912); *English Policy in the Far East: Being* The Times *Special Correspondence* (London: Field & Tuer, The Leadenhall Press, 1885), and *Burma and the Burmans: Or, 'The Best Unopened Market in the World'* (London: Field & Tuer, The Leadenhall Press, 1885).

16 *'H. R. Davies'*: H. R. Davies, *Yunnan: The Link Between India and the Yangtze* (Cambridge: Cambridge University Press, 1909), p. 10.

16 *'The French had similar'*: Milton Osborne, *River Road to China: The Search for the Source of the Mekong, 1866–73* (London: Allen & Unwin, 1975).

18 *'By the beginning'*: On Rangoon history, see Alister McCrae, *Scots in Burma: Golden Times in a Golden Land* (Edinburgh: Kiscadale, 1990); B. R. Pearn, *A History of Rangoon* (Rangoon: American Baptist Mission Press, 1939); Noel F. Singer, *Old Rangoon: City of the Shwedagon* (Gartmore, Scotland: Kiscadale, 1995).

20 *'Rangoon in those days'*: On General Ne Win's 'Burmese Way to Socialism', see Michael W. Charney, *A History of Modern Burma* (Cambridge: Cambridge University Press, 2009), pp. 107–47; David I. Steinberg, *Burma/Myanmar: What Everyone Needs to Know* (Oxford: Oxford University Press, 2010), pp. 62–80, Thant Myint-U, *River of Lost Footsteps: A Personal History of Burma* (New York: Farrar Straus Giroux, 2006; and London: Faber, 2007), chapter 12.

20 *'In 1988'*: On the 1988 uprising, see Bertil Lintner, *Outrage: Burma's Struggle for Democracy* (Hong Kong: Review Publishing, 1989); Maung Maung, *The 1988 Uprising in Burma* (New Haven: Yale University Southeast Asia Studies, 1999).

21 *'New political forces'*: On recent political developments, Charney, *A History of Modern Burma*, pp. 148–200; Steinberg, *Burma/Myanmar*, pp. 81–147; Thant Myint-U, *River of Lost Footsteps*, chapters 2 and 13.

23 *'On 2 May 2008'*: On Cyclone Nargis, see International Crisis Group, 'Burma/Myanmar after Nargis: Time to Normalise Aid Relations', *Asia Report*, No. 161, 20 October 2008.

26 *'In the heart of downtown'*: On the Indian community in Rangoon

and elsewhere in Burma, see Jean A. Berlie, *The Burmanization of Myanmar's Muslims* (Bangkok: White Lotus, 2008); N. R. Chakravarti, *The Indian Minority in Burma* (London: Oxford University Press, 1971); Renauld Egreateau, 'Burmese Indians in Contemporary Burma: Heritage, Influence, and Perceptions since 1988', *Asian Ethnicity*, Vol. 12, No. 1 (February 2011), pp. 33–54.

27 '*There is even*': Ruth Fredman Cernea, *Almost Englishmen: Baghdadi Jews in British Burma* (Plymouth: Lexington Books, 2007), pp. 1–49.

28 '*Most mixed races*': Sir Charles Crosthwaite, 'The Chinese in Burma', *Straits Times Weekly Issue*, 24 May 1892, p. 11.

29 '*Two Oceans*': Li Chenyang and Lye Liang Fook, 'China's Policies towards Myanmar: A Successful Model for Dealing with the Myanmar Issue?', *China: An International Journal*, Vol. 7, No. 2, September 2009, pp. 255–87.

29 '*Malacca Dilemma*': Ian Storey, 'New energy projects help China reduce its "Malacca Dilemma"', *Opinion Asia*, 14 May 2007; Marc Lanteigne, 'China's Maritime Security and the "Malacca Dilemma"', *Asian Security*, Vol. 4, Issue 2, 2008, pp. 143–61

30 '*Chinese plans*': On Sino-Burmese economic ties in recent years, see Maung Aung Myoe, 'Sino-Myanmar Economic Relations Since 1988', Asia Research Institute Working Paper Series, No. 86; Lixin Geng, 'Sino-Myanmar relations: analysis and prospects', *Culture Mandala: The Bulletin of the Centre for East-West Cultural and Economic Studies*, Vol. 7.2, 2001; Toshihiro Kudo, 'Myanmar's Economic Relations with China: Can China Support the Myanmar Economy?', Institute of Developing Economies, Discussion Paper No. 66, July 2006; Poon Kim Shee, 'The Political Economy of China–Myanmar Relations: Strategic and Economic Dimensions', 2002, www.ritsumei.ac.jp/acd/cg/ir/college/bulletin/e-vol1/1-3shee.pdf.

Cousins

36 '*Early Burmese history*': On ancient Burma, see Bob Hudson, 'A Pyu Homeland in the Samon Valley: A New Theory of the Origins of Myanmar's Early Urban System', *Proceedings of the Myanmar Historical Commission Golden Jubilee International Conference*, January 2005; Bob Hudson, 'Thoughts on Some Chronological Markers of Myanmar Archaeology in the Preurban Period', *Journal of the Yangon University Archaeology Department*, Rangoon; G. H. Luce, *Phases of Pre-Pagan Burma: Languages and History*, 2 vols (Oxford: Oxford University Press, 1985); Elizabeth H. Moore, *Early Landscapes of Myanmar* (Bangkok: River Books, 2007), pp. 86–248; Janice Stargardt, *The Ancient Pyu of Burma*, Vol. 1, *Early Pyu Cities in a Man-Made Landscape* (Cambridge: PACSEA, Cambridge, in association with the Institute of Southeast Asian Studies, Singapore, 1990), chapter 7.

41 '*It had once been*': Hsue Hnget, *Straight Lines of Mandalay* (Mandalay: Northern Plain, 2003), pp. 163–4.

44 '*Mandalay had been built*': On Mindon and his reign, see Williams Barretto, *King Mindon* (Rangoon: New Light of Burma Press, 1935); Kyan, 'King Mindon's Councillors', *Journal of the Burma Research Society*, 44 (1961), pp. 43–60; Myo Myint, 'The Politics of Survival in Burma: Diplomacy and Statecraft in the Reign of King Mindon 1853–1878', unpublished Ph.D. dissertation, Cornell University, 1987; Oliver B. Pollak, *Empires in Collision: Anglo-Burmese Relations in the Mid-Nineteenth Century* (Westport, CT: Greenwood Press, 1979); Thaung, 'Burmese Kingship in Theory and Practice Under the Reign of King Mindon', *Journal of the Burma Research Society*, 42 (1959), pp. 171–84; on Mindon's reforms, see Thant Myint-U, *The Making of Modern Burma*, chapters 5 and 6.

45 '*In 1885*': A. T. Q. Stewart, *The Pagoda War: Lord Dufferin and the Fall of the Kingdom of Ava, 1885–6* (London: Faber and Faber, 1972), pp. 76–9.

46 '*George Orwell*': Bernard Crick, *George Orwell: A Life* (London: Secker & Warburg, 1980), chapter 5; Htin Aung, 'George Orwell and Burma', in *The World of George Orwell*, ed. Miriam Gross (London: Weidenfeld and Nicolson, 1971), pp. 26–7.

46 '*Another denizen*': H. R. Robinson, *A Modern de Quincey: Auto-biography of an Opium Addict* (2nd rev. edn) (Bangkok: Orchid Press, 2004).

47 '*Every house*': Clare Boothe, 'The Burma Front', *Life*, 27 April 1942.

48 '*like a field of wind-stirred tulips*': V. C. Scott O'Connor, *Mandalay and Other Cities of the Past in Burma* (London: Hutchinson, 1907), p. 110.

51 '*Later in the 1960s, however*': Roderick MacFarquhar and John King Fairbank (eds), *The Cambridge History of China*, Volume 15: *The People's Republic*, Part 2: *Revolutions Within the Chinese Revolution, 1966–82* (Cambridge: Cambridge University Press, 1991), p. 243.

53 '*Enlightenment finds its way*': George Ernest Morrison, *An Australian in China: Being the Narrative of a Quiet Journey Across China to Burma* (London: Horace Cox, 1895), p. 241.

The Burma Road

58 '*For the British*': On British rule, see John Cady, *A History of Modern Burma* (Ithaca, NY: Cornell University Press, 1958); F. S. V. Donnison, *Public Administration in Burma: A Study of Development During the British Connexion* (London: Royal Institute of International Affairs, 1953); J. S. Furnivall, *Colonial Policy and Practice: A Comparative Study of Burma and Netherlands India* (Cambridge: Cambridge University Press, 1948); G. E. Harvey, *British Rule in Burma, 1824–42* (London: Faber

and Faber, 1946); A. Ireland, *The Province of Burma,* 2 vols (Boston: Houghton, Mifflin, 1907).

59 *'and then the "Stilwell Road"'*: On the Burma and Stilwell roads, see William Donovan, *The Burma Road: The Epic Story of the China-Burma-India Theater in World War II* (New York: Farrar Straus Giroux 2003); see also Brendon I. Koerner, *Now the Hell Will Start: One Soldier's Flight from the Greatest Manhunt of World War II* (New York: Penguin, 2008), on the amazing story of one African-American soldier who went AWOL whilst working on the Ledo Road.

59 *'In the 1700s'*: On the Qing invasions of the 1760s, see Yingcong Dai's seminal study 'A Disguised Defeat: The Myanmar Campaign of the Qing Dynasty', *Modern Asian Studies,* 38:1 (2004), pp. 145-89.

60 *'Through the 1930s'*: On the war, see Louis Allen, *Burma: The Longest War, 1941-45* (London: J. M. Dent & Sons, 1984); Maurice Collis, *Last and First in Burma* (London: Faber and Faber, 1956); and Viscount William Slim, *Defeat into Victory* (London: Cassell, 1956).

61 *'On 5 April'*: Barbara Tuchman, *Stilwell and the American Experience in China, 1911-1945* (New York: Macmillan, 1970), pp. 280-1.

62 *'I have never liked Burma'*: 16 April 1942 letter from Franklin Roosevelt to Winston Churchill, Great Britain Diplomatic Files, Box 37, Franklin D. Roosevelt Presidential Library and Museum.

62 *'Meanwhile, under the'*: Robert Lyman, *Slim, Master of War: Burma and the Birth of Modern Warfare* (London: Constable, 2004).

67 *'The enormous'*: On the Burmese army see Maung Aung Myoe, *Building the Tatmadaw: Myanmar Armed Forces Since 1948* (Singapore: Institute of Southeast Asian Studies, 2009); Andrew Selth, *Burma's Order of Battle: An Interim Assessment* (Canberra, Australia: Strategic and Defence Studies Centre, Australian National University, 2000). On the evolution of the Burmese army and its role in Burmese politics, see especially Mary Callahan, *Making Enemies: War and State-building in Burma* (Ithaca, NY: Cornell University Press, 2003).

71 *'Through the 1990s'*: For an overview of Burma in the 1990s, see David Steinberg, *The Future of Burma: Crisis and Choice in Myanmar* (New York: Asia Society, 1990). On Burma's foreign policy, see Jürgen Haacke, *Myanmar's foreign policy: domestic influences and international implications* (London: Routledge for the Institute for International and Strategic Studies, 2006).

Lords of the Sunset

79 *'In the mountains'*: For a fresh interpretation of lowland-upland relations, see James C. Scott, *The Art of Not Being Governed: An Anarchist History of Upland Southeast Asia* (New Haven: Yale University Press, 2009).

79 *'As with early'*: On Shan history, see Sai Aung Tun, *History of the*

Shan State: From Its Origins to 1962 (Chiangmai: Silkworm, 2009), pp. 89–504; James George Scott, *Gazetteer of Upper Burma and the Shan States*, Volumes 1 and 2 (Rangoon: Printed by the Superintendent, Government Printing, Burma, 1900)

81 *'Hsipaw had been'*: On Hsipaw, see Maurice Collis, *Lords of the Sunset* (London: Faber and Faber, 1938), pp. 167–71; Inge Sargent, *Twilight Over Burma: My Life as a Shan Princess* (Honolulu: University of Hawaii Press, 1994).

85 *'Herbert Hoover'*: *The Memoirs of Herbert Hoover: The years of adventure, 1874–1920* (New York: Macmillan, 1952), p. 91. Herbert Hoover is incidentally one of only three American presidents ever to come to Burma. The first was Civil War hero Ulysses Grant who stopped in Rangoon during his post-retirement round-the-world tour in the 1870s. And the last was Richard Nixon as Dwight D. Eisenhower's Vice President. It was in 1953 and Cold War anti-American feeling among some in the generally left-wing Burmese student community was high. 'Go Home Nixon, Valet of Wall Street', read one of the signs greeting the future president. He paid his respects, shoeless but with socks, at the Shwedagon Pagoda (accompanied by my grandfather, who was then an aide to the Burmese prime minister) and stopped his motorcade on one occasion to debate with placard-waving students.

87 *'The official report'*: Quoted in Shelby Tucker, *Burma: The Curse of Independence* (London: Pluto Press, 2001), p. 124.

87 *'But the country'*: On the civil war, see Bertil Lintner, *Burma in Revolt: Opium and Insurgency Since 1948* (Boulder, CO: Westview Press, 1944); Bertil Lintner, *The Rise and Fall of the Communist Party of Burma (CPB)* (Ithaca, NY: Southeast Asia Program, Cornell University, 1990); Robert H. Taylor, *Foreign and Domestic Consequences of the KMT Intervention in Burma* (Ithaca, NY: Southeast Asia Program, Dept. of Asian Studies, Cornell University, 1973). Martin Smith, *Burma: Insurgency and the Politics of Ethnicity* (London: Zed Books, 1991); Hugh Tinker, *The Union of Burma: A Study of the First Years of Independence* (London: Oxford University Press, 1961); Frank Trager, *Burma from Kingdom to Republic: A Historical and Political Analysis* (London: Pall Mall, 1966).

89 *'And those who stayed'*: On the history of the narcotics trade, see Alfred McCoy, *The Politics of Heroin in Southeast Asia* (New York: Harper, 1973); on more current developments, see Bertil Lintner and Michael Black, *Merchants of Madness: The Methamphetamine Explosion in the Golden Triangle* (Chiangmai: Silkworm, 2009).

92 *'gratuitous act'*: Shan Women's Action Network, *Forbidden Glimpses of Shan State: A Brief Alternative Guide*, November 2009.

New Frontiers

96 'The British botanist': Quoted in Alan Rabinowitz, Life in the Valley of Death: The Fight to Save Tigers in a Land of Guns, Gold, and Greed (Washington DC: Island Press, 2008), pp. 145–6.

101 'Twenty years ago': Rolf Carriere. 'Responding to Myanmar's Silent Emergency: The Urgent Case for International Humanitarian Relief and Development Assistance', in Peter Carey (ed.), Burma: The Challenge of Change in a Divided Society (Basingstoke: Macmillan, 1997), pp. 209–10.

104 'During the early decades': On the China–Burma border in late colonial times, see Beatrix Metford, Where China Meets Burma: Life and Travel in the Burma-China Border Lands (London: Blackie & Son, 1935).

106 'What has emerged': On the various insurgent armies and militias and their recent relations with the Burmese army, see Mary P. Callahan, Political Authority in Burma's Ethnic Minority States: Devolution, Occupation, and Coexistence (Washington DC: East–West Center, 2007); Tom Kramer, The United Wa State Party: Narco-Army or Ethnic Nationalist Party? (Washington DC: East–West Center, 2007); Martin Smith, State of Strife: The Dynamics of Ethnic Conflict in Burma (Washington DC: East–West Center, 2007); Zaw Oo and Win Min, Assessing Burma's Ceasefire Accords (Washington DC: East–West Center, 2007).

108 'Even stranger': Linter and Black, Merchants of Madness, pp. 79–85.

110 'A report in 2010': Xu Ling, 'Wildlife trade on the Vhina–Myanmar border', in State of Wildlife Trade in China 2008, TRAFFIC East Asia China Programme Report 2010) (http://www.traffic.org/general-reports/traffic_pub_gen34.pdf), p. 11; see also Adam H. Oswell, 'The Big Cat Trade in Myanmar and Thailand: A TRAFFIC Southeast Asia Report' (TRAFFIC Southeast Asia, 2010).

111 'illegal trafficking': Juliet Shwe Gaung, 'Forced marriages driving human trafficking, UN says', Myanmar Times, Vol. 26, No. 512, 1–7 March 2010.

111 'Over the past': Jonathan Shieber and Wan Xu, 'China Consortium Starts Work On Myanmar Hydroelectric Project', Dow Jones Newswires, 24 March 2010.

PART TWO Southwestern Barbarians

The Malacca Dilemma

119 'Around the time': Steven F. Sage, Ancient Sichuan and the Unification of China (Albany: State University of New York Press, 1992), pp. 106–16.

120 'In the late 1970s': On modern Chinese history, see John King Fairbank and Merle Goldman, China: A New History (Second Enlarged

Edition) (Cambridge, MA: Harvard University Press, 2006); Jonathan Fenby, *The Penguin History of Modern China: The Fall and Rise of a Great Power, 1850–2009* (London: Penguin, 2009); Immanuel C. Y. Hsü, *The Rise of Modern China* (New York: Oxford University Press, 2000); John Keay, *China: A History* (London: Harper Press, 2008); Jonathan Spence, *The Search for Modern China* (New York: Norton, 1990).

120 *'The results'*: On China's recent 'rise', see C. Fred Bergsten et al., *China's Rise* (Washington, DC: Peterson Institute for International Economics: Center for Strategic and International Studies, 2008); Martin Jacques, *When China Rules the World: The End of the Western World and the Birth of a New Global Order* (London: Allen Lane, 2009); John Kynge, *China Shakes the World: A Titan's Rise and Troubled Future – and the Challenge for America* (New York: First Mariner Books, 2007); Susan L. Shirk, *China, Fragile Superpower: How China's Internal Politics Could Derail Its Peaceful Rise* (New York: Oxford University Press, 2007).

123 *'Beijing is also an old'*: On the history of Beijing, see Lillian M. Li and Alison Dray-Novey, *Beijing: From Imperial Capital to Olympic City* (New York: Palgrave Macmillan, 2007).

124 *'To the south'*: On China's languages, see S. Robert Ramsey, *The Languages of China* (Princeton: Princeton University Press, 1987).

126 *'In November 2006'*: Joseph Kahn, 'China, shy giant, shows signs of shedding its false modesty', *New York Times*, 9 December 2006.

127 *'It's like a man'*: Cui Xiaohuo and Zhang Haizhou, 'Top military officers lash out at US espionage', *China Daily*, 3 November 2009.

128 *'an article in the* Guardian': Jason Burke, 'India's deals with Sri Lanka heighten stakes in "Great Game"' with Beijing', *Guardian*, 9 June 2010.

128 *'Others were more blunt'*: Ian Bremmer, 'Gathering Storm: America and China in 2020', *World Affairs*, July/August 2010. On China's relations with its neighbours, see David C. Kang, *China Rising: Peace, Power, and Order in East Asia* (New York: Columbia University Press, 2008), Chapter Six; David M. Lampton, *Three Faces of Chinese Power: Might, Money, and Minds* (Berkeley: University of California Press, 2008) pp. 164–206.

130 *'The first was the huge'*: *China Statistical Yearbook 2010*; see also 'All the Parties in China: Comparing Chinese provinces with countries', *The Economist*, 24 February 2011 (http://www.economist.com/content/chinese_equivalents).

133 *'Over the past twenty'*: On China's policies towards Burma, see Li Chenyang, 'China's Policies towards Myanmar: A Successful Model for Dealing with the Myanmar Issue?', in *Myanmar: Prospects for Change* (Select Publishing: Singapore, 2010); International Crisis Group, 'China's Myanmar Strategy: Elections, Ethnic Politics and Economics', *Asia Briefing*, No. 112, 21 September 2010.

137 'Chinese civilization': On the expansion of Chinese civilization, see for example, Peter Bellwood, 'Asian Farming Diasporas? Agriculture, Languages, and Genes in China and Southeast Asia', in Mariam T. Stark (ed.), Archaeology of Asia (Malden, MA: Blackwell, 2006), pp. 96–118; C. P. Fitzgerald, The Southern Expansion of the Chinese People (Bangkok: White Lotus, 1972); Jacques Gernet and J. R. Foster, A History of Chinese Civilization (Cambridge: Cambridge University Press, 1996), pp. 1–129; Charles Holcombe, The Genesis of East Asia, 221 BC–AD 907 (Honolulu: University of Hawaii Press, 2001); Harold J. Wiens, Han Chinese Expansion in South China (Hamden, CT: Shoestring Press, 1967. On early trade links to the Indian Ocean, see also Li Qingxin (William W. Wang trans.), Maritime Silk Road (Beijing: China Intercontinental Press, 2000), pp. 7–29.

138 'No one understands': On the southward spread of the Chinese language, see Nicholas Ostler, Empires of the Word: A Language History of the World (New York: Harper, 2005), pp. 134–57.

138 'Wu kingdom': George van Driem, Languages of the Himalayas: An Ethnolinguistic Handbook of the Greater Himalayan Region (London: Brill Academic Publishers, 2002), p. 433.

138 'kingdom of Yue': Edward H. Schafer: The Vermillion Bird: T'ang Images of the South (London: University of California Press, 1967).

South of the Clouds

142 'It was a city': Jim Goodman, The Exploration of Yunnan (Kunming?: Yunnan People's Publishing House, 2002), pp. 251–264; Graham Hutchings, Modern China: A Guide to a Century of Change (Cambridge, MA: Harvard University Press, 2003) pp. 482–3.

146 'Two thousand years': For an exhaustive and fresh overview of Yunnan's history and its regional connections, see Bin Yang, 'Horses, Silver, and Cowries: Yunnan in Global Perspective', Journal of World History, 15:3 (September 2004); Bin Yang, Between Winds and Clouds: The Making of Yunnan (Second Century BCE–Twentieth Century CE) (New York: Columbia University Press, 2009), especially chapter 2.

147 'It was a military society, very hierarchical': Tzehuey Chiou-Peng, 'Horse in the Dian Culture of Yunnan', in Elisabeth A. Bacus, Ian Glover, Peter D. Sharrock (eds), Interpreting Southeast Asia's Past, Volume 2: Monument, Image and Text: Selected Papers from the 10th International Conference of the European Association of Southeast Asian Archaeologists.

147 'During the height': Francis Allard, 'Frontiers and Boundaries: The Han Empire from its Southern Periphery', in Stark, Archaeology of Asia, pp. 233–54.

148 'In the thirteenth': Marco Polo (ed. and trans. Henry Yule), The Book of Ser Marco Polo, the Venetian Concerning the Kingdoms and

Marvels of the East (Cambridge: Cambridge University Press, 2010), Vol. 2, p. 39.

149 '*The Yao*': On Chinese campaigns against the Yao and the Miao, see Mark Elvin, *The Retreat of the Elephants: An Environmental History of China* (New Haven: Yale University Press, 2004), pp. 216–72.

151 '*In Yunnan too there would be rebellions*': Piper Rae Gaubatz, *Beyond the Great Wall: Urban form and transformation on the Chinese frontiers* (Stanford: Stanford University Press, 1996), p. 79.

151 '*The Chinese are*': Quoted in 'The Legacy of Immigration in Southwest China, 1250–1850', *Annales de demographie historique* (1982), pp. 279–304.

152 '*The most important*': On the warlords, see Fenby, *The Penguin History of Modern China*, chapter 8; also David Bonavia, *China's Warlords* (Hong Kong: Oxford University Press, 1995).

152 '*one bedraggled female who said she was American*': Fenby, *The Penguin History of Modern China*, p. 147.

153 '*In 1939 he even responded*': Ernest G. Heppner, *Shanghai Refuge: A Memoir of the World War II Jewish Ghetto* (Lincoln: University of Nebraska Press, 1993), p. 45.

153 '*The Han Chinese*': Nicholas Tapp and Don Cohn, *The Tribal Peoples of Southwest China: Chinese Views of the Other Within* (Bangkok: White Lotus, 2003), pp. 11–18; see also Frank Dikotter, *The Discourse of Race in China* (London: Hurst, 1992), pp. 66–86.

154 '*For a while*': Chien Chiao and Nicholas Tapp (eds), *Ethnicity and Ethnic Groups in China* (Hong Kong: New Asia College, The Chinese University of Hong Kong, 1989).

154 '*Direct rule*': For a sympathetic view of the Chinese take-over of Norsu areas, see Alan Winnington, *The Slaves of the Cool Mountains* (London: Lawrence and Wishart, 1959), pp. 13–125. For his view on the Wa in early post-Communist China, Winnington, ibid., pp. 124–74. See also Erik Mueggler, *The Age of Wild Ghosts: Memory, Violence, and Place in Southwest China* (Berkeley: University of California Press, 2001); Stephen Harrell, 'The History of the History of the Yi', in Stephen Harrell (ed.), *Cultural Encounters on China's Ethnic Frontiers (Studies on Ethnic Groups in China)* (Seattle: University of Washington Press, 2006).

155 '*The Cultural Revolution*': Goodman, *The Exploration of Yunnan*, p. 214.

155 '*In the town*': David Atwill, *The Chinese Sultanate: Islam, Ethnicity, and the Panthay Rebellion in Southwest China, 1856–1873* (Stanford: Stanford University Press, 2005), p. 15.

157 '*There were two aims*': On regional economic integration initiatives, see C. Patterson Giersch, 'From Golden Triangle to Economic Quadrangle: Evaluating Economic Development Schemes From A Historical Perspective', www.ciaonet.org/wps/gpc01/gpc01.html; Thakur,

Ravni, 'The Chinese Perspectives on the Kunming Initiative (BCIM): A Review of Recently Published Literatures', www.ceniseas.org/newasia/ravnipaper.doc; 'The Kunming Initiative for a Growth Quadrangle between China, India, Myanmar and Bangladesh', *China Report*, 14–17 August 1999, Vol. 36, No. 3, 2000.

159 '*Around the time*': Malcolm Moore, 'China corruption trial exposes capital of graft', *Daily Telegraph*, 17 October 2009.

160 '*the worst drought*': William Chang, 'Will China Run Out of Water: The Country is Facing a once-in-a-century drought', *Forbes*, 9 April 2010; Patrick Chovanec, 'Here's What You Need To Know About The Devastating Drought In China's Shangri-La Region', *Business Insider*, 9 April 2010.

161 '*Southern Silk Road*': See also Clifford Coonan, 'Silk Road back on map as China extends bullet train network', *Irish Times*, 17 April 2010; Ananth Krishnan, 'China plans S-E Asia rail links', *The Hindu*, 23 November 2010.

Gandhara

165 '*In the ninth*': Fan Cho, *Man Shu: Book of the Southern Barbarians*, trans. Gordon Luce, Cornell Data Paper Number 44, Southeast Asia Program, Department of Far Eastern Studies, Cornell University (Ithaca, NY, December 1961), pp. 90–1.

166 '*From Dali*': On Nanzhao, see Charles Backus, *The Nan-chao Kingdom and T'ang China's Southwestern Frontier* (Cambridge: Cambridge University Press, 1981); see also Christopher Beckwith, *The Tibetan Empire in Central Asia* (Princeton: Princeton University Press, 1987), especially chapter 6.

167 '*20,000 suits of armour*': Beckwith, *The Tibetan Empire*, p. 157.

167 '*The kings of Dali*': Angela F. Howard, 'The Dharani Pillar of Kunming', *Artibus Asiae*, Vol. 57, No. 1/2 (1997), pp. 33–72.

168 '*storehouses filled, and sixteen thousand dancing girls*': Upendra Thakur, *History of Mithila* (Darbhanga: Mithila Institute of Post-Graduate Studies and Research in Sanskrit Learning, 1956), p. 25.

168 '*A variety*': On Buddhism in China, see Edward Conze, *Buddhism: A Short History* (Oxford: OneWorld Publications, 1980), pp. 52–60, 99–103; Noble Ross Reat, *Buddhism: A History* (Fremont, CA: Jain Publishing, 1994), pp. 133–64; Andrew Skilton, *A Concise History of Buddhism* (Birmingham: Windhorse Publications, 1994), pp. 165–74.

170 '*The creation*': 'China's Han Flock to Theme Parks Featuring Minorities', *New York Times*, 24 February 2010.

171 '*Though the invasion*': Jiangping Wang, 'Concord and Conflict: The Hui Communities of Yunnan Society in a Historical Perspective', *Lund Studies in African and Asian Religions*, Volume 11 (Lund: Lund University, 1996), pp. 42–52.

175 *'In their place'*: John D. Lanlois Jr., 'The Hung-Wu Reign, 1368–1398', in Frederick W. Mote et al. (eds), *The Cambridge History of China: The Ming dynasty, 1368–1644, Part 1* (Cambridge: Cambridge University Press, 1988), pp. 130–9.

175 *'Yunnan's population'*: James Lee, 'Food Supply and Population Growth in Southwest China, 1250–1850', *Journal of Asian Studies*, 41:4 (1982), p. 729.

176 *'Conflict between'*: On the Panthay rebellion, see David Atwill, 'Blinkered Visions: Islamic Identity, Hui Ethnicity, and the Panthay Rebellion in Southwest China, 1856–1873', *Journal of Asian Studies*, 62:4 (2003); see also C. Patterson Giersch, 'A Motley Throng, Social Change on Southwest China's Early Modern Frontier, 1700–1880', *Journal of Asian Studies*, 60:1 (2001).

176 *'a gargantuan civil war'*: Jonathan D. Spence, *God's Chinese Son: The Taiping Heavenly Kingdom of Hong Xiuquan* (New York: W. W. Norton, 1996).

Shangri-La

181 *'Until the communist'*: On the Naxi, see Charles F. McKhann, 'The Naxi and the Nationalities Question', in Stephen Harrell (ed.), *Cultural Encounters on China's Ethnic Frontiers (Studies on Ethnic Groups in China)* (Seattle: University of Washington Press, 2006); William Safran, *Nationalism and ethnoregional identities in China* (London: Frank Cass, 1998), pp. 20–5; Sydney D. White, 'Town and Village: Naxi Identities in the Lijiang Basin', in Susan Blum and Lionel M. Jensen, *China Off Center: Mapping the Margins of the Middle Kingdom* (Honolulu: University of Hawaii Press, 2002). On Naxi language, see Ramsey, *The Languages of China*, pp. 264–8.

182 *'Then the Mongol'*: Fitzgerald, *The Southern Expansion of the Chinese People*, p. 65; Frederick W. Mote, *Imperial China 900–1800* (Cambridge, MA: Harvard University Press, 2003), p. 441; Stephen R. Turnbull, *Genghis Khan & the Mongol Conquests, 1190–1400* (Oxford: Osprey, 2003), p. 61.

185 *'The Naxi'*: Ramsey, *The Languages of China*, p. 266.

186 *'A boom box'*: Sara Davis, 'Dance or Else: China's Simplifying Project', *China Rights Forum*, No. 4 (2006), pp. 38–46.

187 *'To the north'*: On the Tanguts, see Ruth W. Dunnell, *The Great State of White and High: Buddhism and State Formation in Eleventh Century Xia* (Honolulu: University of Hawaii Press, 1996).

188 *'Further back'*: On the earliest relations between Chinese and Tibeto-Burman speakers, see Christopher I. Beckwith, *Empires of the Silk Road: A History of Central Eurasia from the Bronze Age to the Present* (Princeton: Princeton University Press, 2009), pp. 43–8; David Bradley, *Proto-Loloish: Scandinavian Institute of Asian Studies Monograph*

Series No. 39 (London and Malmö: Curzon Press, 1979); Ilia Peiros, 'Lolo-Burmese Linguistic Archeology', unpublished paper, University of Melbourne, August 1996. On the possibility that an early Tibeto-Burman kingdom was the origin of the name 'China', see Geoff Wade, 'The Polity of Yelang and the Origins of the Name "China"', *Sino-Platonic Papers*, No. 188, May 2009 (http://www.sino-platonic.org/complete/spp188_yelang_china.pdf).

189 '*On some of these drums, their rivals to the east*': Terry F. Kleeman, *Great Perfection: Religion and Ethnicity in a Chinese Millennial Kingdom* (Honolulu: University of Hawaii Press, 1998), pp. 19–61.

189 '*the people of Sanxingdui*': van Driem, *Languages of the Himalayas*, p. 433; Lothar von Falkenhausen, 'The External Connections of Sanxingdui', *Journal of East Asian Archaeology*, Vol. 5, Nos 1–4, 2003, pp. 191–245.

189 '*Here have been found*': J. P. Mallory and Victor Mair, The *Tarim Mummies* (London: Thames and Hudson, 2000).

190 '*Pliny*': Pliny the Elder, *Natural History*, chapter 27 (22) – Taprobane (http://www.perseus.tufts.edu/hopper/text?doc=Plin.+Nat.+6.24&redirect=true).

190 '*the final wave of Siberians who journeyed to*': Zhendong Qin et al., 'A mitochondrial revelation of early human migrations to the Tibetan Plateau before and after the last glacial maximum', *American Journal of Physical Anthropology*, published online July 2010; Bo Wen et al., 'Analyses of Genetic Structure of Tibeto-Burman Populations Reveals Sex-Biased Admixture in Southern Tibeto-Burmans', *American Journal of Human Genetics*, May 2004, 74 (5), pp. 856–65.

193 '*The Naxi kingdom*': Joseph F. Rock, *The Ancient Nakhi Kingdom of Southwest China* (Cambridge, MA: Harvard University Press, 1948); Peter Goullart, *Forgotten Kingdom* (London: J. Murray, 1955).

194 '*Part of this*': On the Mosuo, see Eileen Rose Walsh, 'From Nü Guo to Nü'er Guo: Negotiating Desire in the Land of the Mosuo', *Modern China*, 31.4 (2005), pp. 448–86; Steven Harrell, *Ways of Being Ethnic in Southwest China* (Seattle: University of Washington Press, 2002), chapter 12.

196 '*I must tell you*': Marco Polo, *The Book of Ser Marco Polo*, p. 34.

196 '*More than a year*': 'Fire on the roof of the world', *The Economist*, 14 March 2008; 'Tibetan riots spread outside region', *New York Times*, 16 March 2008.

197 '*Tibet has*': Patrick French, *Tibet, Tibet: A personal history of a lost land* (London: Harper Collins, 2003); Tsering Shakya, *The Dragon in the Land of Snows: A History of Modern Tibet Since 1947* (New York: Penguin Compass, 2000).

198 '*July 2009*': Edward Wong, 'Riots in Western China Amid Ethnic Tension', *New York Times*, 5 July 2009.

198 'The Uighurs are a Turkish-speaking': James Millward, Eurasian Crossroads: A History of Xinjiang (New York: Columbia University Press, 2007).

Between China and the Deep Blue Sea

206 'Others from Burma': On Ruili's Muslims, see esp. Berlie, The Burmanization of Myanmar's Muslims, pp. 69–77.

207 'Ruili was once': See for example Anthony Davis, 'Law and Disorder: A Growing Torrent of Guns and Narcotics Overwhelms China', Asiaweek, 25 August 1995; Patrick Tyler, 'Heroin Influx Ignites a Growing AIDS Epidemic in China', New York Times, 28 November 1995.

208 'The Chinese government': 'How much has Yunnan changed in the "Go West" era?', Go Kunming, 6 July 2010 (http://en.kunming.cn/index/content/2010-07/06/content_2215762.htm).

209 'Eurasian Land Bridge': Li Yingqing and Guo Anfei, 'Third land link to Europe envisioned', China Daily, 2 July 2009.

210 'The Ruili River': On the diverse peoples of the borderlands in the early modern era, see C. Patterson Giersch, Asian Borderlands: The Transformation of Qing China's Yunnan Frontier (Cambridge, MA: Harvard University Press, 2006), pp. 21–9.

210 'Up to the 1950s': C. Y. Lee, The Sawbwa and His Secretary (New York: Farrar, Straus, and Cudahy, 1959).

213 'But frontier personalities': Thaw Kaung, 'Palm-leaf Manuscript Record of a Mission Sent by the Myanmar King to the Chinese Emperor in the mid-18th Century', Myanmar Historical Research Journal, No. 20, December 2010, pp. 9–55.

214 'But they also': Chit Hlaing (F. K. Lehman), 'The Central Position of the Shan/Tai as "Knowledge Brokers" in the Inter-ethnic Network of the China–Burma (Myanmar) Borderlands', paper presented at Shan Religion and Culture Conference, 8–10 December, 2007, School of Oriental and African Studies, London University (http://eprints.soas.ac.uk/5293/2/10chitHlaing-Shan_Paper.pdf).

214 'In the fifteenth': Keay, China: A History, pp. 379–86.

217 'Then came': Thomas Fuller, 'Refugees Flee to China as Fighting Breaks Out in Myanmar', New York Times, 28 August 2009; International Crisis Group, 'China's Myanmar Strategy: Elections, Ethnic Politics and Economics', Asia Briefing, No. 112, 21 September 2010.

218 'In the Chinese journal': Ben Blanchard, 'China casts nervous eye at erstwhile ally Myanmar', Reuters News Service, 25 January 2010.

221 'the unswerving policy of his country': 'Hu Jintao Holds Talks with Chairman of Myanmar's State Peace and Development Council Than Shwe', Press statement, Ministry of Foreign Affairs of the People's Republic of China, 10 September 2010.

221 'The Economist': 'China and India: Contest of the Century', *The Economist*, 19 August 2010.

PART THREE The Edge of Hindustan

Looking East

225 *'More and more'*: *Selected Works of Jawaharlal Nehru*, First Series, Vol. I (New Delhi: Orient Longman, 1972), p. 465.

226 *'The origins'*: On the 1962 Sino-Indian war, see Ramachandra Guha, *India After Gandhi: The History of the World's Largest Democracy* (London: Macmillan, 2007), pp. 301–37.

231 *'When I went back'*: On India's recent economic development, see Edward Luce, *In Spite of the Gods: The Strange Rise of Modern India* (London: Little Brown, 2006); Mira Kamdar, *Planet India: The Turbulent Rise of the Largest Democracy and the Future of Our World* (New York: Scribner, 2007).

232 *'Delhi has been'*: On Delhi's history, see Percival Spear et al., *Delhi: Its Monuments and History* (Oxford: Oxford University Press, 2008); also H. C. Fanshawe, *Delhi – Past and Present* (London: J. Murray Hearn, 1902); Gordon Risley, *The Seven Cities of Delhi* (London: W. Thacker, 1906). On Indian history generally, see John Keay, *India: A History* (New York: Harper Collins, 2000); Barbara D. Metcalf and Thomas R. Metcalf, *A Concise Modern History of India* (Cambridge: Cambridge University Press, 2006).

234 *'Goldman Sachs'*: Goldman Sachs, 'Ten Things for India to Achieve its 2050 Potential', Global Economics Paper 169 (http://www2. goldmansachs.com/ideas/brics/ten-things-for-india.html).

234 *'India is currently'*: C. Raja Mohan, 'Chennai-Bangalore industrial corridor launch likely', *Indian Express*, 25 October 2010.

235 *'Move eastward'*: See for example Catriona Purfield, 'Mind the Gap – Is Economic Growth in India Leaving Some States Behind?', International Monetary Fund Working Paper WP/06/103, 2006.

236 *'In the early'*: Ranjit Gupta, 'India's "Look East" Policy', in *Indian Foreign Policy: Challenges and Opportunities* (New Delhi: Academic Foundation and the Foreign Service Institute, 2007).

237 *'A natural partnership'*: For comparisons between India and China and intra-Asian relations generally, see for example, Brahma Chellaney, *Asian Juggernaut: The Rise of China, India, and Japan* (New York: Harper Business, 2006); Bill Emmott, *Rivals: How the Power Struggle Between China, India, and Japan Will Shape Our Next Decade* (New York: Harcourt, 2008); Tarun Khanna, *Billions of Entrepreneurs: How China and India Are Reshaping Their Future and Yours* (Boston: Harvard Business School Press, 2007).

237 *'He has argued'*: Jairam Ramesh, 'Northeast India in a New Asia',

presented at *Gateway to the East: A Symposium on Northeast India and the Look East Policy,* Shillong, 16 June 2005 (http://w ww.india-seminar. com/2005/550/550%20jairam%20ramesh.htm).

241 *'the Emperor Vespasian'*: Andre Wink, *Al Hind: The Making of the Indo-Islamic World,* Vol. 1, *Early Medieval India and the Expansion of Islam, 7th–11th Centuries* (Boston/Leiden: Brill Academic Publishers, 2002), pp. 335–7.

242 *'Recent scholarship'*: Himashu Prabha Ray, 'The Axial Age in South Asia: The Archeology of Buddhism (500 BC – AD 500)', in Stark, *Archaeology of Asia,* pp. 303–23.

242 *'George Coedes'*: George Coedes, *The Indianized States of Southeast Asia* (Honolulu: University of Hawaii Press, 1996), p. xvi. On the spread of Sanskrit to southeast Asia, see also Ostler, *Empires of the Word,* pp. 199–207.

242 *'The Guptas'*: On Gupta India, Keay, , *India: A History,* pp. 129–54; Romila Thapar, *Penguin History of Early India: From the Origins to AD 1300* (London: Penguin, 2002), pp. 245–363.

243 *'Buddhism itself'*: On early Indian Buddhism, see Edward Conze, *Buddhism: A Short History,* pp. 1–44; Donald S. Lopez Jr., *The Story of Buddhism: A Concise Guide to its History & Teachings* (New York: HarperOne, 2001); Noble Ross Reat, *Buddhism: A History,* pp. 1–83; Skilton, *A Concise History of Buddhism,* pp. 13–149.

245 *'into a surprise of life'*: quoted in Jawaharlal Nehru, *The Discovery of India* (Bombay: Asia Publishing House, 1947), p. 211.

Forgotten Partitions

250 *'Calcutta is'*: On Calcutta's history, see Krishna Dutta, *Calcutta: A Cultural History* (Northampton: Interlink, 2003).

251 *'In October 2008'*: 'A new home for the Nano: Protesters force Tata Motors to abandon a car factory in West Bengal', *The Economist,* 9 October 2008.

252 *'one of the very few'*: 'Tortoise That Saw The Rise And The Fall Of The British Empire Dies', *New York Times,* 24 March 2006.

254 *'My great-grandfather'*: On Bengal–Burma relations in colonial times, see Dr Swapna Bhattacharya (Chakraborti), 'A Close View of Encounter between British Burma and British Bengal', unpublished paper presented at the 18th European Conference on Modern South Asian Studies, Lund, Sweden, 6–9 July 2004; S. R. Chakravorty, 'Bengal Revolutionaries in Burma', *Quarterly Review of Historical Studies,* 19:1–2 (1979–80).

255 *'In India it is'*: Quoted in Penny Edwards, 'Gandhiji in Burma and Burma in Gandhiji', in Debjani Ganguly, John Docker (eds), *Rethinking Gandhi and non-violent rationality: A global perspective* (New York: Routledge, 2008).

255 'Rabindranath Tagore, came in 1916': Bhattacharya, 'A Close View of Encounter between British Burma and British Bengal', pp. 42–9.
256 'In ancient times': Ray, 'The Axial Age in South Asia'; Ostler, Empires of the Word, pp. 174–99.
257 'More recent': Richard M. Eaton, The Rise of Islam and the Bengal Frontier 1204–1760 (Berkeley: Univ. of California Press, 1993), pp. 3–10.
259 'Vajrayana or Tantric Buddhism': On Tantric Buddhism, see Conze, Buddhism: A Short History, pp. 61–9; Lopez, The Story of Buddhism, pp. 213–30; Reat, Buddhism: A History, pp. 70–5; Skilton, A Concise History of Buddhism, pp. 135–42.
259 'Nalanda was a very old university': H. D. Sankalia, The University of Nalanda (New Delhi: Oriental Publishers, 1972).
259 'observatories seem to be': quoted in Lal Mani Joshi, Studies in the Buddhistic culture of India during the seventh and eighth centuries (New Delhi: Motilal Banarsidass, 1967), pp. 56–7.
260 'For centuries': On medieval Bengal, see Eaton, The Rise of Islam and the Bengal Frontier, pp. 22–112.
261 'A close relationship': On Arakan's history and its relations with Bengal, see Michael Charney, 'Arakan, Min Yazagyi and the Portuguese: The Relationship Between the Growth of Arakanese Imperial Power and Portuguese Mercenaries on the Fringe of Southeast Asia', SOAS Bulletin of Burma Research, 3:2 (2005); Richard Eaton, 'Locating Arakan and Time, Space and Historical Scholarship', in Jos Gommans and Jacques Leider (eds), The Maritime Frontier of Burma: Exploring Political, Cultural and Commercial Interaction in the Indian Ocean World, 1200–1800 (Amsterdam: KITLV Press, 2002); Harvey, History of Burma, pp. 137–49; Pamela Gutman, Burma's Lost Kingdoms: Splendours of Arakan (Bangkok: Orchid Press, 2001); Sanjay Subrahmanyam, 'And a River Runs Through It: The Mrauk-U Kingdom and Its Bay of Bengal Context', in Gommans and Leider, The Maritime Frontier of Burma.
262 'In August 1947': On partition, see Guha, India After Gandhi, pp. 3–34; Yasmin Khan, The Great Partition: The Making of India and Pakistan (New Haven: Yale University Press, 2007); Narendra Singh Sarila, The Shadow of the Great Game: The Untold Story of India's Partition (London: Constable, 2005); Alex von Tunzelmann, Indian Summer: The Secret History of the End of Empire (London: Simon and Schuster, 2007). On the aftermath of Bengal's partition, see specifically Willem van Schendel, The Bengal Borderland: Beyond State and Nation in South Asia (London: Anthem Press, 2005), pp. 24–85.
263 'Within a quarter': On the 1971 India–Pakistan war, see Guha, India After Gandhi, pp. 449–61.
266 'A US Army': Christopher J. Pehrson, 'A String of Pearls: Meeting the Challenge of China's Rising Power Along the Asian Littoral', Strategic Studies Institute, U.S. Army War College, 2006 (http://www.

strategicstudiesinstitute.army.mil/pdffiles/pub721.pdf). For an overview of recent Sino-Indian relations, Willem van Kemanade, *Détente Between China and India: The Delicate Balance of Geopolitics in Asia* (The Hague: Netherlands Institute of International Relations, 2008).

267 '*In an essay*': Ananth Krishnan, 'Does Beijing really want to "break up" India?', *The Hindu*, 16 August 2009.

268 '*Sixty years*': Sardar Patel letter to Pandit Nehru, 7 November 1950, quoted in Bairaj Krishna, *India's Bismarck: Sardar Vallabhai Patel* (New Delhi: Indus Source Books, 2008), pp. 215–22.

268 '*In the years*': On recent Indo-Burmese relations, see for example Lall Marie, 'Indo-Myanmar Relations in the Era of Pipeline Diplomacy', *Contemporary Southeast Asia*, Vol. 28, No. 3, 2006; Sudha Ramachandran, 'India bends over for Myanmar's generals', *Asia Times Online*, 6 November 2007; Gideon Lundholm, 'Pipeline Politics: India and Myanmar', *The* [Bangladesh] *Daily Star*, 17 November 2007. For one view of India–China competition in Burma, Khanna, *Billions of Entrepreneurs*, pp. 237–56.

271 '*In 1958*': Edgar Snow, *Red China Today* (New York: Random House, 1962), p. 564.

Inner Lines

274 '*In the early*': On Burmese campaigns against Assam, see S. L. Baruah, *A Comprehensive History of Assam* (New Delhi: Munshiram Manoharlal Publishers, 1985), pp. 220–369.

278 '*In ancient times*': On early Assam, see N. N. Acharyya, *Northeast India on* [*sic*] *Historical Perspective* (New Delhi: Omsons Publications, 2006); Edward Albert Gait, *A History of Assam* (Calcutta: Thacker, Spink, 1906), chapters 1 and 2; Promatha Nath Dutta, *Glimpses into the History of Assam* (Calcutta: Vidyodaya Library Private, 1964).

280 '*Scholars believe*': G. Chaubey et al., 'Population Genetic Structure in Indian Austroasiatic speakers: The Role of Landscape Barriers and Sex-specific Admixture', *Journal of Molecular Biology and Evolution*, Vol. 28, No. 2 (Oxford: Oxford University Press, 2010), pp. 1013–24.

280 '*And it was from*': Richard Bernstein, *Ultimate Journey: Retracing the Path of an Ancient Buddhist Monk (Xuanzang) who crossed Asia in Search of Enlightenment* (New York: Alfred A. Knopf, 2001); Mishi Saran, *Chasing the Monk's Shadow: A Journey in the Footsteps of Xuanzang* (London: Penguin, 2005).

281 '*The Ahoms*': On modern Assam history and identity, see Yasmin Saikia, *Fragmented Memories: Struggling to be Tai-Ahom in India* (Durham, NC: Duke University Press, 2004), pp. 1–111.

283 '*The last war*': L. W. Shakespear, *History of Upper Assam, Upper Burmah and North-Eastern Frontier* (London: Macmillan, 1914), pp. 41–4.

285 *'perfect savages'*: Saikia, *Fragmented Memories*, p. 50.
285 *'The belt'*: Laura C. Martin, *Tea: the drink that changed the world* (North Clarendon, VT: Tuttle Publishing, 2007), pp. 154–62.
286 *'Tea was to'*: Manilal Bose, *Social history of Assam* (New Delhi: Ashok Kumar Mittal, 1989), chapter 5; Saikia, *Fragmented Memories*.
288 *'The decades'*: On Assam since independence, see Sanjib Baruah, *India Against Itself: Assam and the Politics of Nationality* (New Delhi: Oxford University Press, 1999).
289 *'An armed group'*: On ULFA and Northeast India insurgency generally, see Sanjib Baruah, *Durable Disorder: Understanding the Politics of Northeast India* (New Delhi: Oxford University Press, 2005), pp. 145–80; Sanjoy Hazarika, *Strangers of the Mist: Tales of War & Peace from India's Northeast* (New Delhi: Penguin, 2004), pp. 167–248.
290 *'This changed soon after'*: Sushanta Talukdar, 'Rajkhowa arrested, brought to Guwahati', *The Hindu*, 5 December 2009; 'An Opportunity in Assam', *The Hindu*, 7 May 2010.

Instruments of Accession

297 *'A few decades'*: On the Burmese campaigns against Manipur, see Gangmumei Kabui, *History of Manipur*, Vol. 1, *Precolonial Period* (New Delhi: National Publishing House, 1991), pp. 194–291.
297 *'And after the Burmese'*: On British views of Manipur in the mid-nineteenth century, see James Johnstone, *My Experiences in Manipur and the Naga Hills* (London: Sampson Low Marston, 1896).
298 *'The Japanese'*: On Imphal, see William Fowler, *We Gave Our Today: Burma 1941–1945* (London: Phoenix, 2009), pp. 128–48; Robert Lyman, *Slim, Master of War: Burma and the Birth of Modern Warfare* (London: Constable, 2004), pp. 199–227.
300 *'As 1948 approached'*: On the accession of princely states, see Guha, *India After Gandhi*, pp. 35–58.
301 *'discussion of the state becoming part of an independent Burma'*: Lokendra Singh, *The Unquiet Valley: Society, Economy, and Politics of Manipur (1891–1950)* (New Delhi: Mittal Publications, 1998), p. 202.
303 *'it is he who has caused all this trouble for the Nagas'*: Saikia, *Fragmented Memories*, pp. 51–2.
303 *'The Nagas would soon'*: On Naga rebellion, see Guha, *India After Gandhi*, pp. 261–78; Hazarika, *Strangers of the Mist*, pp. 88–110.
306 *'The Look East policy originally'*: On the 'Look East' policy and Northeast India, see Sanjib Baruah, *Between South and South East Asia: North East India and The Look East Policy* (Guwahati, India: Centre for North East India, South and Southeast Asia Studies, 2004); also Amit Baruah, 'The Roads to Myanmar', *Frontline*, Vol. 18, No. 5, 3–16 March 2001; Amit Baruah, 'Northeast as Trade Hub', *The Hindu*, 20 September 2004; Mahendra Ved, 'A corner of India that holds the key to Asia',

New Straits Times, 17 November 2007.

312 *'This has had a curious'*: Sunita Akoijam, 'Chopsticks in Manipur', *Himal South Asia*, September 2009.

312 *'Others look for connections'*: See for example, Ian MacKinnon, 'Lost tribe dreams of return to Israel after 2,700 years in exile', *The Times*, 2 April 2005.

313 *'In November 1950'*: Sardar Patel letter to Nehru, 7 November 1950, quoted in Krishna, *India's Bismarck*, pp. 215–22.

Epilogue

317 *'Kipling'*: Rudyard Kipling, *Sea to Sea and Other Sketches: Letters of Travel* (1889), Vol. 1, No. 2 (New York: Doubleday, 1914).

318 *'In October 2010'*: 'An Industrial Project That Could Change Myanmar', *International Herald Tribune*, 26 November 2010.

319 *'plan is tied'*: 'A railway boom promises to tie South-East Asia together—and boost China's sway', *The Economist*, 20 January 2011.

319 *'The Chinese have also'*: Shishir Gupta, 'China beats India to Stilwell Road contract in Myanmar', *Indian Express*, 6 January 2011.

319 *'And India too'*: Nirmala Ganapathy, 'India, Myanmar quietly finalise Kaladan project', *The Economic Times*, 2 November 2007. See also Renauld Egreateau, 'India and China Vying for Influence in Burma: A New Assessment', *India Review*, Vol. 7, No. 1 (January–March 2008), pp. 38–72; Renauld Egreateau, 'India's Ambitions in Burma: More Frustration than Success?', *Asian Survey*, Vol. 48, No. 6 (November–December 2008), pp. 936–57.

322 *'The country's first'*: 'Myanmar's Post-Election Landscape', International Crisis Group Asia, Briefing No. 118, 7 March 2011.

Acknowledgements

I am very grateful to Donald Sommerville for his patient and meticulous copy-editing, to András Bereznay for the excellent maps at the beginning of the book, and especially to Rebecca Lee for her generous assistance and first-rate work. I'd also like to thank Julian Loose, Will Atkinson, Miles Poynton and Rebecca Pearson at Faber and in particular my editor, Walter Donohue, for his support and his perceptive comments and suggestions. Thank you also to Jeff Seroy, Kathy Daneman and Karen Maine at Farrar, Straus and Giroux and to Eric Chinski, for a very early and stimulating discussion about the book that I still remember well. My special thanks to Paul Elie, my editor at FSG, whose guidance from the very start and whose detailed and thoughtful recommendations I have valued greatly. And a special thank you as well to my agent Clare Alexander, for making this book possible and for her unfailing encouragement and wise counsel over the years.

Index